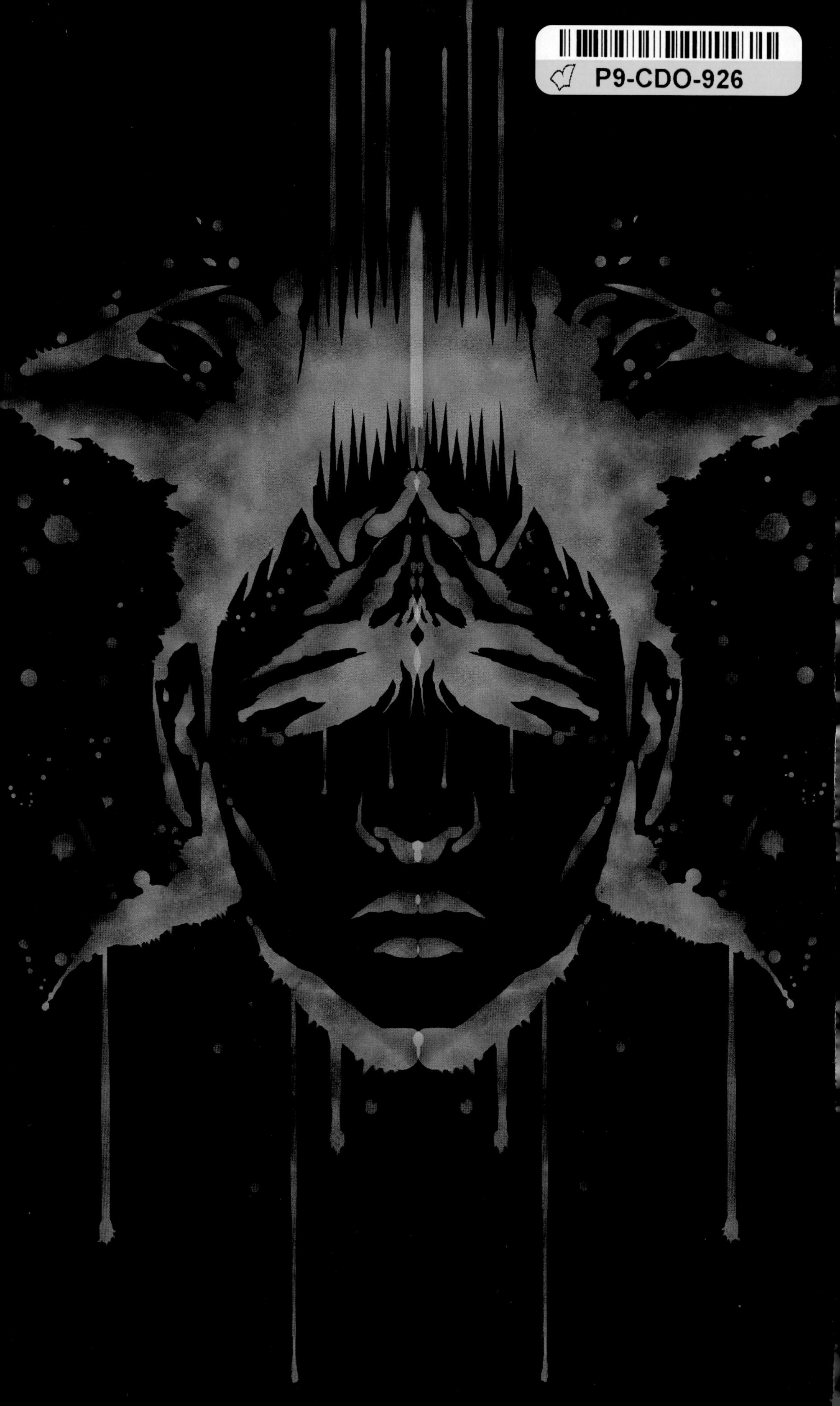

WHISPERS

www.ImageComics.com

www.joshualuna.com

www.facebook.com/joshualunacreations

@Joshua_Luna (Twitter)

WHISPERS. First printing. June 2014. Copyright ® 2014 Joshua Luna. All rights reserved. Published by Image Comics, Inc. Office of publication: 2001 Center Street, Sixth Floor, Berkeley, CA 94704. Originally published in single magazine form as WHISPERS #1-6, by Image Comics. "WHISPERS," its logos, and the likenesses of all characters herein are trademarks of Joshua Luna, unless otherwise noted. "Image" and the Image Comics logos are registered trademarks of Image Comics, Inc. No part of this publication may be reproduced or transmitted, in any form or by any means (except for short excerpts for journalistic or review purposes), without the express written permission of Joshua Luna or Image Comics, Inc. All names, characters, events, and locales in this publication are entirely fictional. Any resemblance to actual persons (living or dead), events, or places, without satiric intent, is coincidental. Printed in the USA. For information regarding the CPSIA on this printed material call: 203-595-3636 and provide reference #RICH-562206. For international rights, contact: foreignlicensing@imagecomics.com. ISBN: 978-1-63215-060-8

JOSHUA LUNA

WRITER

STORY

SCRIPT

LETTERS

ARTIST

COVERS

PENCILS

INKS

COLORS

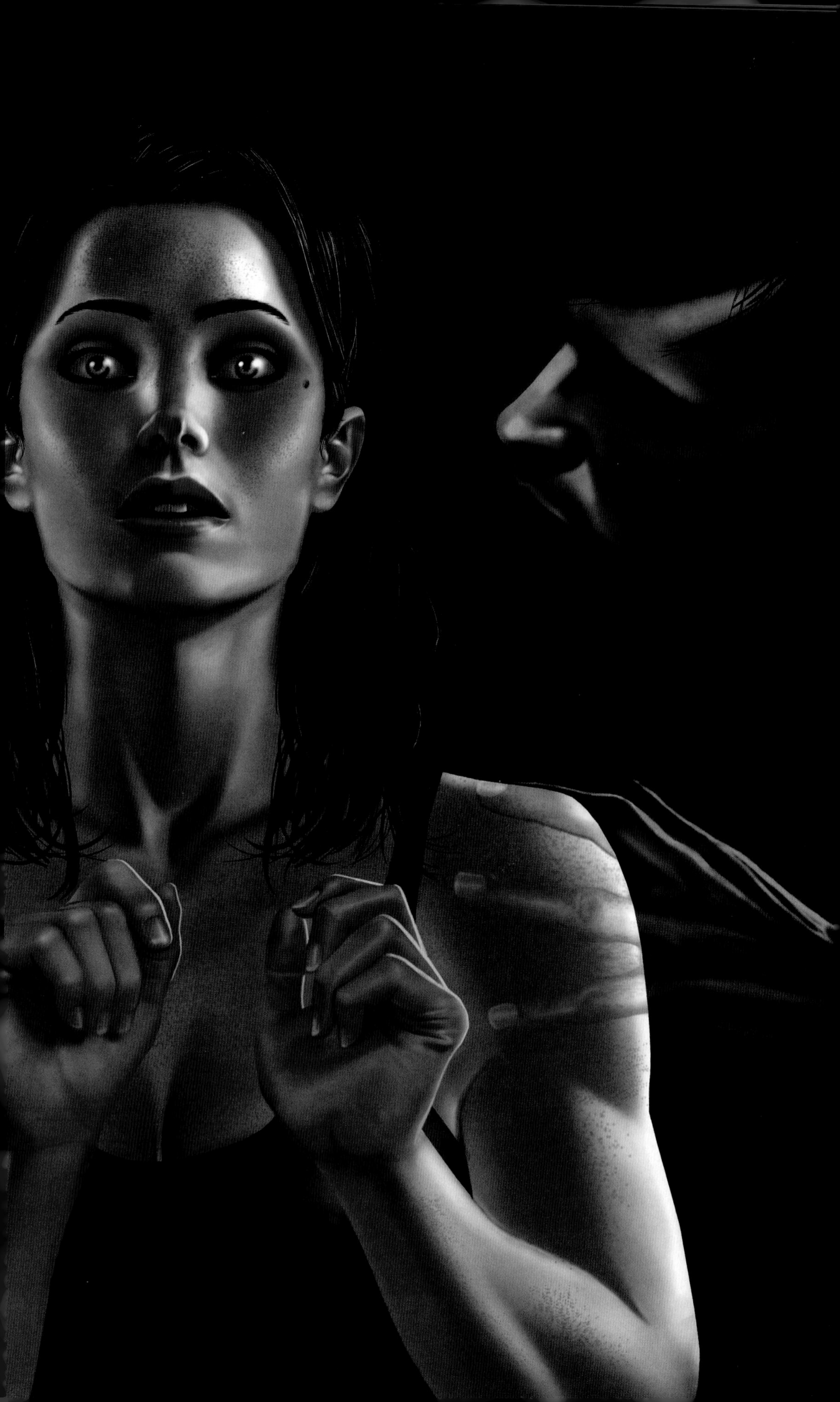

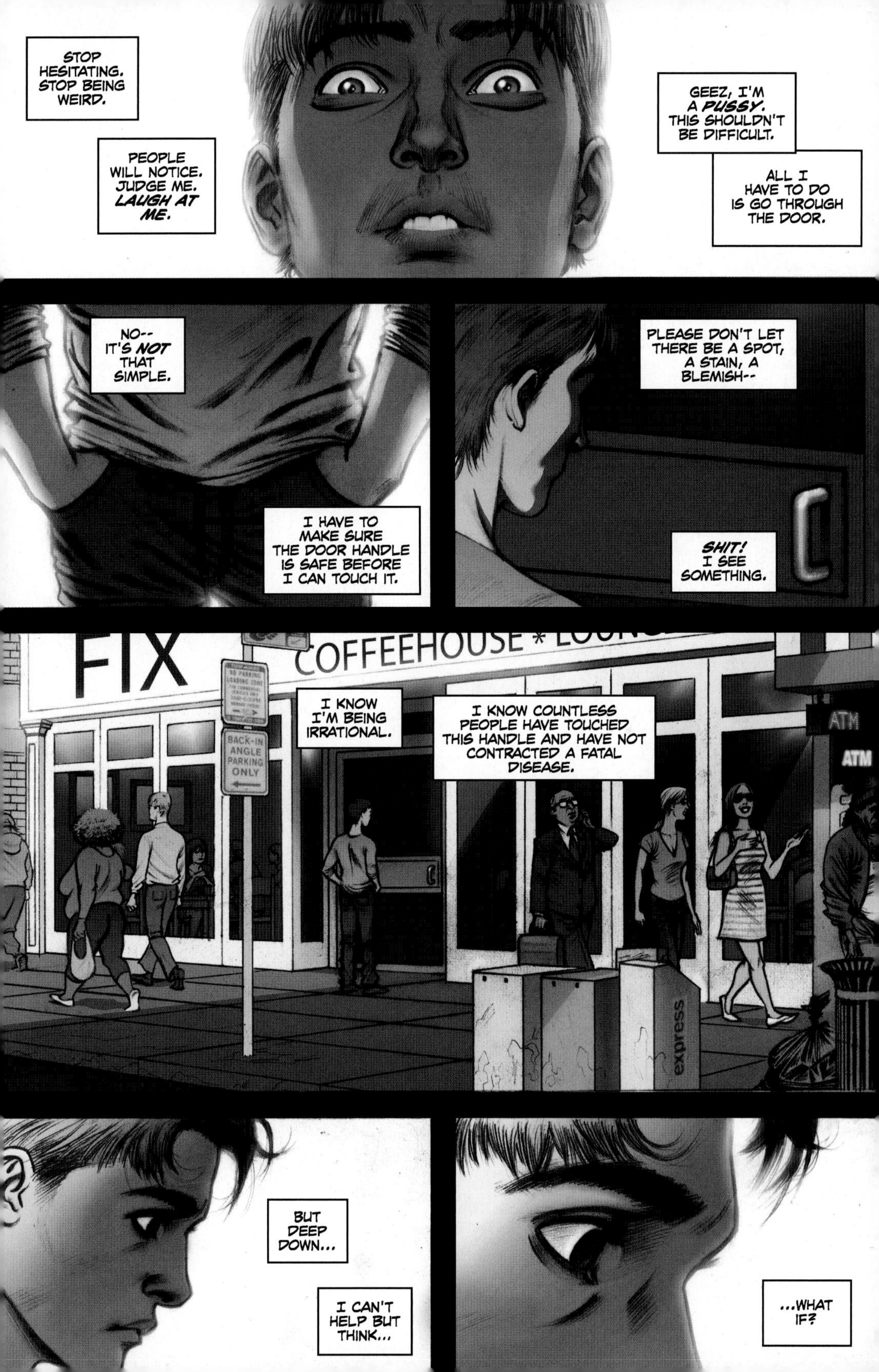

STOP HESITATING. STOP BEING WEIRD.
PEOPLE WILL NOTICE. JUDGE ME. *LAUGH AT ME.*
GEEZ, I'M A *PUSSY*. THIS SHOULDN'T BE DIFFICULT.
ALL I HAVE TO DO IS GO THROUGH THE DOOR.
NO-- IT'S *NOT* THAT SIMPLE.
I HAVE TO MAKE SURE THE DOOR HANDLE IS SAFE BEFORE I CAN TOUCH IT.
PLEASE DON'T LET THERE BE A SPOT, A STAIN, A BLEMISH--
SHIT! I SEE SOMETHING.
FIX
COFFEEHOUSE * LOUNG
BACK-IN ANGLE PARKING ONLY
ATM
ATM
express
I KNOW I'M BEING IRRATIONAL.
I KNOW COUNTLESS PEOPLE HAVE TOUCHED THIS HANDLE AND HAVE NOT CONTRACTED A FATAL DISEASE.
BUT DEEP DOWN...
I CAN'T HELP BUT THINK...
...WHAT IF?

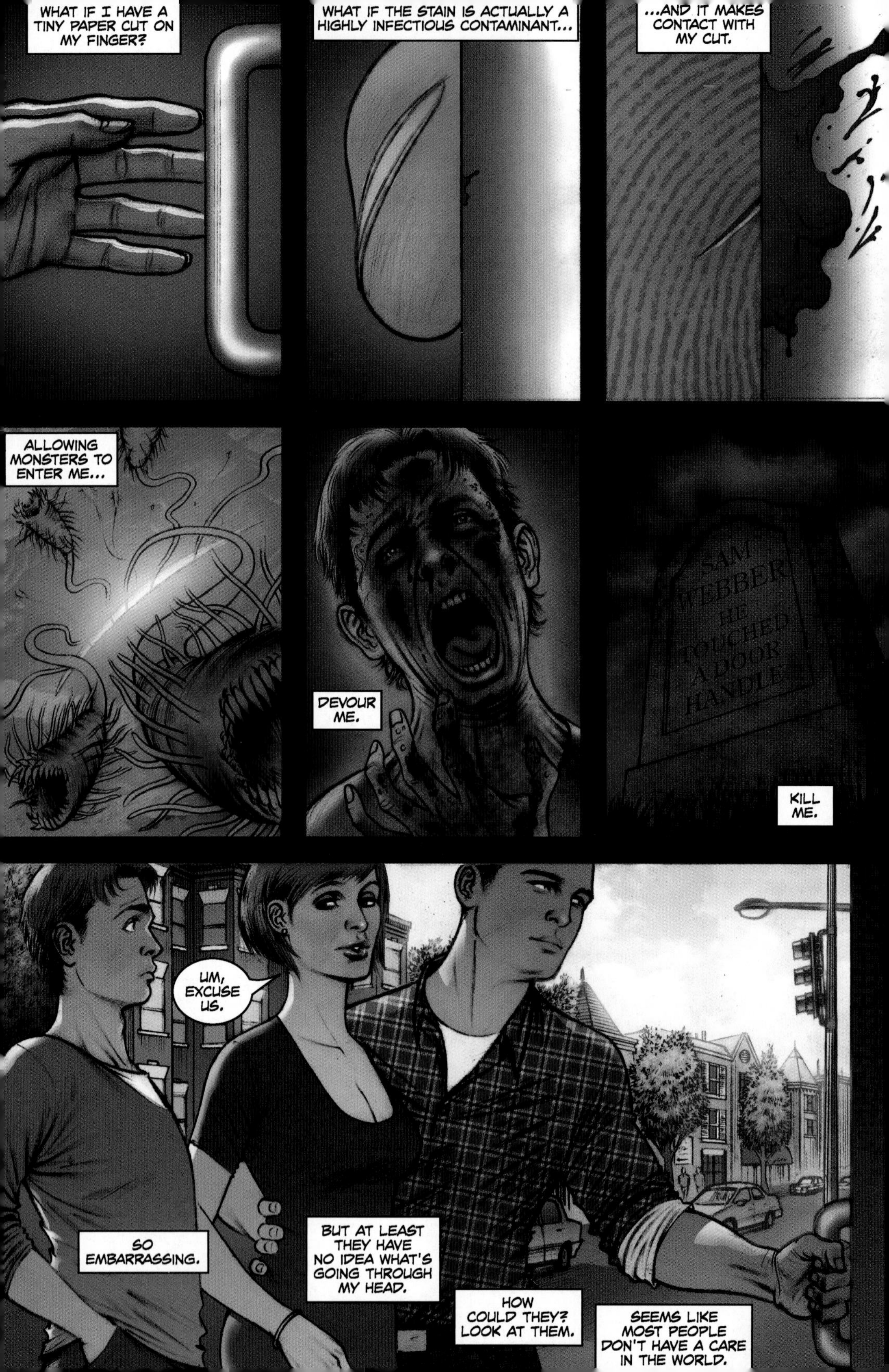
WHAT IF I HAVE A TINY PAPER CUT ON MY FINGER?
WHAT IF THE STAIN IS ACTUALLY A HIGHLY INFECTIOUS CONTAMINANT...
...AND IT MAKES CONTACT WITH MY CUT.
ALLOWING MONSTERS TO ENTER ME...
DEVOUR ME.
SAM WEBBER HE TOUCHED A DOOR HANDLE
KILL ME.
UM, EXCUSE US.
SO EMBARRASSING.
BUT AT LEAST THEY HAVE NO IDEA WHAT'S GOING THROUGH MY HEAD.
HOW COULD THEY? LOOK AT THEM.
SEEMS LIKE MOST PEOPLE DON'T HAVE A CARE IN THE WORLD.

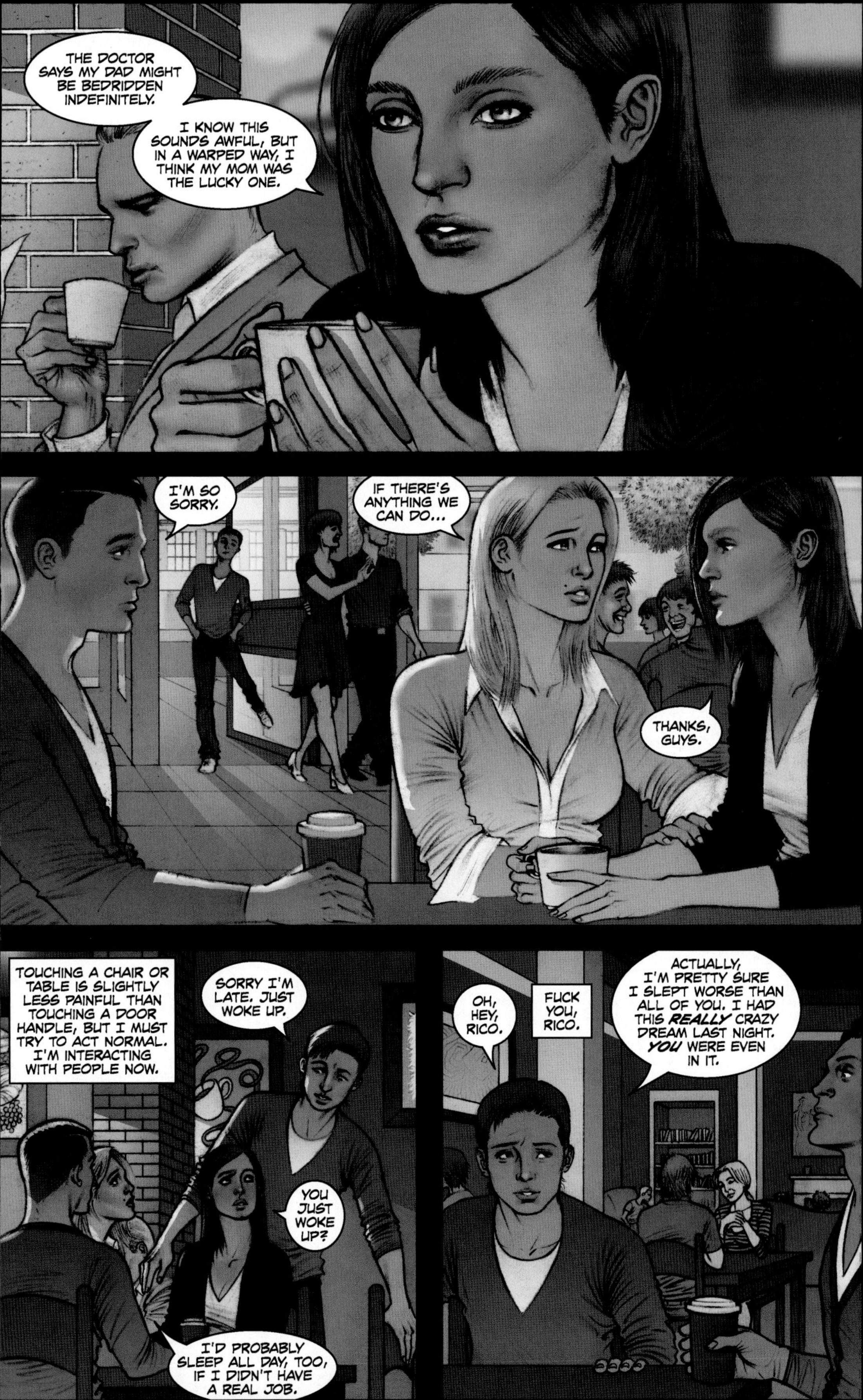
THE DOCTOR SAYS MY DAD MIGHT BE BEDRIDDEN INDEFINITELY.
I KNOW THIS SOUNDS AWFUL, BUT IN A WARPED WAY, I THINK MY MOM WAS THE LUCKY ONE.
I'M SO SORRY.
IF THERE'S ANYTHING WE CAN DO...
THANKS, GUYS.
TOUCHING A CHAIR OR TABLE IS SLIGHTLY LESS PAINFUL THAN TOUCHING A DOOR HANDLE, BUT I MUST TRY TO ACT NORMAL. I'M INTERACTING WITH PEOPLE NOW.
SORRY I'M LATE. JUST WOKE UP.
YOU JUST WOKE UP?
I'D PROBABLY SLEEP ALL DAY, TOO, IF I DIDN'T HAVE A REAL JOB.
OH, HEY, RICO.
FUCK YOU, RICO.
ACTUALLY, I'M PRETTY SURE I SLEPT WORSE THAN ALL OF YOU. I HAD THIS *REALLY* CRAZY DREAM LAST NIGHT. *YOU* WERE EVEN IN IT.

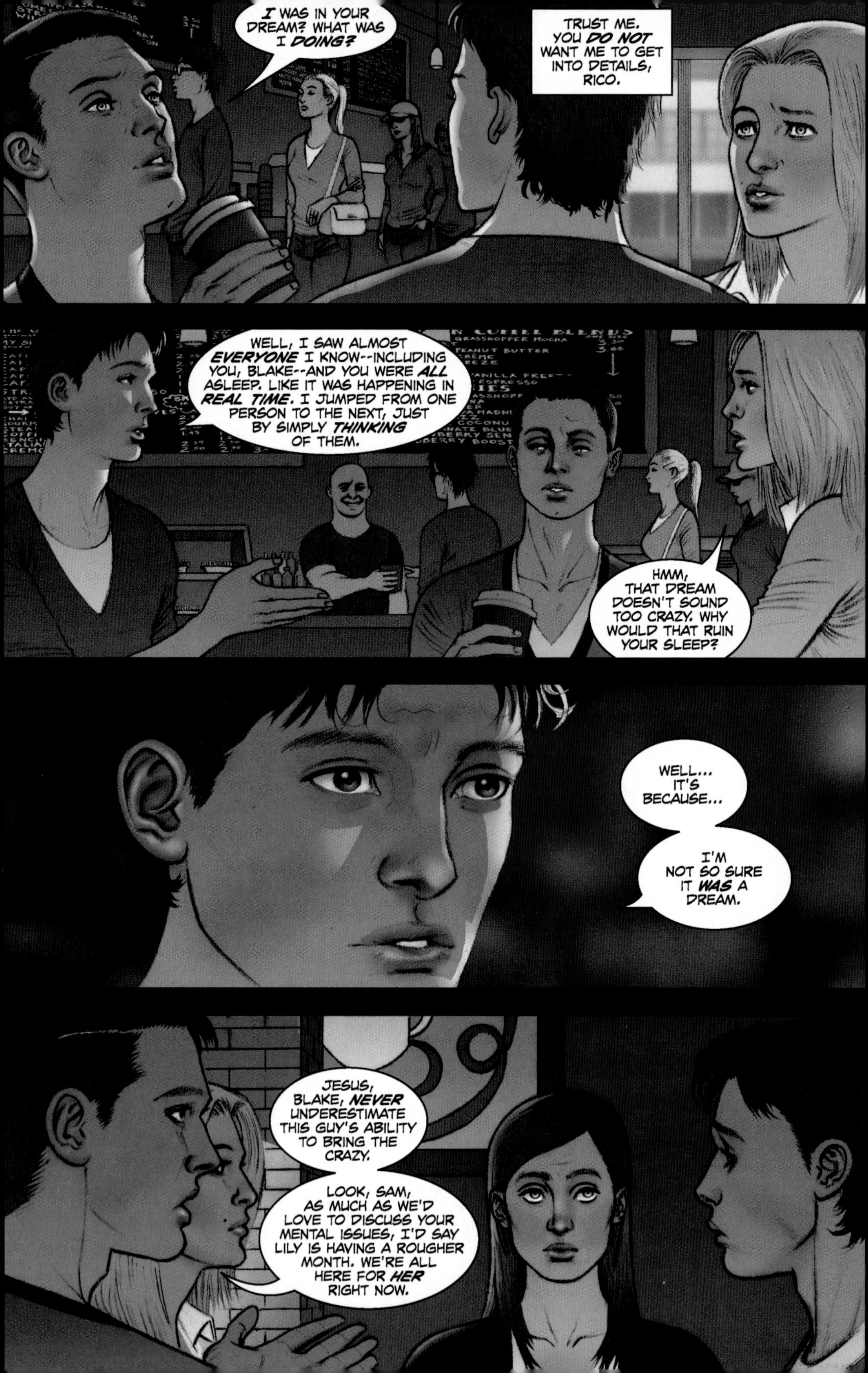
I WAS IN YOUR DREAM? WHAT WAS I DOING?
TRUST ME. YOU DO NOT WANT ME TO GET INTO DETAILS, RICO.
WELL, I SAW ALMOST EVERYONE I KNOW--INCLUDING YOU, BLAKE--AND YOU WERE ALL ASLEEP. LIKE IT WAS HAPPENING IN REAL TIME. I JUMPED FROM ONE PERSON TO THE NEXT, JUST BY SIMPLY THINKING OF THEM.
HMM, THAT DREAM DOESN'T SOUND TOO CRAZY. WHY WOULD THAT RUIN YOUR SLEEP?
WELL... IT'S BECAUSE...
I'M NOT SO SURE IT WAS A DREAM.
JESUS, BLAKE, NEVER UNDERESTIMATE THIS GUY'S ABILITY TO BRING THE CRAZY.
LOOK, SAM, AS MUCH AS WE'D LOVE TO DISCUSS YOUR MENTAL ISSUES, I'D SAY LILY IS HAVING A ROUGHER MONTH. WE'RE ALL HERE FOR HER RIGHT NOW.

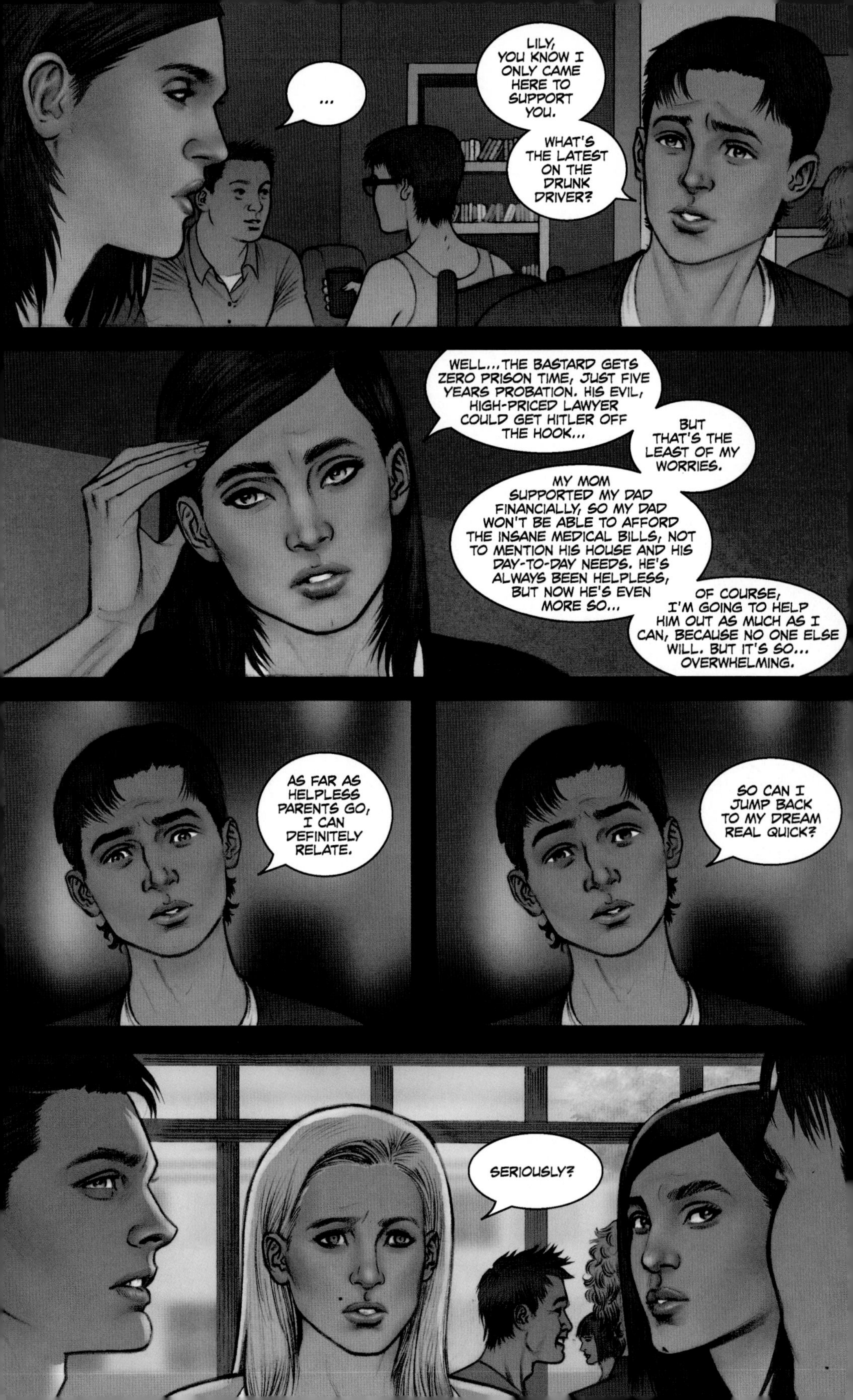
...
LILY, YOU KNOW I ONLY CAME HERE TO SUPPORT YOU.
WHAT'S THE LATEST ON THE DRUNK DRIVER?
WELL...THE BASTARD GETS ZERO PRISON TIME, JUST FIVE YEARS PROBATION. HIS EVIL, HIGH-PRICED LAWYER COULD GET HITLER OFF THE HOOK...
BUT THAT'S THE LEAST OF MY WORRIES.
MY MOM SUPPORTED MY DAD FINANCIALLY, SO MY DAD WON'T BE ABLE TO AFFORD THE INSANE MEDICAL BILLS, NOT TO MENTION HIS HOUSE AND HIS DAY-TO-DAY NEEDS. HE'S ALWAYS BEEN HELPLESS, BUT NOW HE'S EVEN MORE SO...
OF COURSE, I'M GOING TO HELP HIM OUT AS MUCH AS I CAN, BECAUSE NO ONE ELSE WILL. BUT IT'S SO... OVERWHELMING.
AS FAR AS HELPLESS PARENTS GO, I CAN DEFINITELY RELATE.
SO CAN I JUMP BACK TO MY DREAM REAL QUICK?
SERIOUSLY?

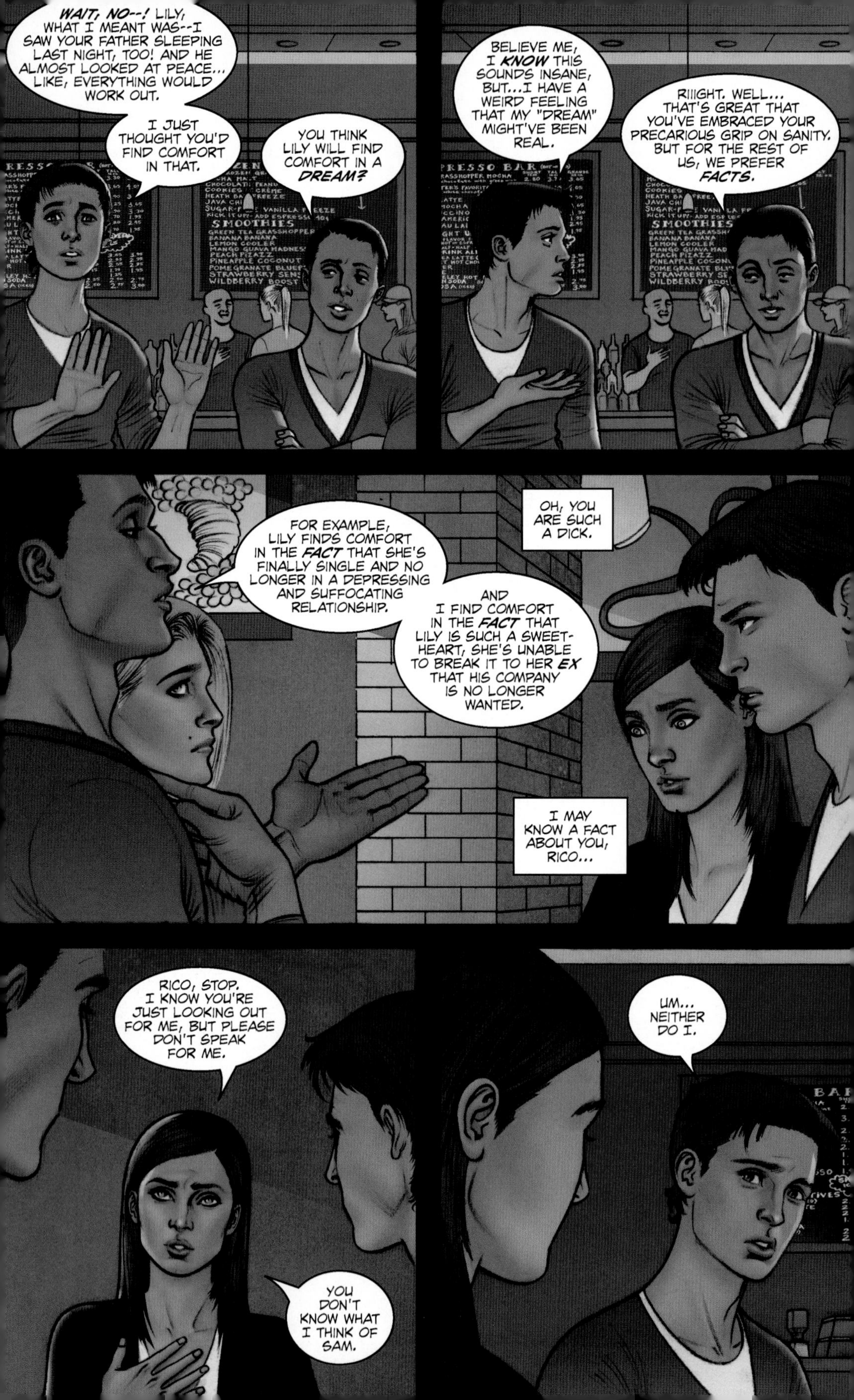
WAIT, NO--! LILY, WHAT I MEANT WAS--I SAW YOUR FATHER SLEEPING LAST NIGHT, TOO! AND HE ALMOST LOOKED AT PEACE... LIKE, EVERYTHING WOULD WORK OUT.
I JUST THOUGHT YOU'D FIND COMFORT IN THAT.
YOU THINK LILY WILL FIND COMFORT IN A DREAM?
BELIEVE ME, I KNOW THIS SOUNDS INSANE, BUT...I HAVE A WEIRD FEELING THAT MY "DREAM" MIGHT'VE BEEN REAL.
RIIIGHT. WELL... THAT'S GREAT THAT YOU'VE EMBRACED YOUR PRECARIOUS GRIP ON SANITY. BUT FOR THE REST OF US, WE PREFER FACTS.
FOR EXAMPLE, LILY FINDS COMFORT IN THE FACT THAT SHE'S FINALLY SINGLE AND NO LONGER IN A DEPRESSING AND SUFFOCATING RELATIONSHIP.
AND I FIND COMFORT IN THE FACT THAT LILY IS SUCH A SWEET-HEART, SHE'S UNABLE TO BREAK IT TO HER EX THAT HIS COMPANY IS NO LONGER WANTED.
OH, YOU ARE SUCH A DICK.
I MAY KNOW A FACT ABOUT YOU, RICO...
RICO, STOP. I KNOW YOU'RE JUST LOOKING OUT FOR ME, BUT PLEASE DON'T SPEAK FOR ME.
YOU DON'T KNOW WHAT I THINK OF SAM.
UM... NEITHER DO I.

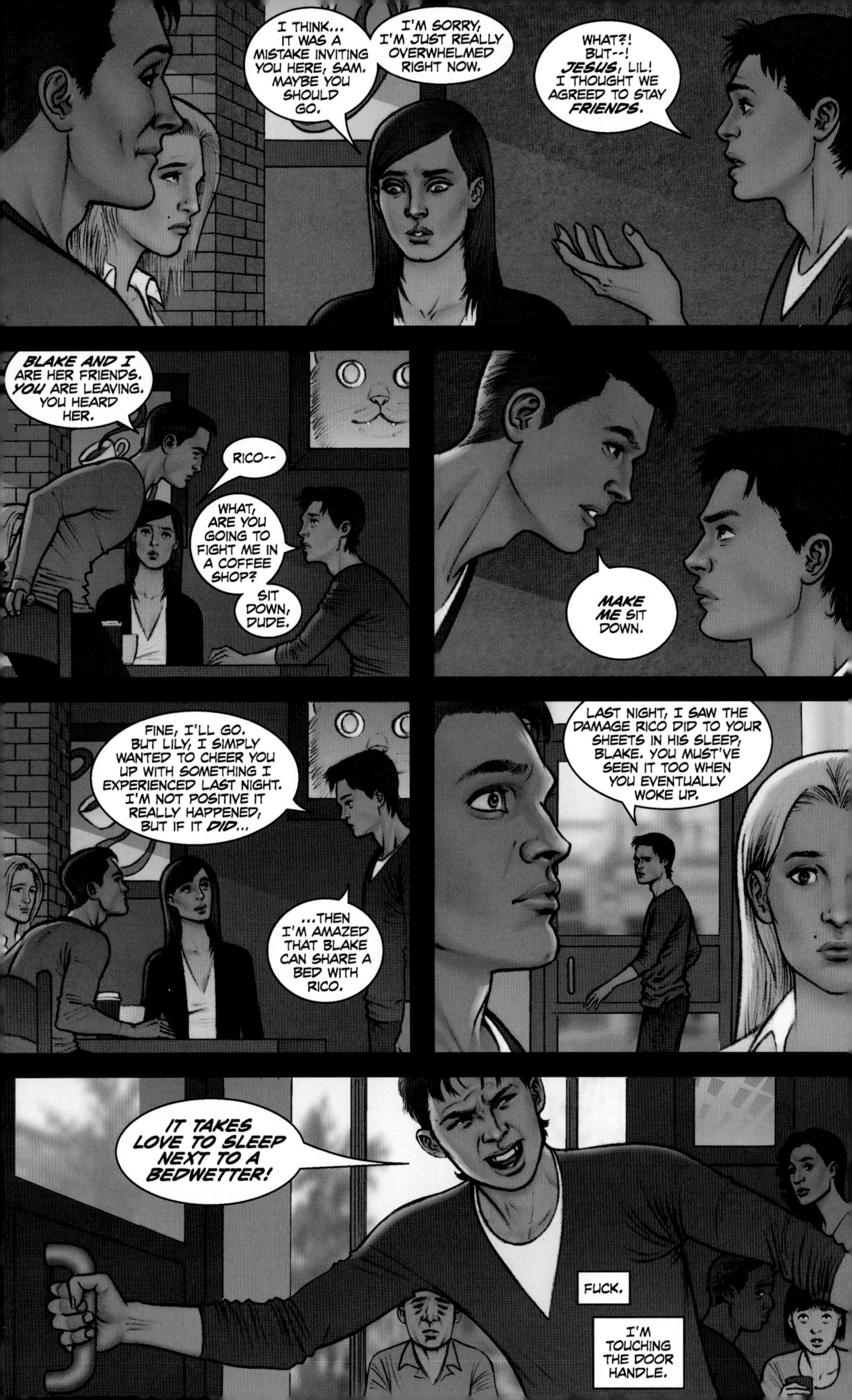

I THINK... IT WAS A MISTAKE INVITING YOU HERE, SAM. MAYBE YOU SHOULD GO.
I'M SORRY, I'M JUST REALLY OVERWHELMED RIGHT NOW.
WHAT?! BUT--! JESUS, LIL! I THOUGHT WE AGREED TO STAY FRIENDS.
BLAKE AND I ARE HER FRIENDS. YOU ARE LEAVING. YOU HEARD HER.
RICO--
WHAT, ARE YOU GOING TO FIGHT ME IN A COFFEE SHOP?
SIT DOWN, DUDE.
MAKE ME SIT DOWN.
FINE, I'LL GO. BUT LILY, I SIMPLY WANTED TO CHEER YOU UP WITH SOMETHING I EXPERIENCED LAST NIGHT. I'M NOT POSITIVE IT REALLY HAPPENED, BUT IF IT DID...
...THEN I'M AMAZED THAT BLAKE CAN SHARE A BED WITH RICO.
LAST NIGHT, I SAW THE DAMAGE RICO DID TO YOUR SHEETS IN HIS SLEEP, BLAKE. YOU MUST'VE SEEN IT TOO WHEN YOU EVENTUALLY WOKE UP.
IT TAKES LOVE TO SLEEP NEXT TO A BEDWETTER!
FUCK.
I'M TOUCHING THE DOOR HANDLE.

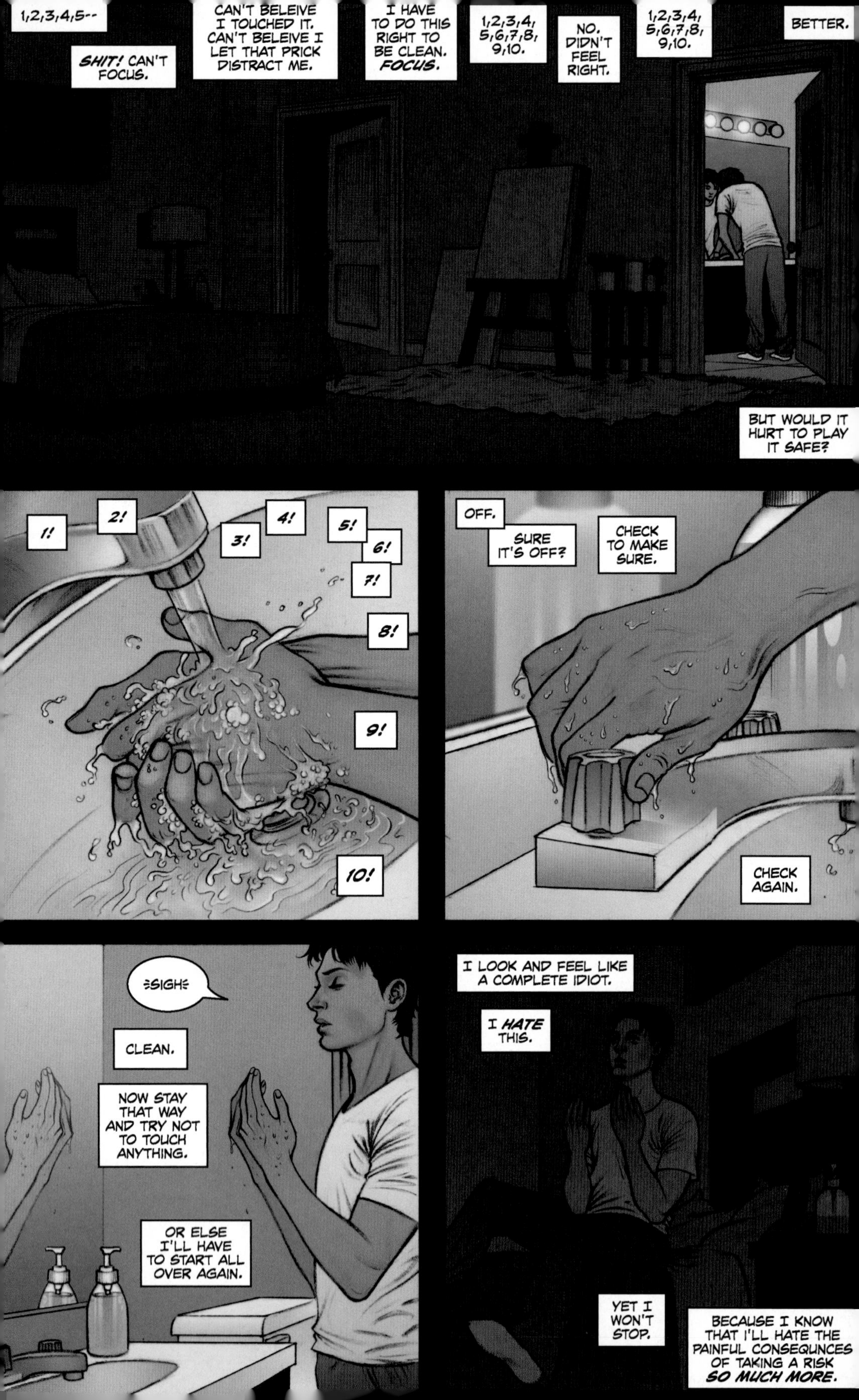
1,2,3,4,5--
SHIT! CAN'T FOCUS.
CAN'T BELEIVE I TOUCHED IT. CAN'T BELEIVE I LET THAT PRICK DISTRACT ME.
I HAVE TO DO THIS RIGHT TO BE CLEAN. FOCUS.
1,2,3,4, 5,6,7,8, 9,10.
NO. DIDN'T FEEL RIGHT.
1,2,3,4, 5,6,7,8, 9,10.
BETTER.
BUT WOULD IT HURT TO PLAY IT SAFE?
1!
2!
3!
4!
5!
6!
7!
8!
9!
10!
OFF.
SURE IT'S OFF?
CHECK TO MAKE SURE.
CHECK AGAIN.
≈SIGH≈
CLEAN.
NOW STAY THAT WAY AND TRY NOT TO TOUCH ANYTHING.
OR ELSE I'LL HAVE TO START ALL OVER AGAIN.
I LOOK AND FEEL LIKE A COMPLETE IDIOT.
I HATE THIS.
YET I WON'T STOP.
BECAUSE I KNOW THAT I'LL HATE THE PAINFUL CONSEQUNCES OF TAKING A RISK SO MUCH MORE.

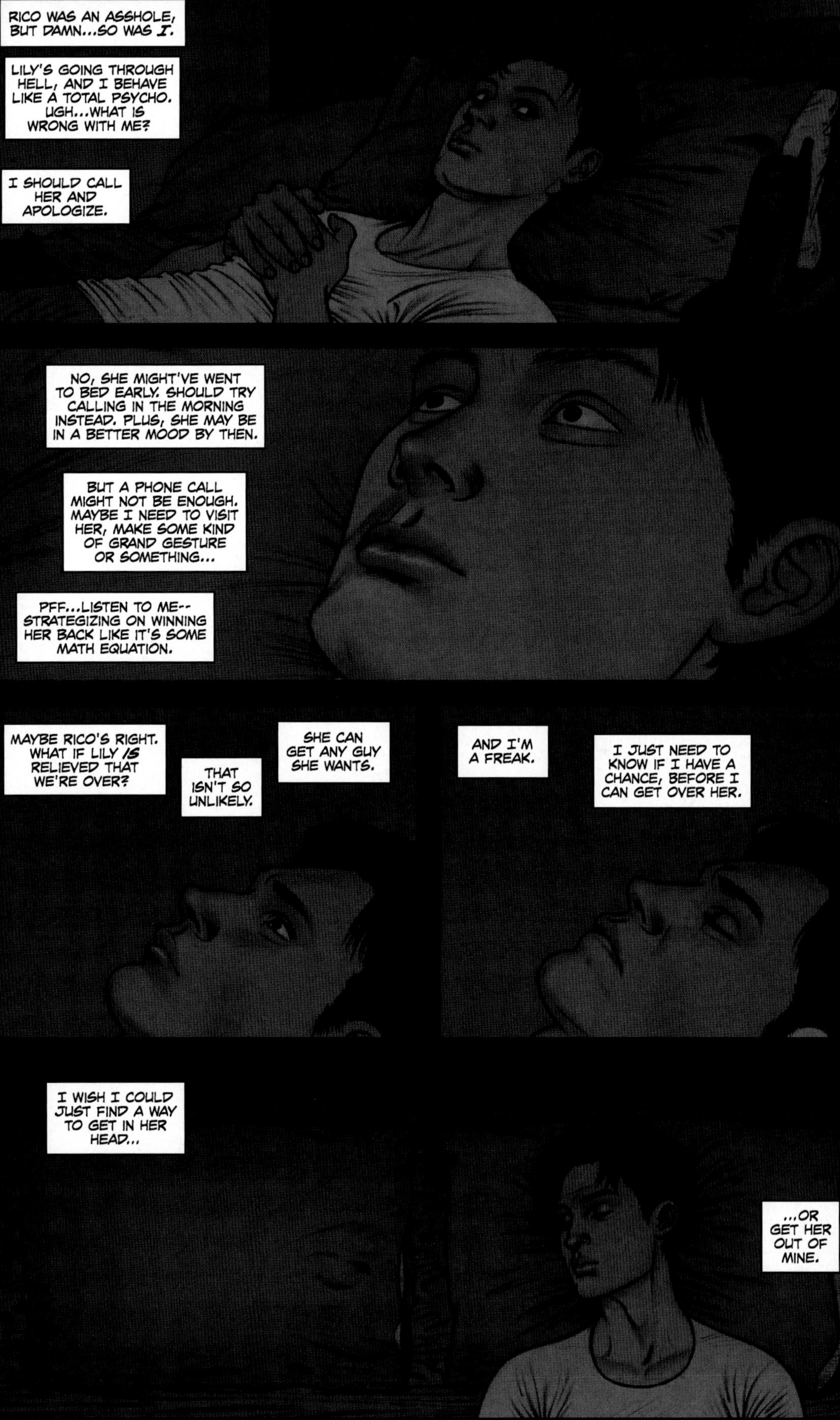
RICO WAS AN ASSHOLE, BUT DAMN...SO WAS *I*.
LILY'S GOING THROUGH HELL, AND I BEHAVE LIKE A TOTAL PSYCHO. UGH...WHAT IS WRONG WITH ME?
I SHOULD CALL HER AND APOLOGIZE.
NO, SHE MIGHT'VE WENT TO BED EARLY. SHOULD TRY CALLING IN THE MORNING INSTEAD. PLUS, SHE MAY BE IN A BETTER MOOD BY THEN.
BUT A PHONE CALL MIGHT NOT BE ENOUGH. MAYBE I NEED TO VISIT HER, MAKE SOME KIND OF GRAND GESTURE OR SOMETHING...
PFF...LISTEN TO ME--STRATEGIZING ON WINNING HER BACK LIKE IT'S SOME MATH EQUATION.
MAYBE RICO'S RIGHT. WHAT IF LILY *IS* RELIEVED THAT WE'RE OVER?
THAT ISN'T SO UNLIKELY.
SHE CAN GET ANY GUY SHE WANTS.
AND I'M A FREAK.
I JUST NEED TO KNOW IF I HAVE A CHANCE, BEFORE I CAN GET OVER HER.
I WISH I COULD JUST FIND A WAY TO GET IN HER HEAD...
...OR GET HER OUT OF MINE.

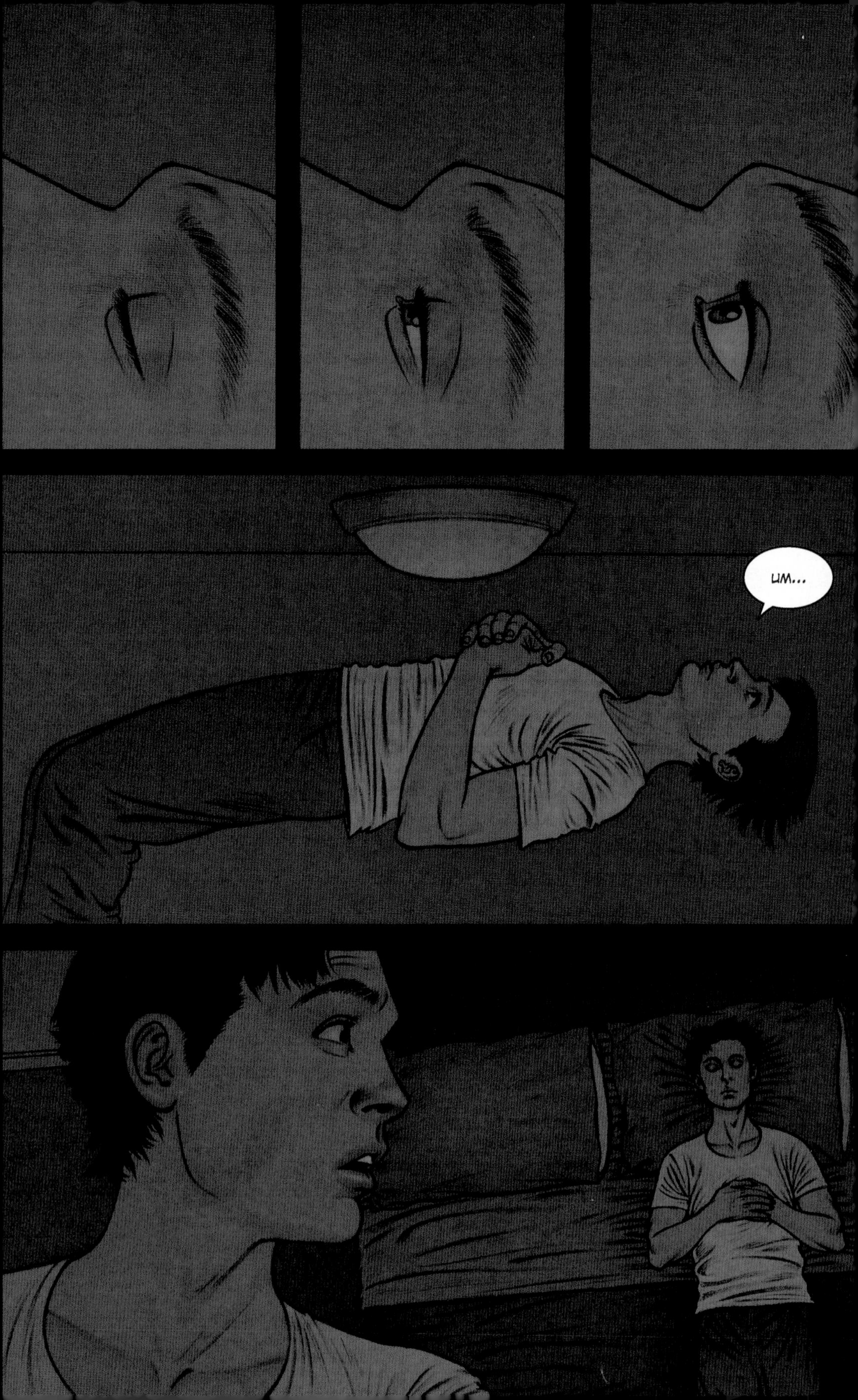
UM...

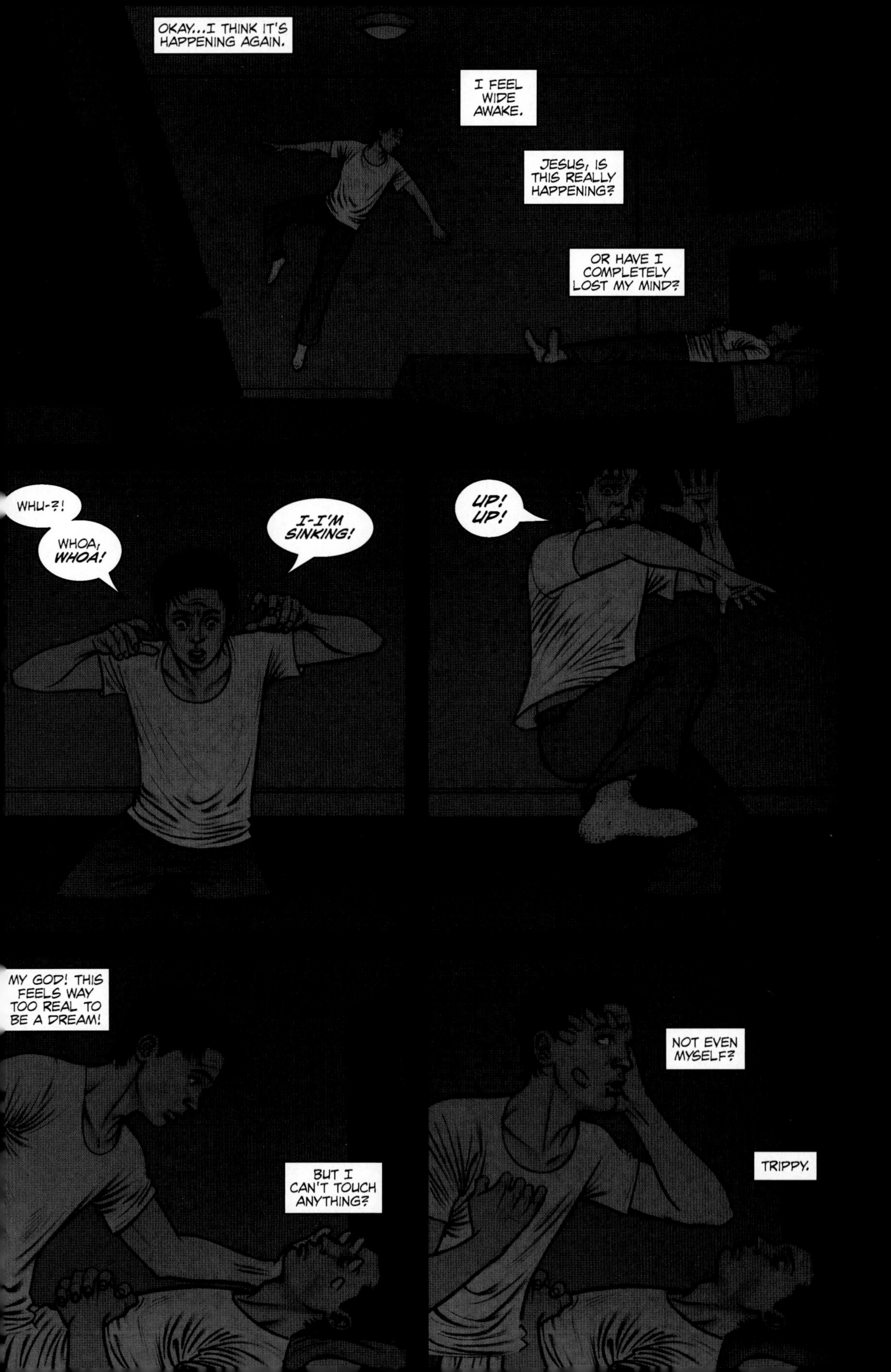
OKAY...I THINK IT'S HAPPENING AGAIN.
I FEEL WIDE AWAKE.
JESUS, IS THIS REALLY HAPPENING?
OR HAVE I COMPLETELY LOST MY MIND?
WHU-?!
WHOA, *WHOA!*
I-I'M SINKING!
UP! UP!
MY GOD! THIS FEELS WAY TOO REAL TO BE A DREAM!
BUT I CAN'T TOUCH ANYTHING?
NOT EVEN MYSELF?
TRIPPY.

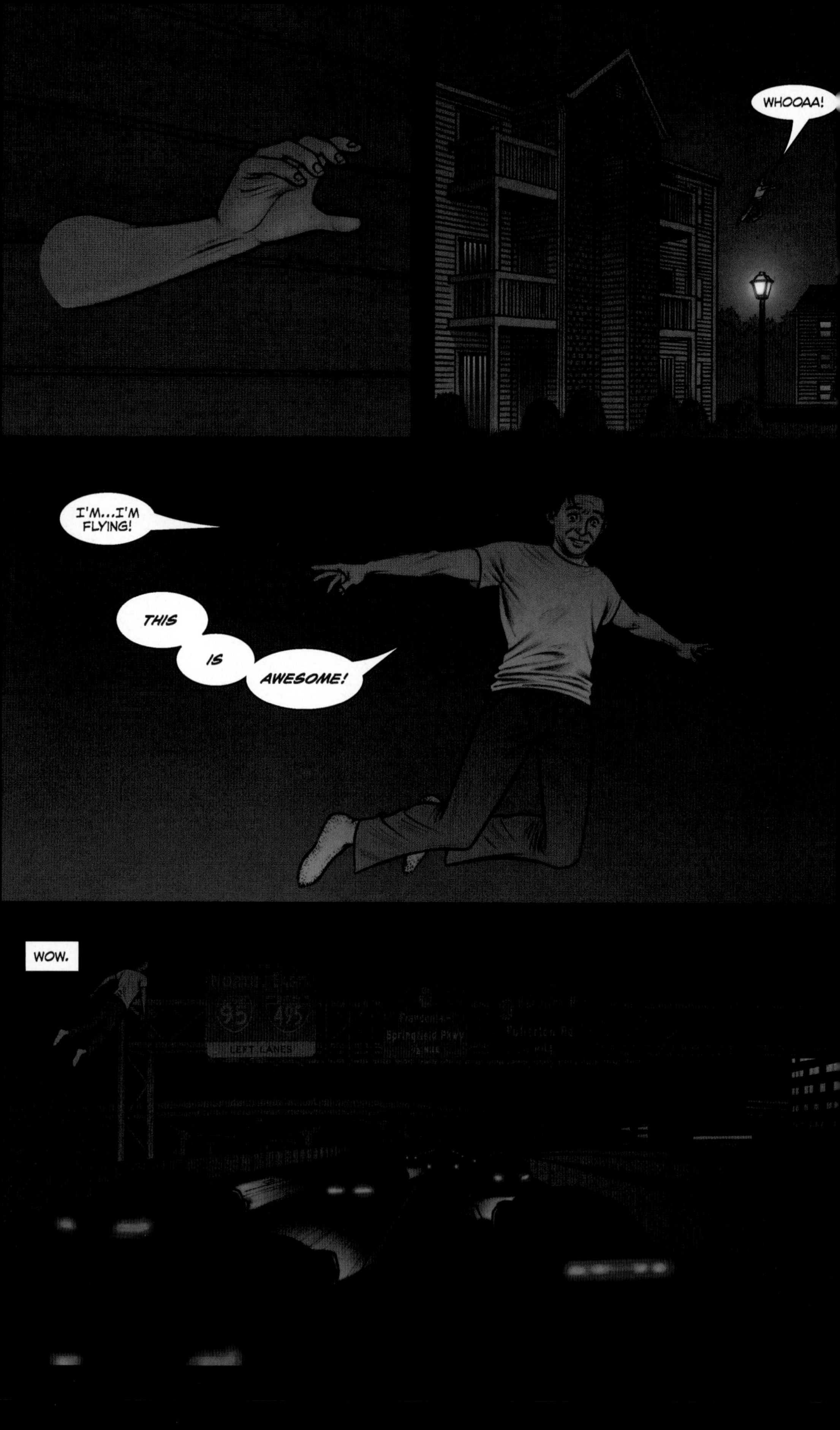
WHOOAA!
I'M...I'M FLYING!
THIS IS AWESOME!
WOW.
95
495
LEFT LANES

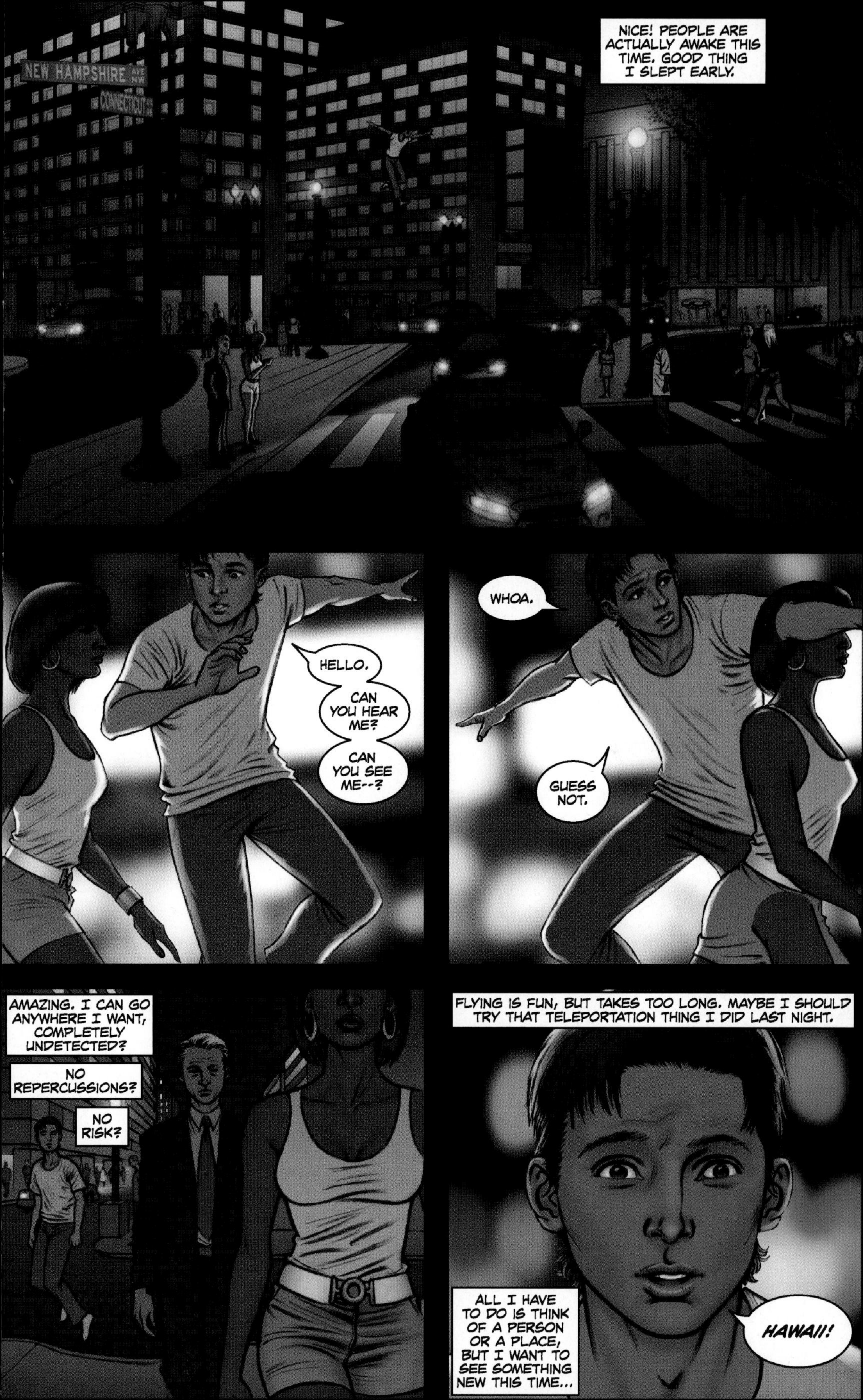
NEW HAMPSHIRE AVE NW
CONNECTICUT AVE
NICE! PEOPLE ARE ACTUALLY AWAKE THIS TIME. GOOD THING I SLEPT EARLY.
HELLO.
CAN YOU HEAR ME?
CAN YOU SEE ME--?
WHOA.
GUESS NOT.
AMAZING. I CAN GO ANYWHERE I WANT, COMPLETELY UNDETECTED?
NO REPERCUSSIONS?
NO RISK?
FLYING IS FUN, BUT TAKES TOO LONG. MAYBE I SHOULD TRY THAT TELEPORTATION THING I DID LAST NIGHT.
ALL I HAVE TO DO IS THINK OF A PERSON OR A PLACE, BUT I WANT TO SEE SOMETHING NEW THIS TIME...
HAWAII!

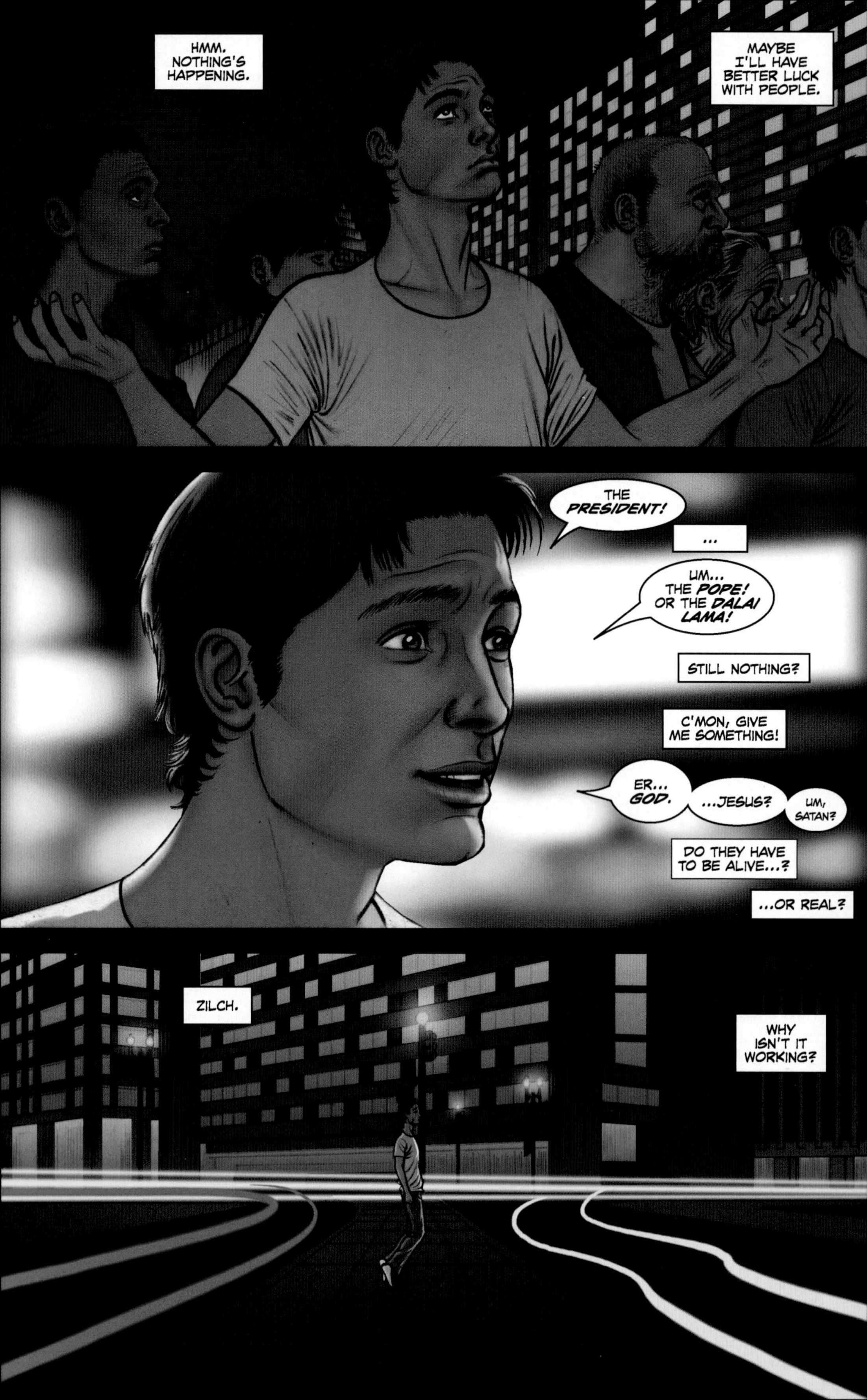
HMM. NOTHING'S HAPPENING.
MAYBE I'LL HAVE BETTER LUCK WITH PEOPLE.
THE *PRESIDENT!*
...
UM... THE *POPE!* OR THE *DALAI LAMA!*
STILL NOTHING?
C'MON, GIVE ME SOMETHING!
ER... *GOD.*
...JESUS?
UM, SATAN?
DO THEY HAVE TO BE ALIVE...?
...OR REAL?
ZILCH.
WHY ISN'T IT WORKING?

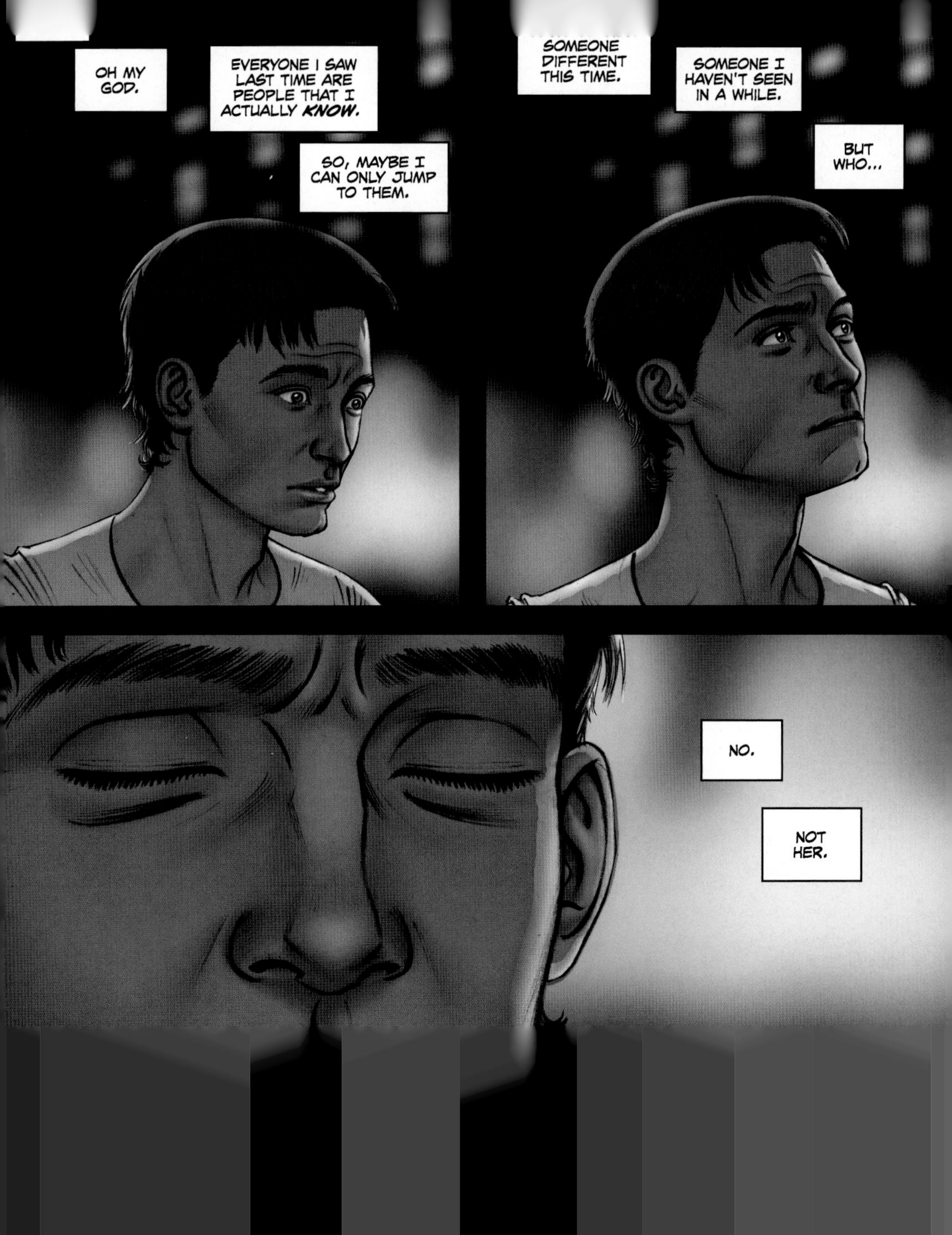
OH MY GOD.
EVERYONE I SAW LAST TIME ARE PEOPLE THAT I ACTUALLY *KNOW*.
SO, MAYBE I CAN ONLY JUMP TO THEM.
SOMEONE DIFFERENT THIS TIME.
SOMEONE I HAVEN'T SEEN IN A WHILE.
BUT WHO...
NO.
NOT HER.

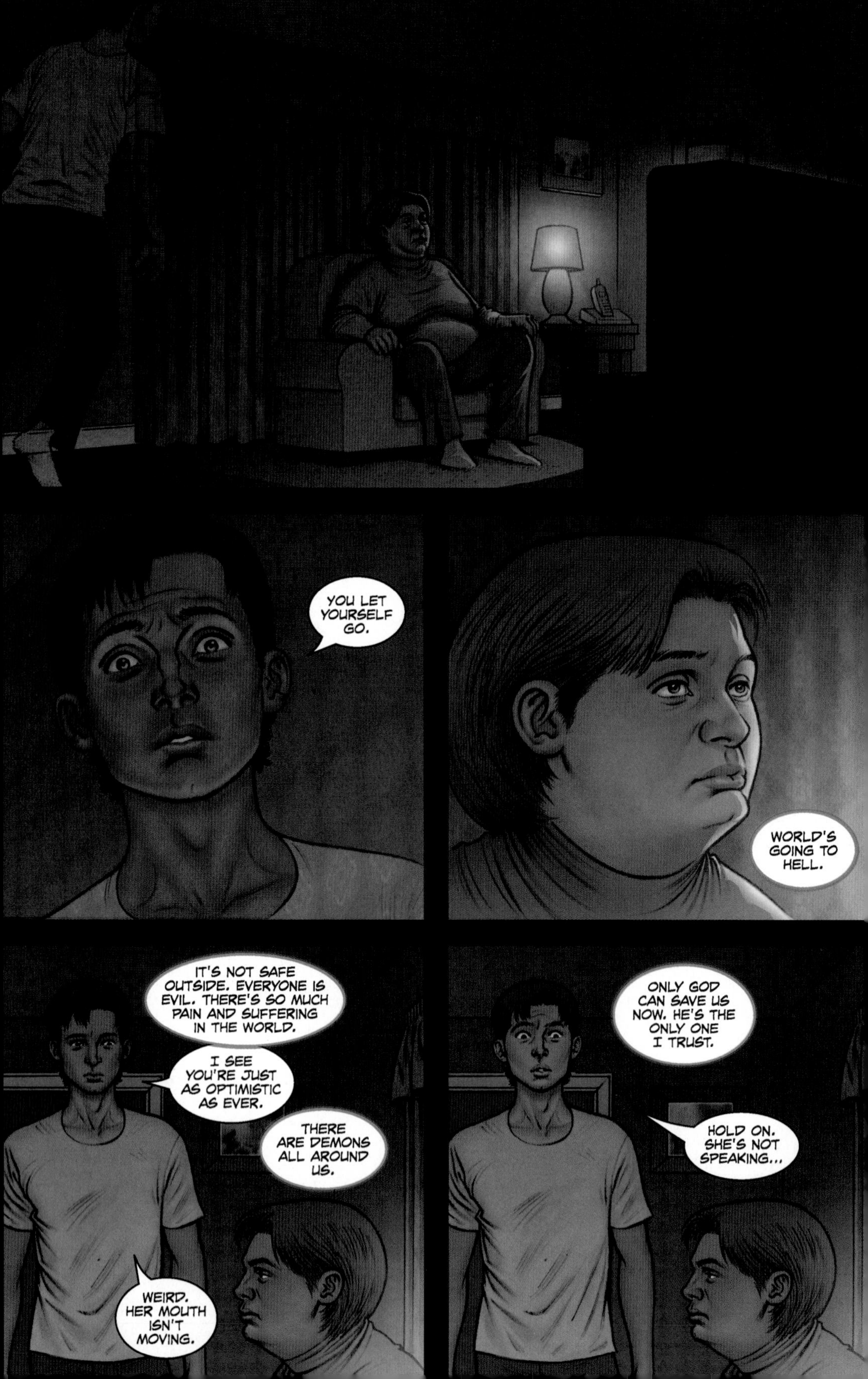
YOU LET YOURSELF GO.
WORLD'S GOING TO HELL.
IT'S NOT SAFE OUTSIDE. EVERYONE IS EVIL. THERE'S SO MUCH PAIN AND SUFFERING IN THE WORLD.
I SEE YOU'RE JUST AS OPTIMISTIC AS EVER.
THERE ARE DEMONS ALL AROUND US.
WEIRD. HER MOUTH ISN'T MOVING.
ONLY GOD CAN SAVE US NOW. HE'S THE ONLY ONE I TRUST.
HOLD ON. SHE'S NOT SPEAKING...

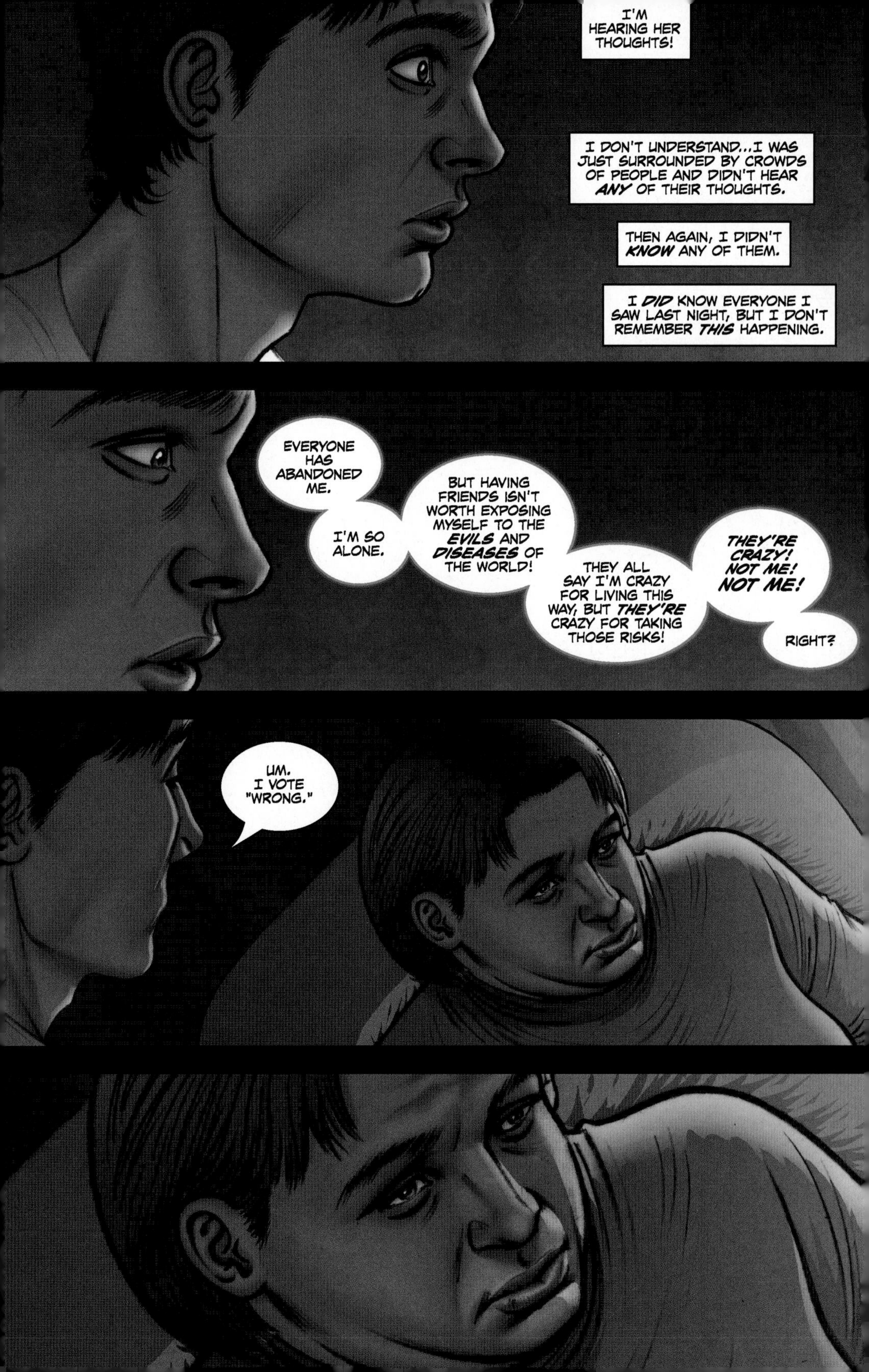
I'M HEARING HER THOUGHTS!
I DON'T UNDERSTAND...I WAS JUST SURROUNDED BY CROWDS OF PEOPLE AND DIDN'T HEAR *ANY* OF THEIR THOUGHTS.
THEN AGAIN, I DIDN'T *KNOW* ANY OF THEM.
I *DID* KNOW EVERYONE I SAW LAST NIGHT, BUT I DON'T REMEMBER *THIS* HAPPENING.
EVERYONE HAS ABANDONED ME.
I'M SO ALONE.
BUT HAVING FRIENDS ISN'T WORTH EXPOSING MYSELF TO THE *EVILS* AND *DISEASES* OF THE WORLD!
THEY ALL SAY I'M CRAZY FOR LIVING THIS WAY, BUT *THEY'RE* CRAZY FOR TAKING THOSE RISKS!
THEY'RE CRAZY! NOT ME! ***NOT ME!***
RIGHT?
UM. I VOTE "WRONG."

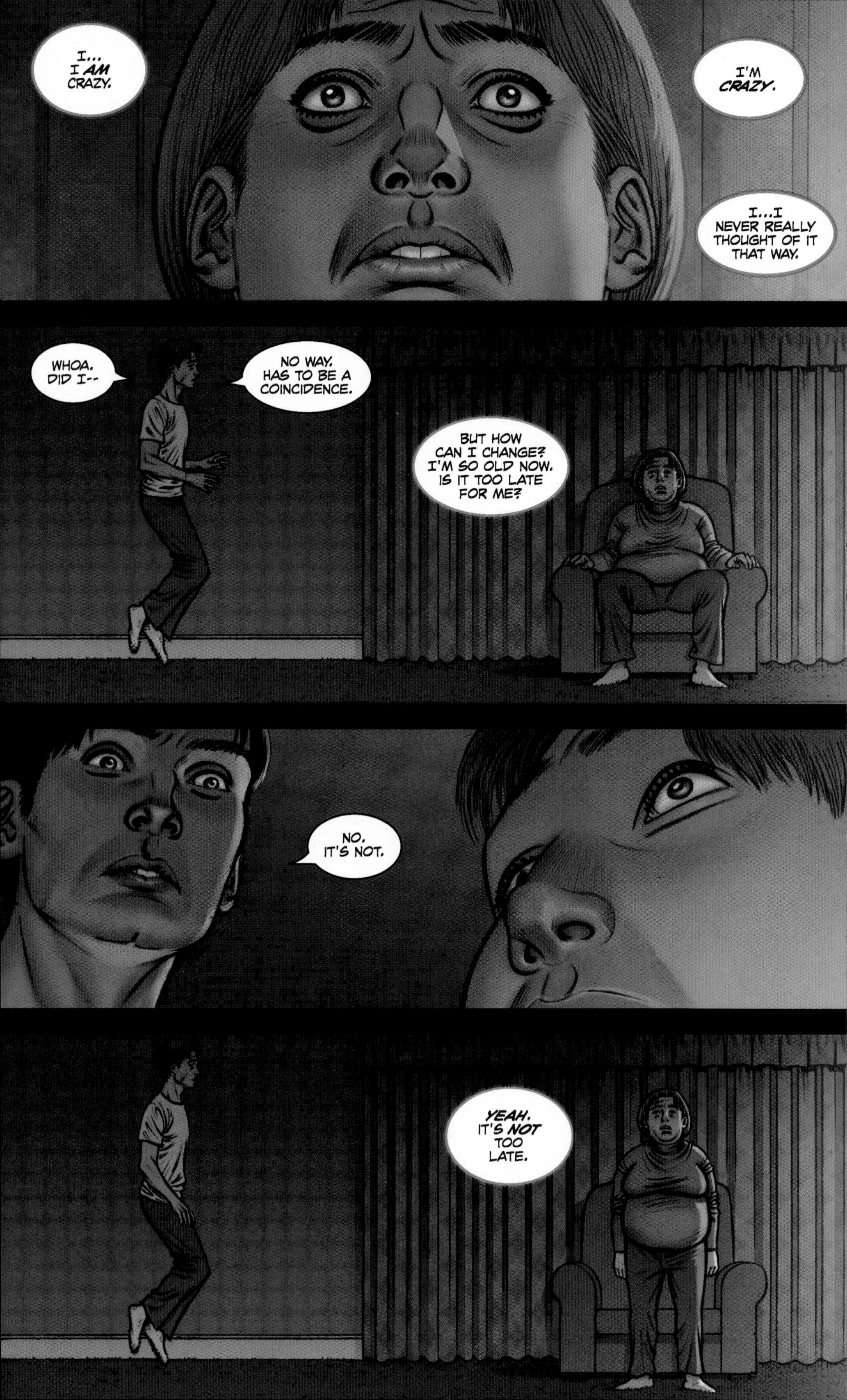
I... I AM CRAZY.
I'M CRAZY.
I...I NEVER REALLY THOUGHT OF IT THAT WAY.
WHOA. DID I--
NO WAY. HAS TO BE A COINCIDENCE.
BUT HOW CAN I CHANGE? I'M SO OLD NOW. IS IT TOO LATE FOR ME?
NO. IT'S NOT.
YEAH. IT'S NOT TOO LATE.

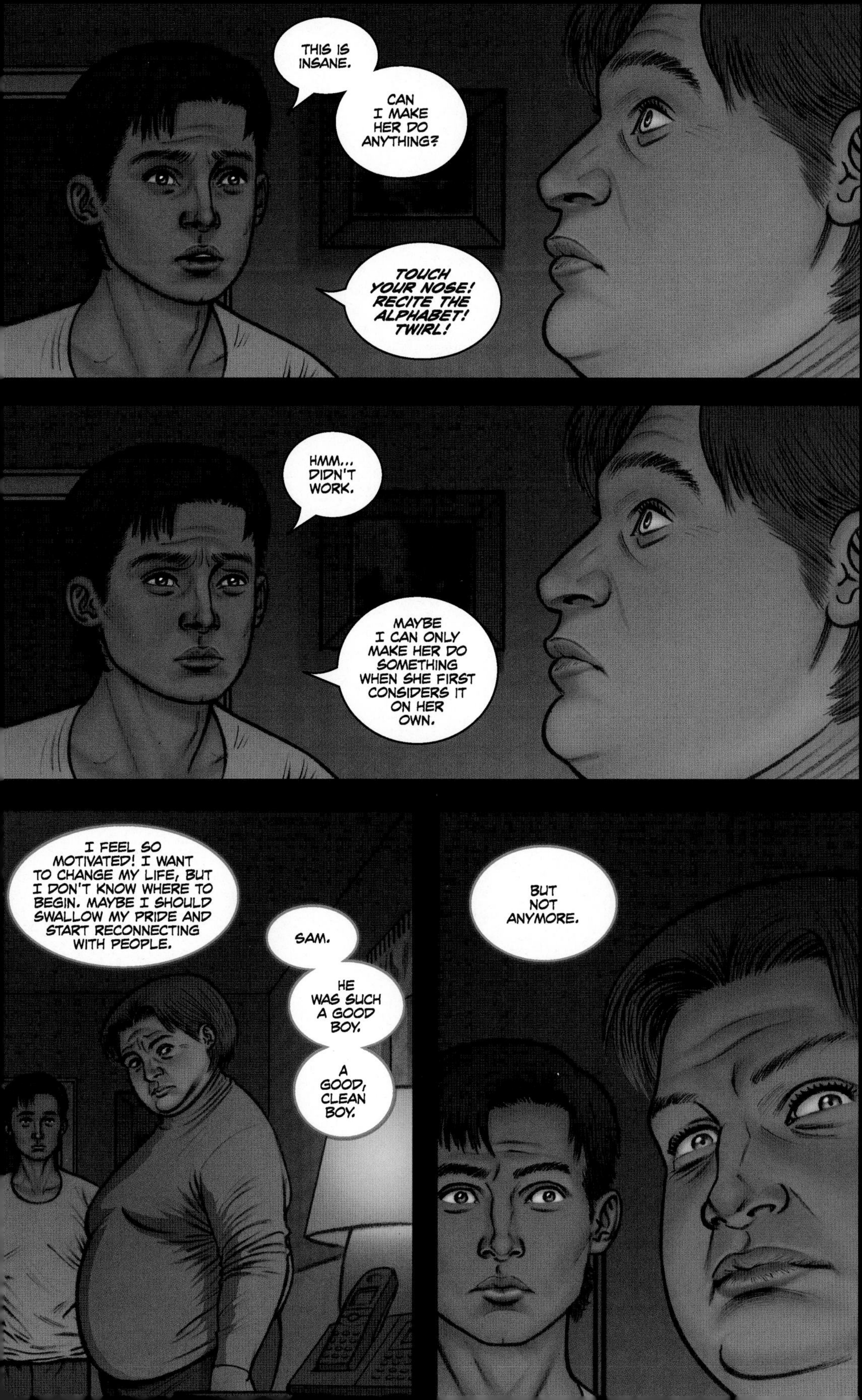
THIS IS INSANE.
CAN I MAKE HER DO ANYTHING?
TOUCH YOUR NOSE! RECITE THE ALPHABET! TWIRL!
HMM... DIDN'T WORK.
MAYBE I CAN ONLY MAKE HER DO SOMETHING WHEN SHE FIRST CONSIDERS IT ON HER OWN.
I FEEL SO MOTIVATED! I WANT TO CHANGE MY LIFE, BUT I DON'T KNOW WHERE TO BEGIN. MAYBE I SHOULD SWALLOW MY PRIDE AND START RECONNECTING WITH PEOPLE.
SAM.
HE WAS SUCH A GOOD BOY.
A GOOD, CLEAN BOY.
BUT NOT ANYMORE.

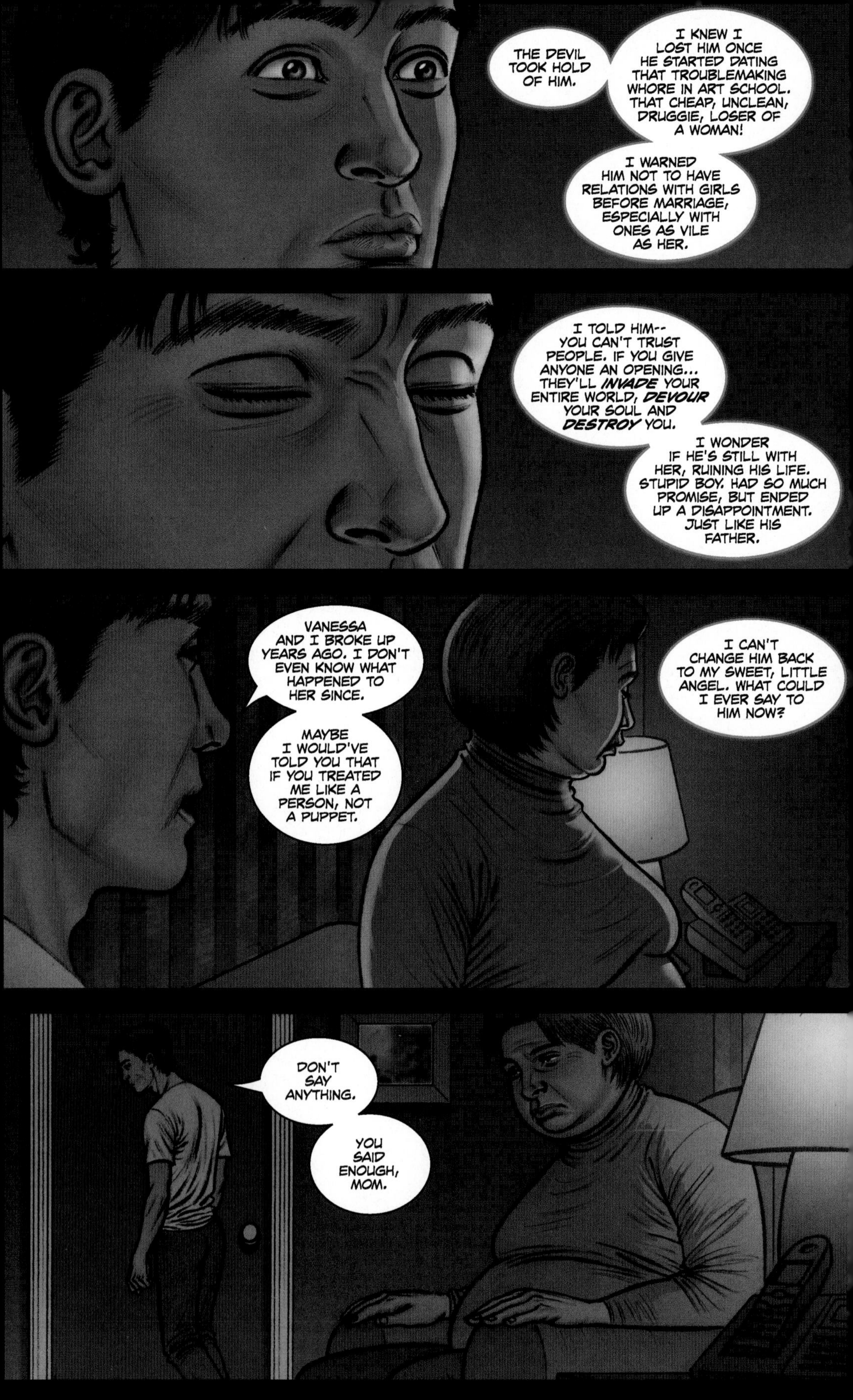
THE DEVIL TOOK HOLD OF HIM.
I KNEW I LOST HIM ONCE HE STARTED DATING THAT TROUBLEMAKING WHORE IN ART SCHOOL. THAT CHEAP, UNCLEAN, DRUGGIE, LOSER OF A WOMAN!
I WARNED HIM NOT TO HAVE RELATIONS WITH GIRLS BEFORE MARRIAGE, ESPECIALLY WITH ONES AS VILE AS HER.
I TOLD HIM-- YOU CAN'T TRUST PEOPLE. IF YOU GIVE ANYONE AN OPENING... THEY'LL *INVADE* YOUR ENTIRE WORLD, *DEVOUR* YOUR SOUL AND *DESTROY* YOU.
I WONDER IF HE'S STILL WITH HER, RUINING HIS LIFE. STUPID BOY. HAD SO MUCH PROMISE, BUT ENDED UP A DISAPPOINTMENT. JUST LIKE HIS FATHER.
VANESSA AND I BROKE UP YEARS AGO. I DON'T EVEN KNOW WHAT HAPPENED TO HER SINCE.
MAYBE I WOULD'VE TOLD YOU THAT IF YOU TREATED ME LIKE A PERSON, NOT A PUPPET.
I CAN'T CHANGE HIM BACK TO MY SWEET, LITTLE ANGEL. WHAT COULD I EVER SAY TO HIM NOW?
DON'T SAY ANYTHING.
YOU SAID ENOUGH, MOM.

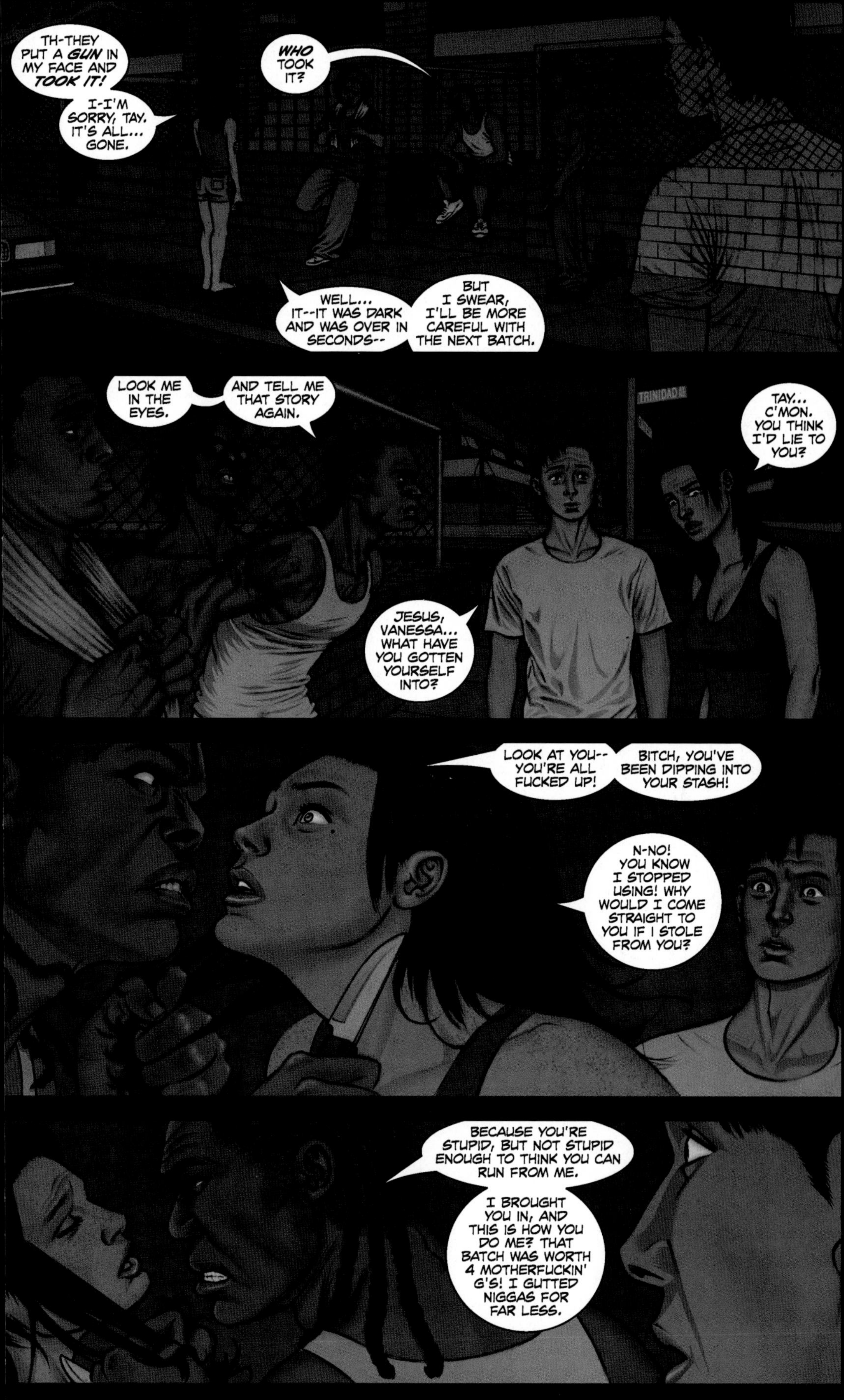
TH-THEY PUT A *GUN* IN MY FACE AND *TOOK IT!*
I-I'M SORRY, TAY. IT'S ALL... GONE.
WHO TOOK IT?
WELL... IT--IT WAS DARK AND WAS OVER IN SECONDS--
BUT I SWEAR, I'LL BE MORE CAREFUL WITH THE NEXT BATCH.
LOOK ME IN THE EYES.
AND TELL ME THAT STORY AGAIN.
TRINIDAD
TAY... C'MON. YOU THINK I'D LIE TO YOU?
JESUS, VANESSA... WHAT HAVE YOU GOTTEN YOURSELF INTO?
LOOK AT YOU--YOU'RE ALL FUCKED UP!
BITCH, YOU'VE BEEN DIPPING INTO YOUR STASH!
N-NO! YOU KNOW I STOPPED USING! WHY WOULD I COME STRAIGHT TO YOU IF I STOLE FROM YOU?
BECAUSE YOU'RE STUPID, BUT NOT STUPID ENOUGH TO THINK YOU CAN RUN FROM ME.
I BROUGHT YOU IN, AND THIS IS HOW YOU DO ME? THAT BATCH WAS WORTH 4 MOTHERFUCKIN' G'S! I GUTTED NIGGAS FOR FAR LESS.

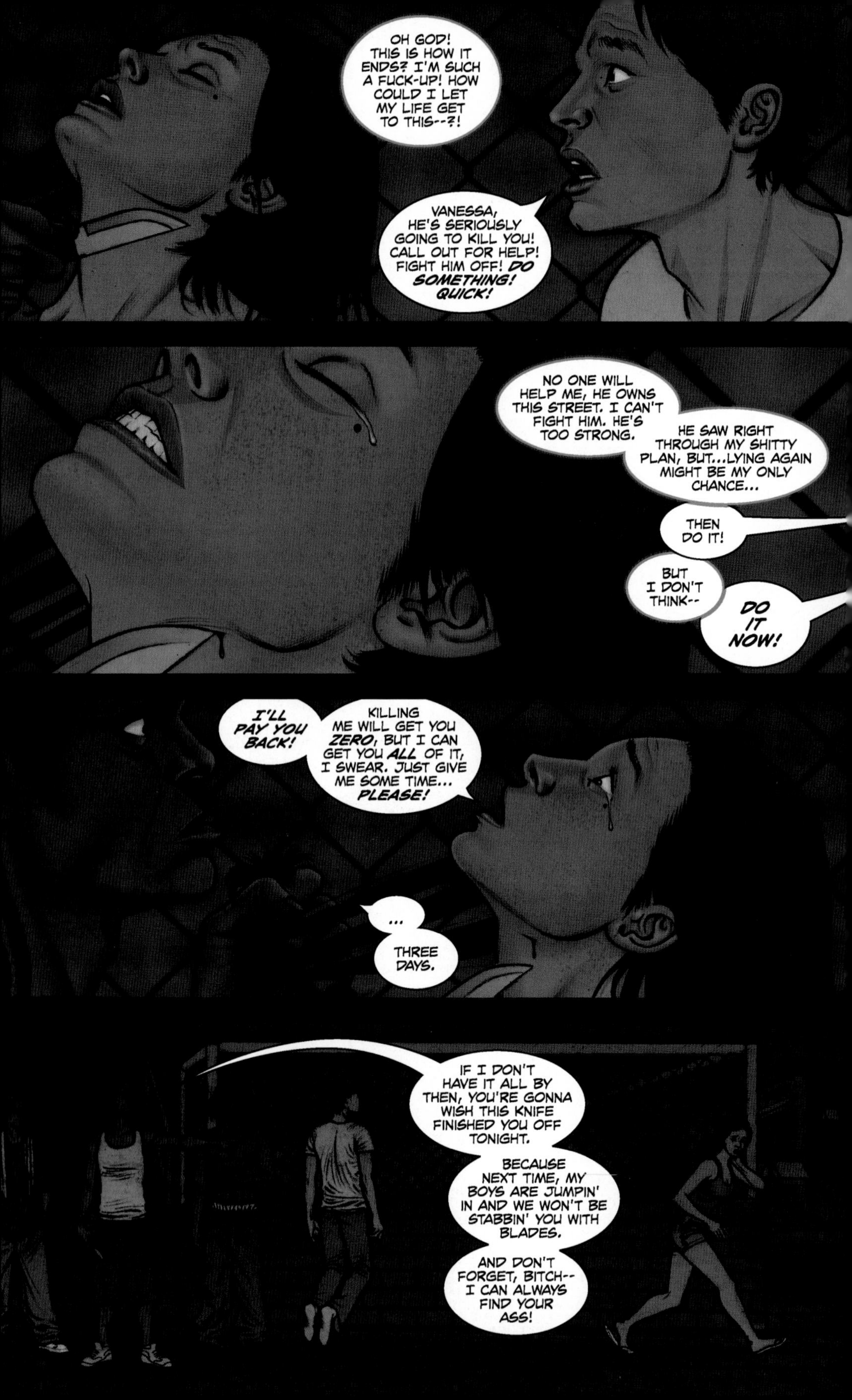
OH GOD! THIS IS HOW IT ENDS? I'M SUCH A FUCK-UP! HOW COULD I LET MY LIFE GET TO THIS--?!
VANESSA, HE'S SERIOUSLY GOING TO KILL YOU! CALL OUT FOR HELP! FIGHT HIM OFF! DO SOMETHING! QUICK!
NO ONE WILL HELP ME, HE OWNS THIS STREET. I CAN'T FIGHT HIM. HE'S TOO STRONG.
HE SAW RIGHT THROUGH MY SHITTY PLAN, BUT...LYING AGAIN MIGHT BE MY ONLY CHANCE...
THEN DO IT!
BUT I DON'T THINK--
DO IT NOW!
I'LL PAY YOU BACK!
KILLING ME WILL GET YOU ZERO, BUT I CAN GET YOU ALL OF IT, I SWEAR. JUST GIVE ME SOME TIME... PLEASE!
...
THREE DAYS.
IF I DON'T HAVE IT ALL BY THEN, YOU'RE GONNA WISH THIS KNIFE FINISHED YOU OFF TONIGHT.
BECAUSE NEXT TIME, MY BOYS ARE JUMPIN' IN AND WE WON'T BE STABBIN' YOU WITH BLADES.
AND DON'T FORGET, BITCH-- I CAN ALWAYS FIND YOUR ASS!

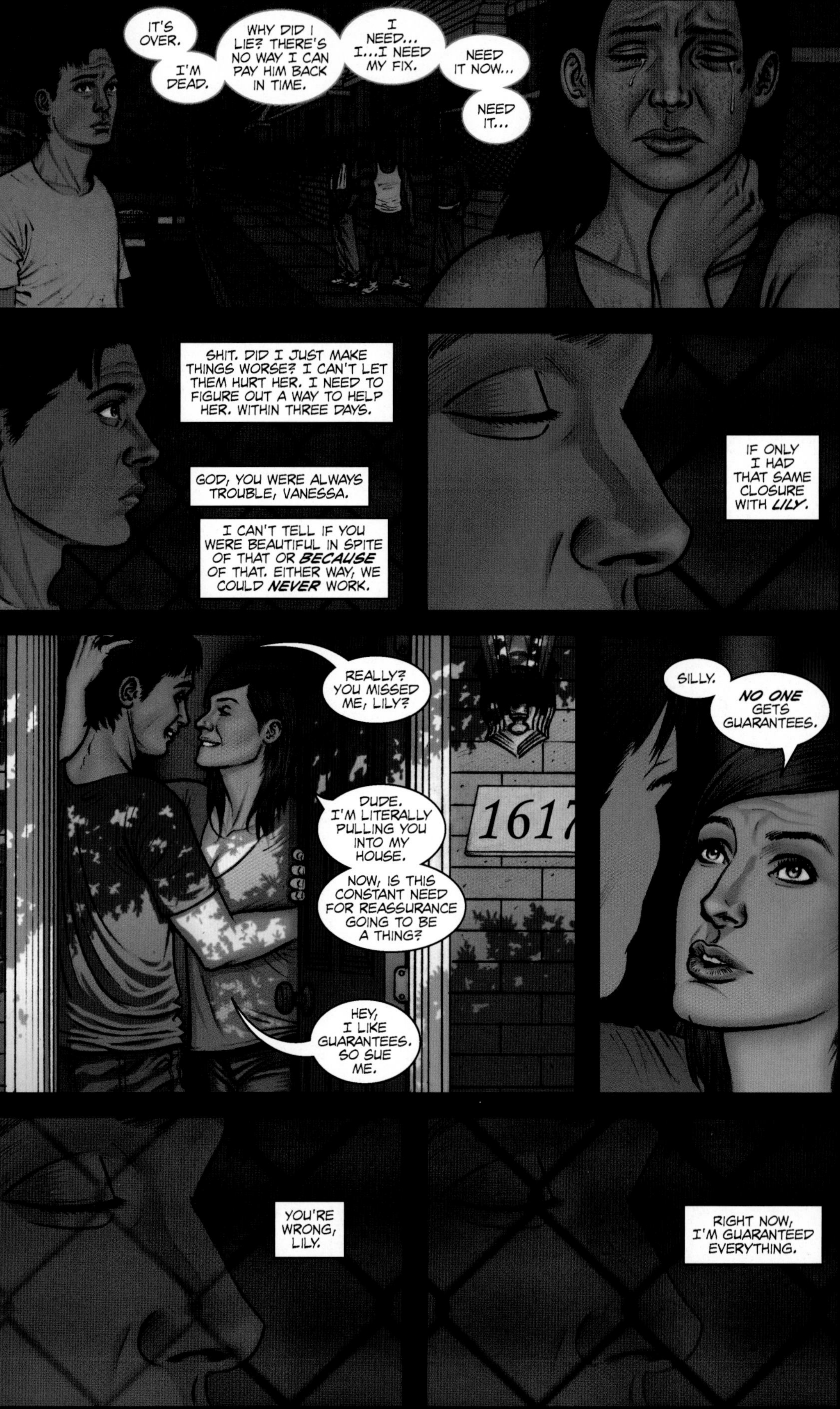
IT'S OVER.
I'M DEAD.
WHY DID I LIE? THERE'S NO WAY I CAN PAY HIM BACK IN TIME.
I NEED... I...I NEED MY FIX.
NEED IT NOW...
NEED IT...
SHIT. DID I JUST MAKE THINGS WORSE? I CAN'T LET THEM HURT HER. I NEED TO FIGURE OUT A WAY TO HELP HER. WITHIN THREE DAYS.
GOD, YOU WERE ALWAYS TROUBLE, VANESSA.
I CAN'T TELL IF YOU WERE BEAUTIFUL IN SPITE OF THAT OR BECAUSE OF THAT. EITHER WAY, WE COULD NEVER WORK.
IF ONLY I HAD THAT SAME CLOSURE WITH LILY.
REALLY? YOU MISSED ME, LILY?
DUDE. I'M LITERALLY PULLING YOU INTO MY HOUSE.
NOW, IS THIS CONSTANT NEED FOR REASSURANCE GOING TO BE A THING?
HEY, I LIKE GUARANTEES. SO SUE ME.
1617
SILLY.
NO ONE GETS GUARANTEES.
YOU'RE WRONG, LILY.
RIGHT NOW, I'M GUARANTEED EVERYTHING.

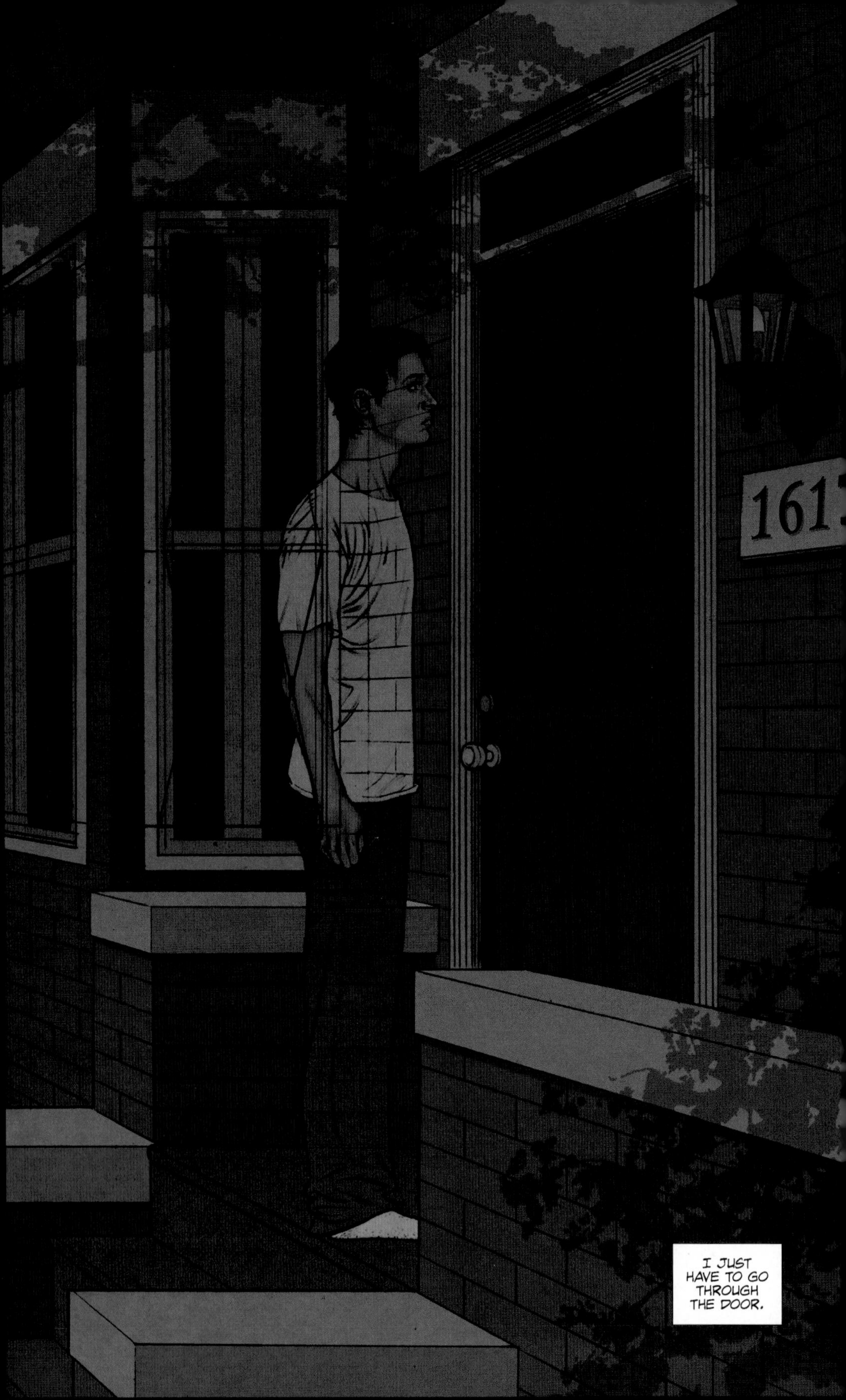
161
I JUST HAVE TO GO THROUGH THE DOOR.

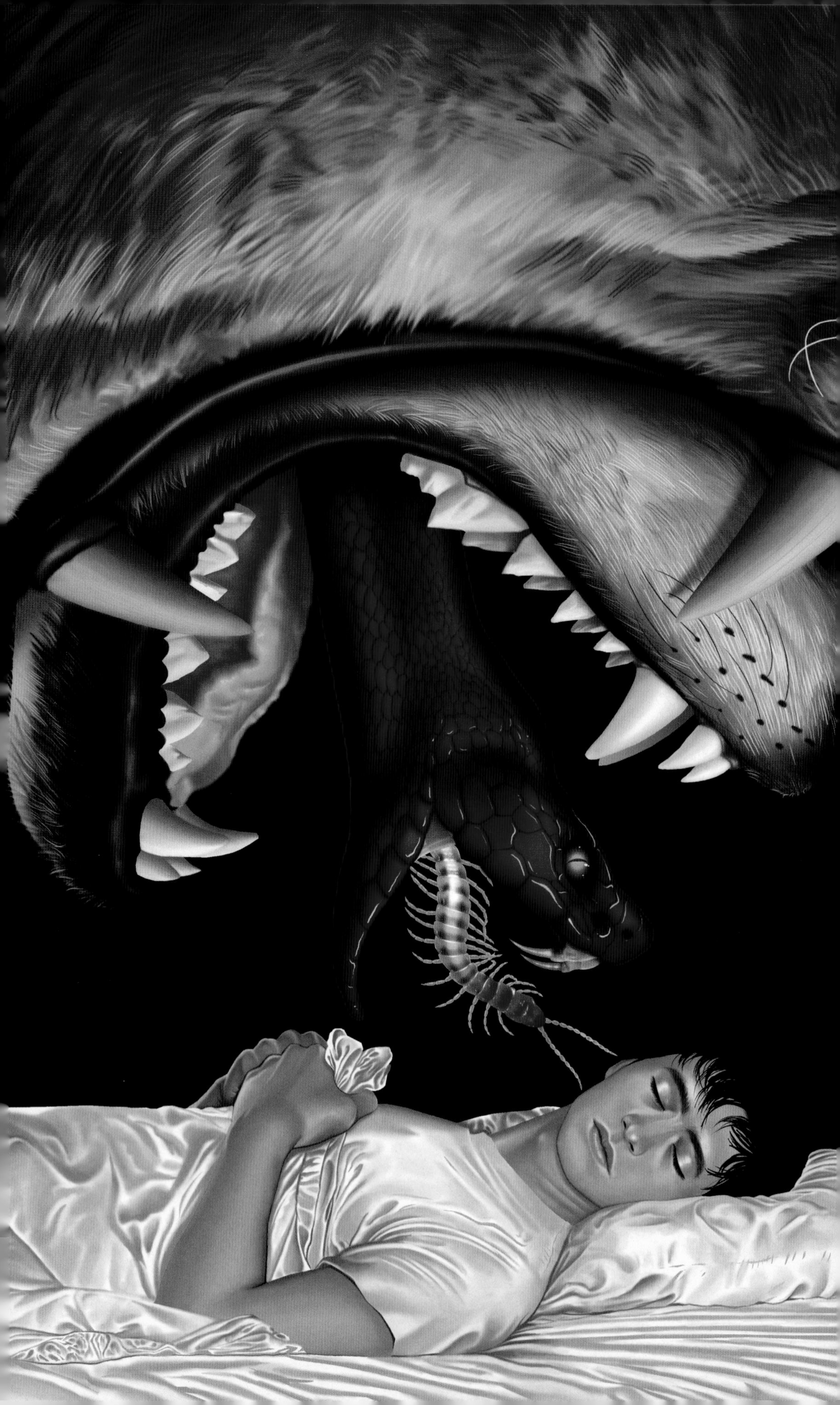

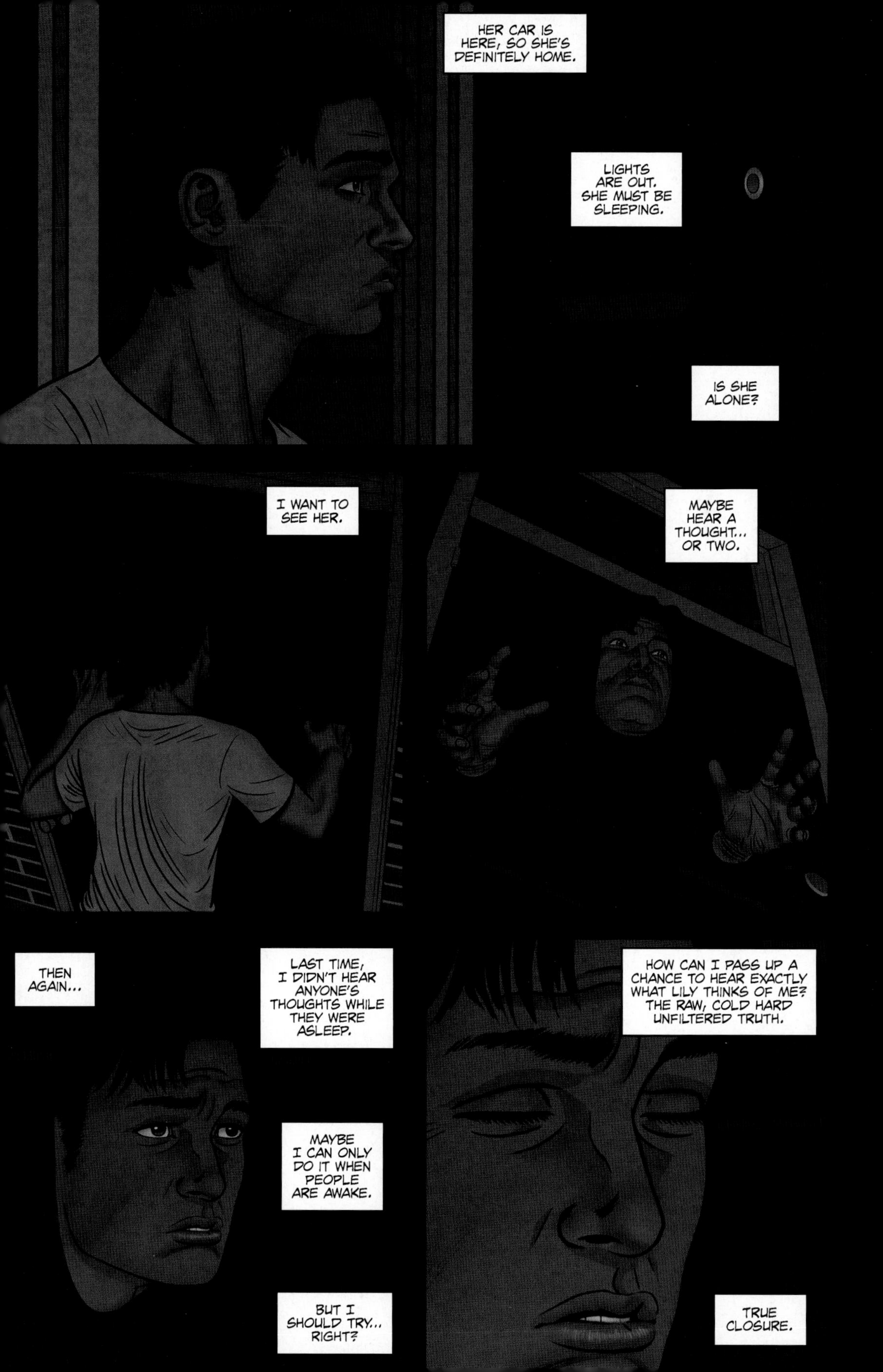
HER CAR IS HERE, SO SHE'S DEFINITELY HOME.
LIGHTS ARE OUT. SHE MUST BE SLEEPING.
IS SHE ALONE?
I WANT TO SEE HER.
MAYBE HEAR A THOUGHT... OR TWO.
THEN AGAIN...
LAST TIME, I DIDN'T HEAR ANYONE'S THOUGHTS WHILE THEY WERE ASLEEP.
MAYBE I CAN ONLY DO IT WHEN PEOPLE ARE AWAKE.
BUT I SHOULD TRY... RIGHT?
HOW CAN I PASS UP A CHANCE TO HEAR EXACTLY WHAT LILY THINKS OF ME? THE RAW, COLD HARD UNFILTERED TRUTH.
TRUE CLOSURE.

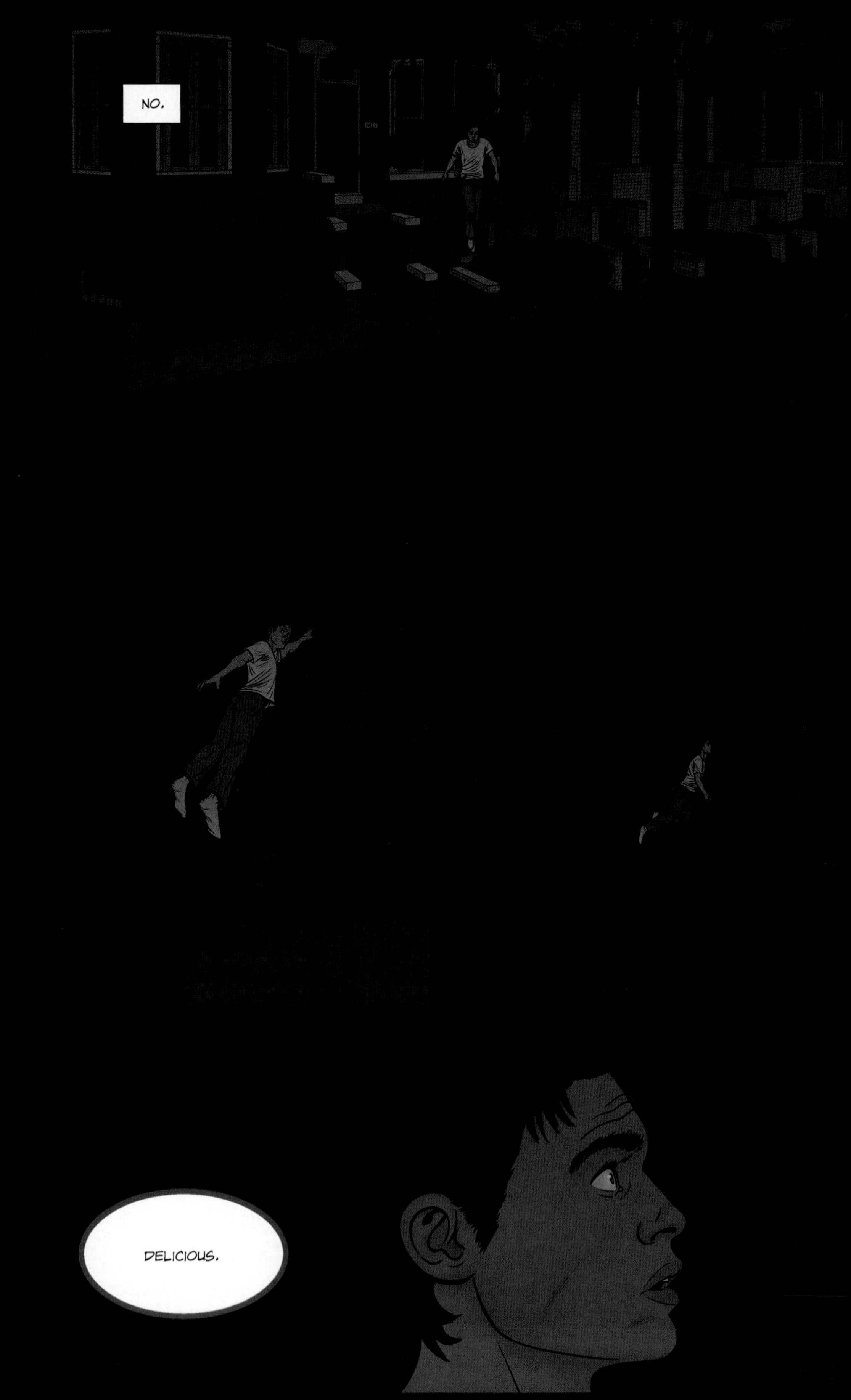
NO.
DELICIOUS.

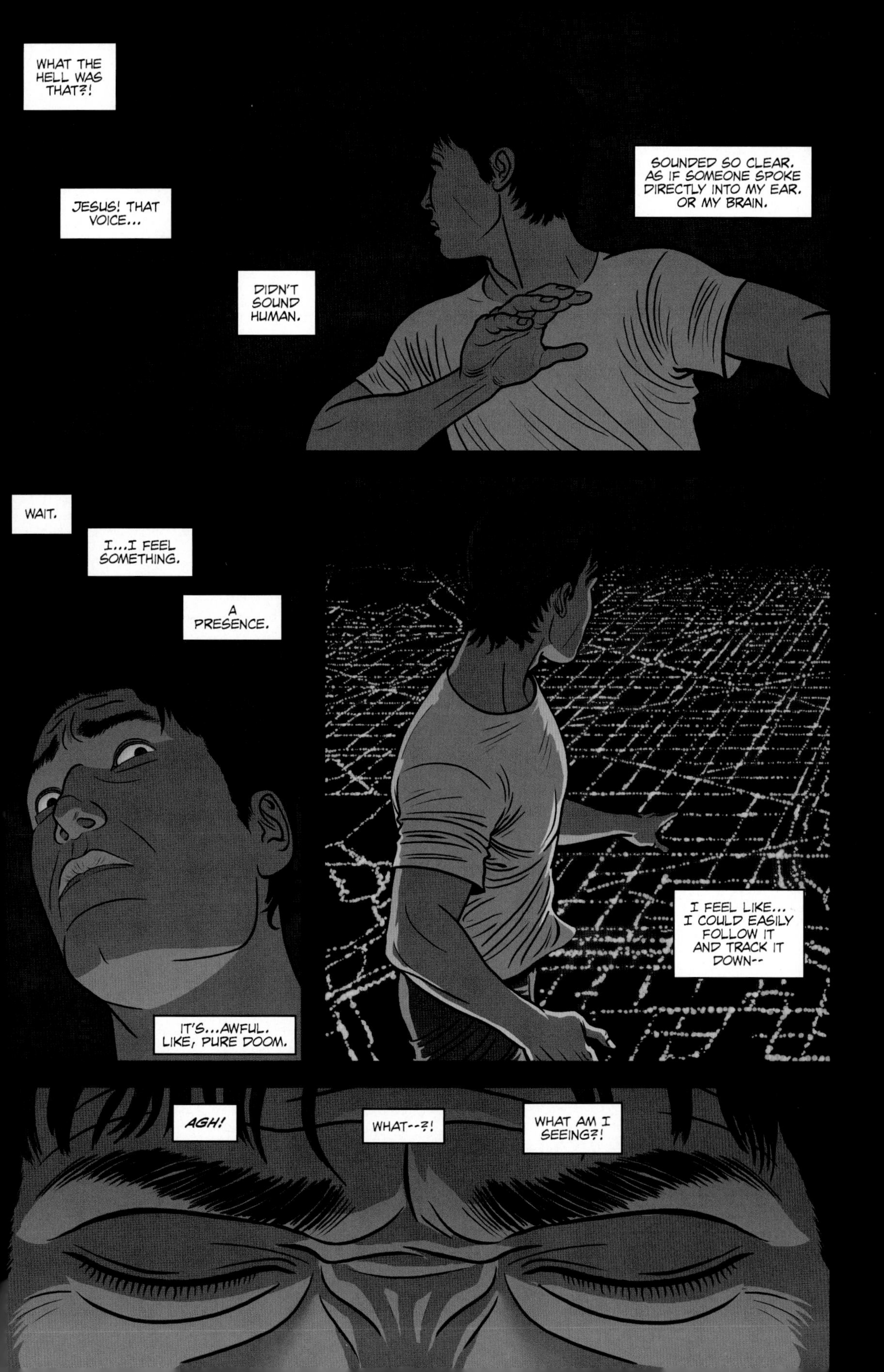
WHAT THE HELL WAS THAT?!
JESUS! THAT VOICE...
DIDN'T SOUND HUMAN.
SOUNDED SO CLEAR. AS IF SOMEONE SPOKE DIRECTLY INTO MY EAR. OR MY BRAIN.
WAIT.
I...I FEEL SOMETHING.
A PRESENCE.
IT'S...AWFUL. LIKE, PURE DOOM.
I FEEL LIKE... I COULD EASILY FOLLOW IT AND TRACK IT DOWN--
AGH!
WHAT--?!
WHAT AM I SEEING?!

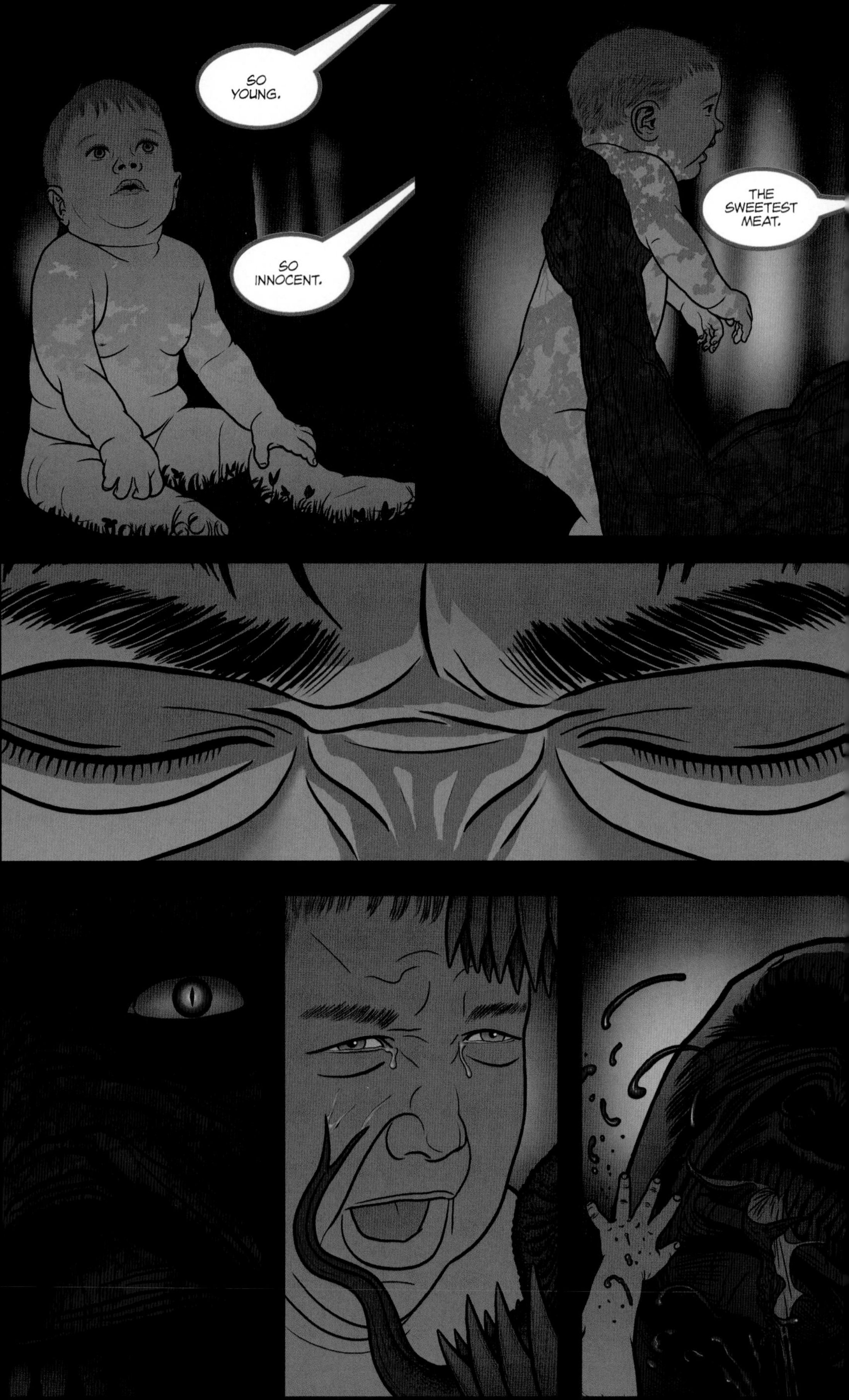
SO YOUNG.
SO INNOCENT.
THE SWEETEST MEAT.

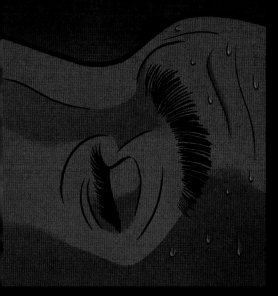

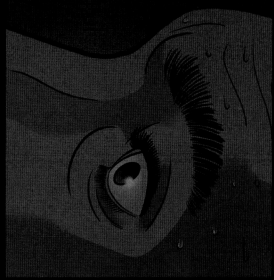

WHAT THE FUCK WAS THAT?!

≷HUFF≷
≷HUFF≷

WAS I SEEING SOMEONE'S THOUGHTS? THAT...MONSTER CAN'T BE REAL SO THAT WASN'T ACTUALLY HAPPENING... RIGHT?!

I KNOW THAT WASN'T ALL IN MY HEAD. I DON'T KNOW WHAT THAT LAST PART WAS ABOUT, BUT THE FIRST HALF WAS DEFINITELY REAL. I CAN PROVE IT!

I JUST HOPE I STILL HAVE THAT NUMBER.

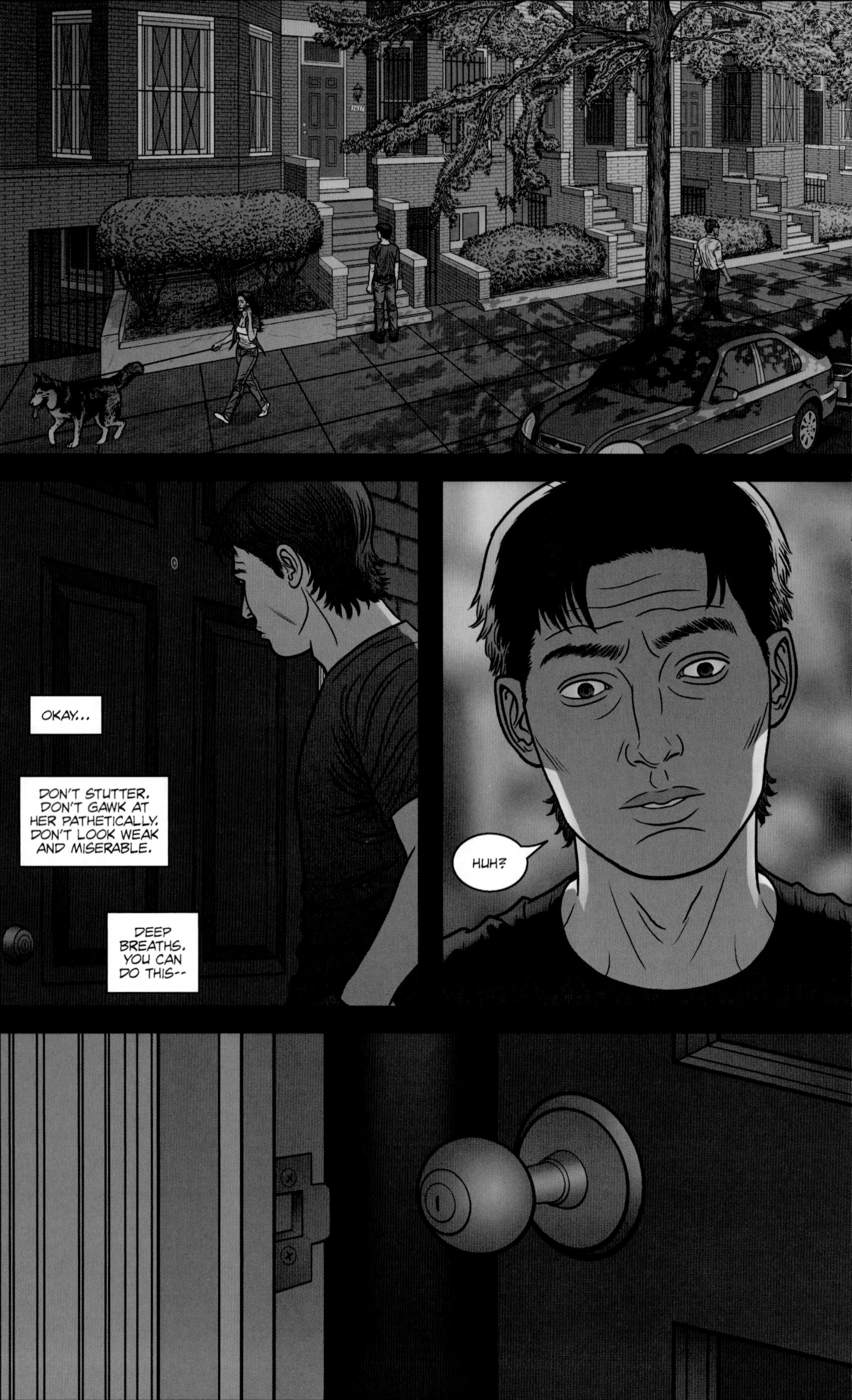
OKAY...
DON'T STUTTER. DON'T GAWK AT HER PATHETICALLY. DON'T LOOK WEAK AND MISERABLE.
DEEP BREATHS. YOU CAN DO THIS--
HUH?

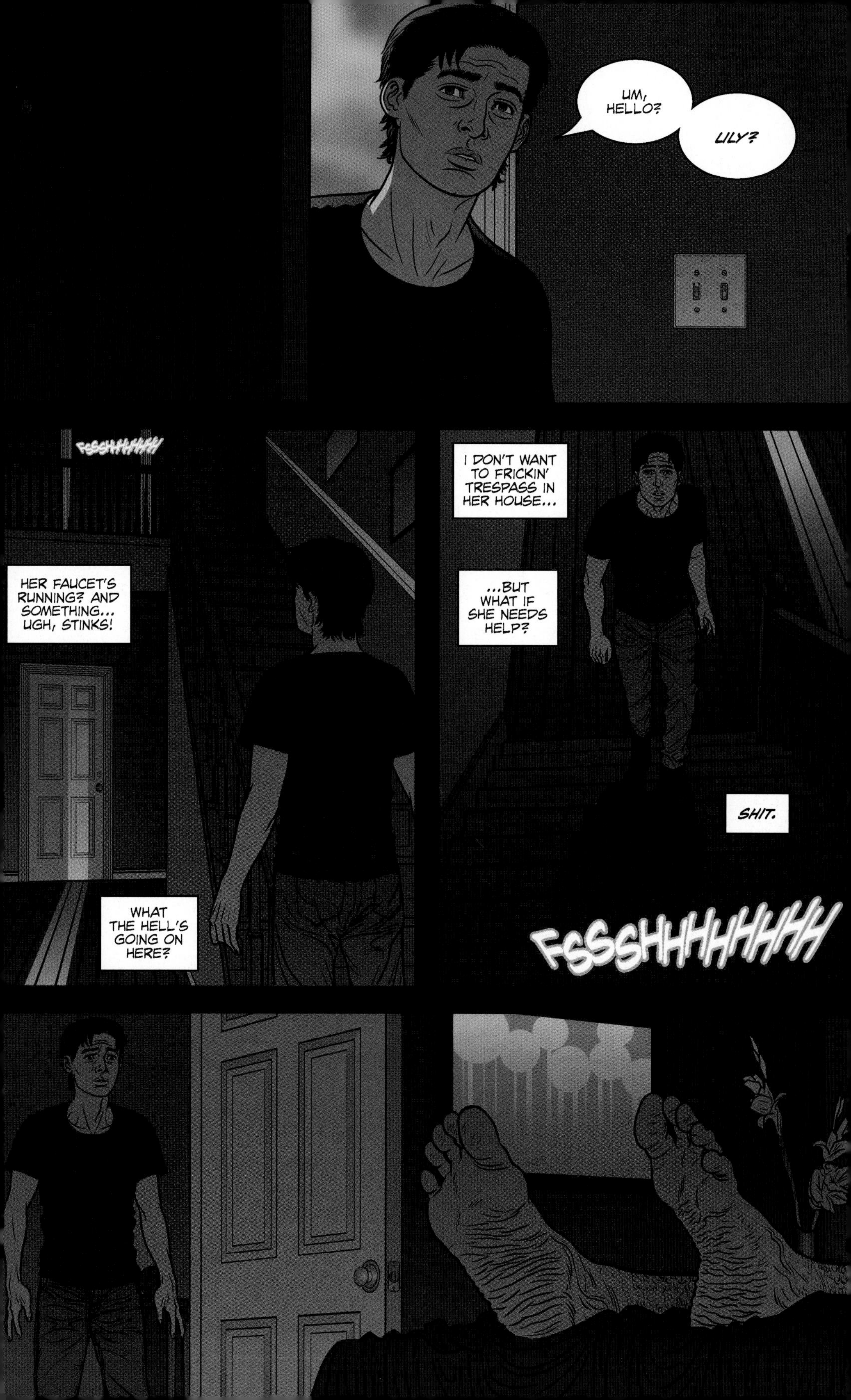
UM, HELLO?
LILY?
FSSSHHHHHHH
HER FAUCET'S RUNNING? AND SOMETHING... UGH, STINKS!
WHAT THE HELL'S GOING ON HERE?
I DON'T WANT TO FRICKIN' TRESPASS IN HER HOUSE...
...BUT WHAT IF SHE NEEDS HELP?
SHIT.
FSSSHHHHHHHH

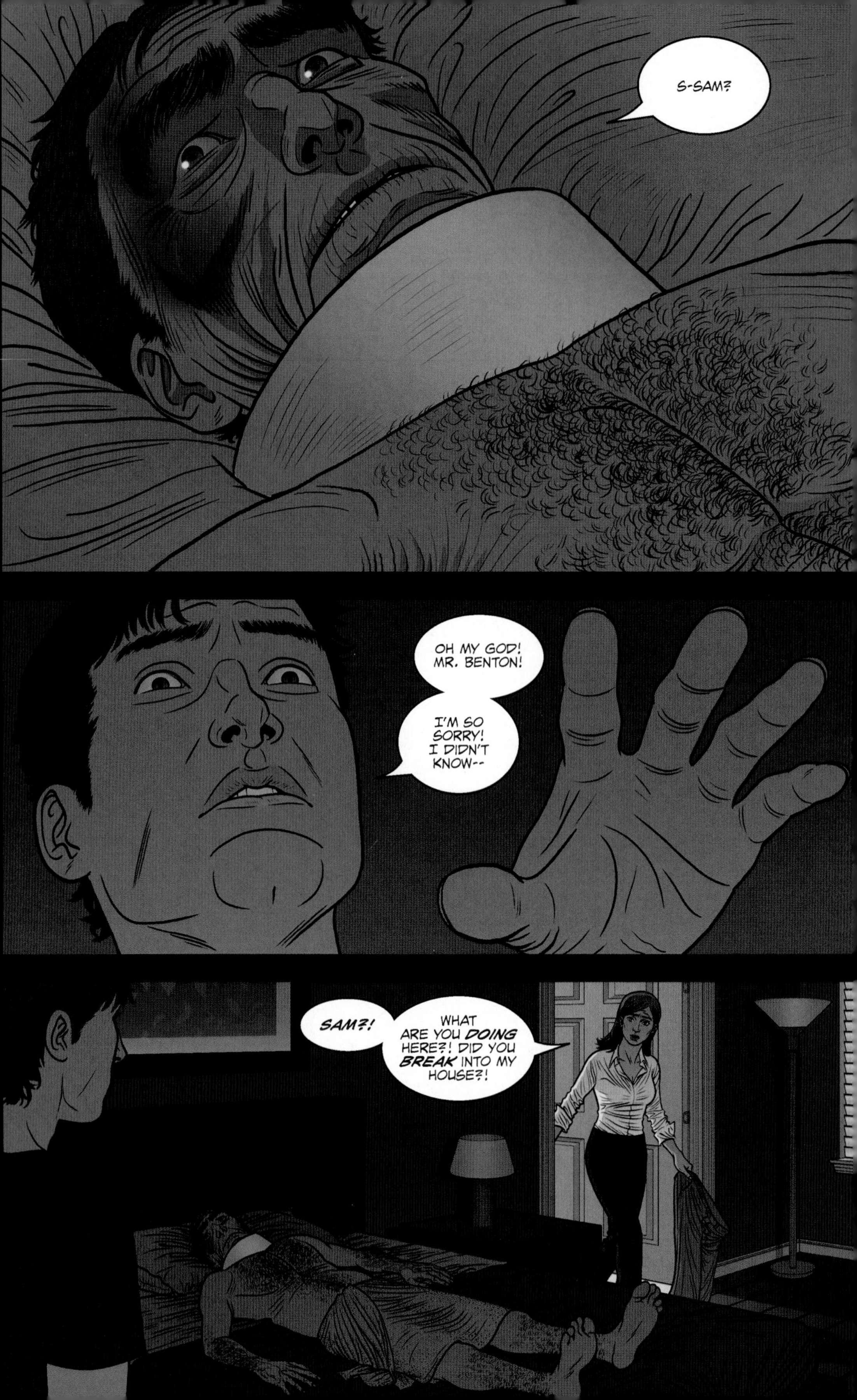
S-SAM?
OH MY GOD! MR. BENTON!
I'M SO SORRY! I DIDN'T KNOW--
SAM?!
WHAT ARE YOU DOING HERE?! DID YOU BREAK INTO MY HOUSE?!

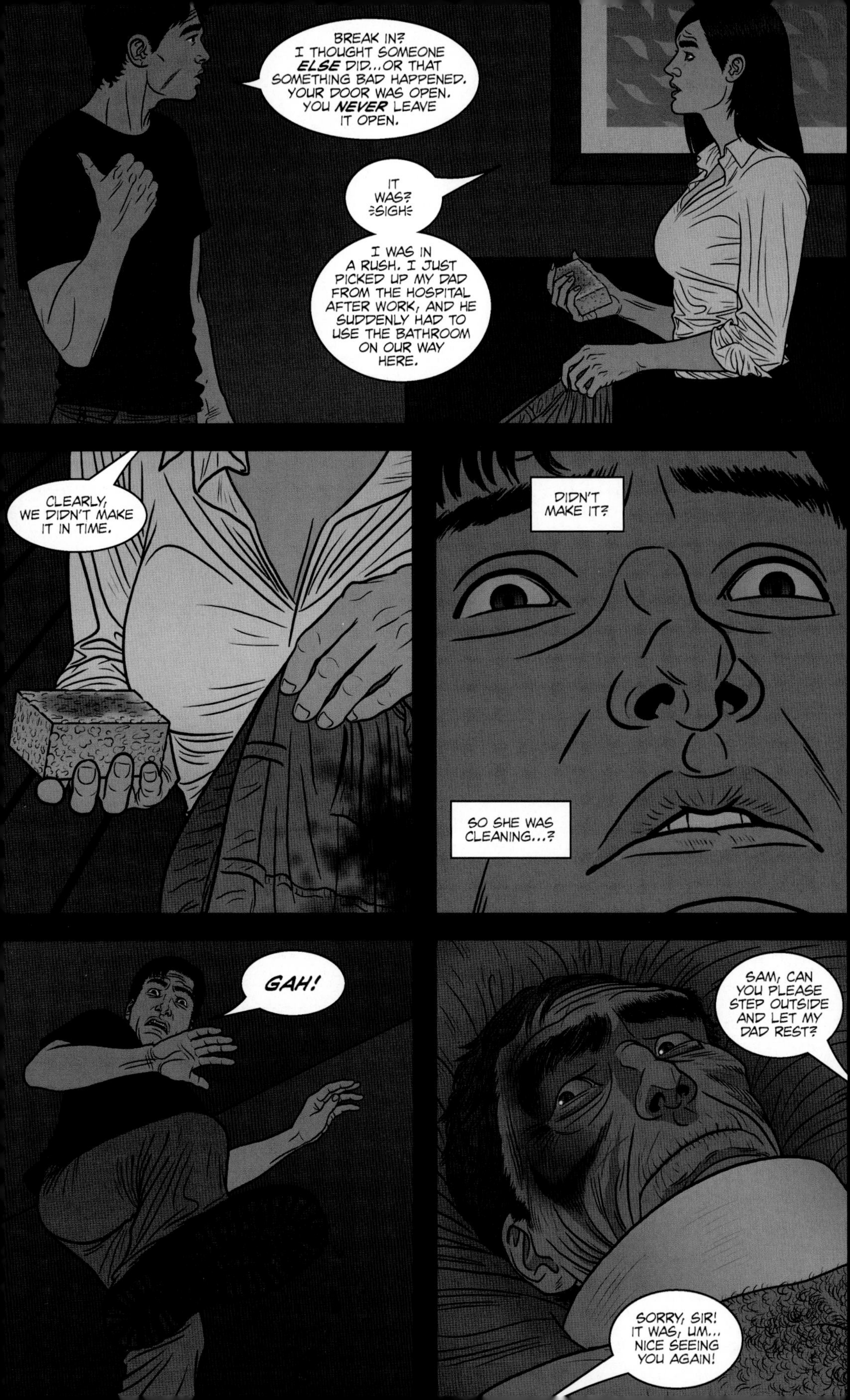
BREAK IN? I THOUGHT SOMEONE *ELSE* DID...OR THAT SOMETHING BAD HAPPENED. YOUR DOOR WAS OPEN. YOU *NEVER* LEAVE IT OPEN.
IT WAS? ≶SIGH≷
I WAS IN A RUSH. I JUST PICKED UP MY DAD FROM THE HOSPITAL AFTER WORK, AND HE SUDDENLY HAD TO USE THE BATHROOM ON OUR WAY HERE.
CLEARLY, WE DIDN'T MAKE IT IN TIME.
DIDN'T MAKE IT?
SO SHE WAS CLEANING...?
GAH!
SAM, CAN YOU PLEASE STEP OUTSIDE AND LET MY DAD REST?
SORRY, SIR! IT WAS, UM... NICE SEEING YOU AGAIN!

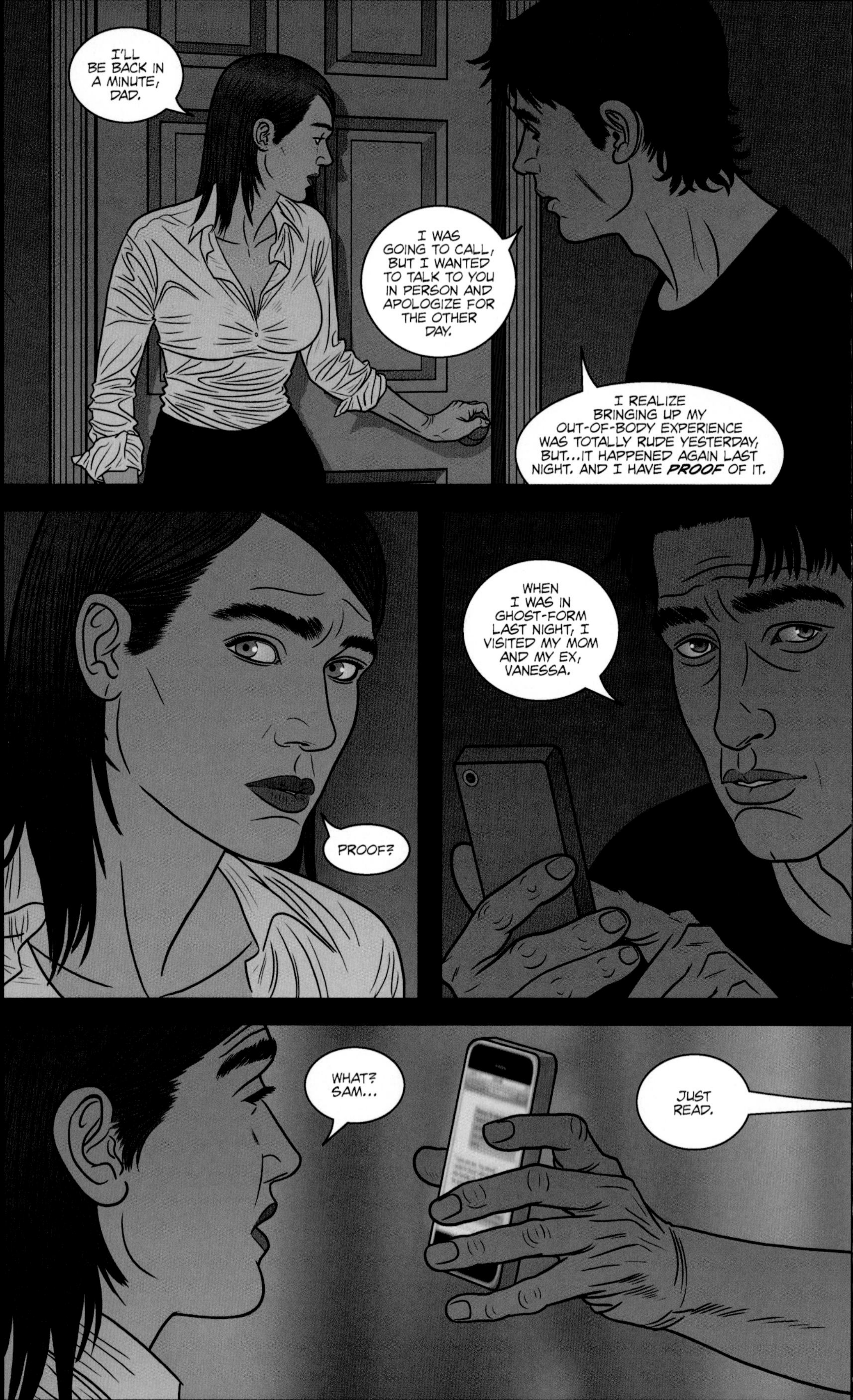
I'LL BE BACK IN A MINUTE, DAD.
I WAS GOING TO CALL, BUT I WANTED TO TALK TO YOU IN PERSON AND APOLOGIZE FOR THE OTHER DAY.
I REALIZE BRINGING UP MY OUT-OF-BODY EXPERIENCE WAS TOTALLY RUDE YESTERDAY, BUT...IT HAPPENED AGAIN LAST NIGHT. AND I HAVE *PROOF* OF IT.
PROOF?
WHEN I WAS IN GHOST-FORM LAST NIGHT, I VISITED MY MOM AND MY EX, VANESSA.
WHAT? SAM...
JUST READ.

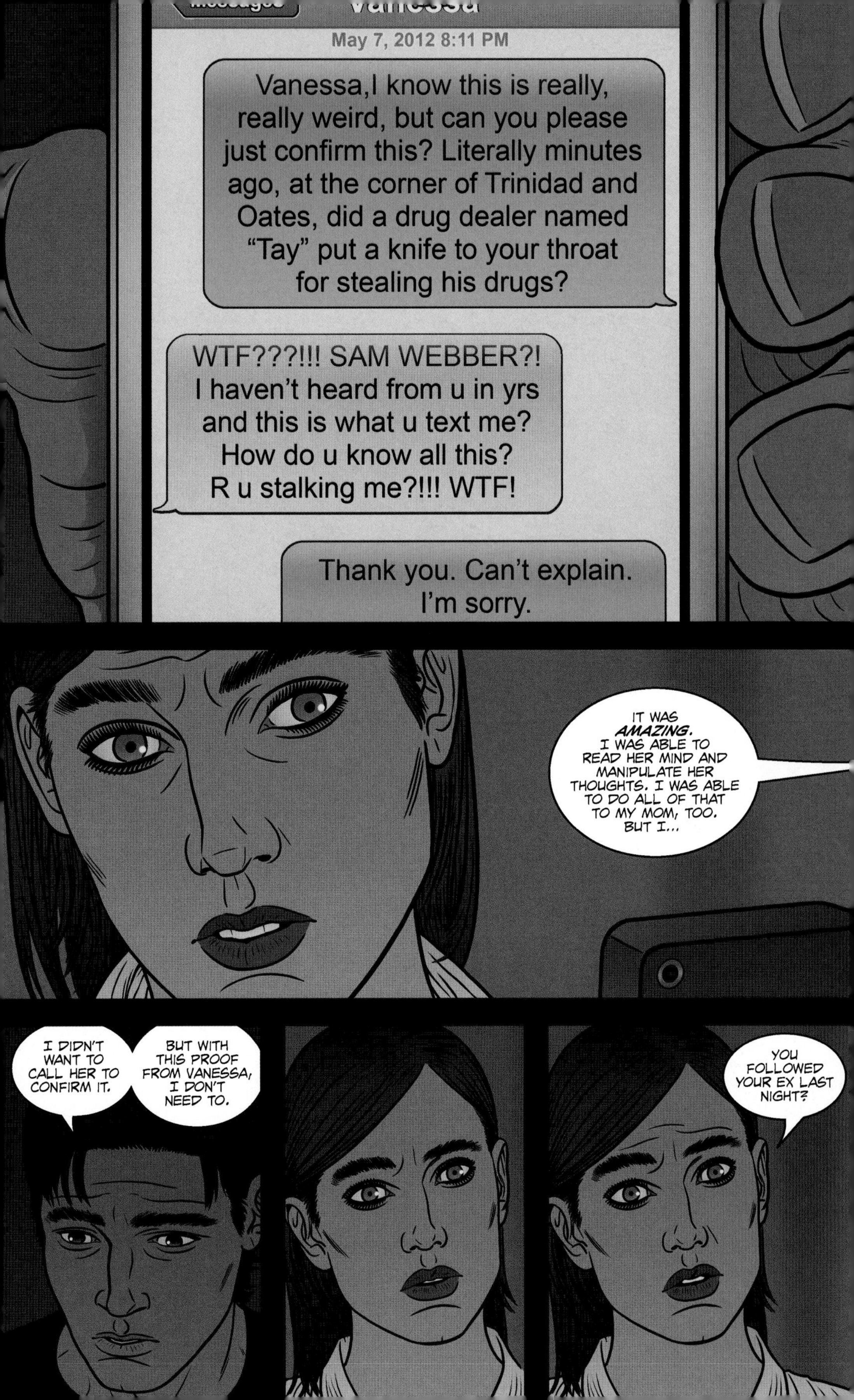
May 7, 2012 8:11 PM
Vanessa,I know this is really, really weird, but can you please just confirm this? Literally minutes ago, at the corner of Trinidad and Oates, did a drug dealer named "Tay" put a knife to your throat for stealing his drugs?
WTF???!!! SAM WEBBER?! I haven't heard from u in yrs and this is what u text me? How do u know all this? R u stalking me?!!! WTF!
Thank you. Can't explain. I'm sorry.
IT WAS AMAZING. I WAS ABLE TO READ HER MIND AND MANIPULATE HER THOUGHTS. I WAS ABLE TO DO ALL OF THAT TO MY MOM, TOO. BUT I...
I DIDN'T WANT TO CALL HER TO CONFIRM IT.
BUT WITH THIS PROOF FROM VANESSA, I DON'T NEED TO.
YOU FOLLOWED YOUR EX LAST NIGHT?

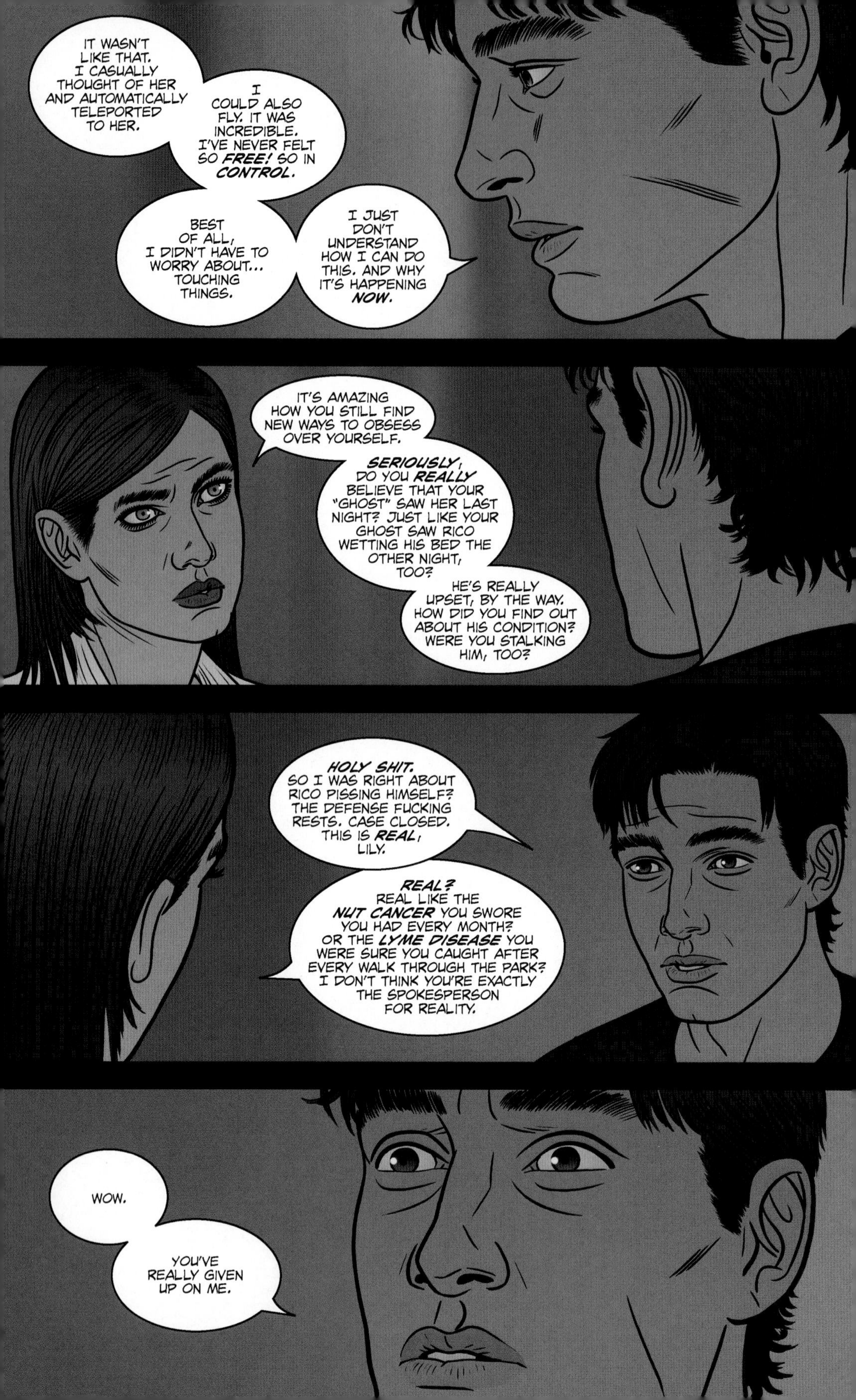
IT WASN'T LIKE THAT. I CASUALLY THOUGHT OF HER AND AUTOMATICALLY TELEPORTED TO HER.
I COULD ALSO FLY. IT WAS INCREDIBLE. I'VE NEVER FELT SO FREE! SO IN CONTROL.
BEST OF ALL, I DIDN'T HAVE TO WORRY ABOUT... TOUCHING THINGS.
I JUST DON'T UNDERSTAND HOW I CAN DO THIS. AND WHY IT'S HAPPENING NOW.
IT'S AMAZING HOW YOU STILL FIND NEW WAYS TO OBSESS OVER YOURSELF.
SERIOUSLY, DO YOU REALLY BELIEVE THAT YOUR "GHOST" SAW HER LAST NIGHT? JUST LIKE YOUR GHOST SAW RICO WETTING HIS BED THE OTHER NIGHT, TOO?
HE'S REALLY UPSET, BY THE WAY. HOW DID YOU FIND OUT ABOUT HIS CONDITION? WERE YOU STALKING HIM, TOO?
HOLY SHIT. SO I WAS RIGHT ABOUT RICO PISSING HIMSELF? THE DEFENSE FUCKING RESTS. CASE CLOSED. THIS IS REAL, LILY.
REAL? REAL LIKE THE NUT CANCER YOU SWORE YOU HAD EVERY MONTH? OR THE LYME DISEASE YOU WERE SURE YOU CAUGHT AFTER EVERY WALK THROUGH THE PARK? I DON'T THINK YOU'RE EXACTLY THE SPOKESPERSON FOR REALITY.
WOW.
YOU'VE REALLY GIVEN UP ON ME.

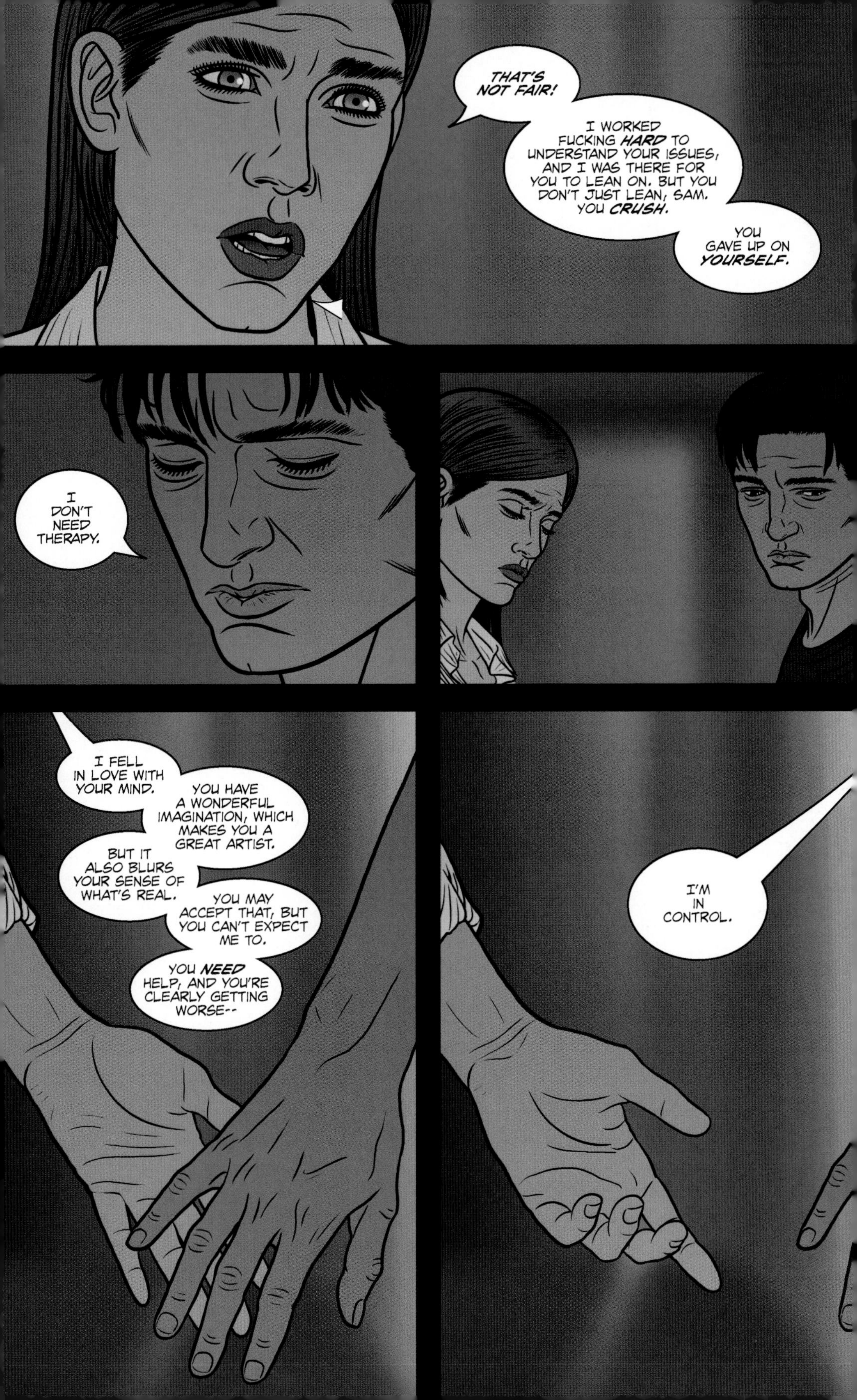

THAT'S NOT FAIR!
I WORKED FUCKING HARD TO UNDERSTAND YOUR ISSUES, AND I WAS THERE FOR YOU TO LEAN ON. BUT YOU DON'T JUST LEAN, SAM. YOU CRUSH.
YOU GAVE UP ON YOURSELF.
I DON'T NEED THERAPY.
I FELL IN LOVE WITH YOUR MIND.
YOU HAVE A WONDERFUL IMAGINATION, WHICH MAKES YOU A GREAT ARTIST.
BUT IT ALSO BLURS YOUR SENSE OF WHAT'S REAL.
YOU MAY ACCEPT THAT, BUT YOU CAN'T EXPECT ME TO.
YOU NEED HELP, AND YOU'RE CLEARLY GETTING WORSE--
I'M IN CONTROL.

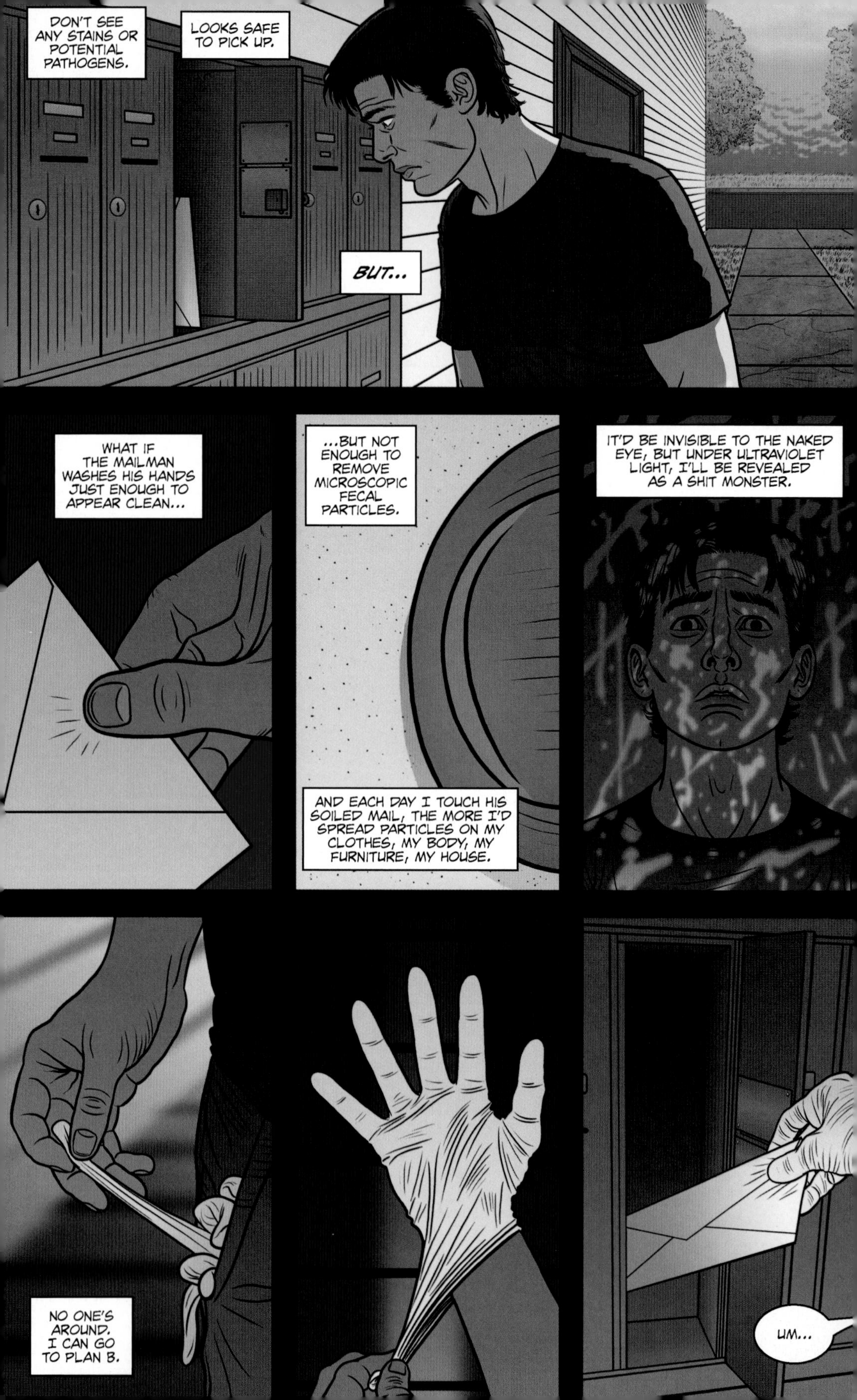
DON'T SEE ANY STAINS OR POTENTIAL PATHOGENS.
LOOKS SAFE TO PICK UP.
BUT...
WHAT IF THE MAILMAN WASHES HIS HANDS JUST ENOUGH TO APPEAR CLEAN...
...BUT NOT ENOUGH TO REMOVE MICROSCOPIC FECAL PARTICLES.
AND EACH DAY I TOUCH HIS SOILED MAIL, THE MORE I'D SPREAD PARTICLES ON MY CLOTHES, MY BODY, MY FURNITURE, MY HOUSE.
IT'D BE INVISIBLE TO THE NAKED EYE, BUT UNDER ULTRAVIOLET LIGHT, I'LL BE REVEALED AS A SHIT MONSTER.
NO ONE'S AROUND. I CAN GO TO PLAN B.
UM...

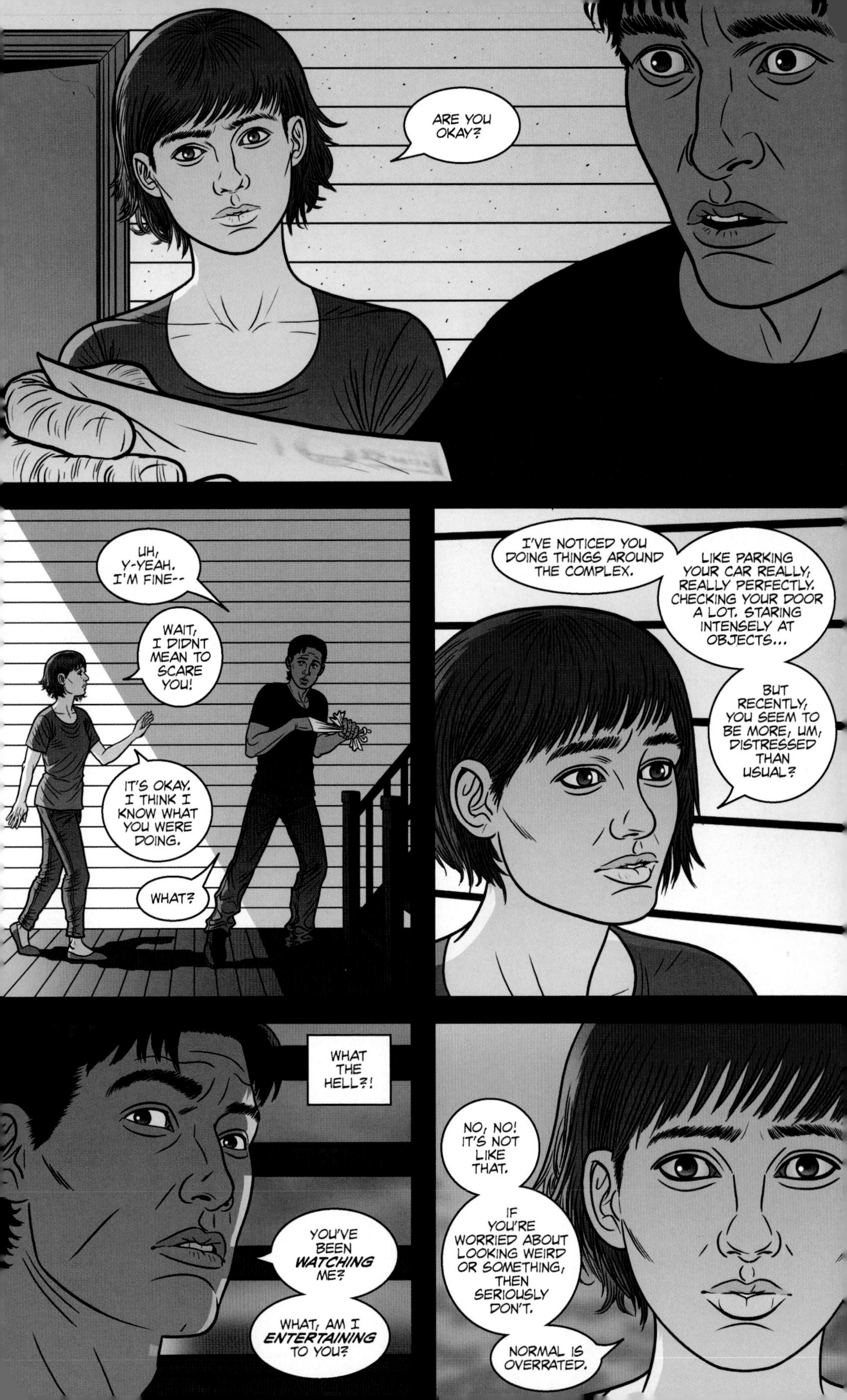
ARE YOU OKAY?
UH, Y-YEAH. I'M FINE--
WAIT, I DIDNT MEAN TO SCARE YOU!
IT'S OKAY. I THINK I KNOW WHAT YOU WERE DOING.
WHAT?
I'VE NOTICED YOU DOING THINGS AROUND THE COMPLEX.
LIKE PARKING YOUR CAR REALLY, REALLY PERFECTLY. CHECKING YOUR DOOR A LOT. STARING INTENSELY AT OBJECTS...
BUT RECENTLY, YOU SEEM TO BE MORE, UM, DISTRESSED THAN USUAL?
WHAT THE HELL?!
YOU'VE BEEN WATCHING ME?
WHAT, AM I ENTERTAINING TO YOU?
NO, NO! IT'S NOT LIKE THAT.
IF YOU'RE WORRIED ABOUT LOOKING WEIRD OR SOMETHING, THEN SERIOUSLY DON'T.
NORMAL IS OVERRATED.

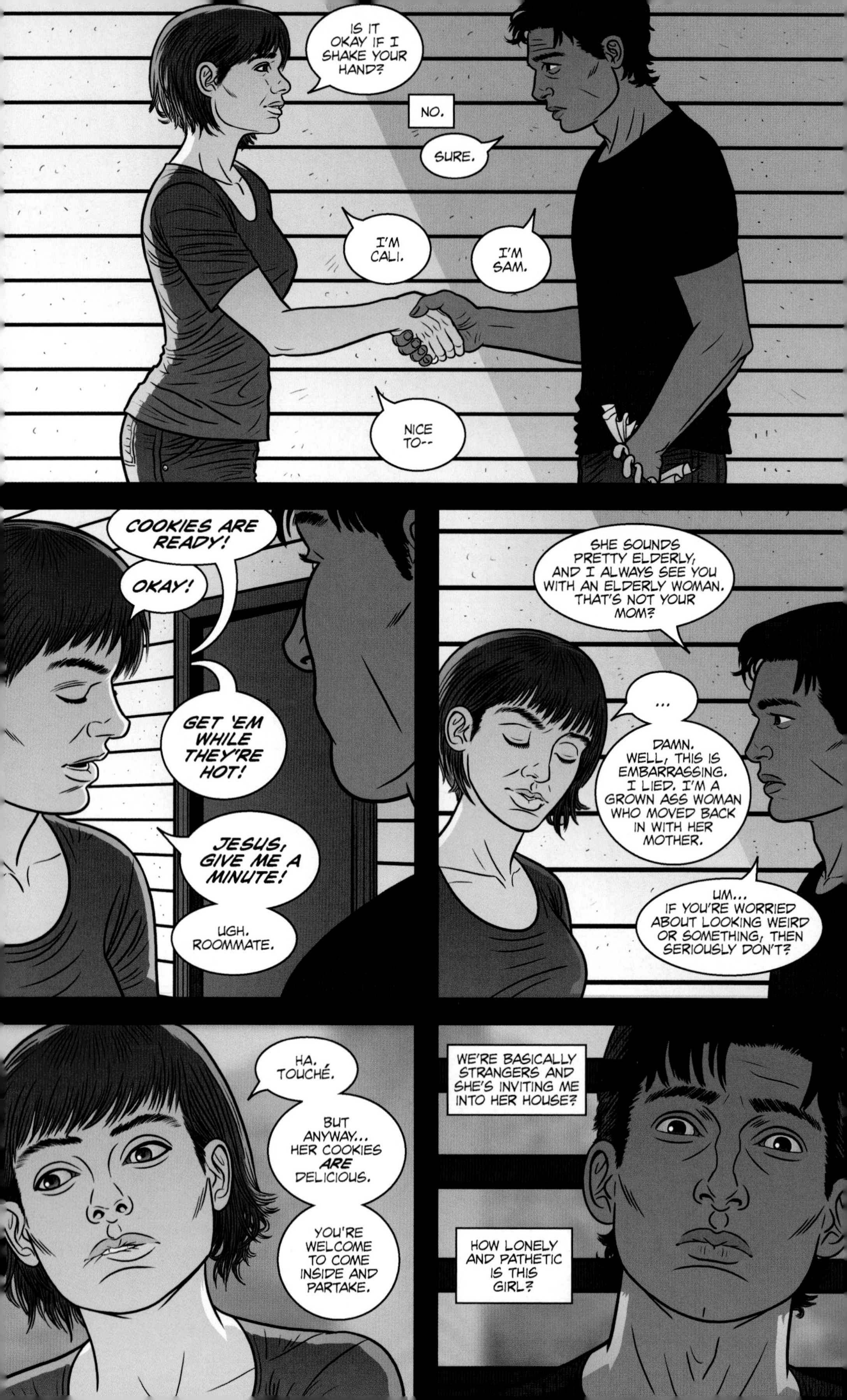

IS IT OKAY IF I SHAKE YOUR HAND?
NO.
SURE.
I'M CALI.
I'M SAM.
NICE TO--
COOKIES ARE READY!
OKAY!
GET 'EM WHILE THEY'RE HOT!
JESUS, GIVE ME A MINUTE!
UGH. ROOMMATE.
SHE SOUNDS PRETTY ELDERLY, AND I ALWAYS SEE YOU WITH AN ELDERLY WOMAN. THAT'S NOT YOUR MOM?
...
DAMN. WELL, THIS IS EMBARRASSING. I LIED. I'M A GROWN ASS WOMAN WHO MOVED BACK IN WITH HER MOTHER.
UM... IF YOU'RE WORRIED ABOUT LOOKING WEIRD OR SOMETHING, THEN SERIOUSLY DON'T?
HA. TOUCHÉ.
BUT ANYWAY... HER COOKIES ARE DELICIOUS.
YOU'RE WELCOME TO COME INSIDE AND PARTAKE.
WE'RE BASICALLY STRANGERS AND SHE'S INVITING ME INTO HER HOUSE?
HOW LONELY AND PATHETIC IS THIS GIRL?

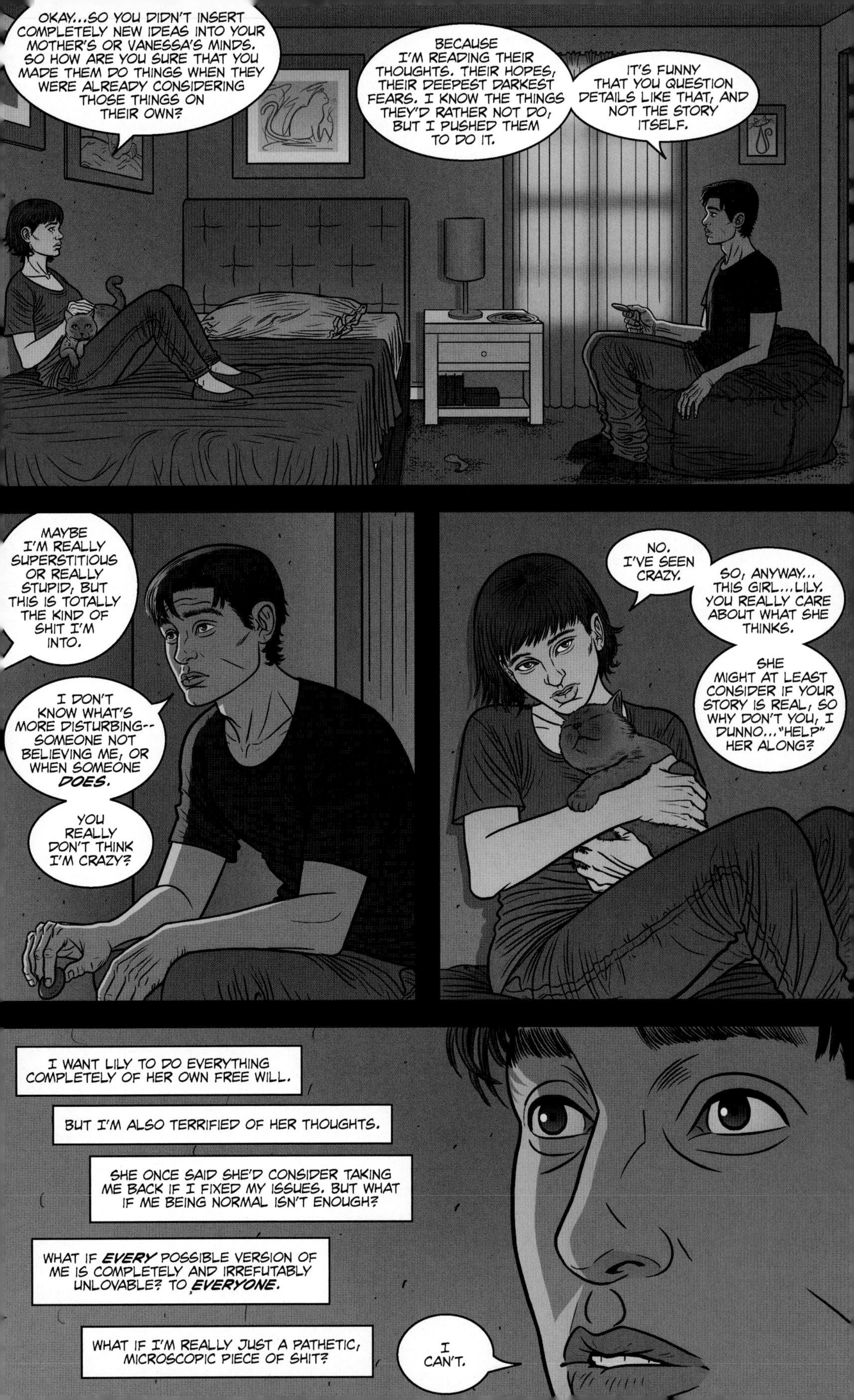
OKAY...SO YOU DIDN'T INSERT COMPLETELY NEW IDEAS INTO YOUR MOTHER'S OR VANESSA'S MINDS. SO HOW ARE YOU SURE THAT YOU MADE THEM DO THINGS WHEN THEY WERE ALREADY CONSIDERING THOSE THINGS ON THEIR OWN?
BECAUSE I'M READING THEIR THOUGHTS. THEIR HOPES, THEIR DEEPEST DARKEST FEARS. I KNOW THE THINGS THEY'D RATHER NOT DO, BUT I PUSHED THEM TO DO IT.
IT'S FUNNY THAT YOU QUESTION DETAILS LIKE THAT, AND NOT THE STORY ITSELF.
MAYBE I'M REALLY SUPERSTITIOUS OR REALLY STUPID, BUT THIS IS TOTALLY THE KIND OF SHIT I'M INTO.
I DON'T KNOW WHAT'S MORE DISTURBING-- SOMEONE NOT BELIEVING ME, OR WHEN SOMEONE **DOES**.
YOU REALLY DON'T THINK I'M CRAZY?
NO. I'VE SEEN CRAZY.
SO, ANYWAY... THIS GIRL...LILY. YOU REALLY CARE ABOUT WHAT SHE THINKS.
SHE MIGHT AT LEAST CONSIDER IF YOUR STORY IS REAL, SO WHY DON'T YOU, I DUNNO..."HELP" HER ALONG?
I WANT LILY TO DO EVERYTHING COMPLETELY OF HER OWN FREE WILL.
BUT I'M ALSO TERRIFIED OF HER THOUGHTS.
SHE ONCE SAID SHE'D CONSIDER TAKING ME BACK IF I FIXED MY ISSUES. BUT WHAT IF ME BEING NORMAL ISN'T ENOUGH?
WHAT IF ***EVERY*** POSSIBLE VERSION OF ME IS COMPLETELY AND IRREFUTABLY UNLOVABLE? TO ***EVERYONE***.
WHAT IF I'M REALLY JUST A PATHETIC, MICROSCOPIC PIECE OF SHIT?
I CAN'T.

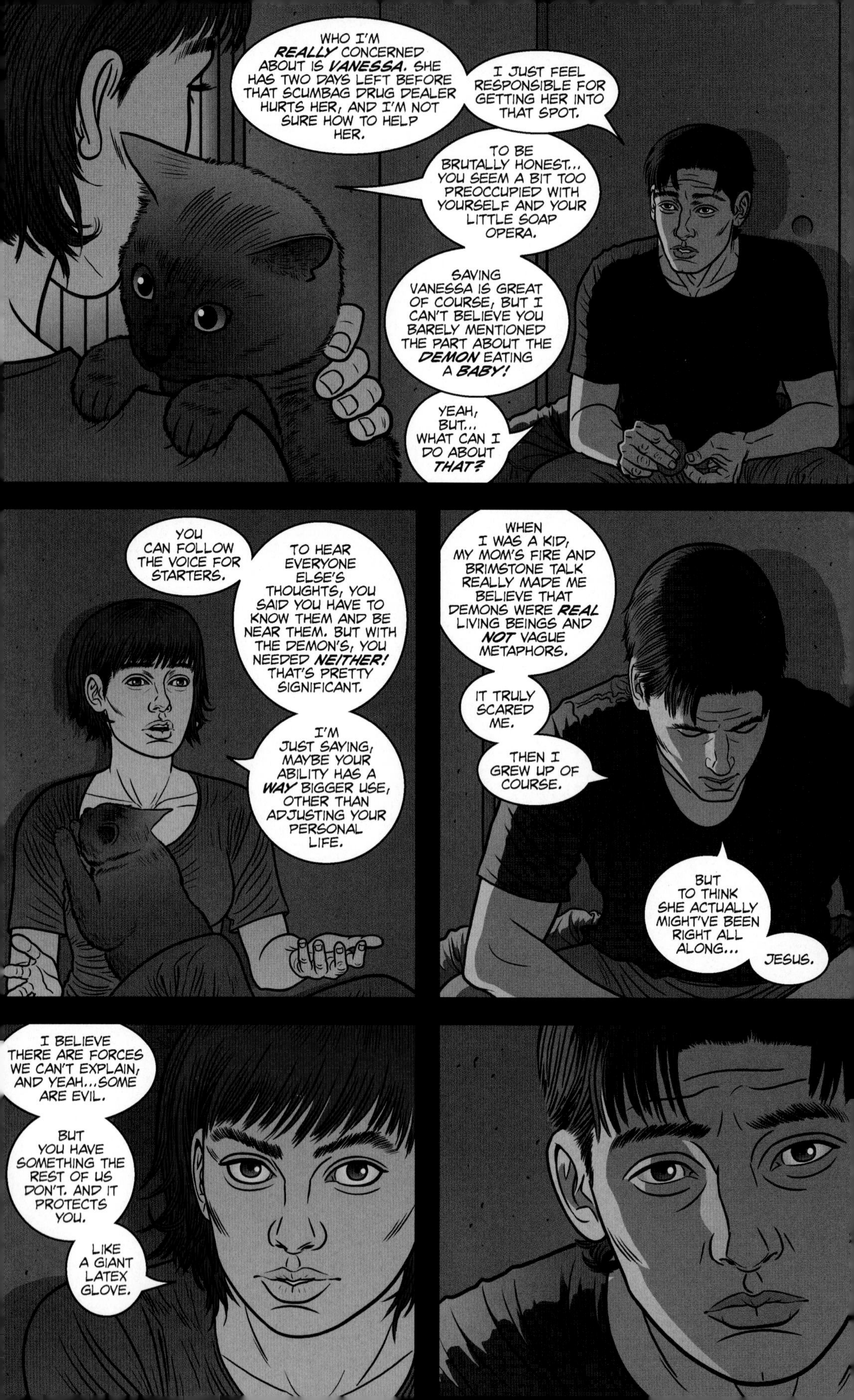
WHO I'M REALLY CONCERNED ABOUT IS VANESSA. SHE HAS TWO DAYS LEFT BEFORE THAT SCUMBAG DRUG DEALER HURTS HER, AND I'M NOT SURE HOW TO HELP HER.
I JUST FEEL RESPONSIBLE FOR GETTING HER INTO THAT SPOT.
TO BE BRUTALLY HONEST... YOU SEEM A BIT TOO PREOCCUPIED WITH YOURSELF AND YOUR LITTLE SOAP OPERA.
SAVING VANESSA IS GREAT OF COURSE, BUT I CAN'T BELIEVE YOU BARELY MENTIONED THE PART ABOUT THE DEMON EATING A BABY!
YEAH, BUT... WHAT CAN I DO ABOUT THAT?
YOU CAN FOLLOW THE VOICE FOR STARTERS.
TO HEAR EVERYONE ELSE'S THOUGHTS, YOU SAID YOU HAVE TO KNOW THEM AND BE NEAR THEM. BUT WITH THE DEMON'S, YOU NEEDED NEITHER! THAT'S PRETTY SIGNIFICANT.
I'M JUST SAYING, MAYBE YOUR ABILITY HAS A WAY BIGGER USE, OTHER THAN ADJUSTING YOUR PERSONAL LIFE.
WHEN I WAS A KID, MY MOM'S FIRE AND BRIMSTONE TALK REALLY MADE ME BELIEVE THAT DEMONS WERE REAL LIVING BEINGS AND NOT VAGUE METAPHORS.
IT TRULY SCARED ME.
THEN I GREW UP OF COURSE.
BUT TO THINK SHE ACTUALLY MIGHT'VE BEEN RIGHT ALL ALONG...
JESUS.
I BELIEVE THERE ARE FORCES WE CAN'T EXPLAIN, AND YEAH...SOME ARE EVIL.
BUT YOU HAVE SOMETHING THE REST OF US DON'T. AND IT PROTECTS YOU.
LIKE A GIANT LATEX GLOVE.

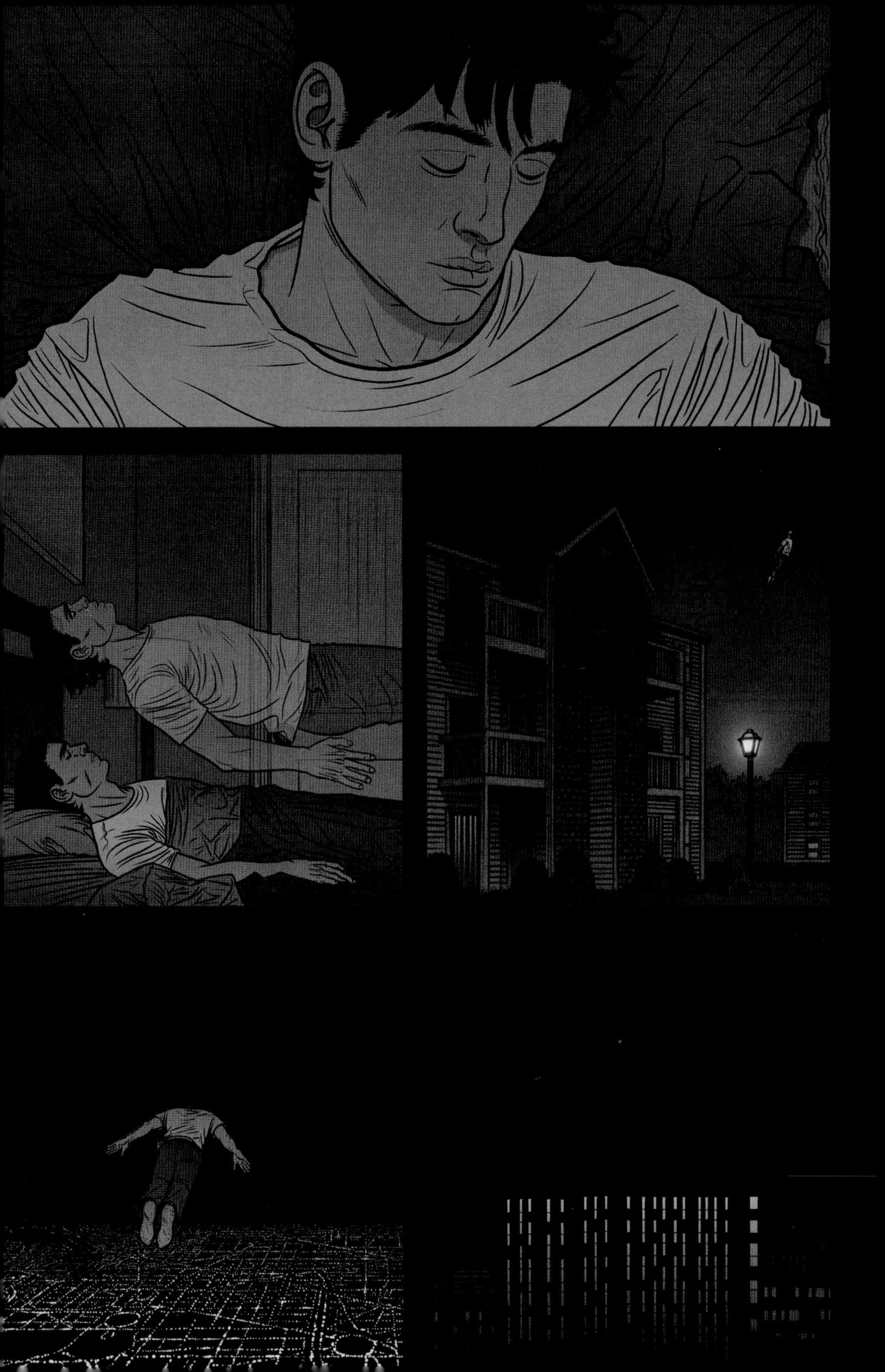

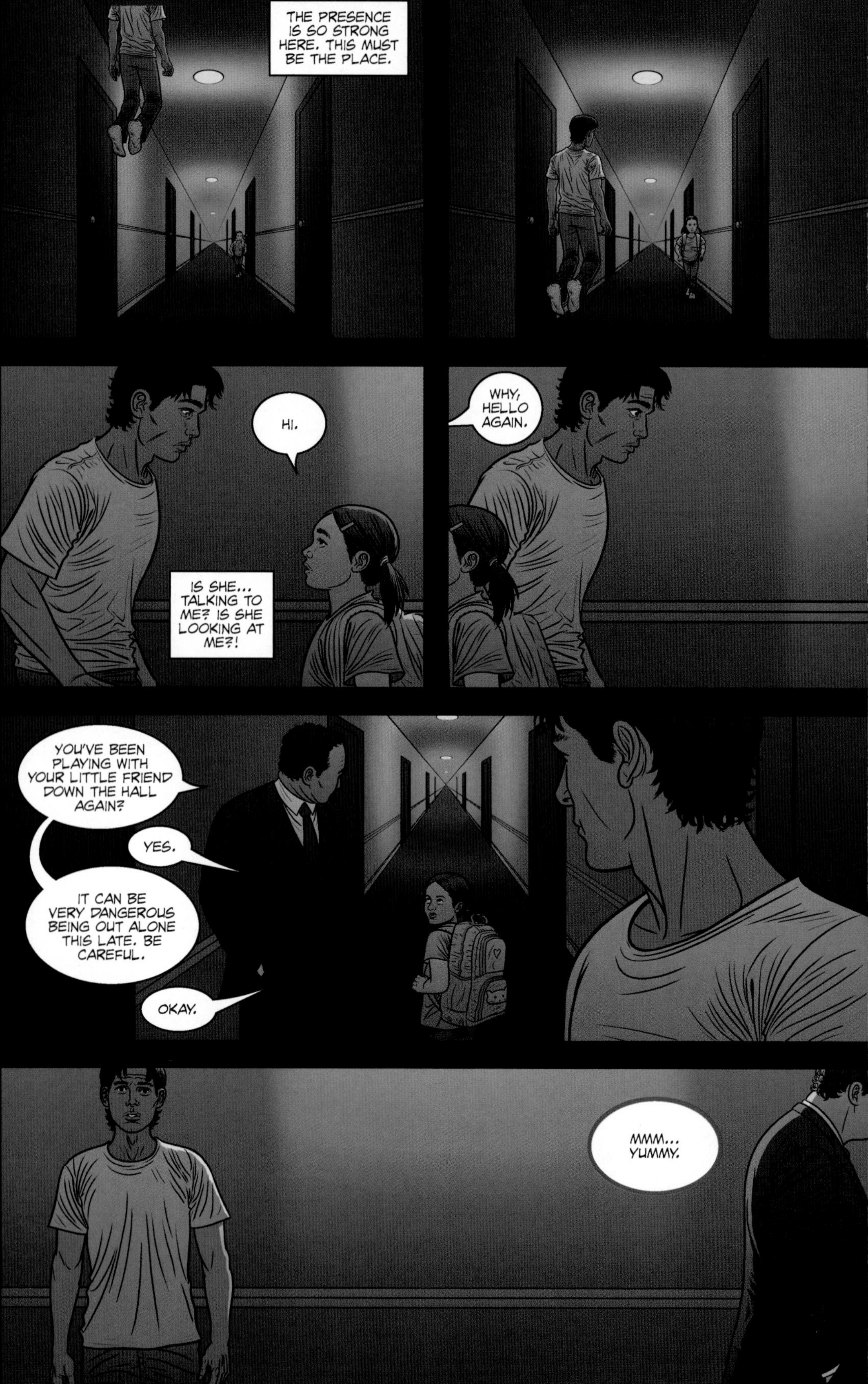
THE PRESENCE IS SO STRONG HERE. THIS MUST BE THE PLACE.
HI.
IS SHE... TALKING TO ME? IS SHE LOOKING AT ME?!
WHY, HELLO AGAIN.
YOU'VE BEEN PLAYING WITH YOUR LITTLE FRIEND DOWN THE HALL AGAIN?
YES.
IT CAN BE VERY DANGEROUS BEING OUT ALONE THIS LATE. BE CAREFUL.
OKAY.
MMM... YUMMY.

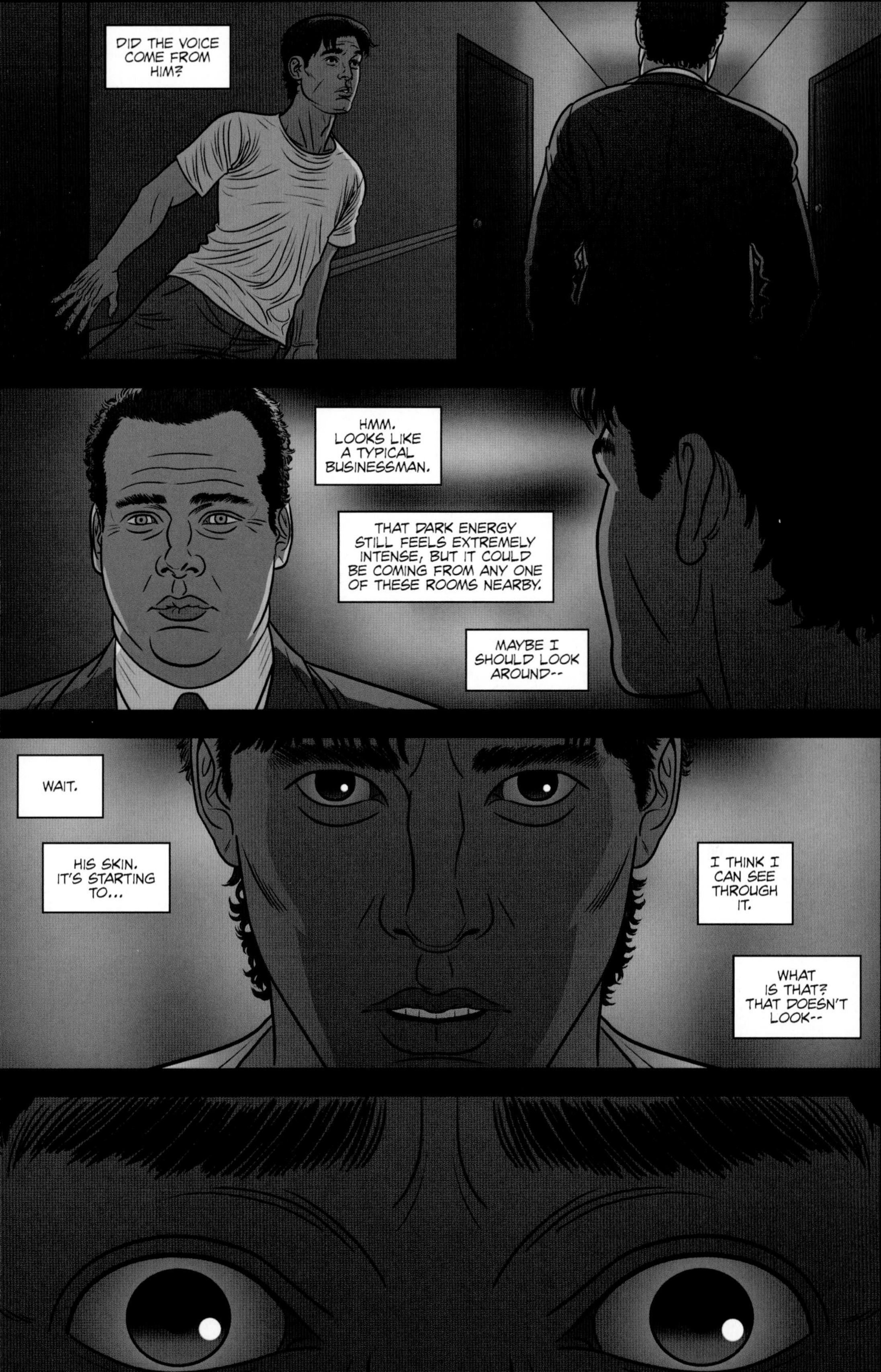
DID THE VOICE COME FROM HIM?
HMM. LOOKS LIKE A TYPICAL BUSINESSMAN.
THAT DARK ENERGY STILL FEELS EXTREMELY INTENSE, BUT IT COULD BE COMING FROM ANY ONE OF THESE ROOMS NEARBY.
MAYBE I SHOULD LOOK AROUND--
WAIT.
HIS SKIN. IT'S STARTING TO...
I THINK I CAN SEE THROUGH IT.
WHAT IS THAT? THAT DOESN'T LOOK--

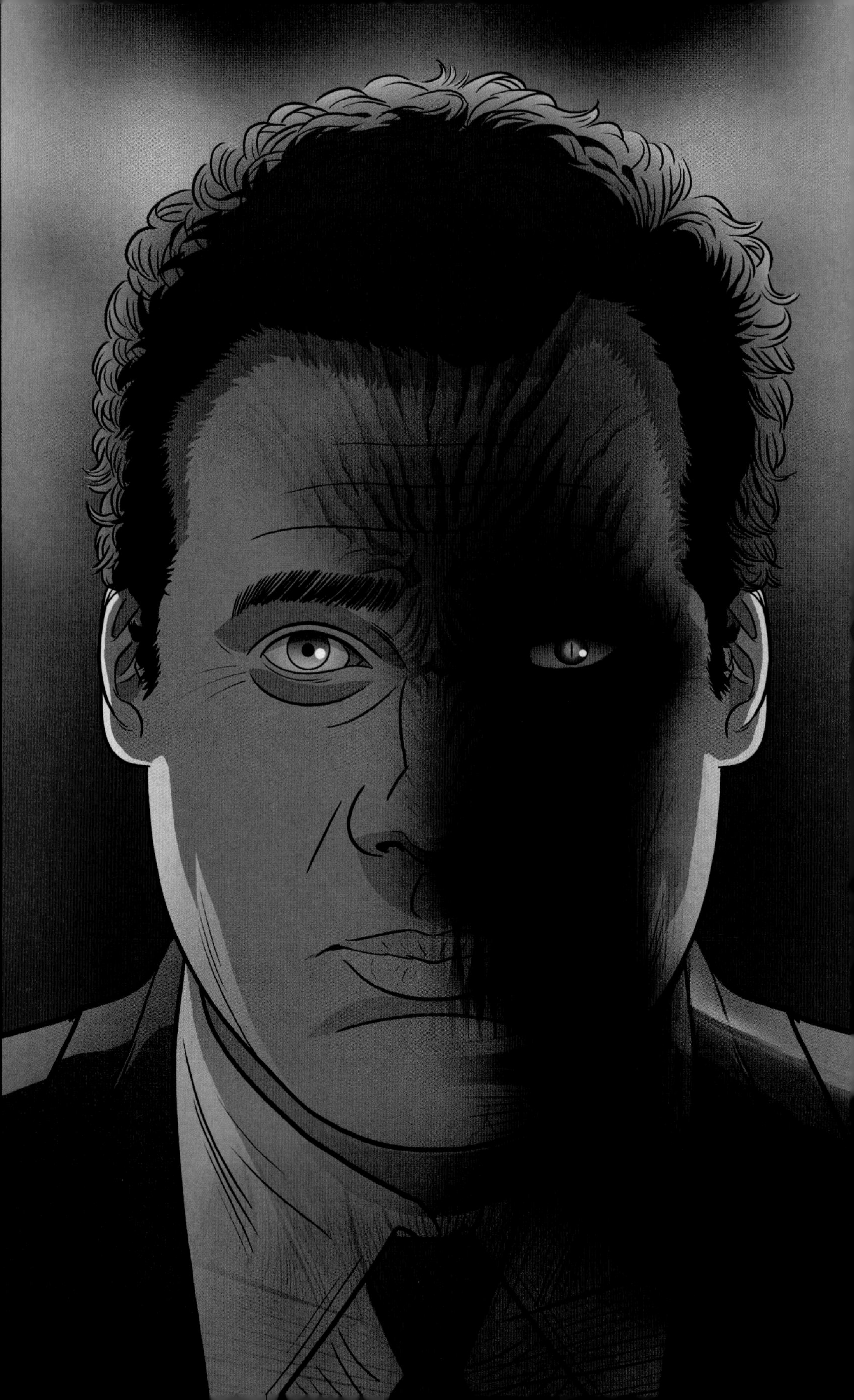

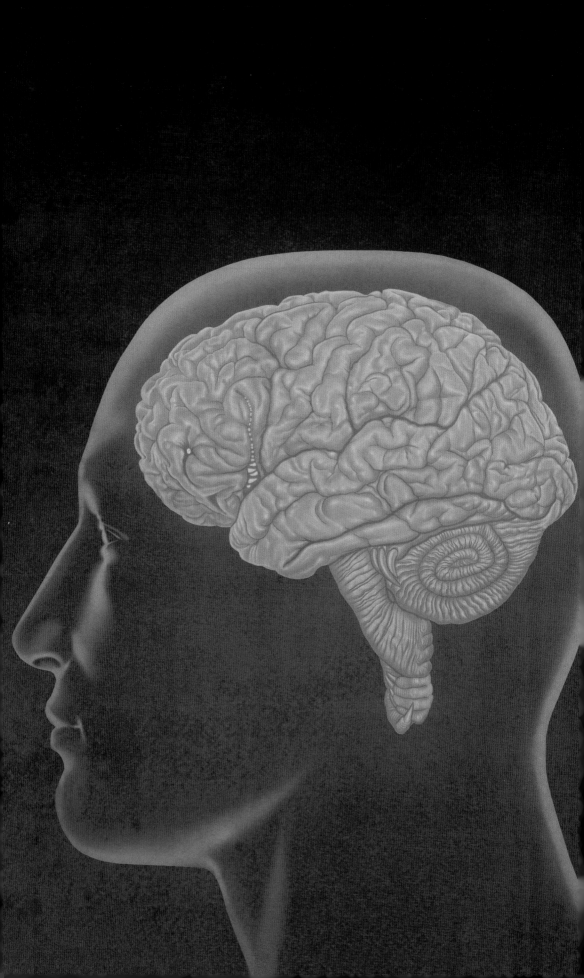

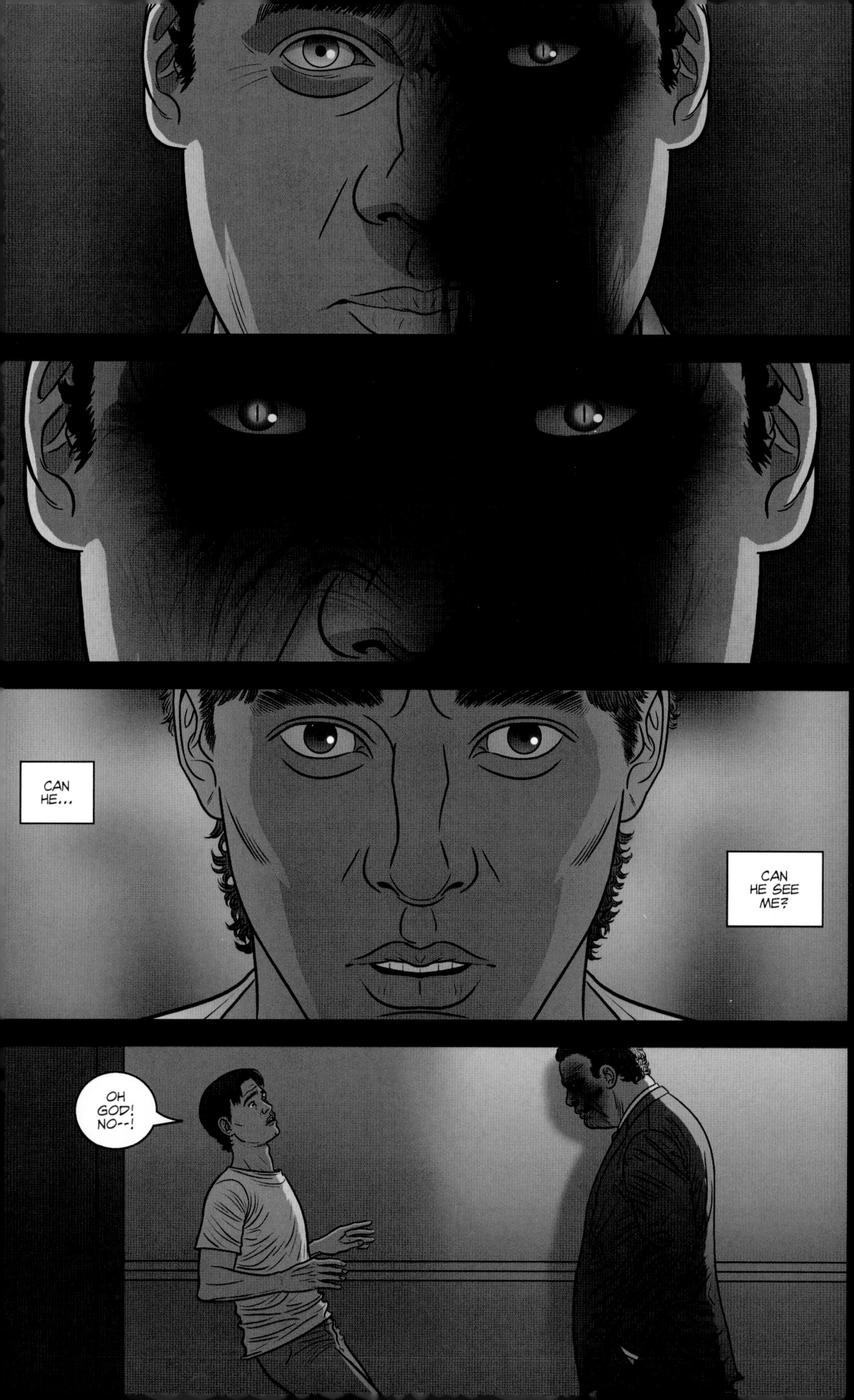
CAN HE...
CAN HE SEE ME?
OH GOD! NO--!

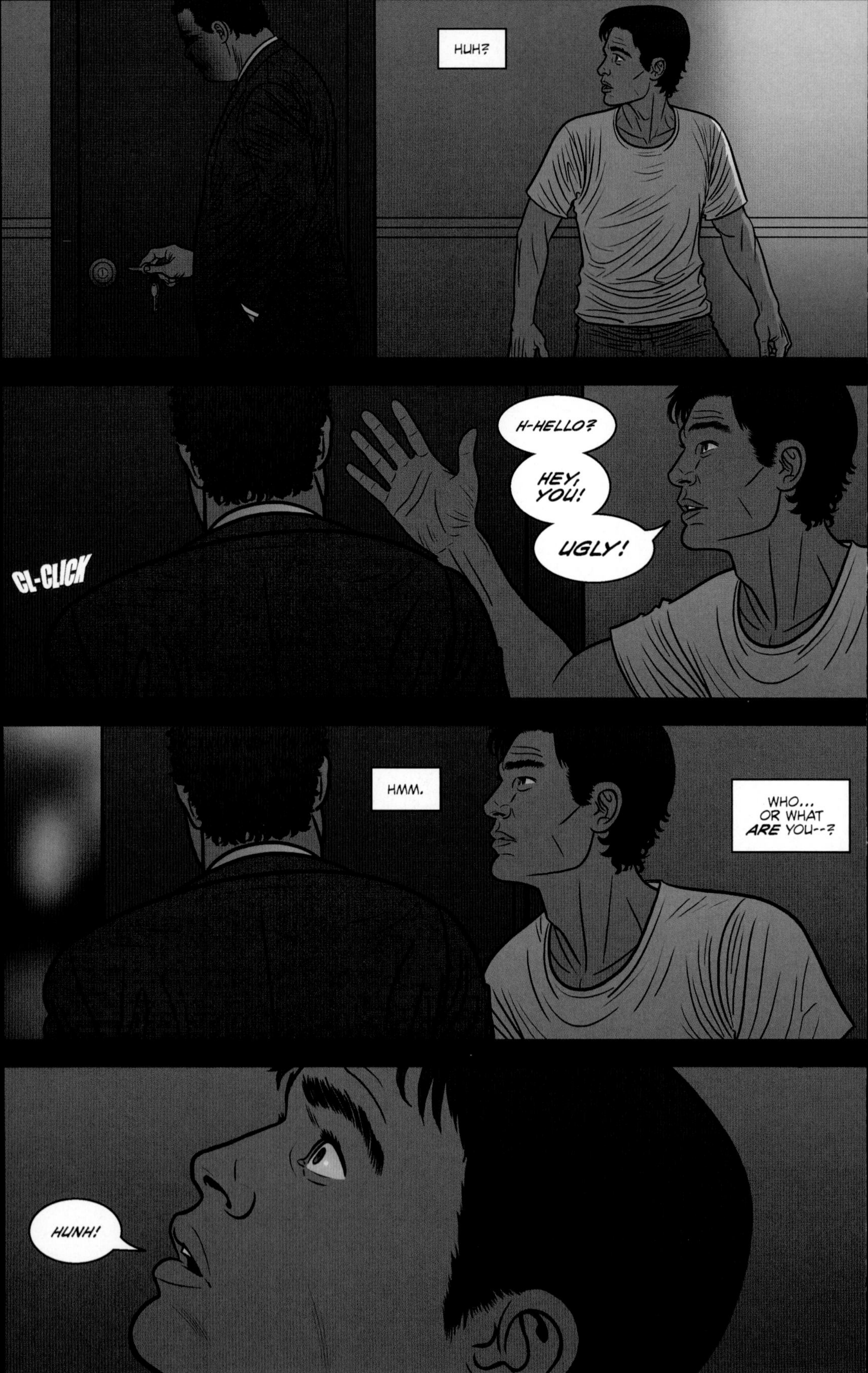
HUH?
H-HELLO?
HEY, YOU!
UGLY!
CL-CLICK
HMM.
WHO... OR WHAT ARE YOU--?
HUNH!

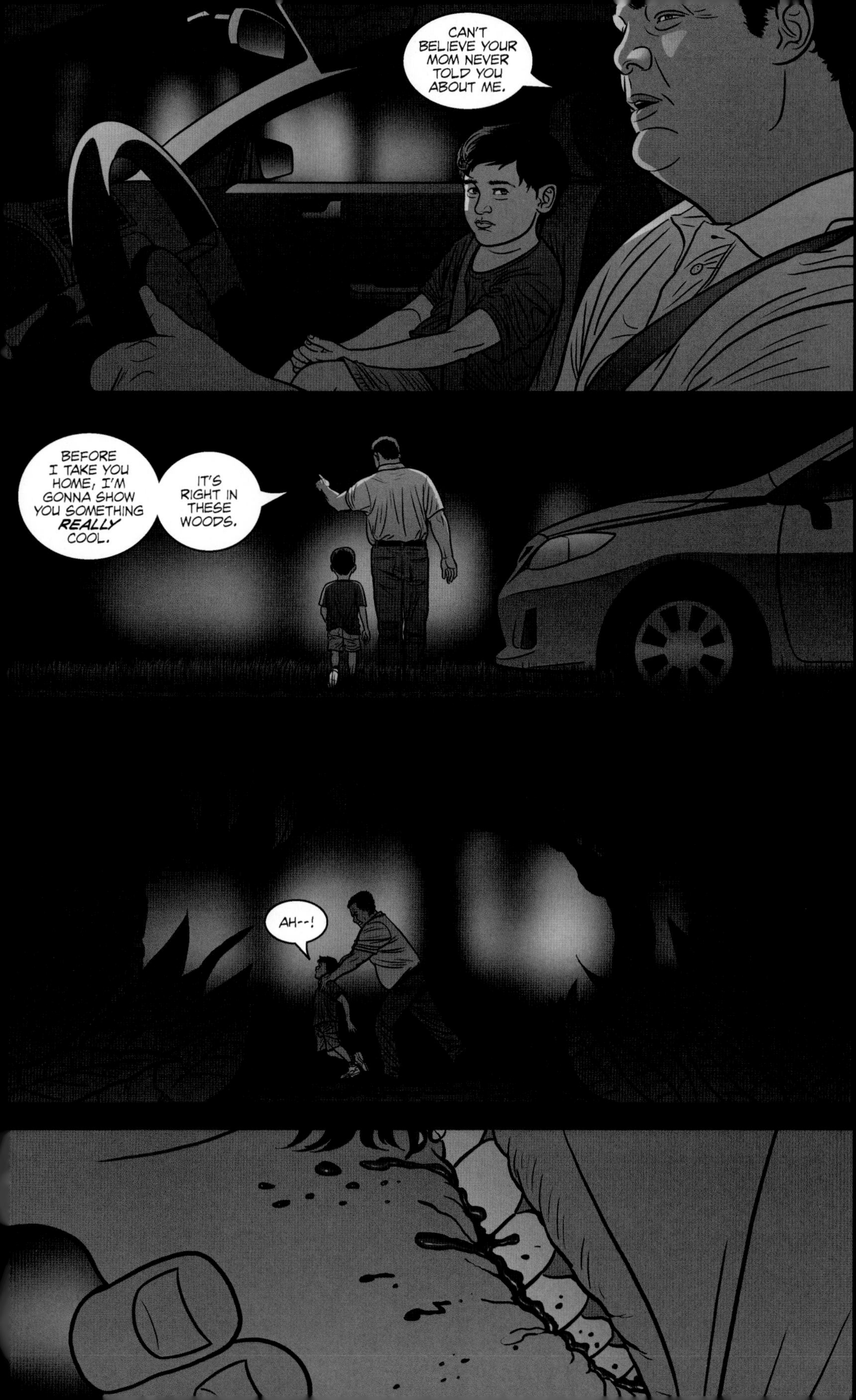
CAN'T BELIEVE YOUR MOM NEVER TOLD YOU ABOUT ME.
BEFORE I TAKE YOU HOME, I'M GONNA SHOW YOU SOMETHING REALLY COOL.
IT'S RIGHT IN THESE WOODS.
AH--!

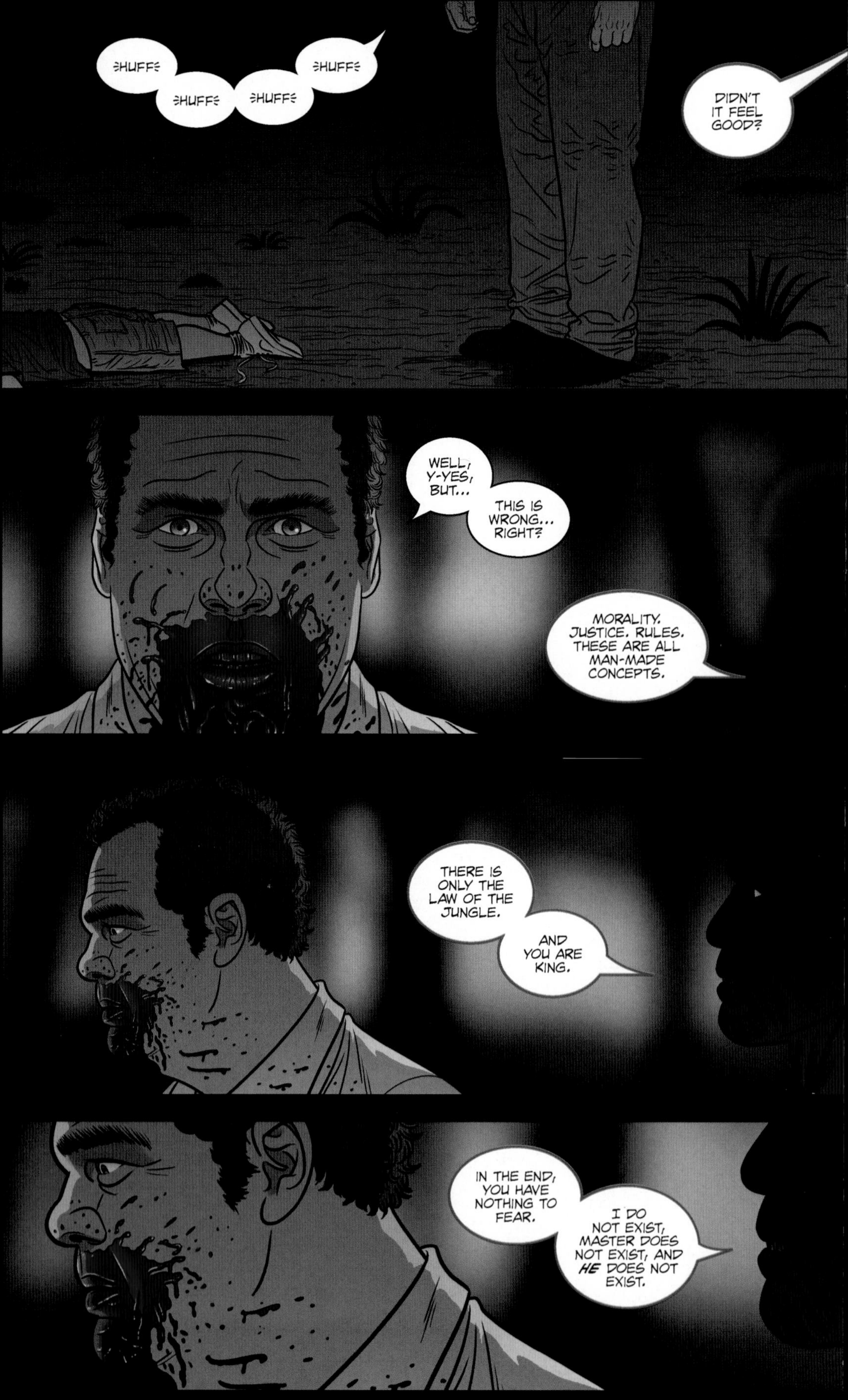

=HUFF=
=HUFF=
=HUFF=
=HUFF=
DIDN'T IT FEEL GOOD?
WELL, Y-YES, BUT...
THIS IS WRONG... RIGHT?
MORALITY. JUSTICE. RULES. THESE ARE ALL MAN-MADE CONCEPTS.
THERE IS ONLY THE LAW OF THE JUNGLE.
AND YOU ARE KING.
IN THE END, YOU HAVE NOTHING TO FEAR.
I DO NOT EXIST, MASTER DOES NOT EXIST, AND *HE* DOES NOT EXIST.

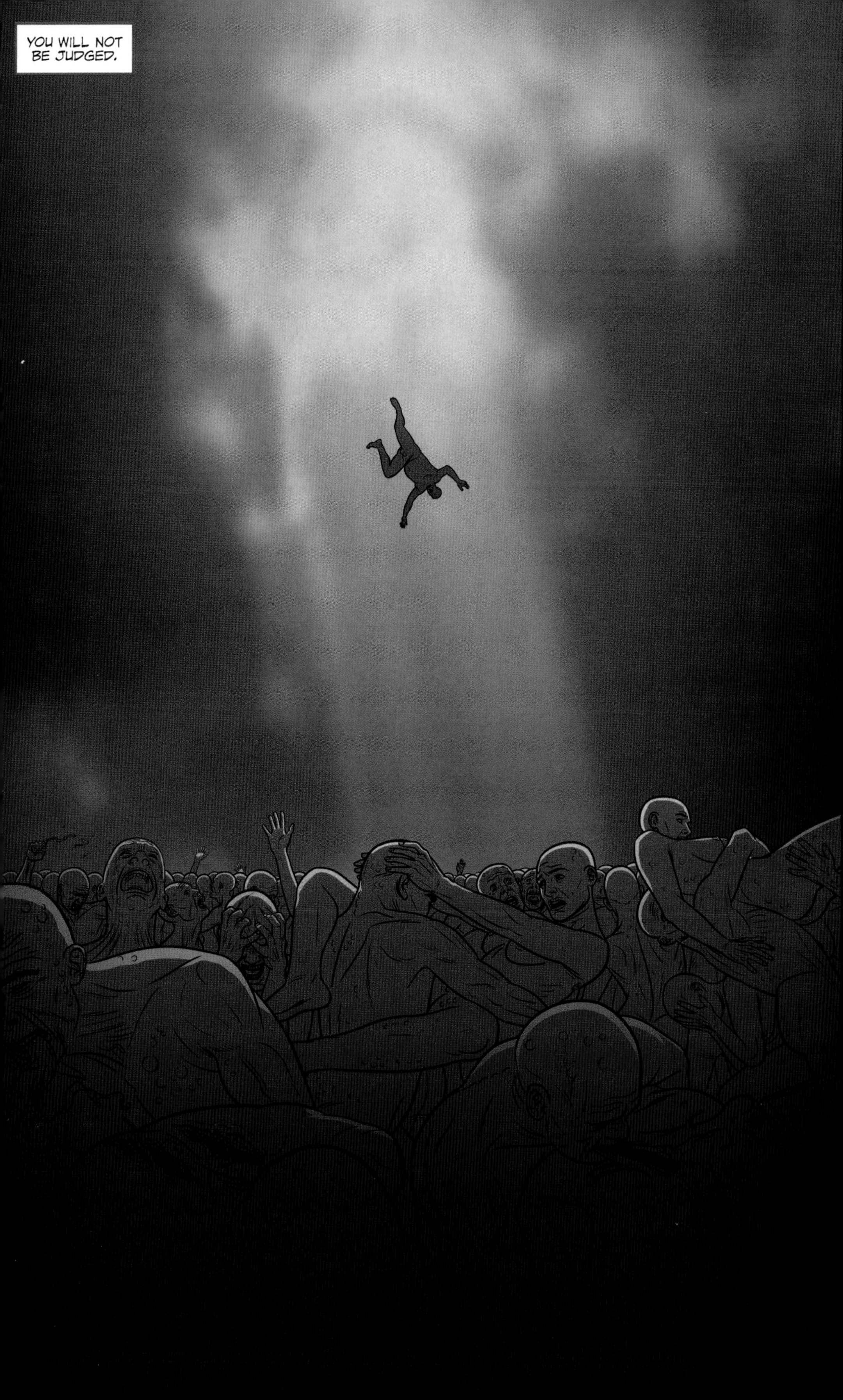
YOU WILL NOT BE JUDGED.

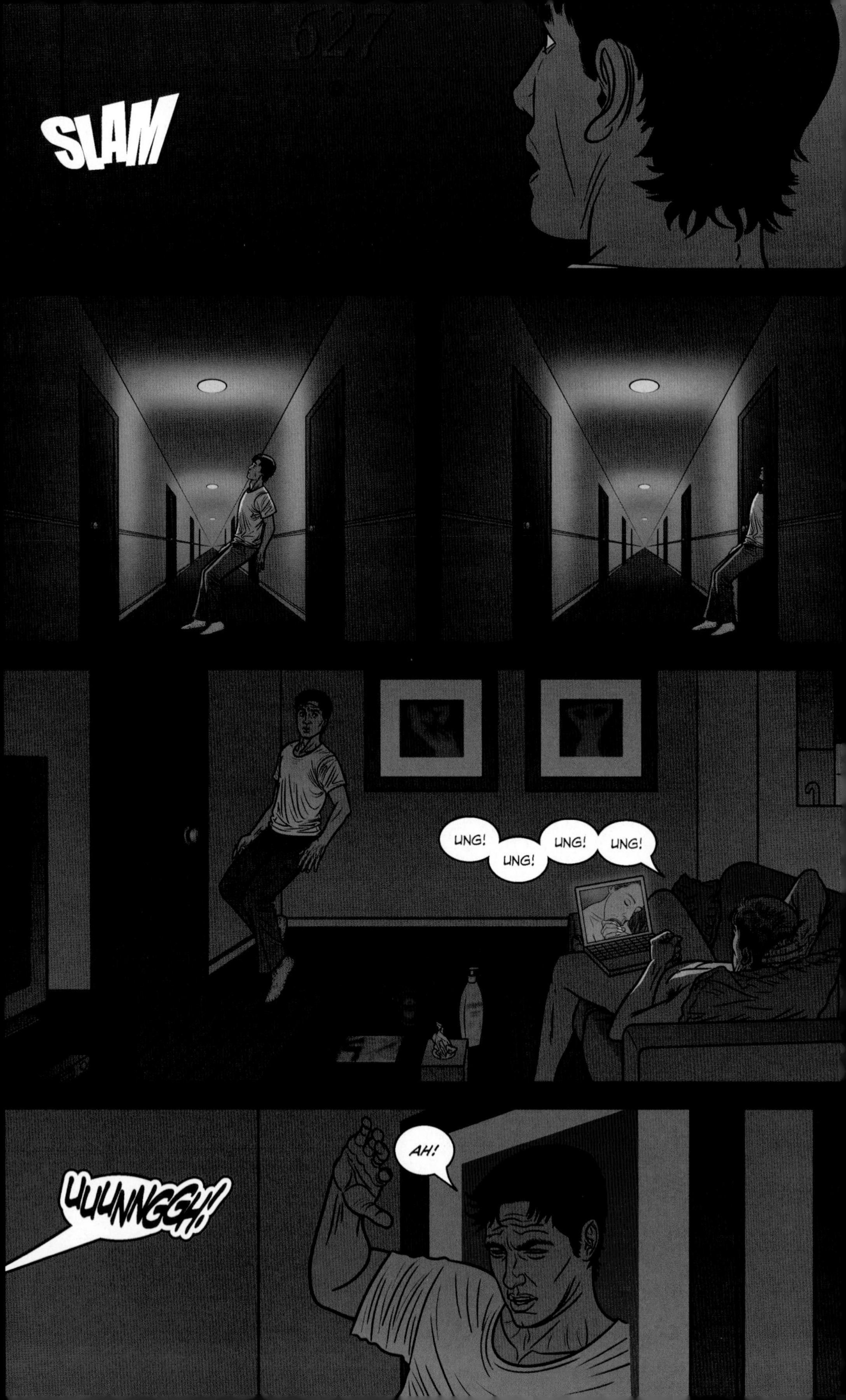
SLAM
UNG!
UNG!
UNG!
UNG!
UUUNNGGH!
AH!

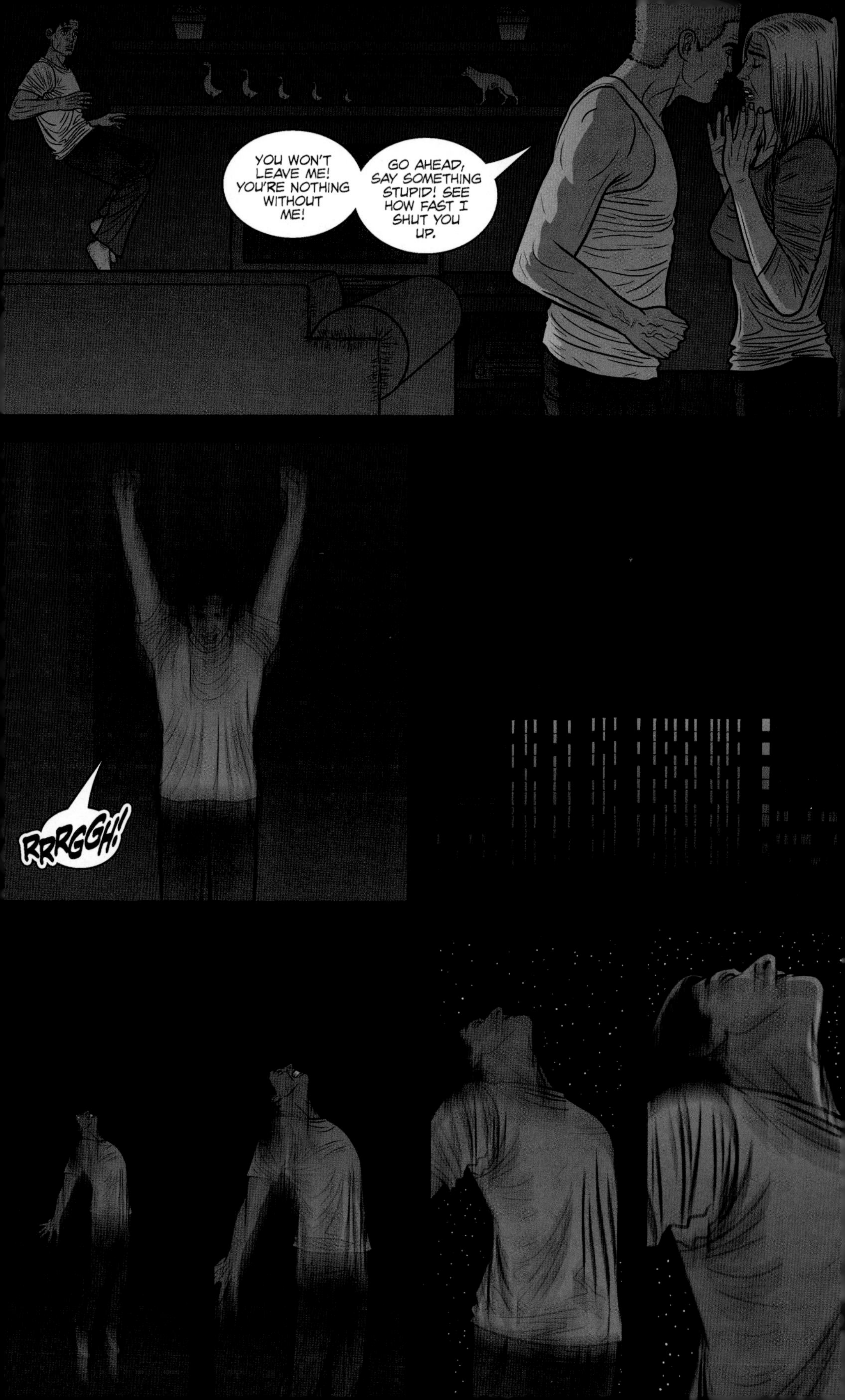

YOU WON'T LEAVE ME! YOU'RE NOTHING WITHOUT ME!
GO AHEAD, SAY SOMETHING STUPID! SEE HOW FAST I SHUT YOU UP.
RRRGGH!

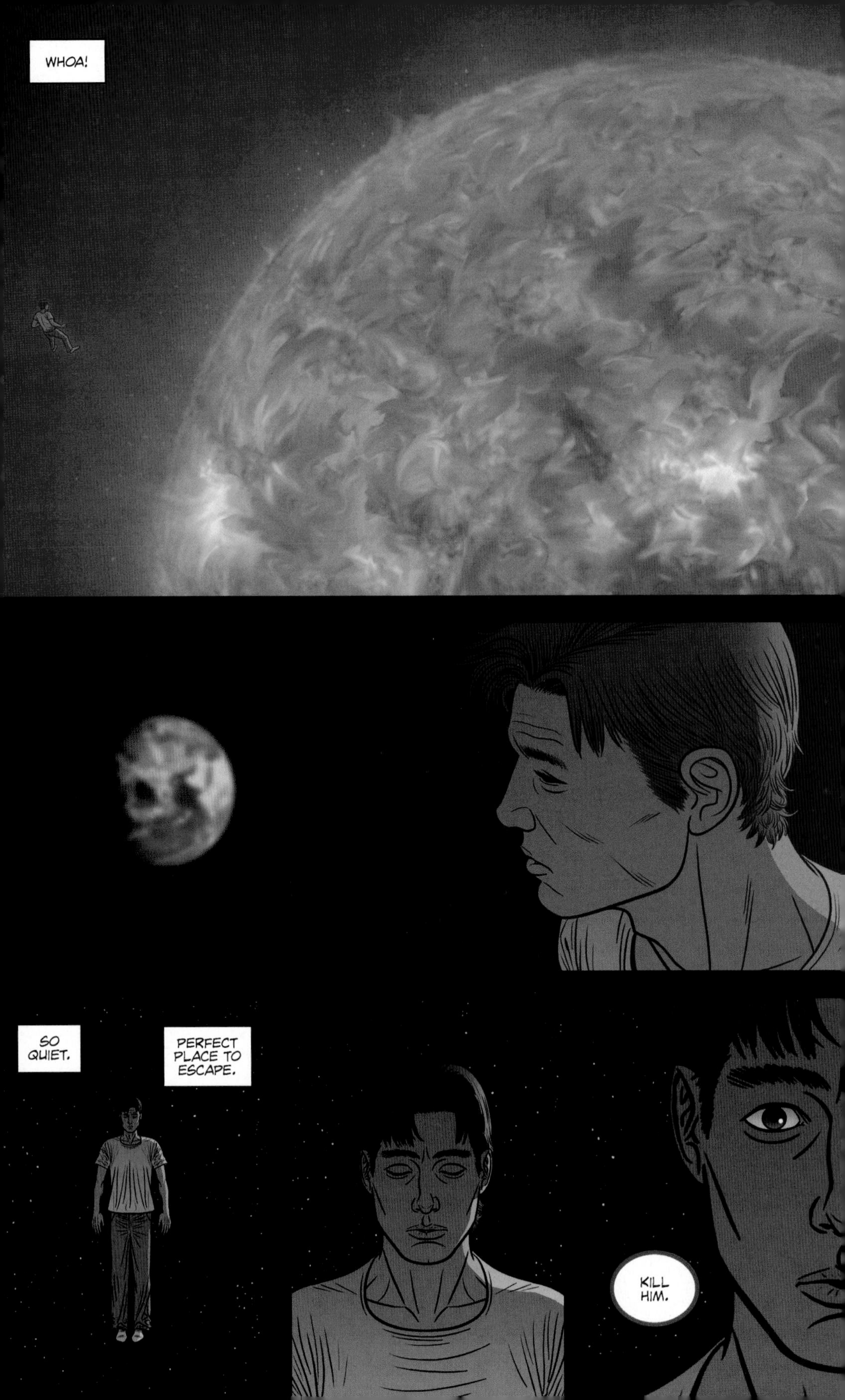
WHOA!
SO QUIET.
PERFECT PLACE TO ESCAPE.
KILL HIM.

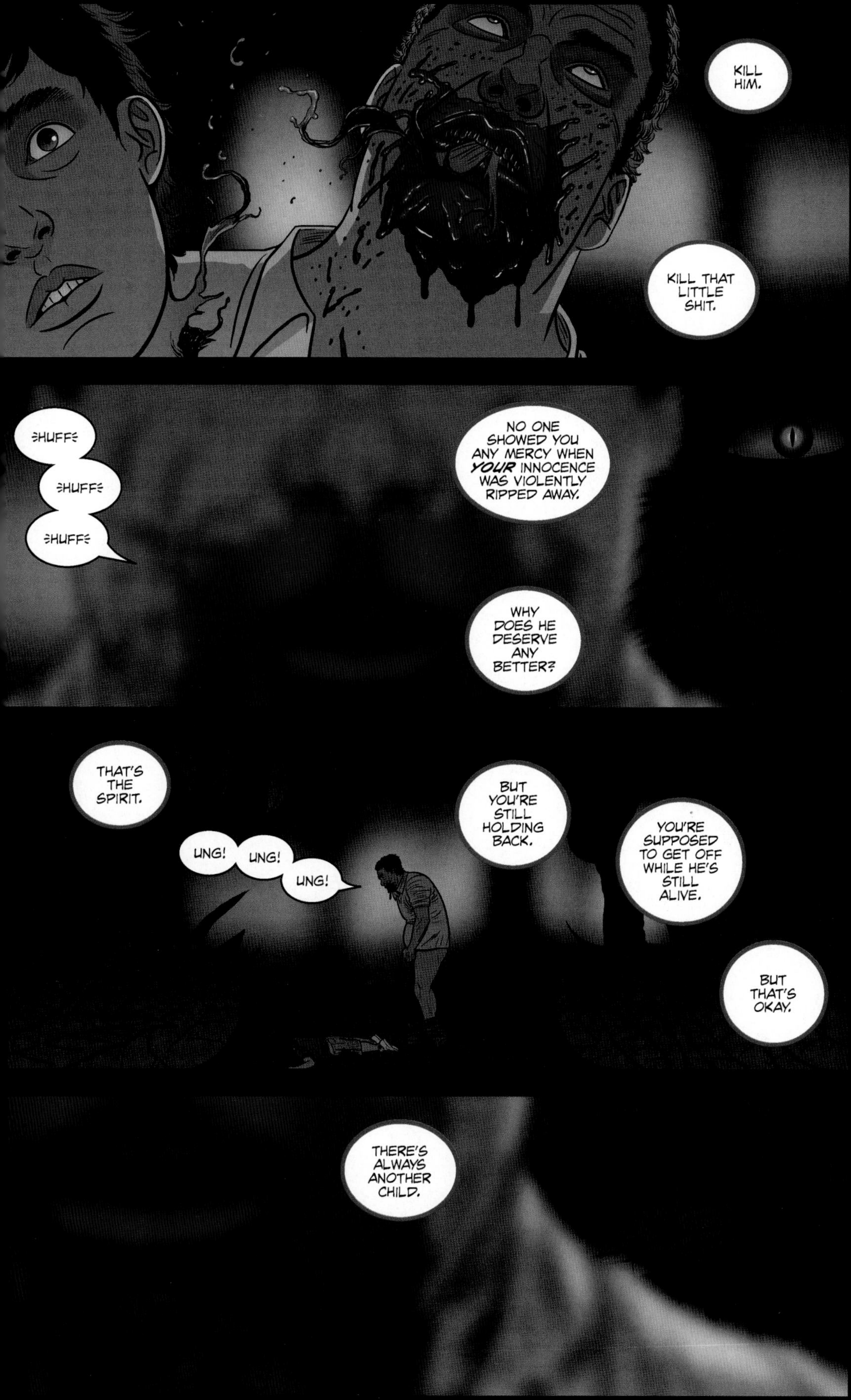
KILL HIM.
KILL THAT LITTLE SHIT.
=HUFF=
=HUFF=
=HUFF=
NO ONE SHOWED YOU ANY MERCY WHEN YOUR INNOCENCE WAS VIOLENTLY RIPPED AWAY.
WHY DOES HE DESERVE ANY BETTER?
THAT'S THE SPIRIT.
UNG!
UNG!
UNG!
BUT YOU'RE STILL HOLDING BACK.
YOU'RE SUPPOSED TO GET OFF WHILE HE'S STILL ALIVE.
BUT THAT'S OKAY.
THERE'S ALWAYS ANOTHER CHILD.

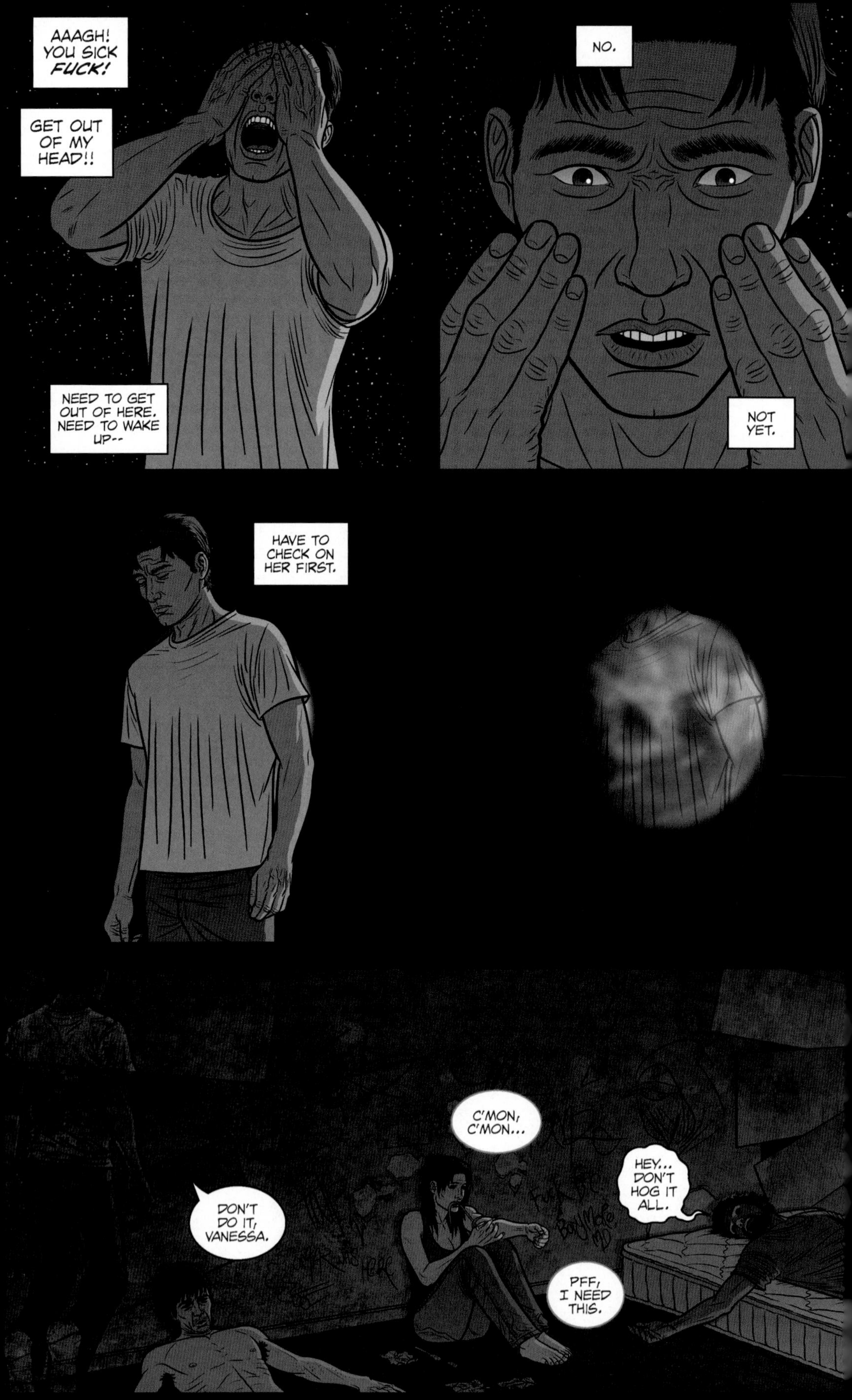

AAAGH! YOU SICK FUCK!
GET OUT OF MY HEAD!!
NEED TO GET OUT OF HERE. NEED TO WAKE UP--
NO.
NOT YET.
HAVE TO CHECK ON HER FIRST.
C'MON, C'MON...
HEY... DON'T HOG IT ALL.
DON'T DO IT, VANESSA.
PFF, I NEED THIS.

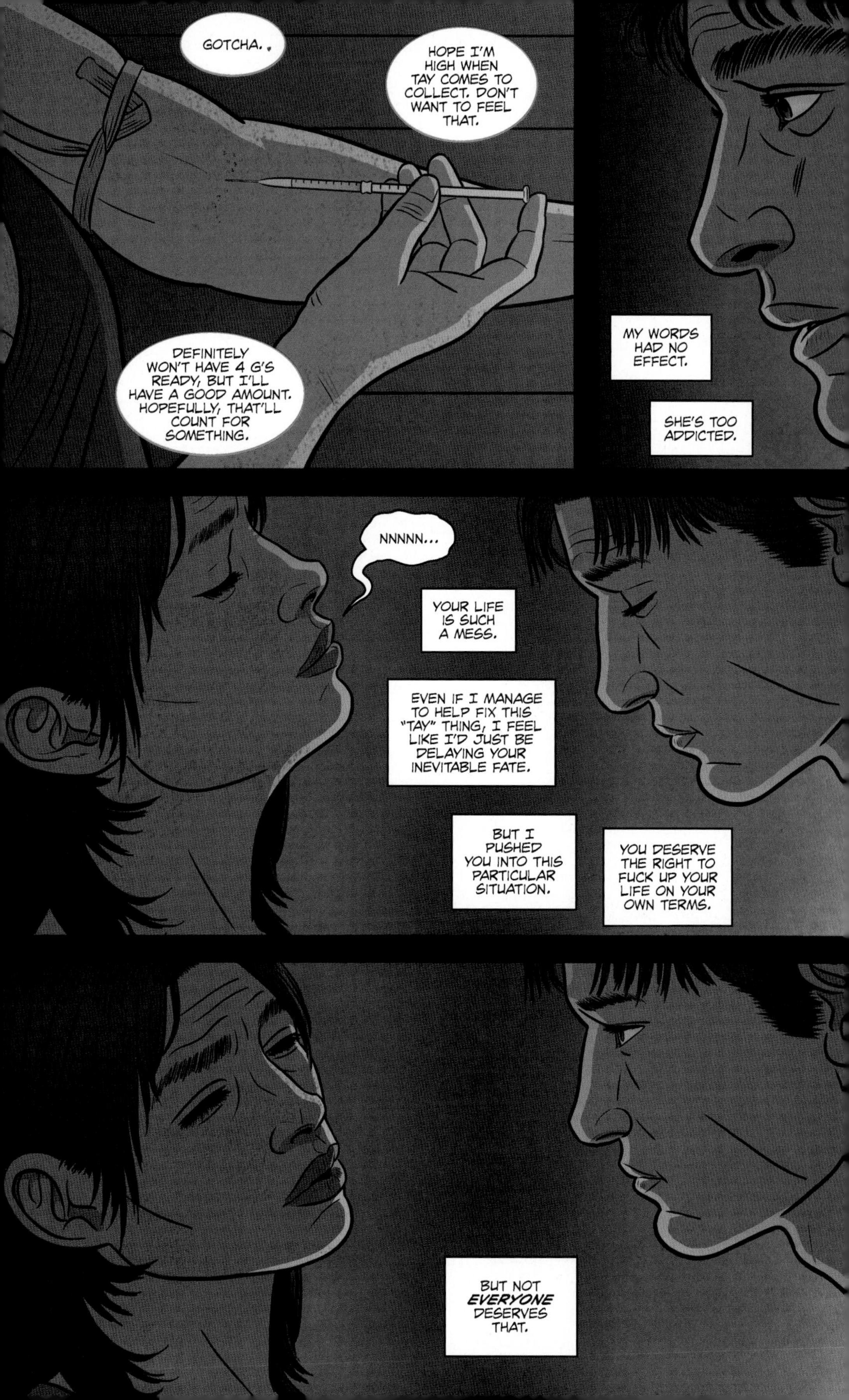
GOTCHA.
HOPE I'M HIGH WHEN TAY COMES TO COLLECT. DON'T WANT TO FEEL THAT.
DEFINITELY WON'T HAVE 4 G'S READY, BUT I'LL HAVE A GOOD AMOUNT. HOPEFULLY, THAT'LL COUNT FOR SOMETHING.
MY WORDS HAD NO EFFECT.
SHE'S TOO ADDICTED.
NNNNN...
YOUR LIFE IS SUCH A MESS.
EVEN IF I MANAGE TO HELP FIX THIS "TAY" THING, I FEEL LIKE I'D JUST BE DELAYING YOUR INEVITABLE FATE.
BUT I PUSHED YOU INTO THIS PARTICULAR SITUATION.
YOU DESERVE THE RIGHT TO FUCK UP YOUR LIFE ON YOUR OWN TERMS.
BUT NOT *EVERYONE* DESERVES THAT.

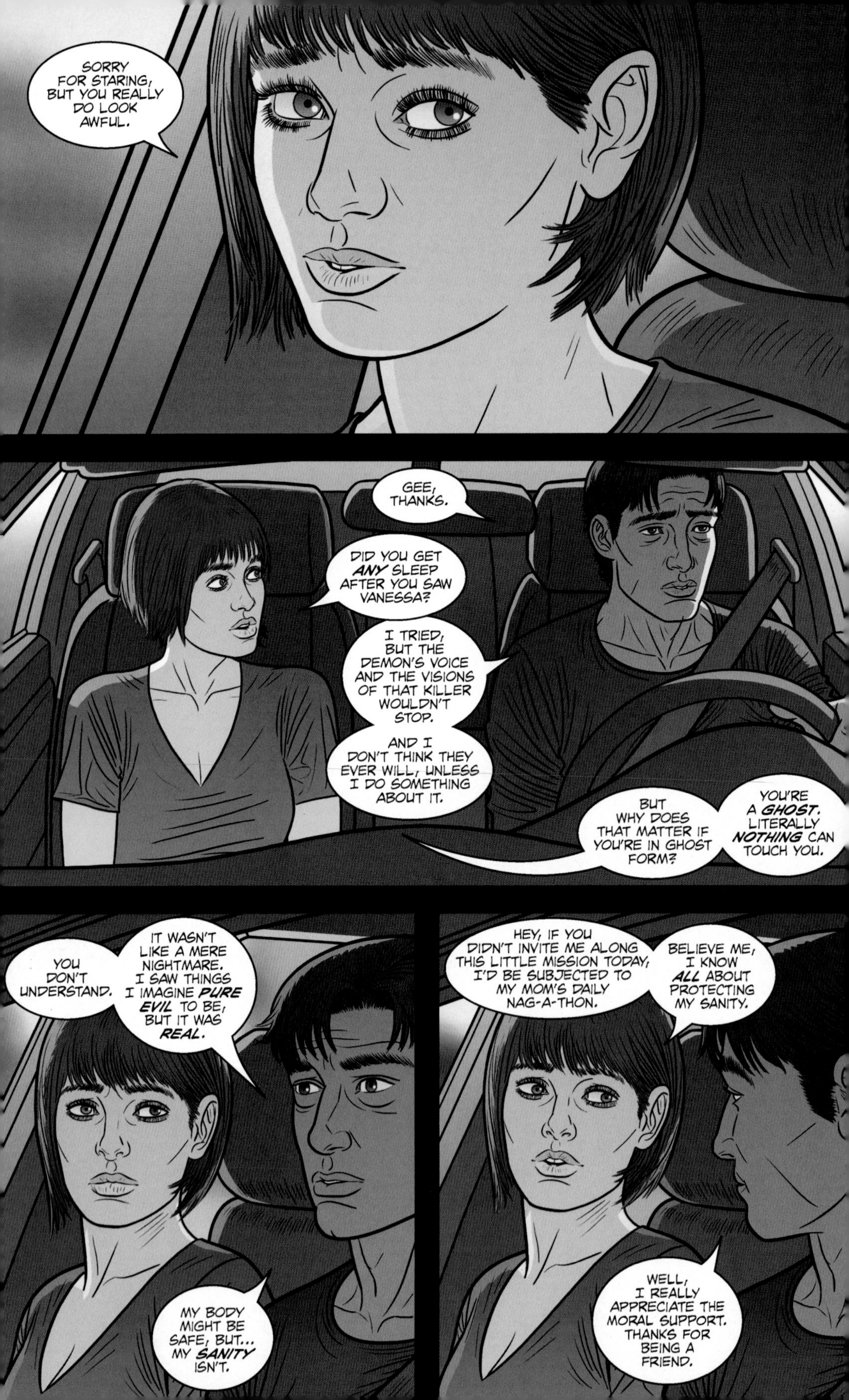
SORRY FOR STARING, BUT YOU REALLY DO LOOK AWFUL.
GEE, THANKS.
DID YOU GET ANY SLEEP AFTER YOU SAW VANESSA?
I TRIED, BUT THE DEMON'S VOICE AND THE VISIONS OF THAT KILLER WOULDN'T STOP.
AND I DON'T THINK THEY EVER WILL, UNLESS I DO SOMETHING ABOUT IT.
BUT WHY DOES THAT MATTER IF YOU'RE IN GHOST FORM?
YOU'RE A GHOST. LITERALLY NOTHING CAN TOUCH YOU.
YOU DON'T UNDERSTAND.
IT WASN'T LIKE A MERE NIGHTMARE. I SAW THINGS I IMAGINE PURE EVIL TO BE, BUT IT WAS REAL.
MY BODY MIGHT BE SAFE, BUT... MY SANITY ISN'T.
HEY, IF YOU DIDN'T INVITE ME ALONG THIS LITTLE MISSION TODAY, I'D BE SUBJECTED TO MY MOM'S DAILY NAG-A-THON.
BELIEVE ME, I KNOW ALL ABOUT PROTECTING MY SANITY.
WELL, I REALLY APPRECIATE THE MORAL SUPPORT. THANKS FOR BEING A FRIEND.

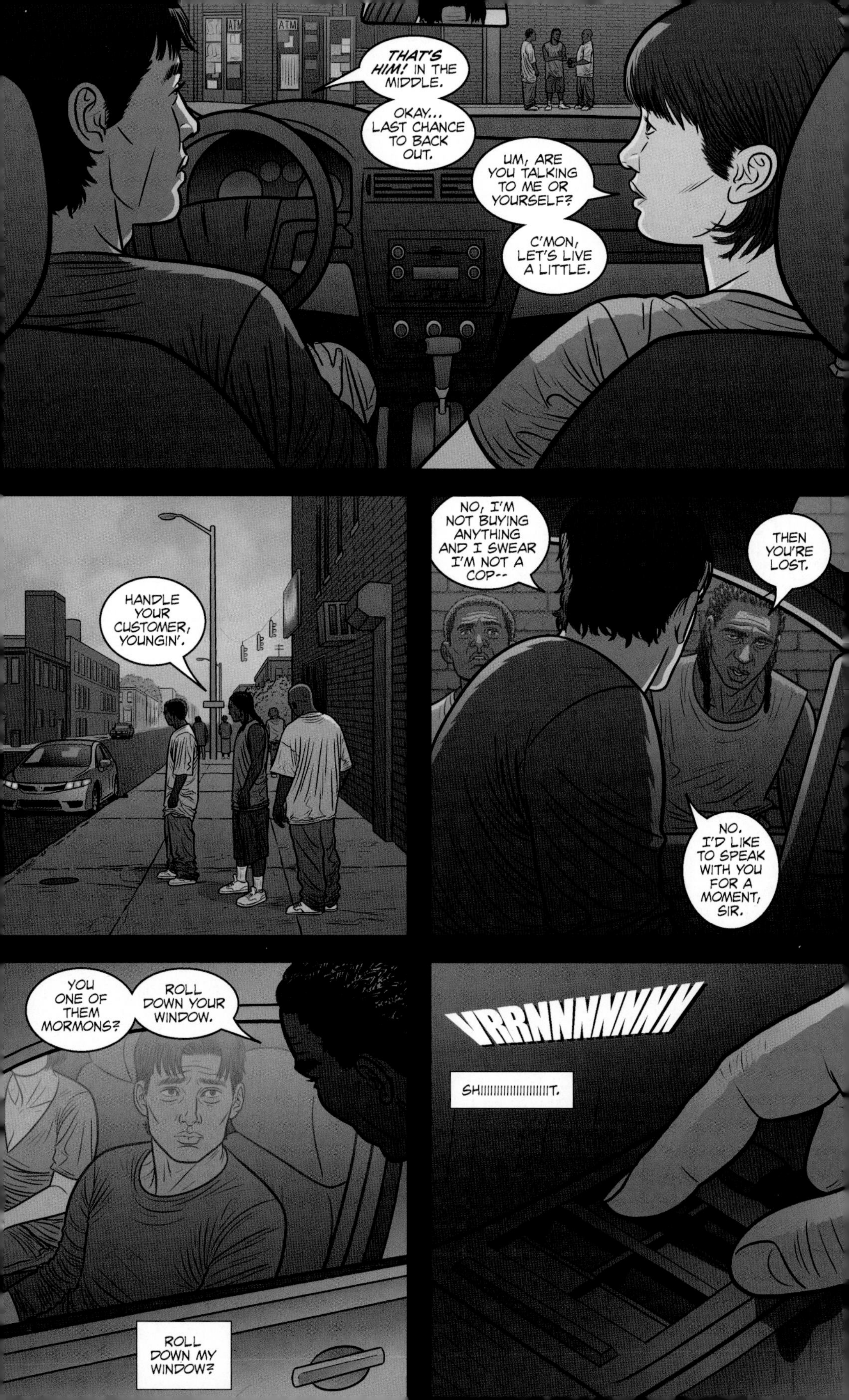
THAT'S HIM! IN THE MIDDLE.
OKAY... LAST CHANCE TO BACK OUT.
UM, ARE YOU TALKING TO ME OR YOURSELF?
C'MON, LET'S LIVE A LITTLE.
HANDLE YOUR CUSTOMER, YOUNGIN'.
NO, I'M NOT BUYING ANYTHING AND I SWEAR I'M NOT A COP--
THEN YOU'RE LOST.
NO. I'D LIKE TO SPEAK WITH YOU FOR A MOMENT, SIR.
YOU ONE OF THEM MORMONS?
ROLL DOWN YOUR WINDOW.
ROLL DOWN MY WINDOW?
VRRNNNNNNNN
SHIIIIIIIIIIIIIIIIIIIT.

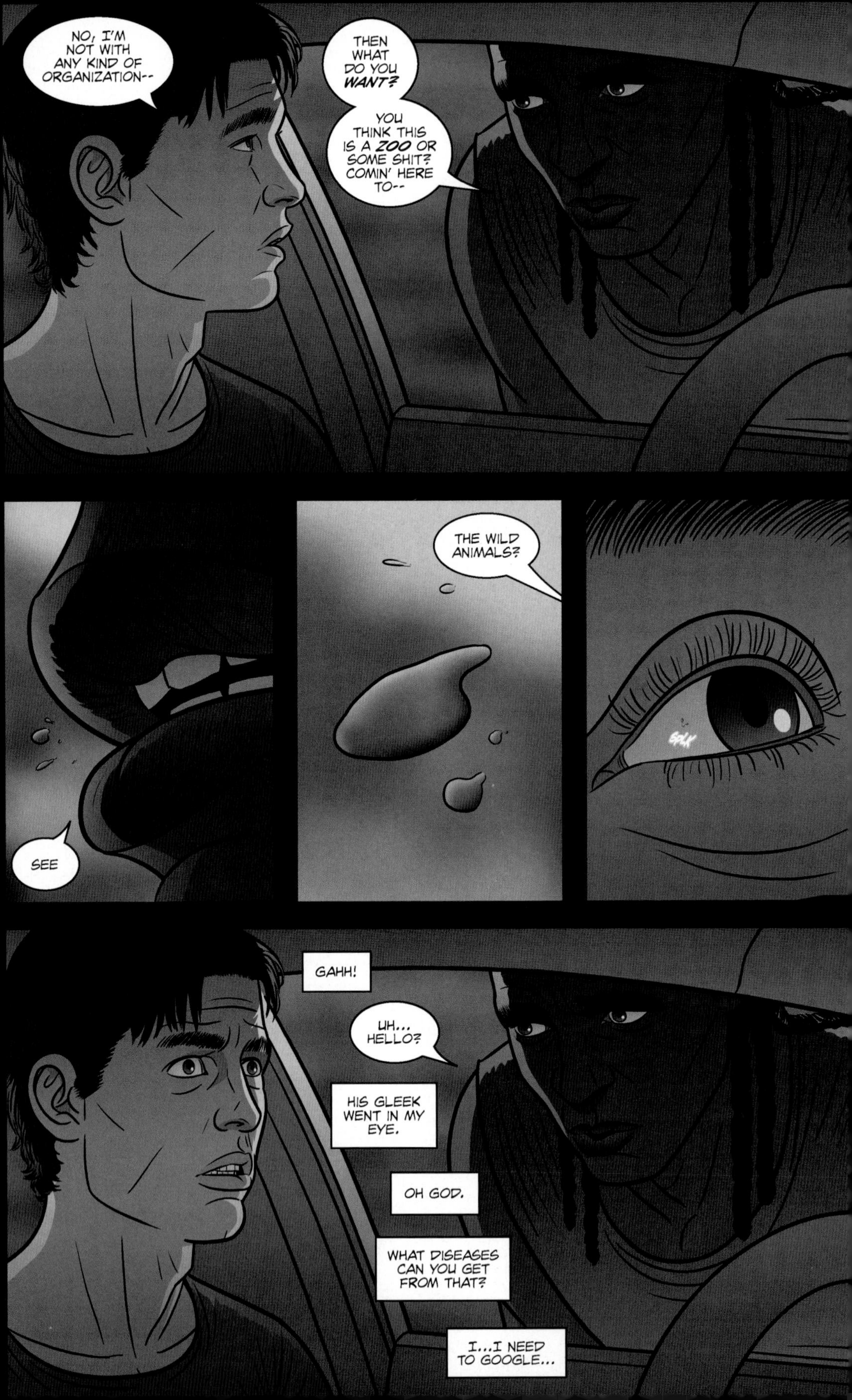
NO, I'M NOT WITH ANY KIND OF ORGANIZATION--
THEN WHAT DO YOU *WANT?*
YOU THINK THIS IS A *ZOO* OR SOME SHIT? COMIN' HERE TO--
SEE
THE WILD ANIMALS?
SPLK
GAHH!
UH... HELLO?
HIS GLEEK WENT IN MY EYE.
OH GOD.
WHAT DISEASES CAN YOU GET FROM THAT?
I...I NEED TO GOOGLE...

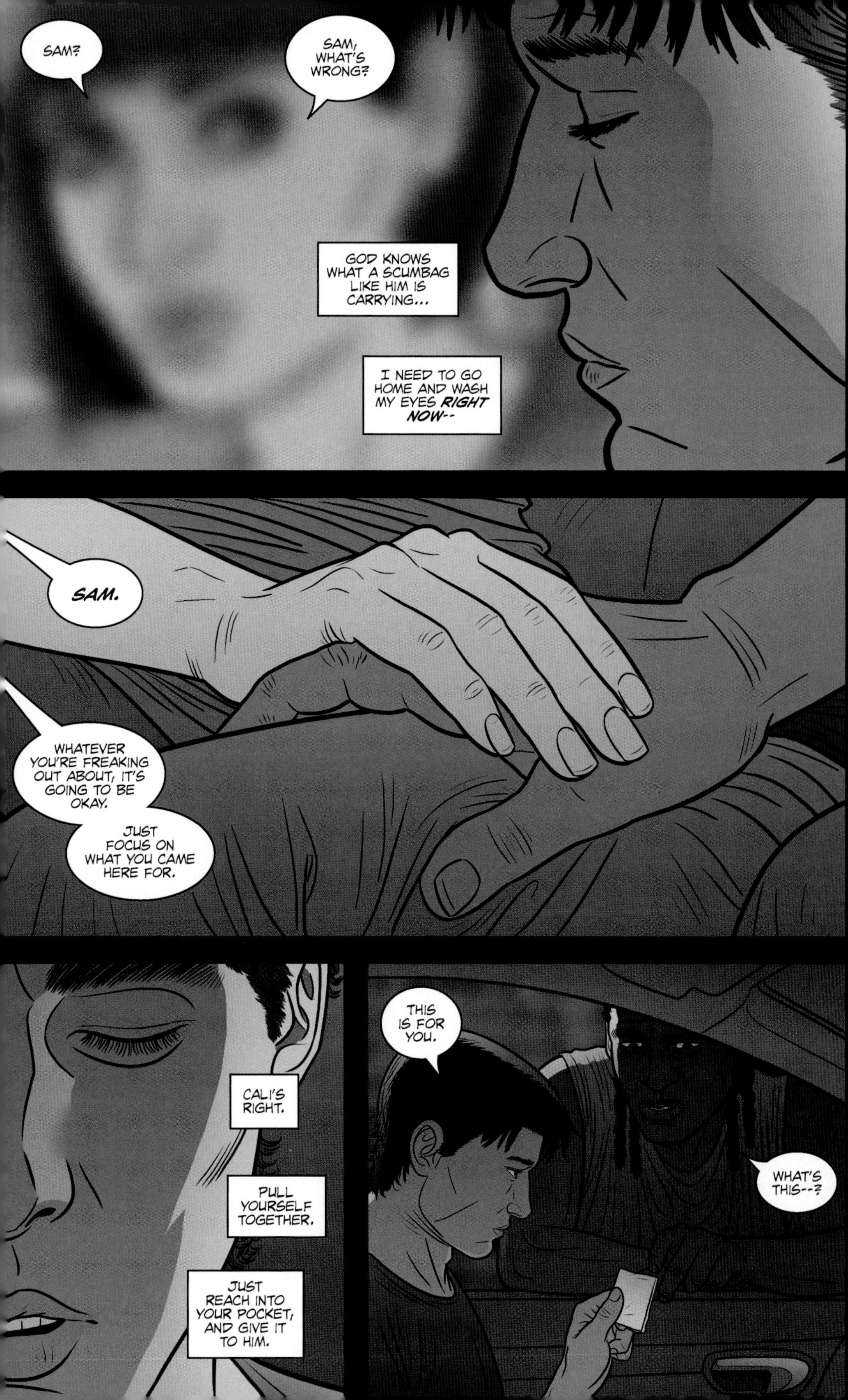
SAM?
SAM, WHAT'S WRONG?
GOD KNOWS WHAT A SCUMBAG LIKE HIM IS CARRYING...
I NEED TO GO HOME AND WASH MY EYES *RIGHT NOW*--
SAM.
WHATEVER YOU'RE FREAKING OUT ABOUT, IT'S GOING TO BE OKAY.
JUST FOCUS ON WHAT YOU CAME HERE FOR.
CALI'S RIGHT.
PULL YOURSELF TOGETHER.
JUST REACH INTO YOUR POCKET, AND GIVE IT TO HIM.
THIS IS FOR YOU.
WHAT'S THIS--?

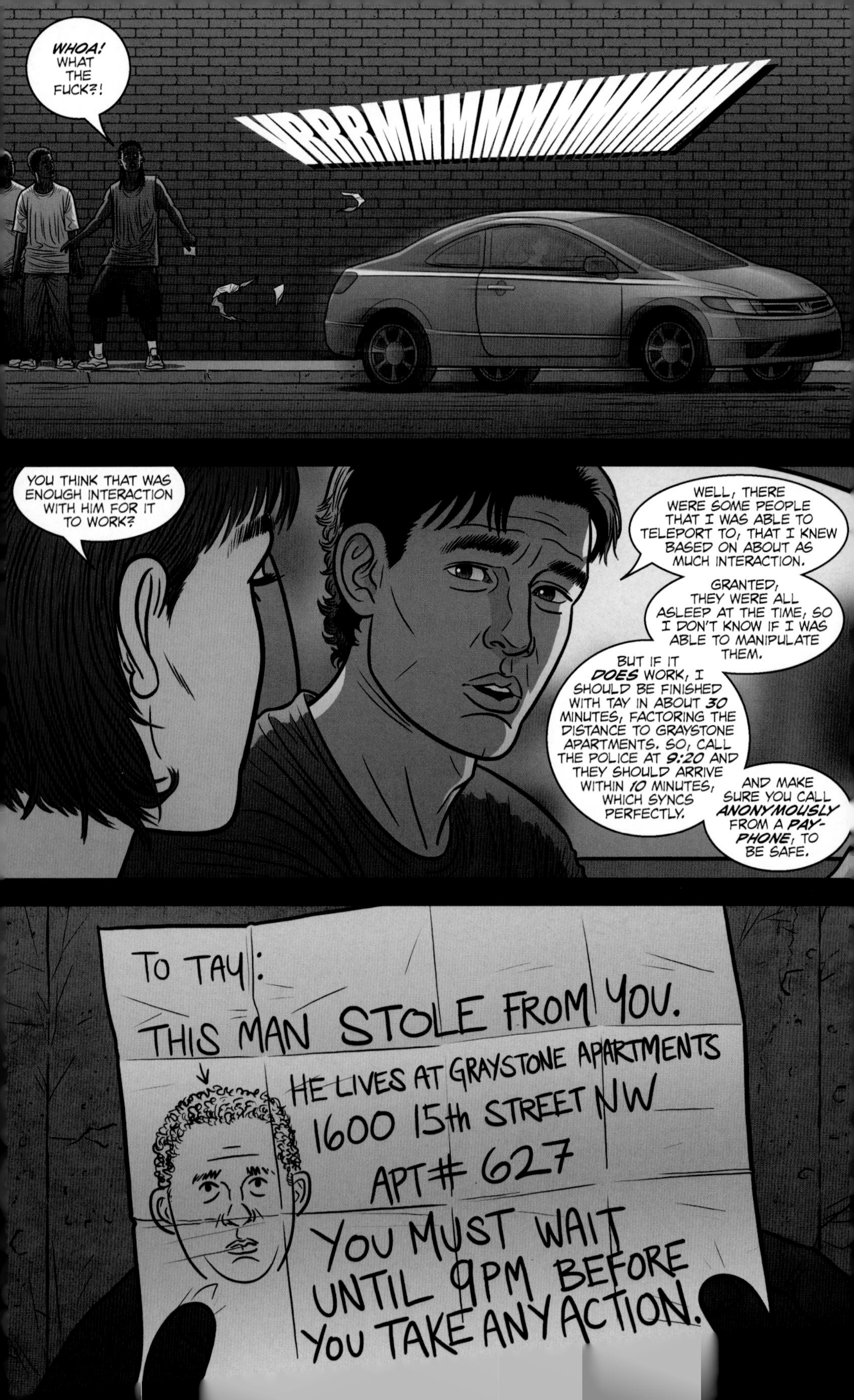
WHOA! WHAT THE FUCK?!
VRRRMMMMMMHHHHH
YOU THINK THAT WAS ENOUGH INTERACTION WITH HIM FOR IT TO WORK?
WELL, THERE WERE SOME PEOPLE THAT I WAS ABLE TO TELEPORT TO, THAT I KNEW BASED ON ABOUT AS MUCH INTERACTION.
GRANTED, THEY WERE ALL ASLEEP AT THE TIME, SO I DON'T KNOW IF I WAS ABLE TO MANIPULATE THEM.
BUT IF IT DOES WORK, I SHOULD BE FINISHED WITH TAY IN ABOUT 30 MINUTES, FACTORING THE DISTANCE TO GRAYSTONE APARTMENTS. SO, CALL THE POLICE AT 9:20 AND THEY SHOULD ARRIVE WITHIN 10 MINUTES, WHICH SYNCS PERFECTLY.
AND MAKE SURE YOU CALL ANONYMOUSLY FROM A PAY-PHONE, TO BE SAFE.
TO TAY:
THIS MAN STOLE FROM YOU.
HE LIVES AT GRAYSTONE APARTMENTS
1600 15th STREET NW
APT # 627
YOU MUST WAIT UNTIL 9PM BEFORE YOU TAKE ANY ACTION.

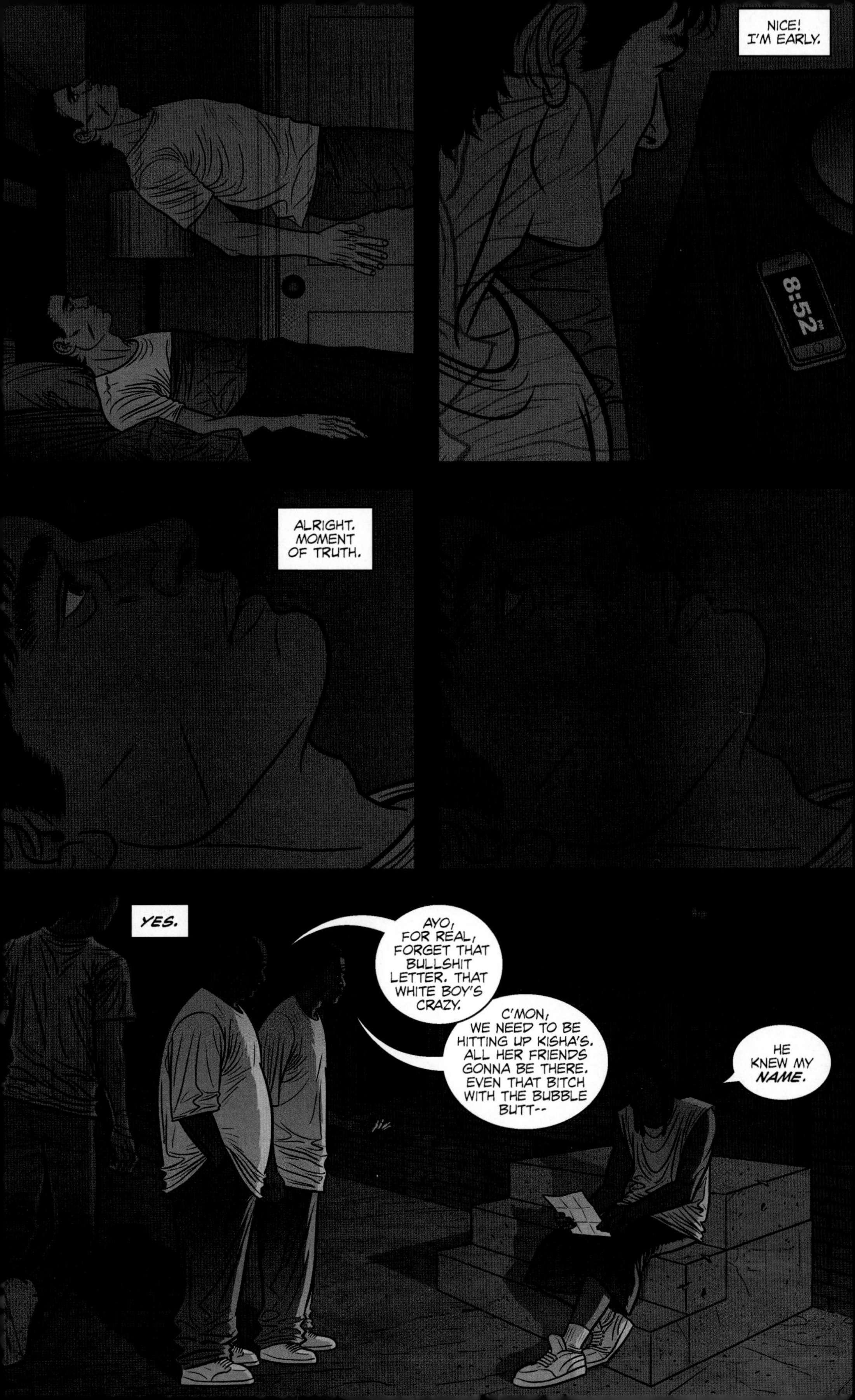
NICE! I'M EARLY.
8:52
ALRIGHT. MOMENT OF TRUTH.
YES.
AYO, FOR REAL, FORGET THAT BULLSHIT LETTER. THAT WHITE BOY'S CRAZY.
C'MON, WE NEED TO BE HITTING UP KISHA'S. ALL HER FRIENDS GONNA BE THERE. EVEN THAT BITCH WITH THE BUBBLE BUTT--
HE KNEW MY NAME.

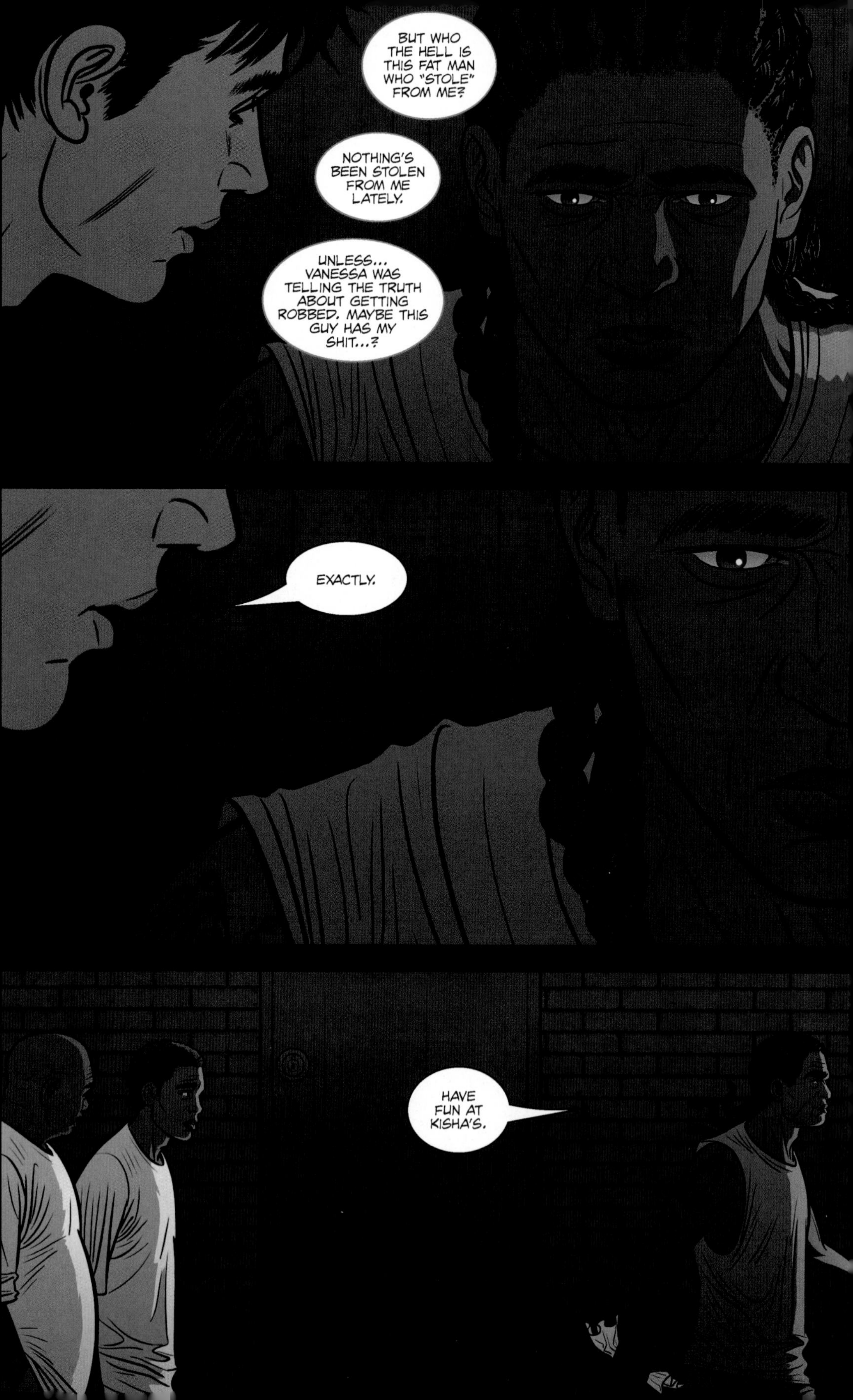
BUT WHO THE HELL IS THIS FAT MAN WHO "STOLE" FROM ME?
NOTHING'S BEEN STOLEN FROM ME LATELY.
UNLESS... VANESSA WAS TELLING THE TRUTH ABOUT GETTING ROBBED. MAYBE THIS GUY HAS MY SHIT...?
EXACTLY.
HAVE FUN AT KISHA'S.

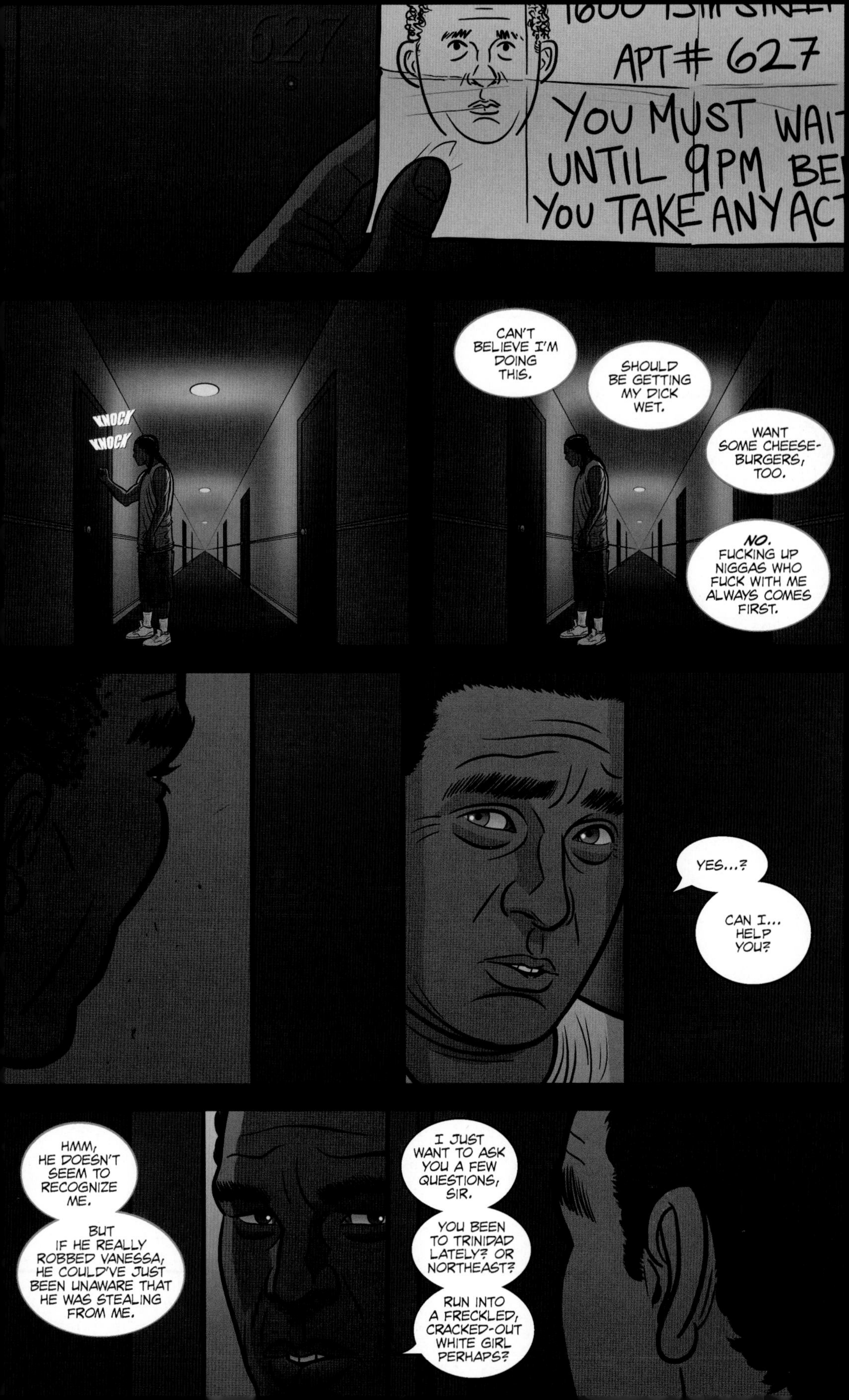
1600 13TH STREET
APT# 627
YOU MUST WAIT
UNTIL 9PM BE
YOU TAKE ANY ACT
KNOCK
KNOCK
CAN'T BELIEVE I'M DOING THIS.
SHOULD BE GETTING MY DICK WET.
WANT SOME CHEESE-BURGERS, TOO.
NO. FUCKING UP NIGGAS WHO FUCK WITH ME ALWAYS COMES FIRST.
YES...?
CAN I... HELP YOU?
HMM, HE DOESN'T SEEM TO RECOGNIZE ME.
BUT IF HE REALLY ROBBED VANESSA, HE COULD'VE JUST BEEN UNAWARE THAT HE WAS STEALING FROM ME.
I JUST WANT TO ASK YOU A FEW QUESTIONS, SIR.
YOU BEEN TO TRINIDAD LATELY? OR NORTHEAST?
RUN INTO A FRECKLED, CRACKED-OUT WHITE GIRL PERHAPS?

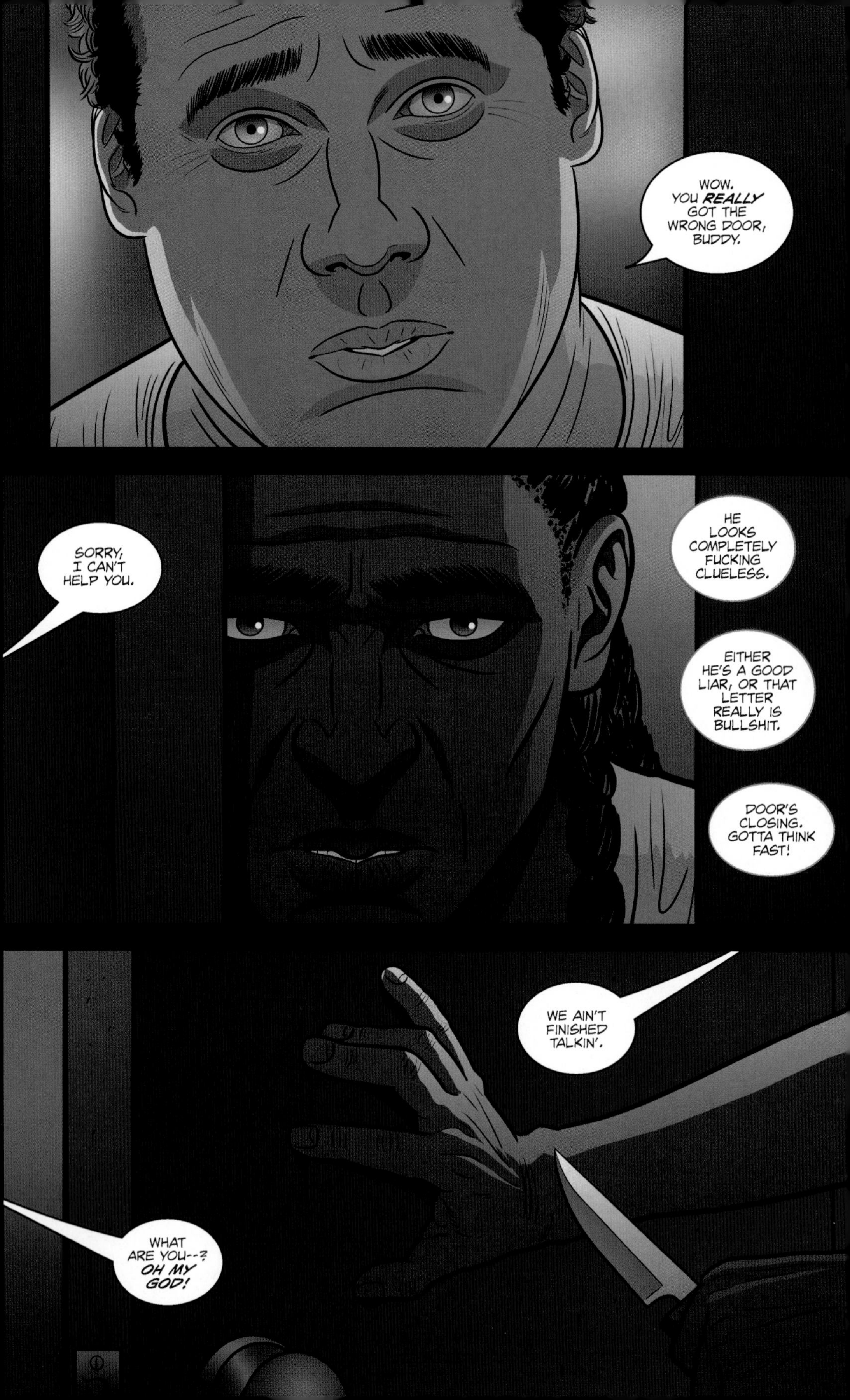
WOW. YOU **REALLY** GOT THE WRONG DOOR, BUDDY.
SORRY, I CAN'T HELP YOU.
HE LOOKS COMPLETELY FUCKING CLUELESS.
EITHER HE'S A GOOD LIAR, OR THAT LETTER REALLY IS BULLSHIT.
DOOR'S CLOSING. GOTTA THINK FAST!
WE AIN'T FINISHED TALKIN'.
WHAT ARE YOU--? ***OH MY GOD!***

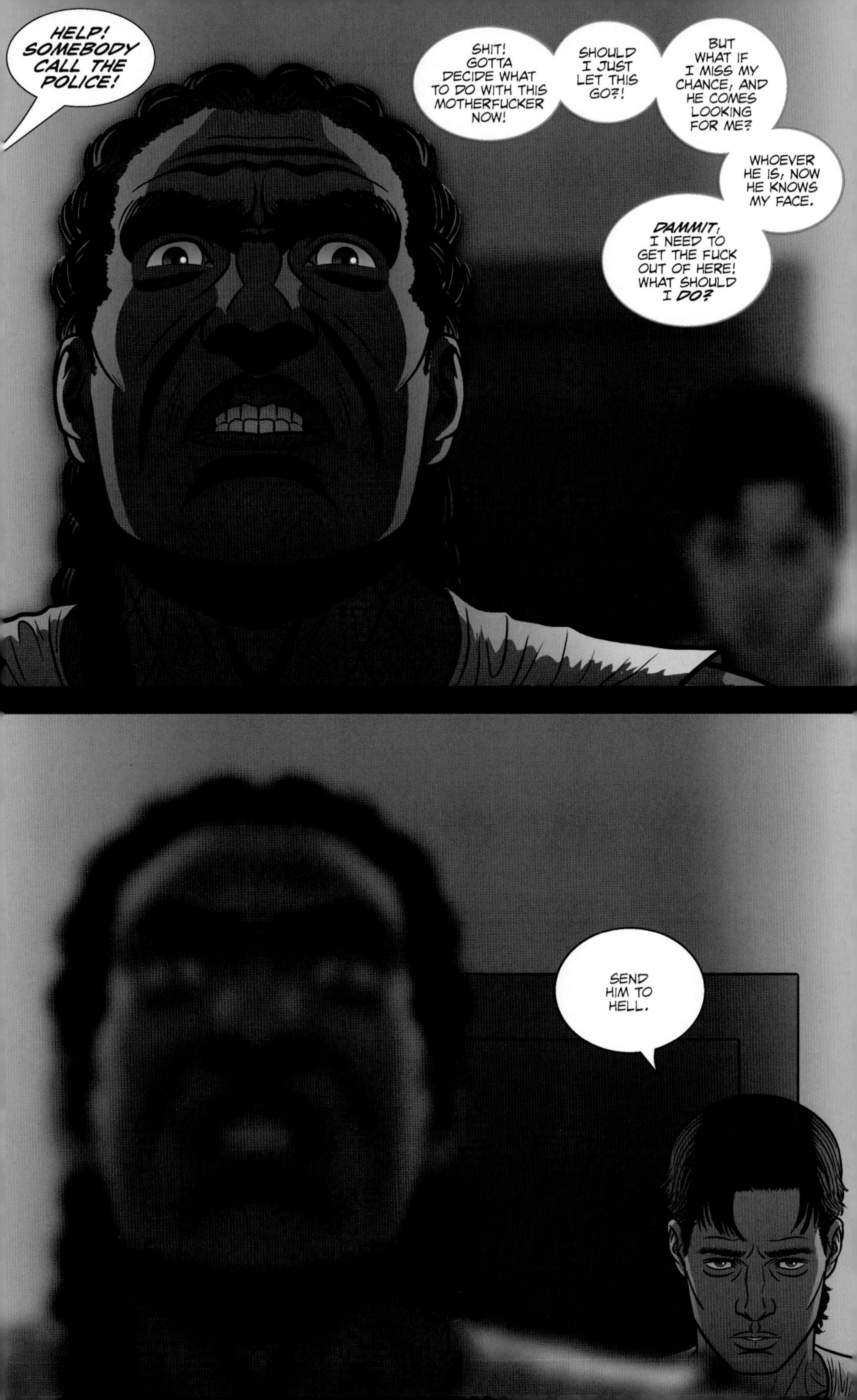
HELP! SOMEBODY CALL THE POLICE!
SHIT! GOTTA DECIDE WHAT TO DO WITH THIS MOTHERFUCKER NOW!
SHOULD I JUST LET THIS GO?!
BUT WHAT IF I MISS MY CHANCE, AND HE COMES LOOKING FOR ME?
WHOEVER HE IS, NOW HE KNOWS MY FACE.
DAMMIT, I NEED TO GET THE FUCK OUT OF HERE! WHAT SHOULD I DO?
SEND HIM TO HELL.

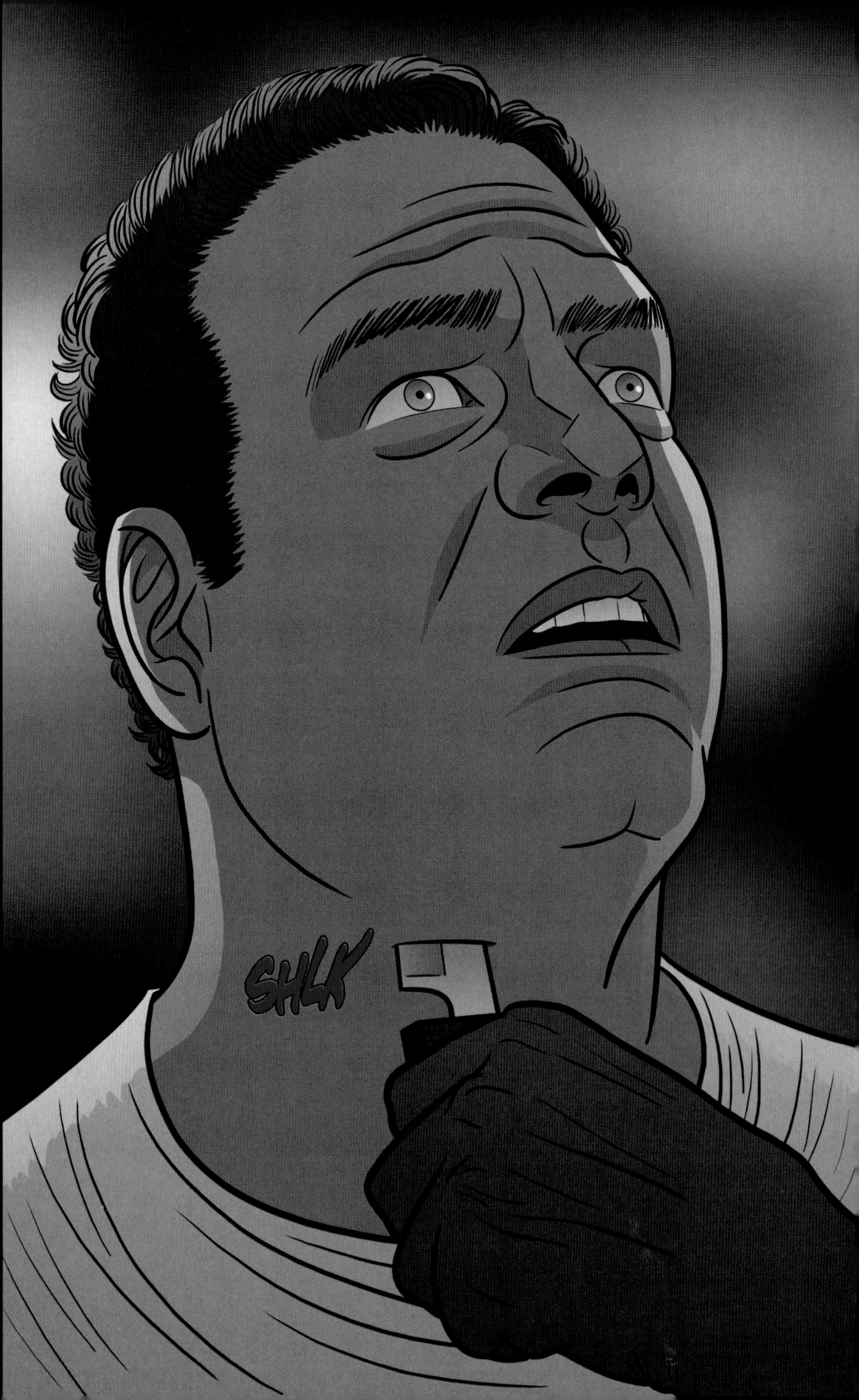
SHLK

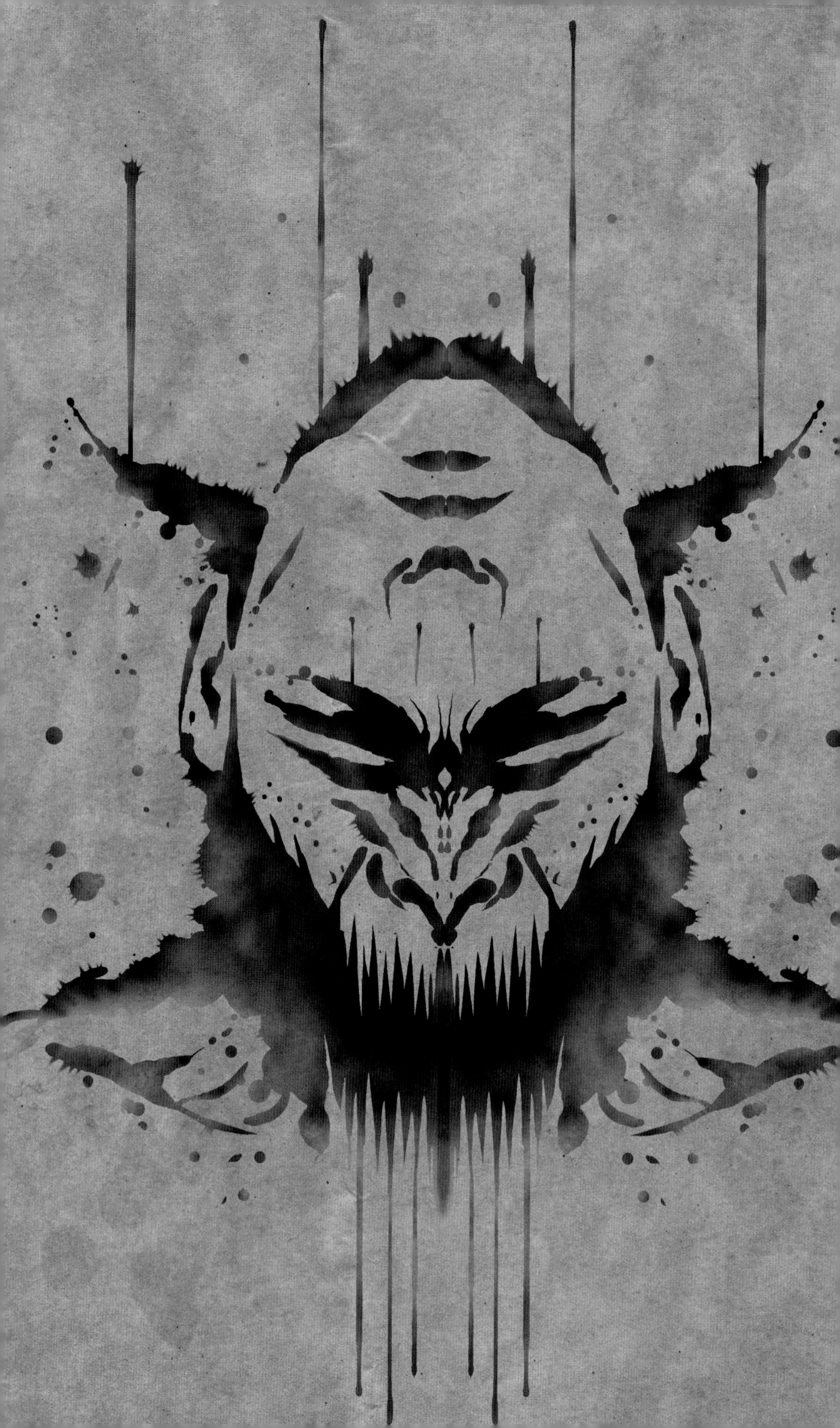

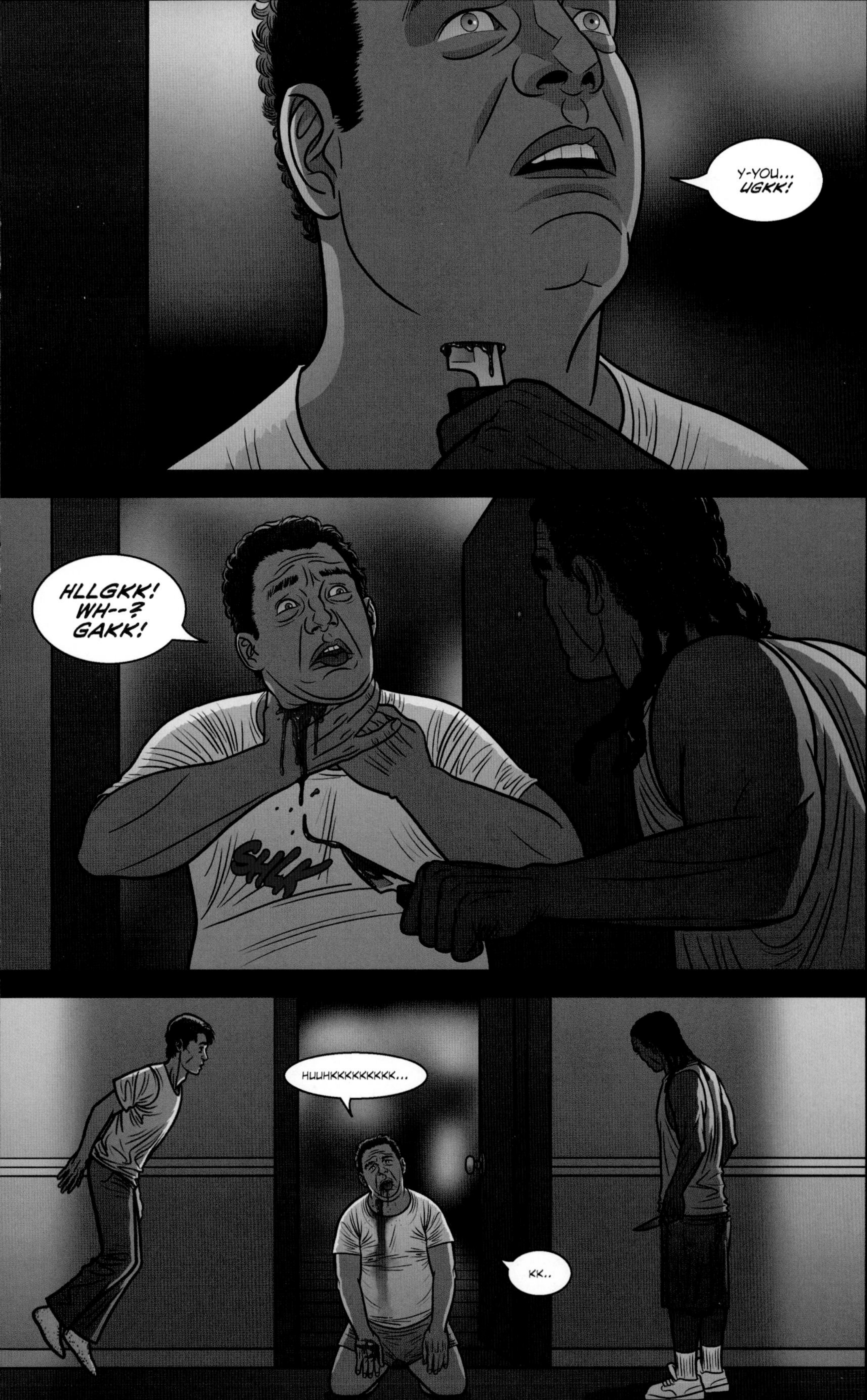
Y-YOU... UGKK!
HLLGKK! WH--? GAKK!
SHLK
HUUHKKKKKKKKK...
KK..

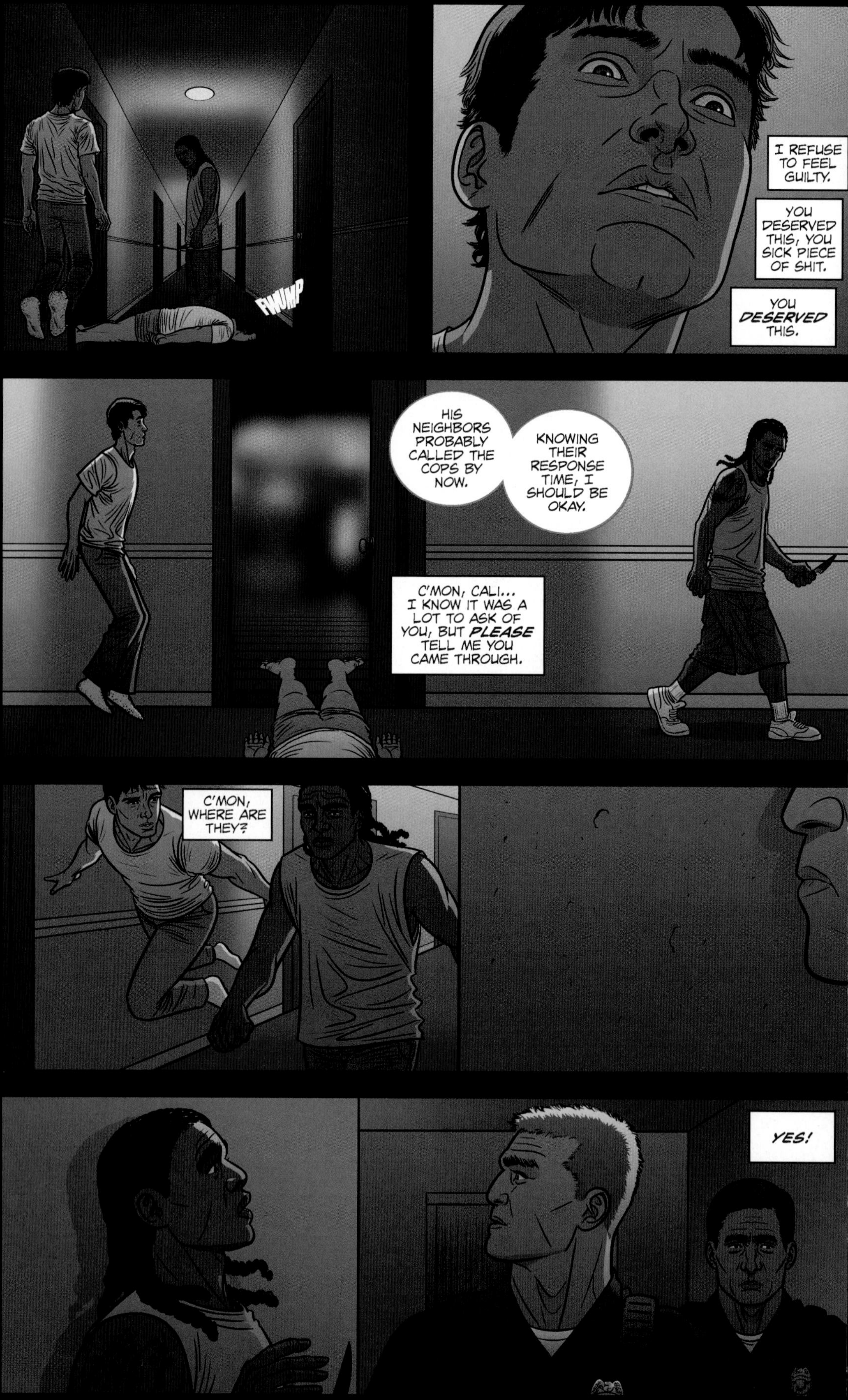
FWUMP
I REFUSE TO FEEL GUILTY.
YOU DESERVED THIS, YOU SICK PIECE OF SHIT.
YOU DESERVED THIS.
HIS NEIGHBORS PROBABLY CALLED THE COPS BY NOW.
KNOWING THEIR RESPONSE TIME, I SHOULD BE OKAY.
C'MON, CALI... I KNOW IT WAS A LOT TO ASK OF YOU, BUT PLEASE TELL ME YOU CAME THROUGH.
C'MON, WHERE ARE THEY?
YES!

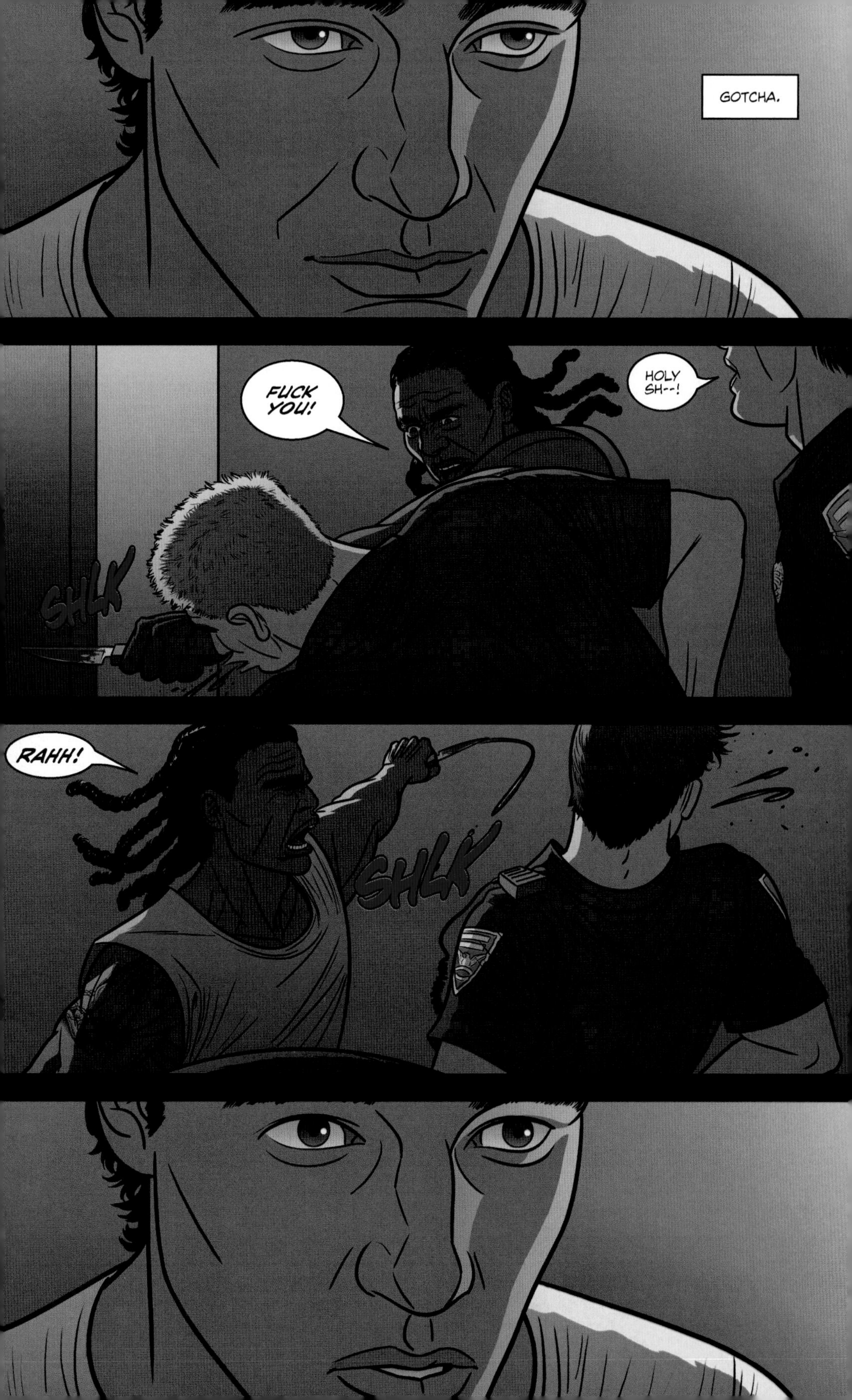
GOTCHA.
FUCK YOU!
HOLY SH--!
SHLK
RAHH!
SHLK

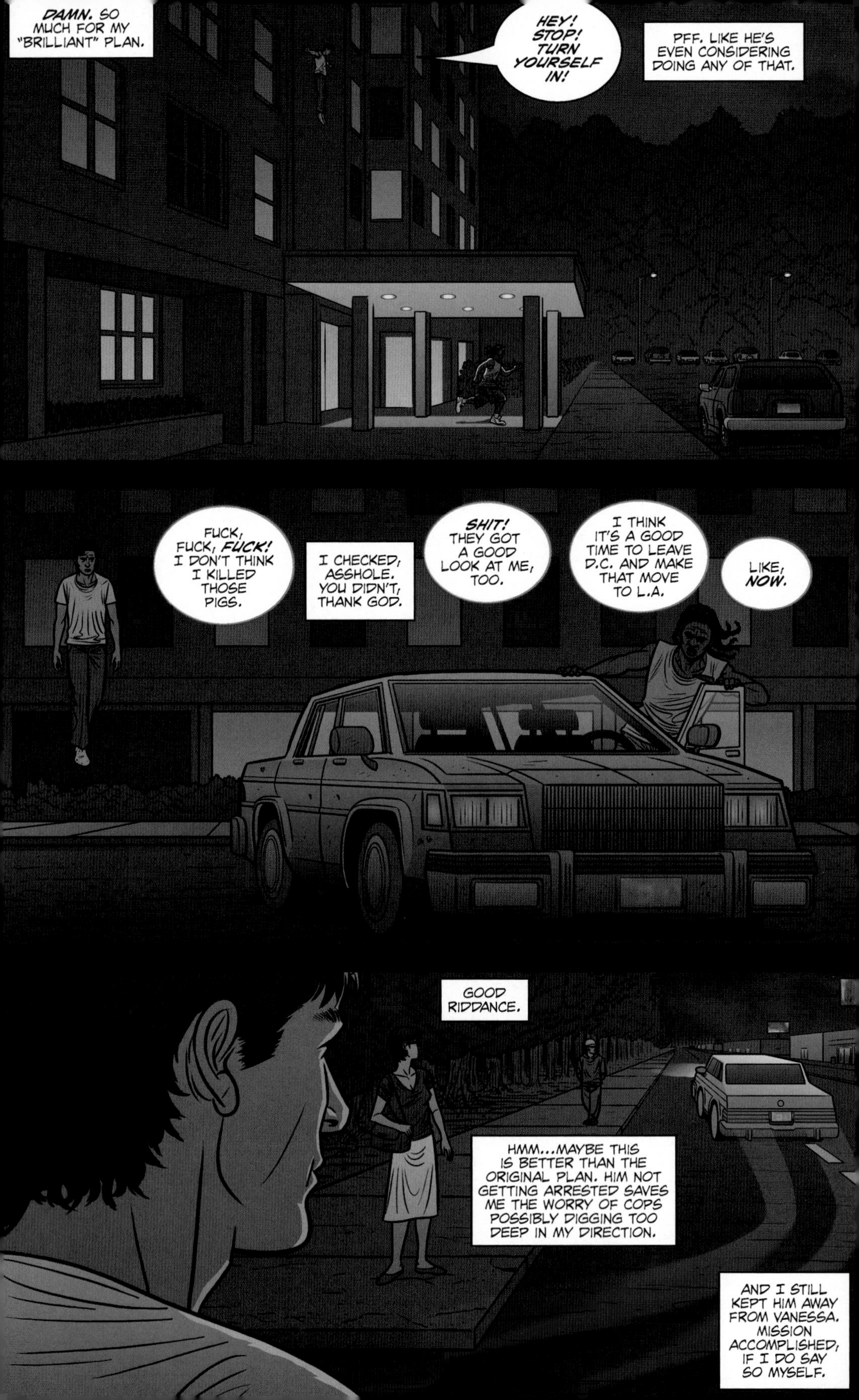
DAMN. SO MUCH FOR MY "BRILLIANT" PLAN.
HEY! STOP! TURN YOURSELF IN!
PFF. LIKE HE'S EVEN CONSIDERING DOING ANY OF THAT.
FUCK, FUCK, FUCK! I DON'T THINK I KILLED THOSE PIGS.
I CHECKED, ASSHOLE. YOU DIDN'T, THANK GOD.
SHIT! THEY GOT A GOOD LOOK AT ME, TOO.
I THINK IT'S A GOOD TIME TO LEAVE D.C. AND MAKE THAT MOVE TO L.A.
LIKE, NOW.
GOOD RIDDANCE.
HMM...MAYBE THIS IS BETTER THAN THE ORIGINAL PLAN. HIM NOT GETTING ARRESTED SAVES ME THE WORRY OF COPS POSSIBLY DIGGING TOO DEEP IN MY DIRECTION.
AND I STILL KEPT HIM AWAY FROM VANESSA. MISSION ACCOMPLISHED, IF I DO SAY SO MYSELF.

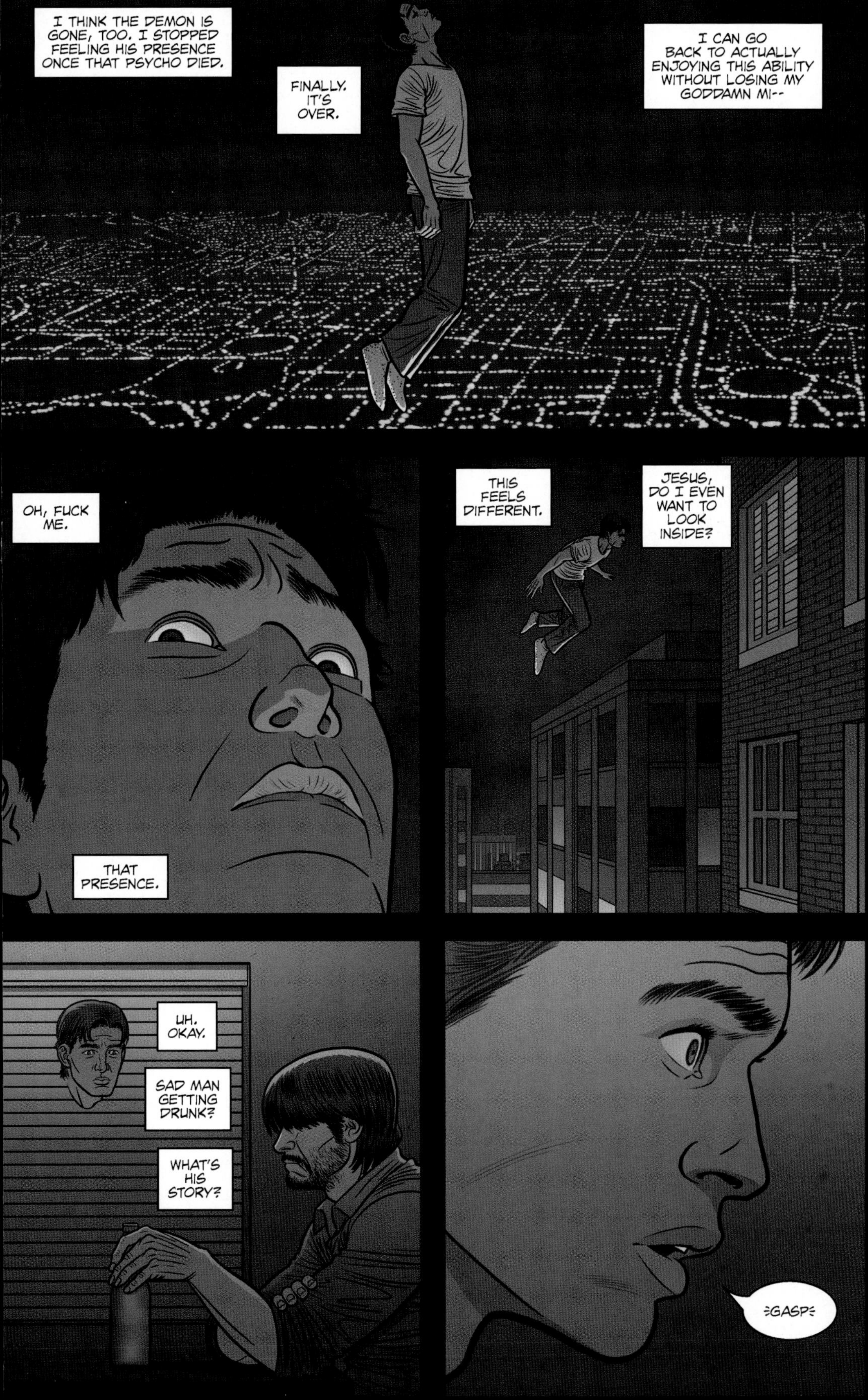
I THINK THE DEMON IS GONE, TOO. I STOPPED FEELING HIS PRESENCE ONCE THAT PSYCHO DIED.
FINALLY. IT'S OVER.
I CAN GO BACK TO ACTUALLY ENJOYING THIS ABILITY WITHOUT LOSING MY GODDAMN MI--
OH, FUCK ME.
THAT PRESENCE.
THIS FEELS DIFFERENT.
JESUS, DO I EVEN WANT TO LOOK INSIDE?
UH. OKAY.
SAD MAN GETTING DRUNK?
WHAT'S HIS STORY?
GASP

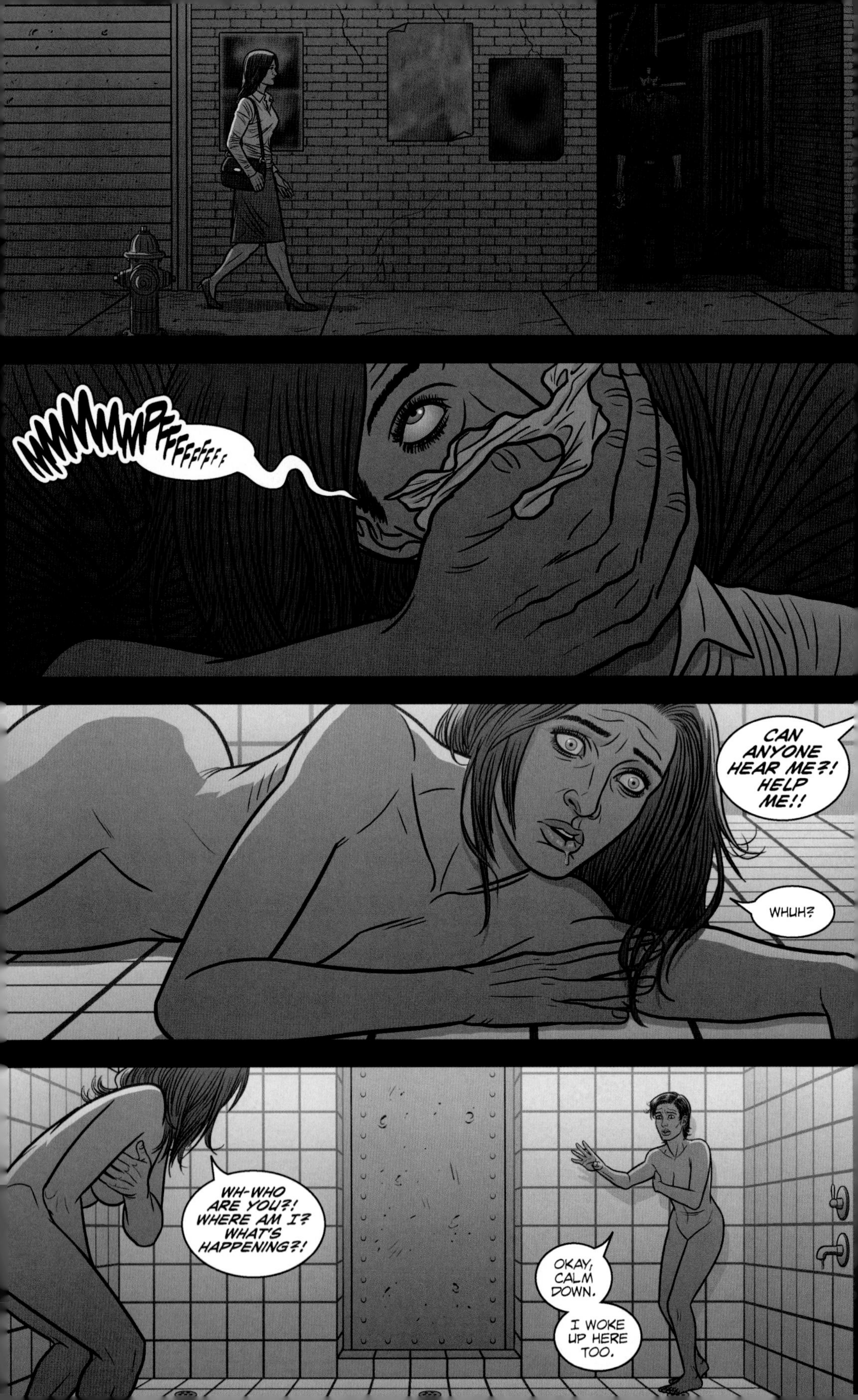
MMMMMMPFFFFFFF
CAN ANYONE HEAR ME?! HELP ME!!
WHUH?
WH-WHO ARE YOU?! WHERE AM I? WHAT'S HAPPENING?!
OKAY, CALM DOWN.
I WOKE UP HERE TOO.

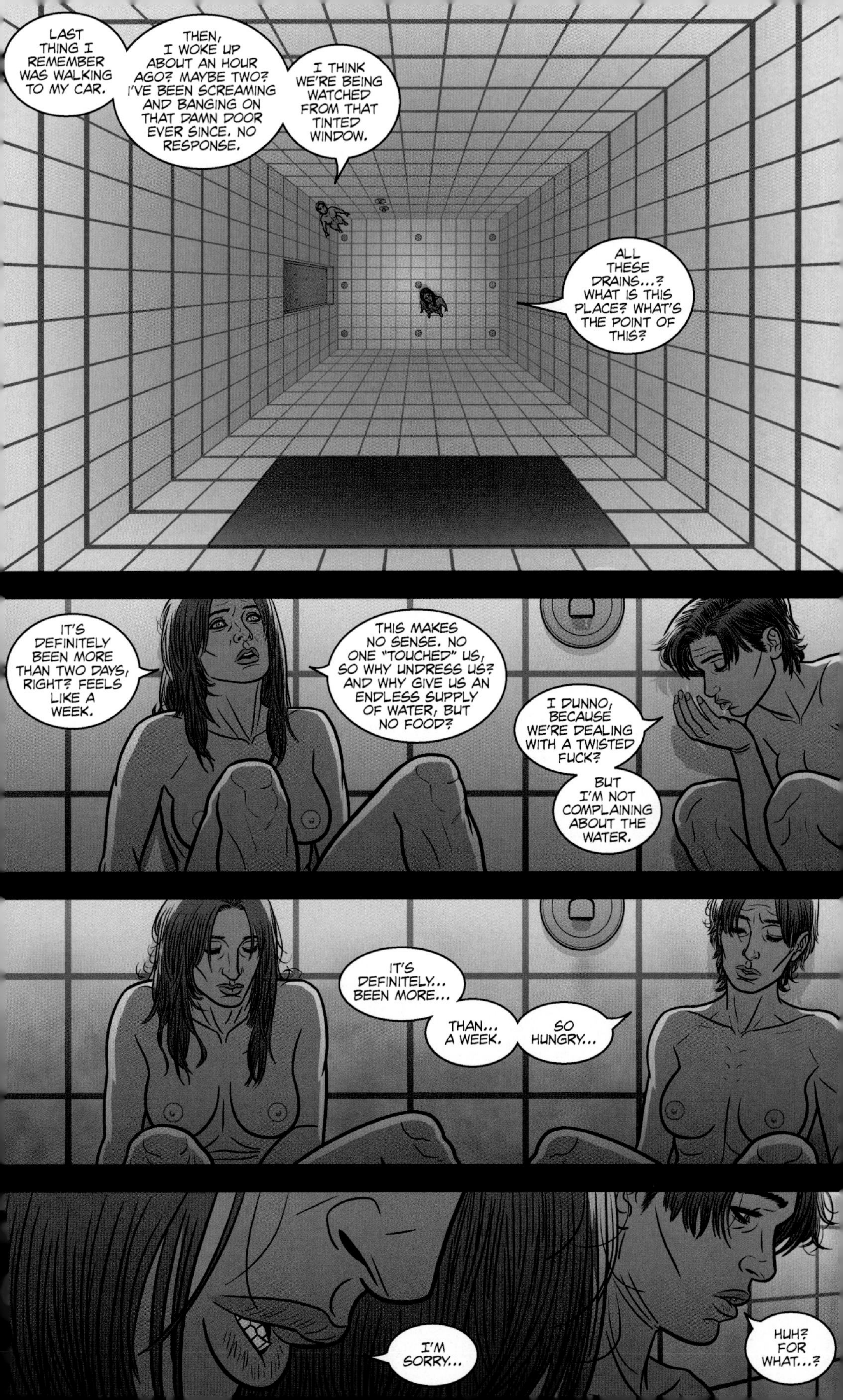
LAST THING I REMEMBER WAS WALKING TO MY CAR.
THEN, I WOKE UP ABOUT AN HOUR AGO? MAYBE TWO? I'VE BEEN SCREAMING AND BANGING ON THAT DAMN DOOR EVER SINCE. NO RESPONSE.
I THINK WE'RE BEING WATCHED FROM THAT TINTED WINDOW.
ALL THESE DRAINS...? WHAT IS THIS PLACE? WHAT'S THE POINT OF THIS?
IT'S DEFINITELY BEEN MORE THAN TWO DAYS, RIGHT? FEELS LIKE A WEEK.
THIS MAKES NO SENSE. NO ONE "TOUCHED" US, SO WHY UNDRESS US? AND WHY GIVE US AN ENDLESS SUPPLY OF WATER, BUT NO FOOD?
I DUNNO, BECAUSE WE'RE DEALING WITH A TWISTED FUCK?
BUT I'M NOT COMPLAINING ABOUT THE WATER.
IT'S DEFINITELY... BEEN MORE...
THAN... A WEEK.
SO HUNGRY...
I'M SORRY...
HUH? FOR WHAT...?

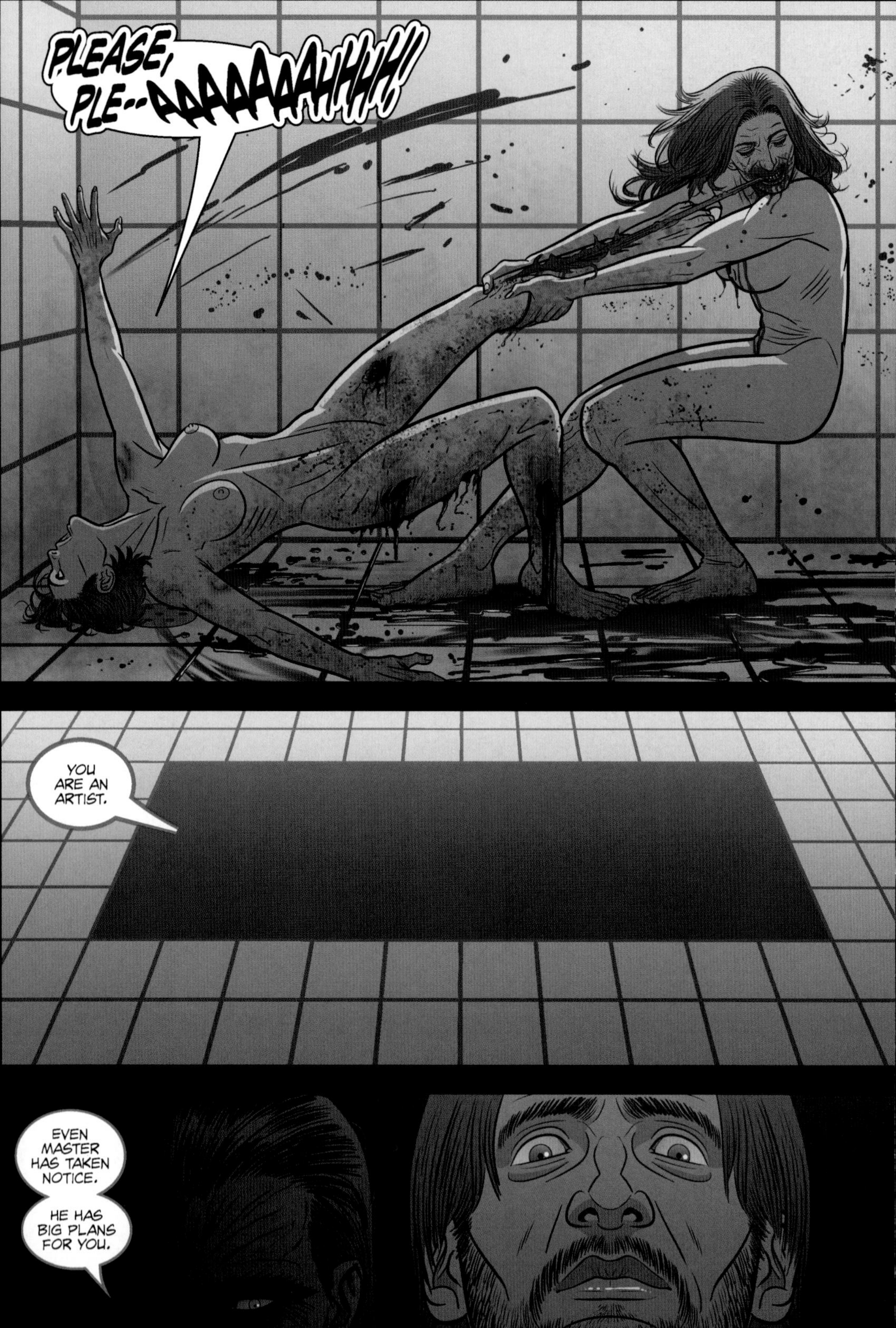
PLEASE, PLE--AAAAAAAHHHH!!
YOU ARE AN ARTIST.
EVEN MASTER HAS TAKEN NOTICE.
HE HAS BIG PLANS FOR YOU.

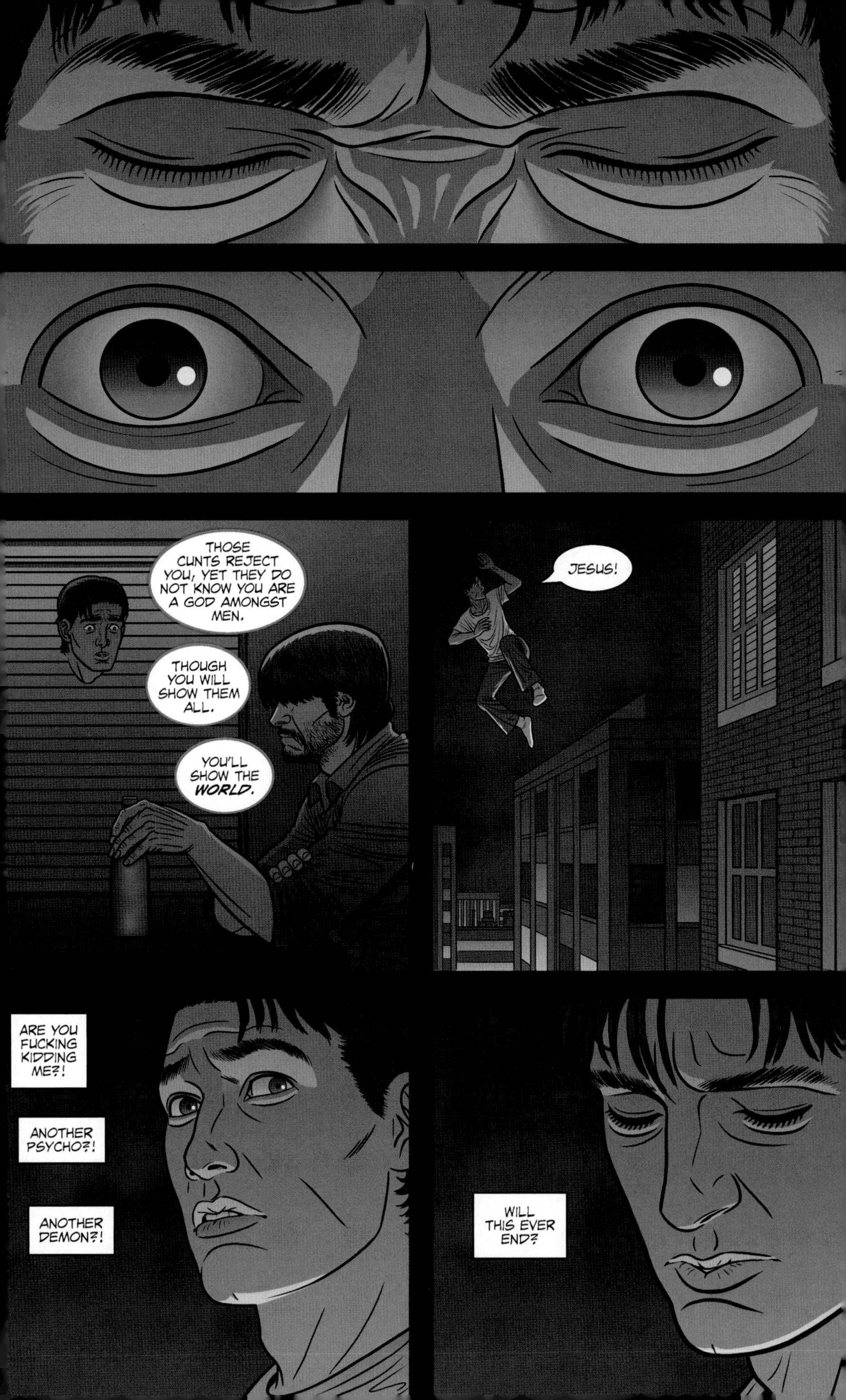
THOSE CUNTS REJECT YOU, YET THEY DO NOT KNOW YOU ARE A GOD AMONGST MEN.
THOUGH YOU WILL SHOW THEM ALL.
YOU'LL SHOW THE *WORLD.*
JESUS!
ARE YOU FUCKING KIDDING ME?!
ANOTHER PSYCHO?!
ANOTHER DEMON?!
WILL THIS EVER END?

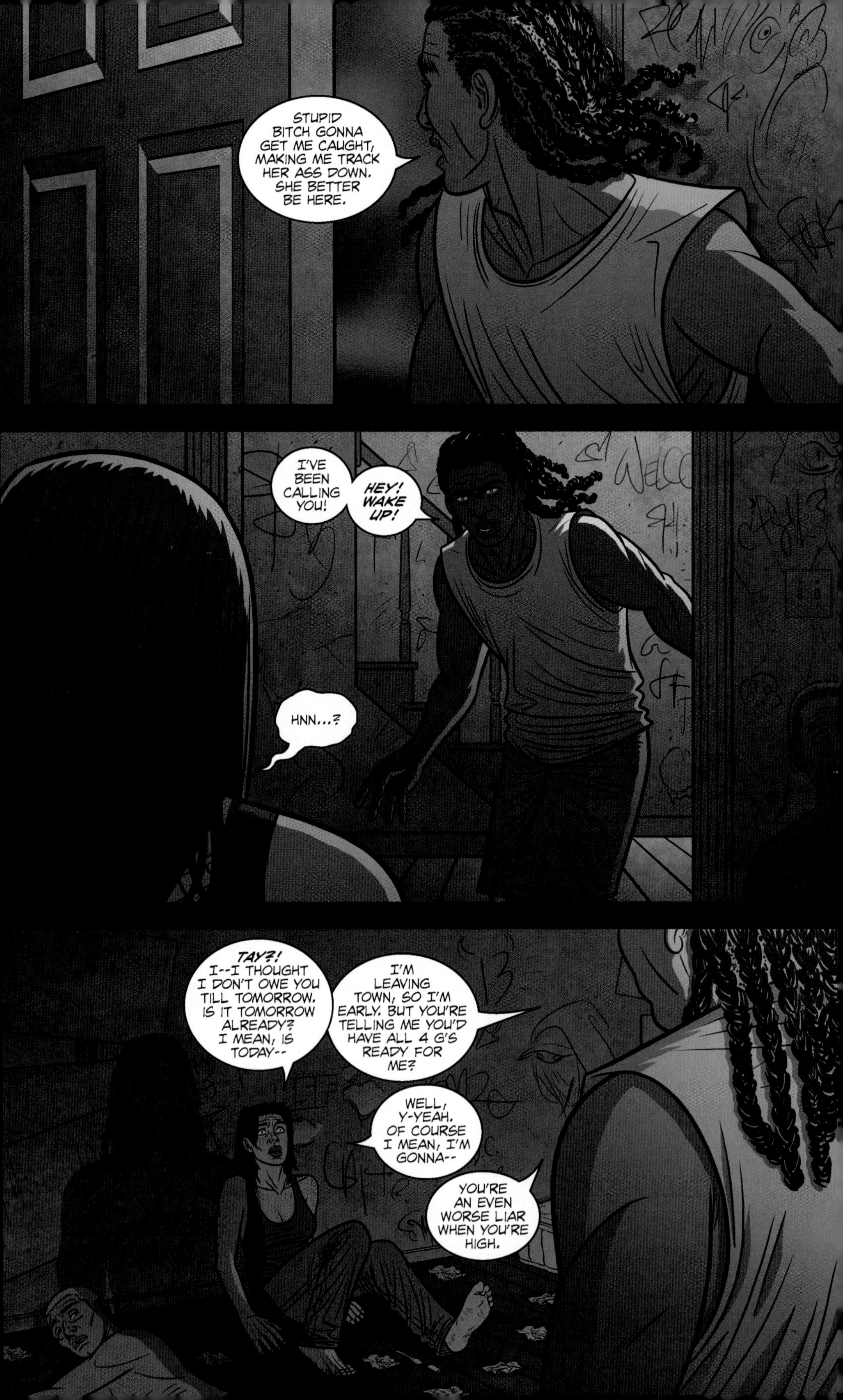
STUPID BITCH GONNA GET ME CAUGHT, MAKING ME TRACK HER ASS DOWN. SHE BETTER BE HERE.
I'VE BEEN CALLING YOU!
HEY! WAKE UP!
HNN...?
TAY?! I--I THOUGHT I DON'T OWE YOU TILL TOMORROW. IS IT TOMORROW ALREADY? I MEAN, IS TODAY--
I'M LEAVING TOWN, SO I'M EARLY. BUT YOU'RE TELLING ME YOU'D HAVE ALL 4 G'S READY FOR ME?
WELL, Y-YEAH. OF COURSE I MEAN, I'M GONNA--
YOU'RE AN EVEN WORSE LIAR WHEN YOU'RE HIGH.

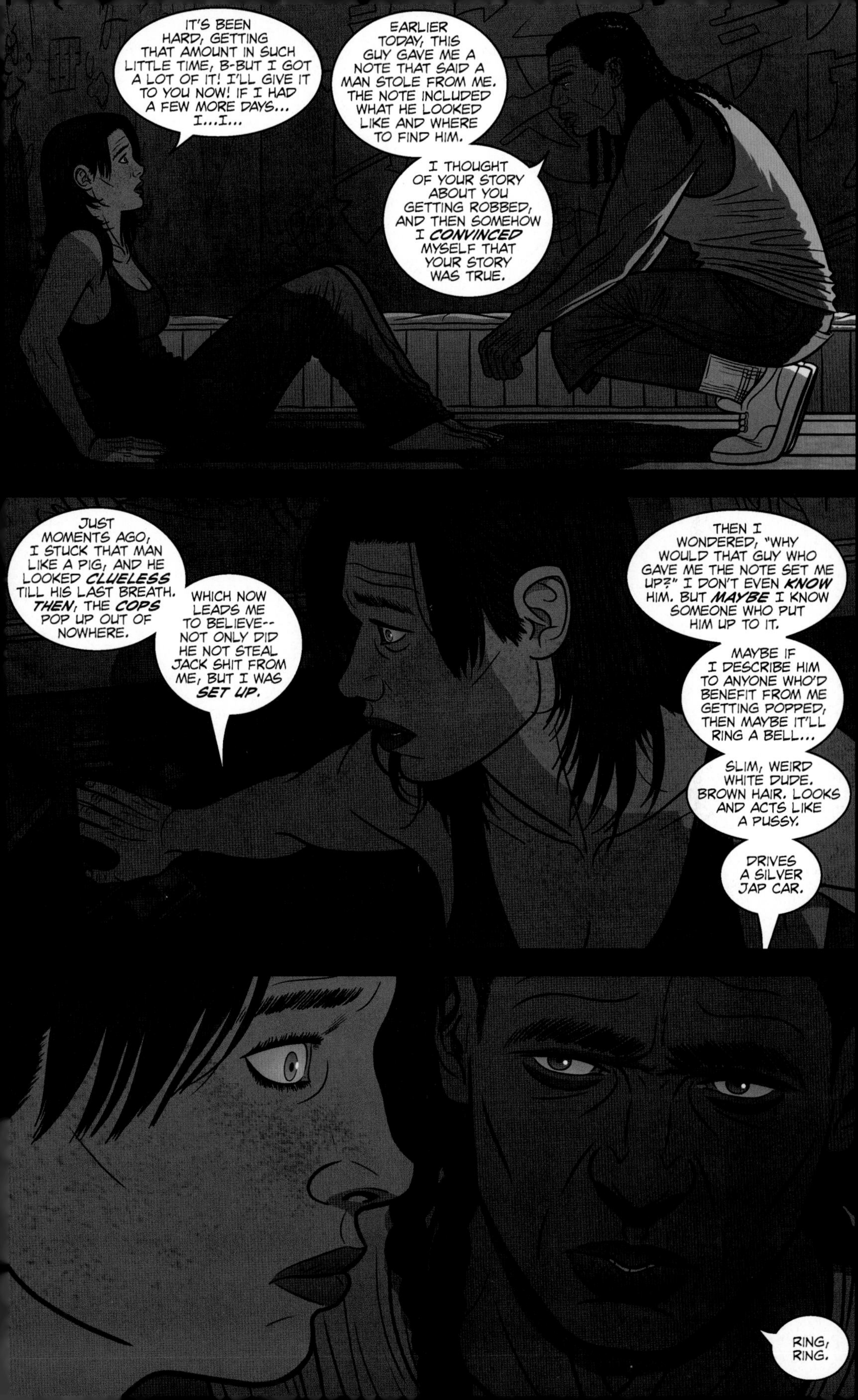
IT'S BEEN HARD, GETTING THAT AMOUNT IN SUCH LITTLE TIME, B-BUT I GOT A LOT OF IT! I'LL GIVE IT TO YOU NOW! IF I HAD A FEW MORE DAYS... I...I...
EARLIER TODAY, THIS GUY GAVE ME A NOTE THAT SAID A MAN STOLE FROM ME. THE NOTE INCLUDED WHAT HE LOOKED LIKE AND WHERE TO FIND HIM.
I THOUGHT OF YOUR STORY ABOUT YOU GETTING ROBBED, AND THEN SOMEHOW I CONVINCED MYSELF THAT YOUR STORY WAS TRUE.
JUST MOMENTS AGO, I STUCK THAT MAN LIKE A PIG, AND HE LOOKED CLUELESS TILL HIS LAST BREATH. THEN, THE COPS POP UP OUT OF NOWHERE.
WHICH NOW LEADS ME TO BELIEVE-- NOT ONLY DID HE NOT STEAL JACK SHIT FROM ME, BUT I WAS SET UP.
THEN I WONDERED, "WHY WOULD THAT GUY WHO GAVE ME THE NOTE SET ME UP?" I DON'T EVEN KNOW HIM. BUT MAYBE I KNOW SOMEONE WHO PUT HIM UP TO IT.
MAYBE IF I DESCRIBE HIM TO ANYONE WHO'D BENEFIT FROM ME GETTING POPPED, THEN MAYBE IT'LL RING A BELL...
SLIM, WEIRD WHITE DUDE. BROWN HAIR. LOOKS AND ACTS LIKE A PUSSY.
DRIVES A SILVER JAP CAR.
RING, RING.

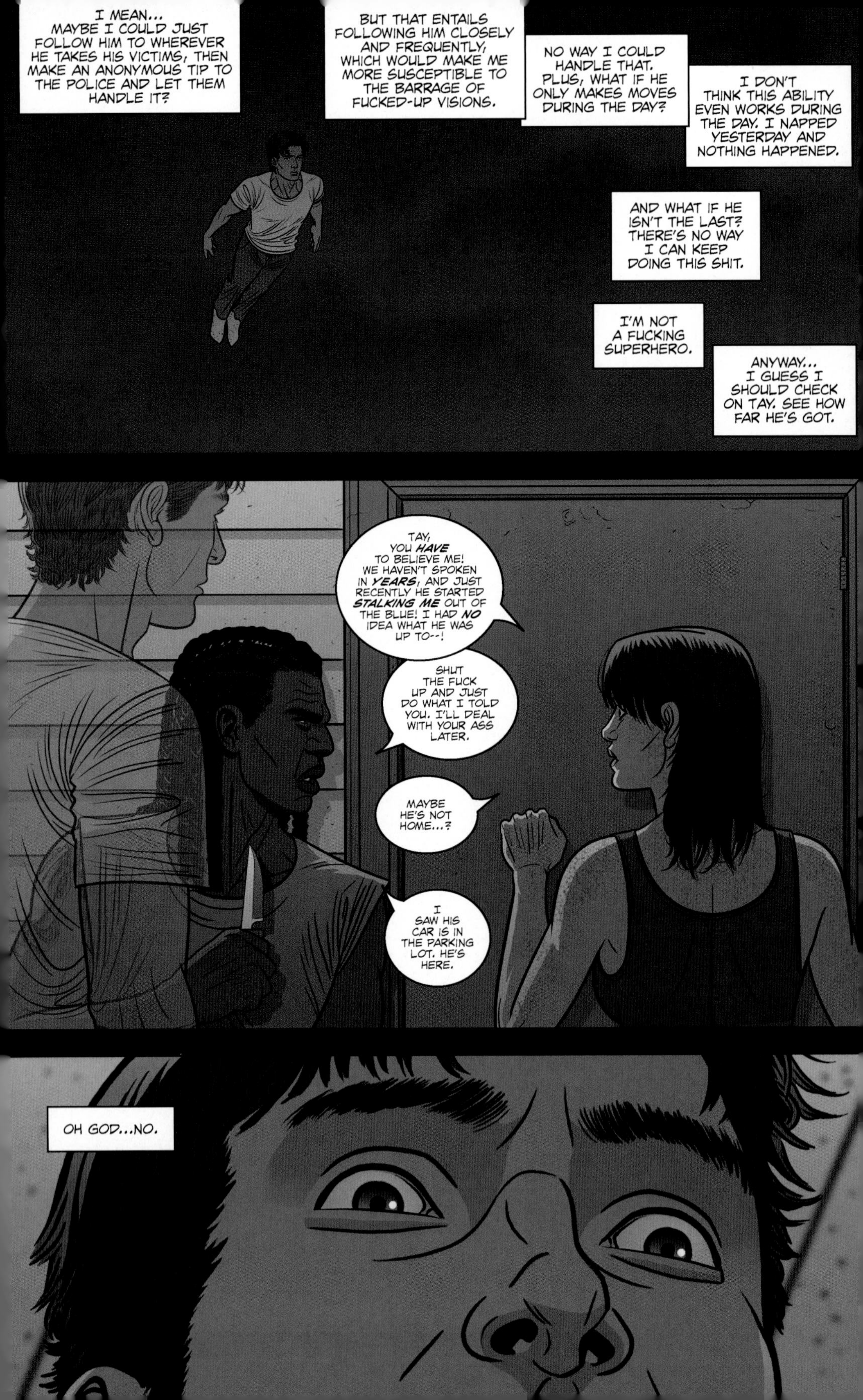
I MEAN... MAYBE I COULD JUST FOLLOW HIM TO WHEREVER HE TAKES HIS VICTIMS, THEN MAKE AN ANONYMOUS TIP TO THE POLICE AND LET THEM HANDLE IT?
BUT THAT ENTAILS FOLLOWING HIM CLOSELY AND FREQUENTLY, WHICH WOULD MAKE ME MORE SUSCEPTIBLE TO THE BARRAGE OF FUCKED-UP VISIONS.
NO WAY I COULD HANDLE THAT. PLUS, WHAT IF HE ONLY MAKES MOVES DURING THE DAY?
I DON'T THINK THIS ABILITY EVEN WORKS DURING THE DAY. I NAPPED YESTERDAY AND NOTHING HAPPENED.
AND WHAT IF HE ISN'T THE LAST? THERE'S NO WAY I CAN KEEP DOING THIS SHIT.
I'M NOT A FUCKING SUPERHERO.
ANYWAY... I GUESS I SHOULD CHECK ON TAY. SEE HOW FAR HE'S GOT.
TAY, YOU **HAVE** TO BELIEVE ME! WE HAVEN'T SPOKEN IN **YEARS**, AND JUST RECENTLY HE STARTED **STALKING ME** OUT OF THE BLUE! I HAD **NO** IDEA WHAT HE WAS UP TO--!
SHUT THE FUCK UP AND JUST DO WHAT I TOLD YOU. I'LL DEAL WITH YOUR ASS LATER.
MAYBE HE'S NOT HOME...?
I SAW HIS CAR IS IN THE PARKING LOT. HE'S HERE.
OH GOD...NO.

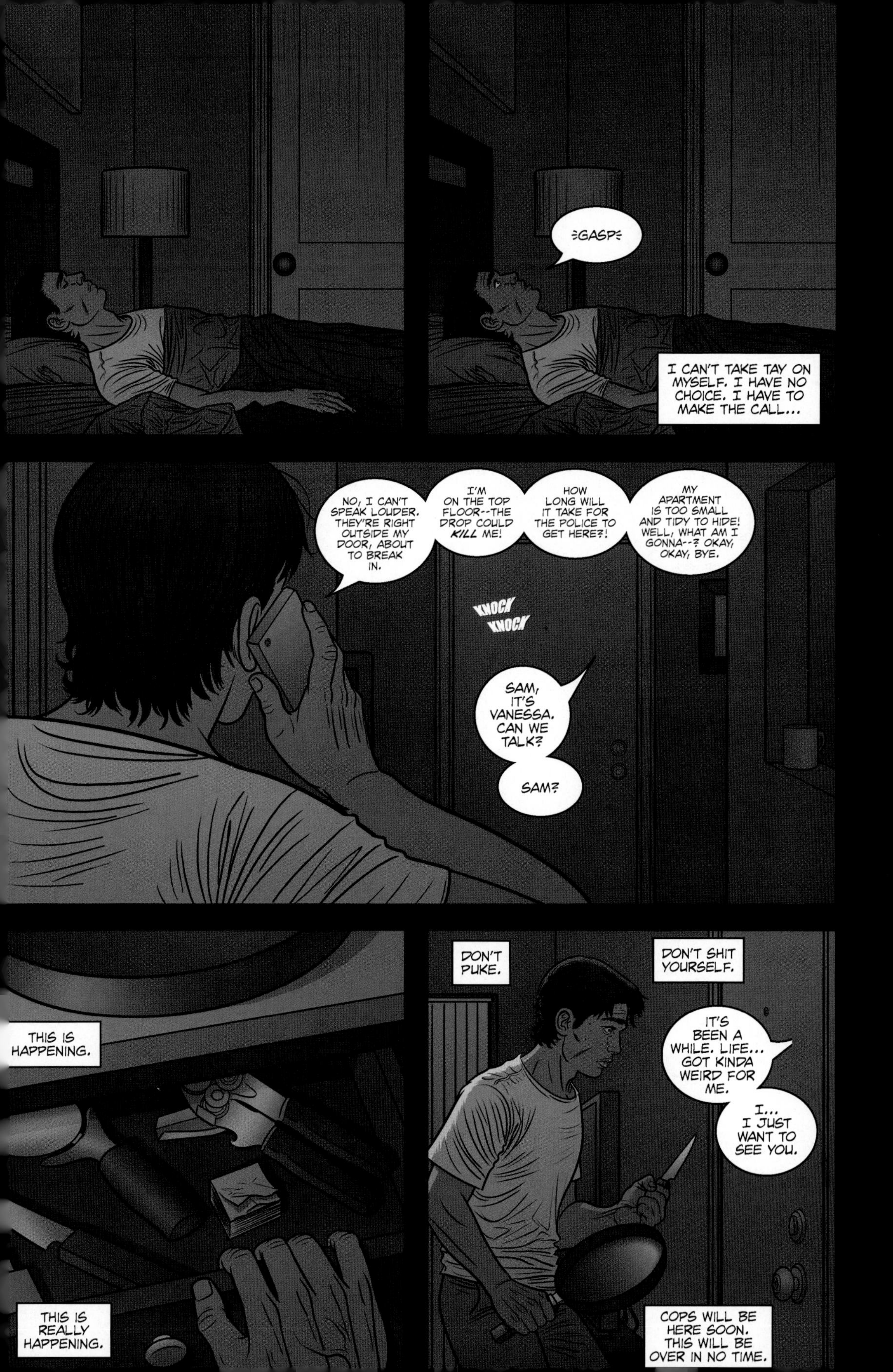

GASP
I CAN'T TAKE TAY ON MYSELF. I HAVE NO CHOICE. I HAVE TO MAKE THE CALL...
NO, I CAN'T SPEAK LOUDER. THEY'RE RIGHT OUTSIDE MY DOOR, ABOUT TO BREAK IN.
I'M ON THE TOP FLOOR--THE DROP COULD KILL ME!
HOW LONG WILL IT TAKE FOR THE POLICE TO GET HERE?!
MY APARTMENT IS TOO SMALL AND TIDY TO HIDE! WELL, WHAT AM I GONNA--? OKAY, OKAY, BYE.
KNOCK KNOCK
SAM, IT'S VANESSA. CAN WE TALK?
SAM?
THIS IS HAPPENING.
THIS IS REALLY HAPPENING.
DON'T PUKE.
DON'T SHIT YOURSELF.
IT'S BEEN A WHILE. LIFE... GOT KINDA WEIRD FOR ME.
I... I JUST WANT TO SEE YOU.
COPS WILL BE HERE SOON. THIS WILL BE OVER IN NO TIME.

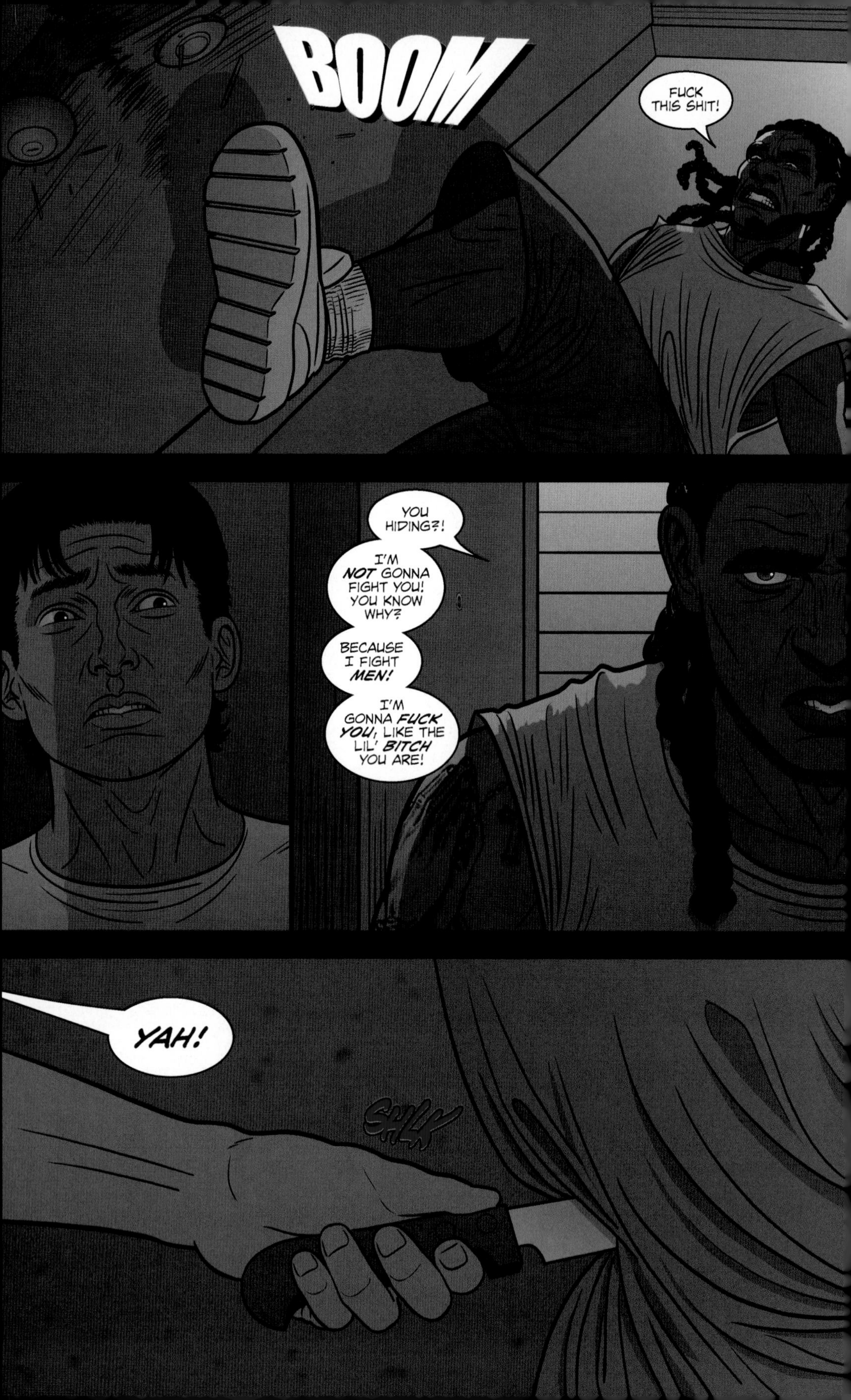
BOOM
FUCK THIS SHIT!
YOU HIDING?!
I'M NOT GONNA FIGHT YOU! YOU KNOW WHY?
BECAUSE I FIGHT MEN!
I'M GONNA FUCK YOU, LIKE THE LIL' BITCH YOU ARE!
YAH!
SHLK

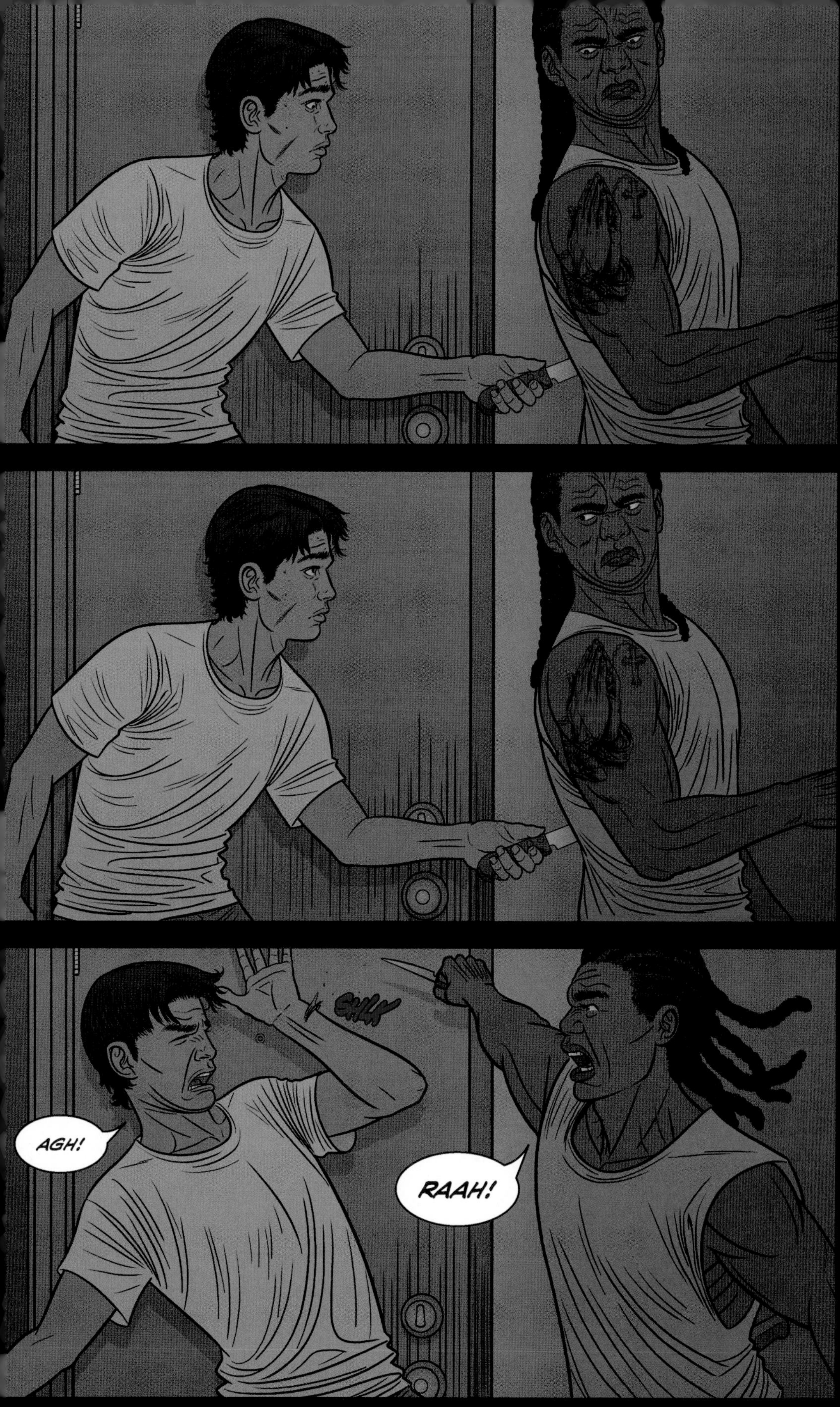
SHIK
AGH!
RAAH!

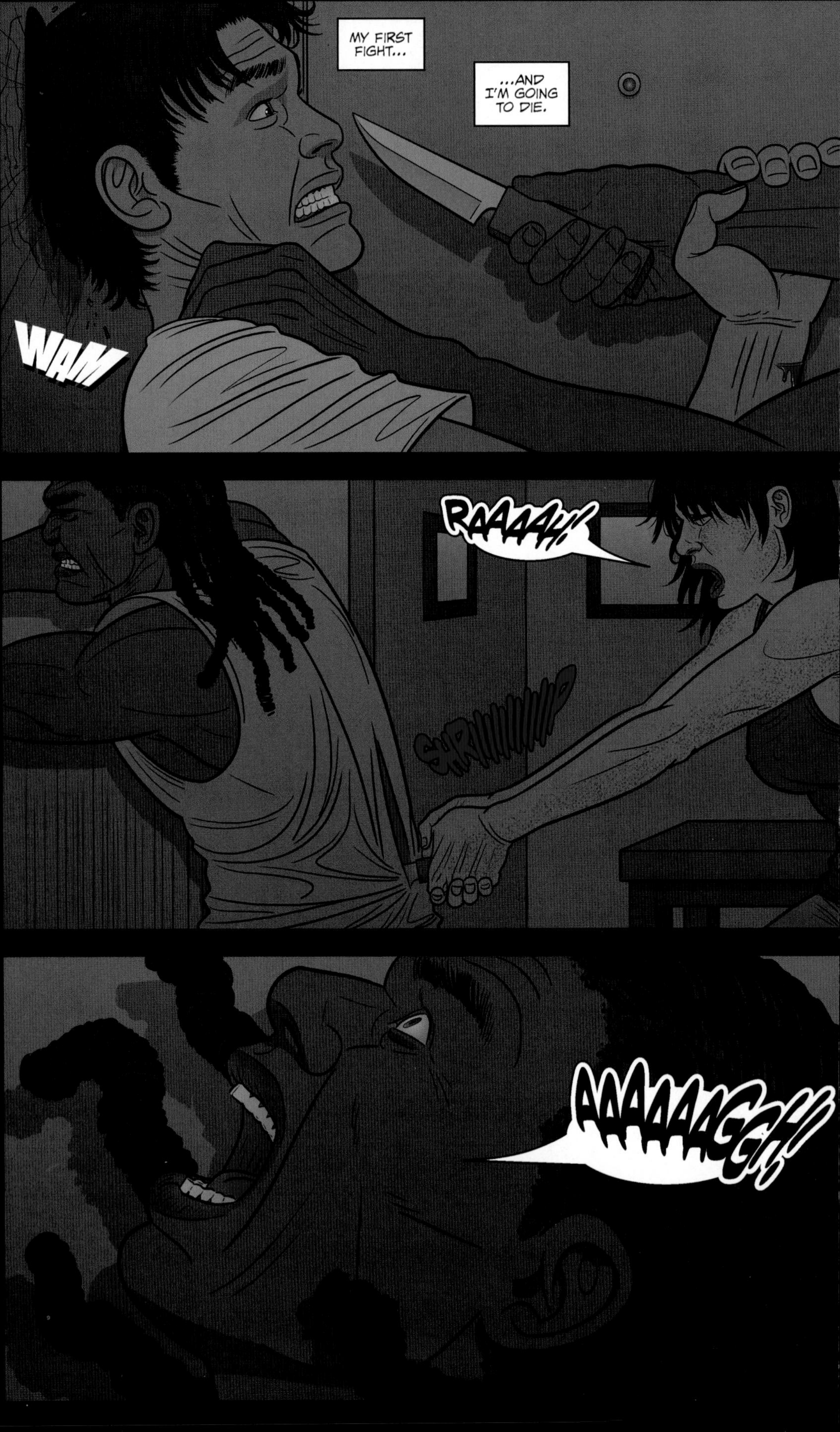
MY FIRST FIGHT...
...AND I'M GOING TO DIE.
WAM
RAAAAH!
AAAAAAGGH!

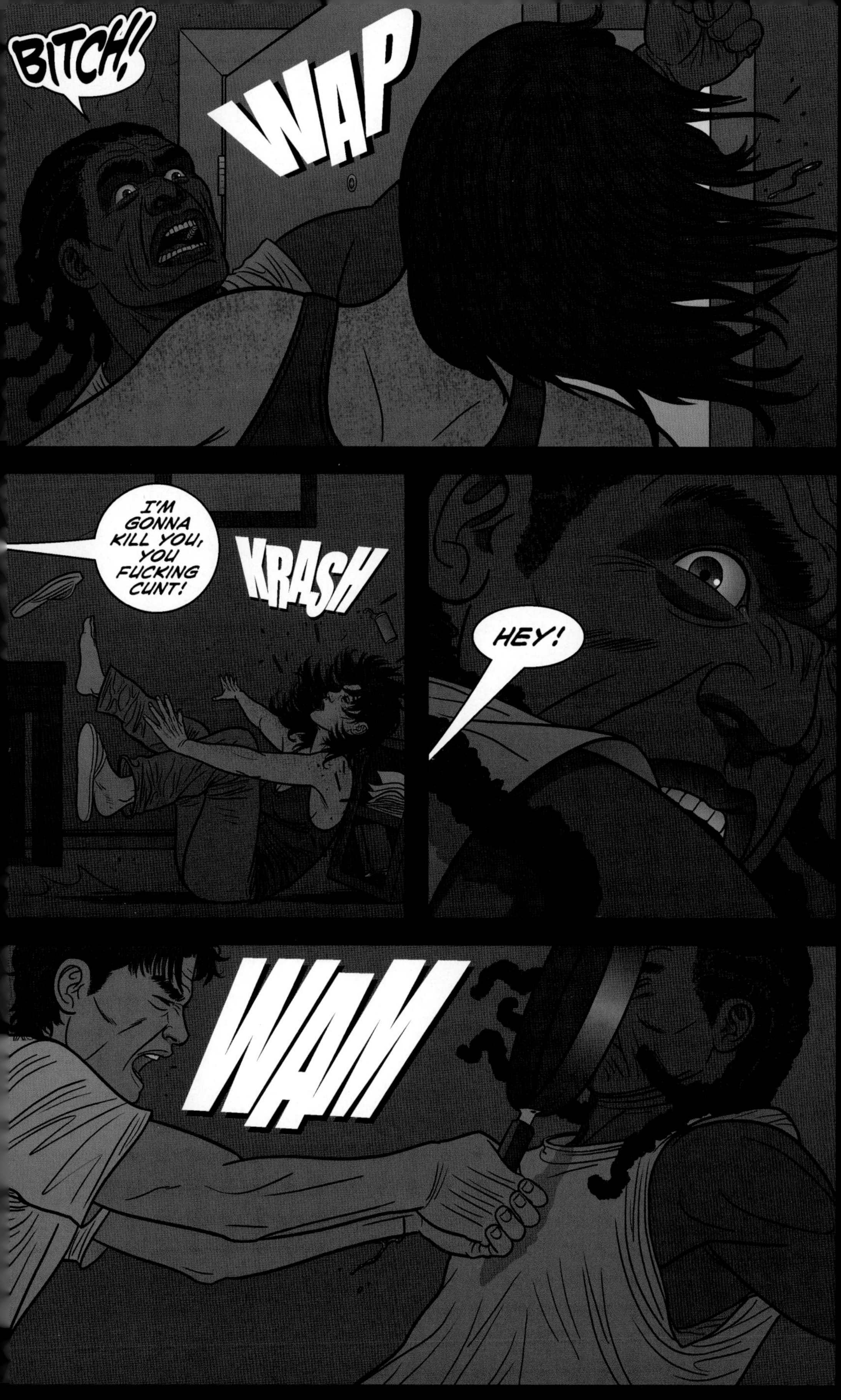
BITCH!!
WAP
I'M GONNA KILL YOU, YOU FUCKING CUNT!
KRASH
HEY!
WAM

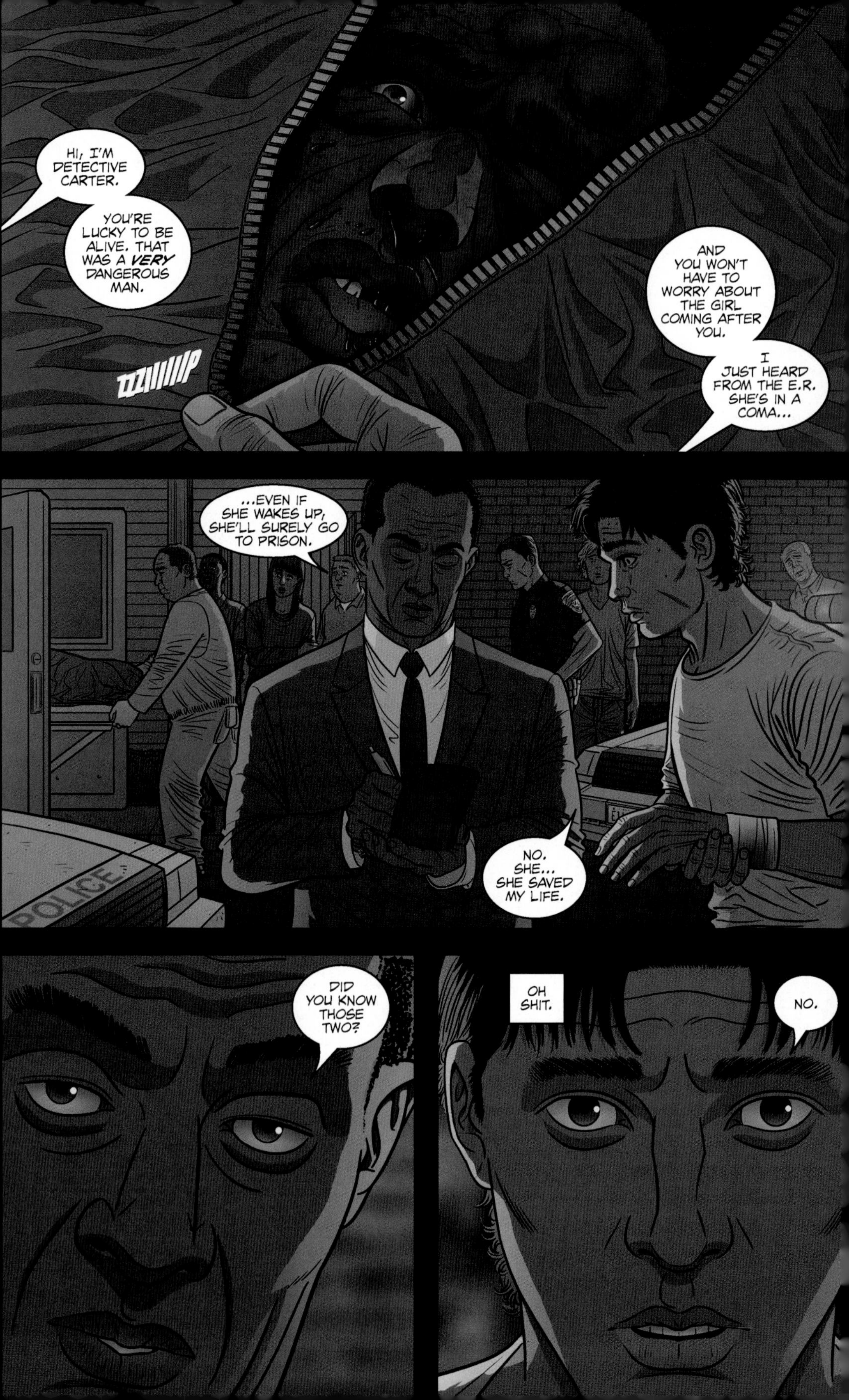
HI, I'M DETECTIVE CARTER.
YOU'RE LUCKY TO BE ALIVE. THAT WAS A *VERY* DANGEROUS MAN.
TZZIIIIIIIP
AND YOU WON'T HAVE TO WORRY ABOUT THE GIRL COMING AFTER YOU.
I JUST HEARD FROM THE E.R. SHE'S IN A COMA...
...EVEN IF SHE WAKES UP, SHE'LL SURELY GO TO PRISON.
NO. SHE... SHE SAVED MY LIFE.
POLICE
DID YOU KNOW THOSE TWO?
OH SHIT.
NO.

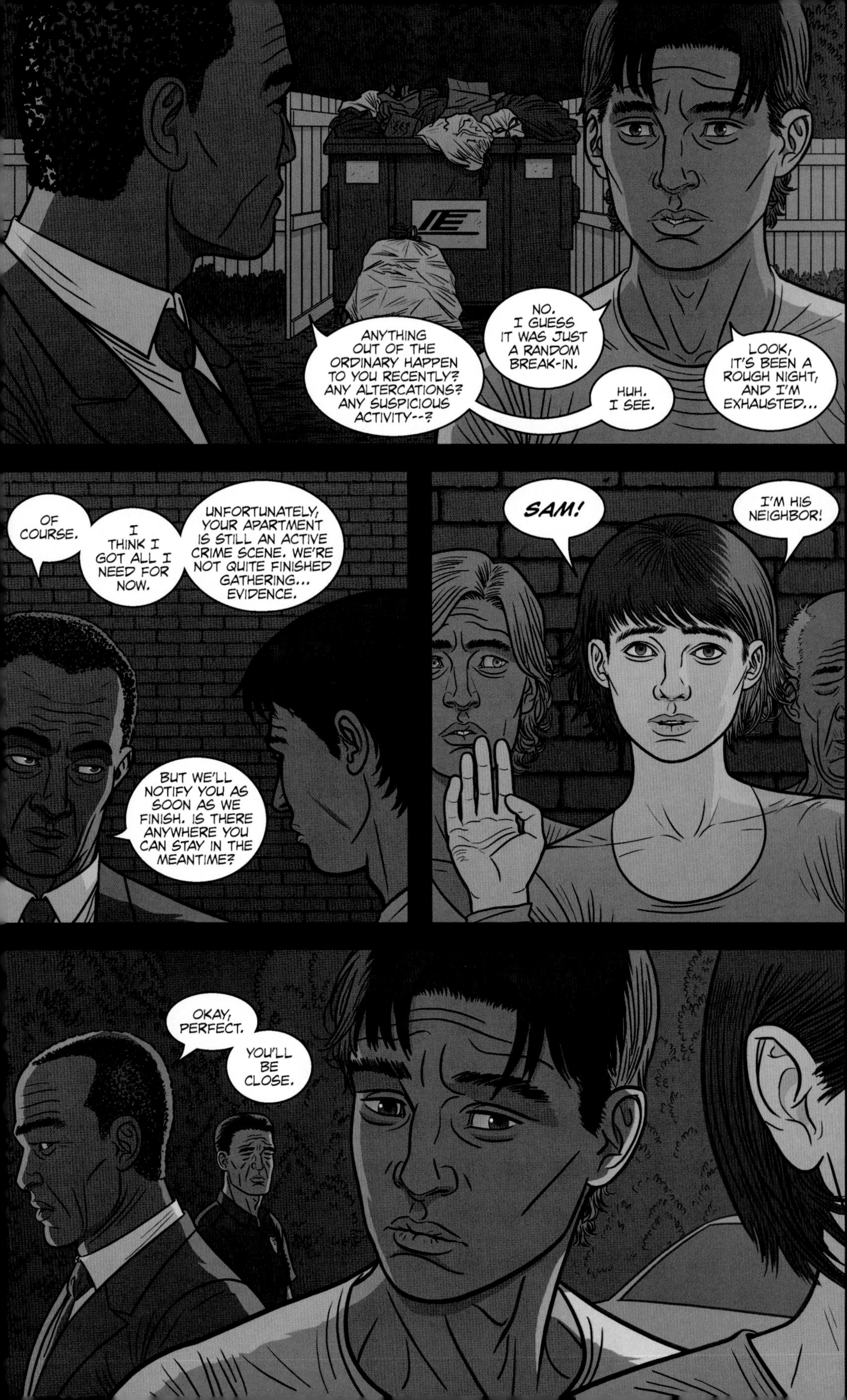
ANYTHING OUT OF THE ORDINARY HAPPEN TO YOU RECENTLY? ANY ALTERCATIONS? ANY SUSPICIOUS ACTIVITY--?
NO. I GUESS IT WAS JUST A RANDOM BREAK-IN.
HUH. I SEE.
LOOK, IT'S BEEN A ROUGH NIGHT, AND I'M EXHAUSTED...
OF COURSE.
I THINK I GOT ALL I NEED FOR NOW.
UNFORTUNATELY, YOUR APARTMENT IS STILL AN ACTIVE CRIME SCENE. WE'RE NOT QUITE FINISHED GATHERING... EVIDENCE.
BUT WE'LL NOTIFY YOU AS SOON AS WE FINISH. IS THERE ANYWHERE YOU CAN STAY IN THE MEANTIME?
SAM!
I'M HIS NEIGHBOR!
OKAY, PERFECT.
YOU'LL BE CLOSE.

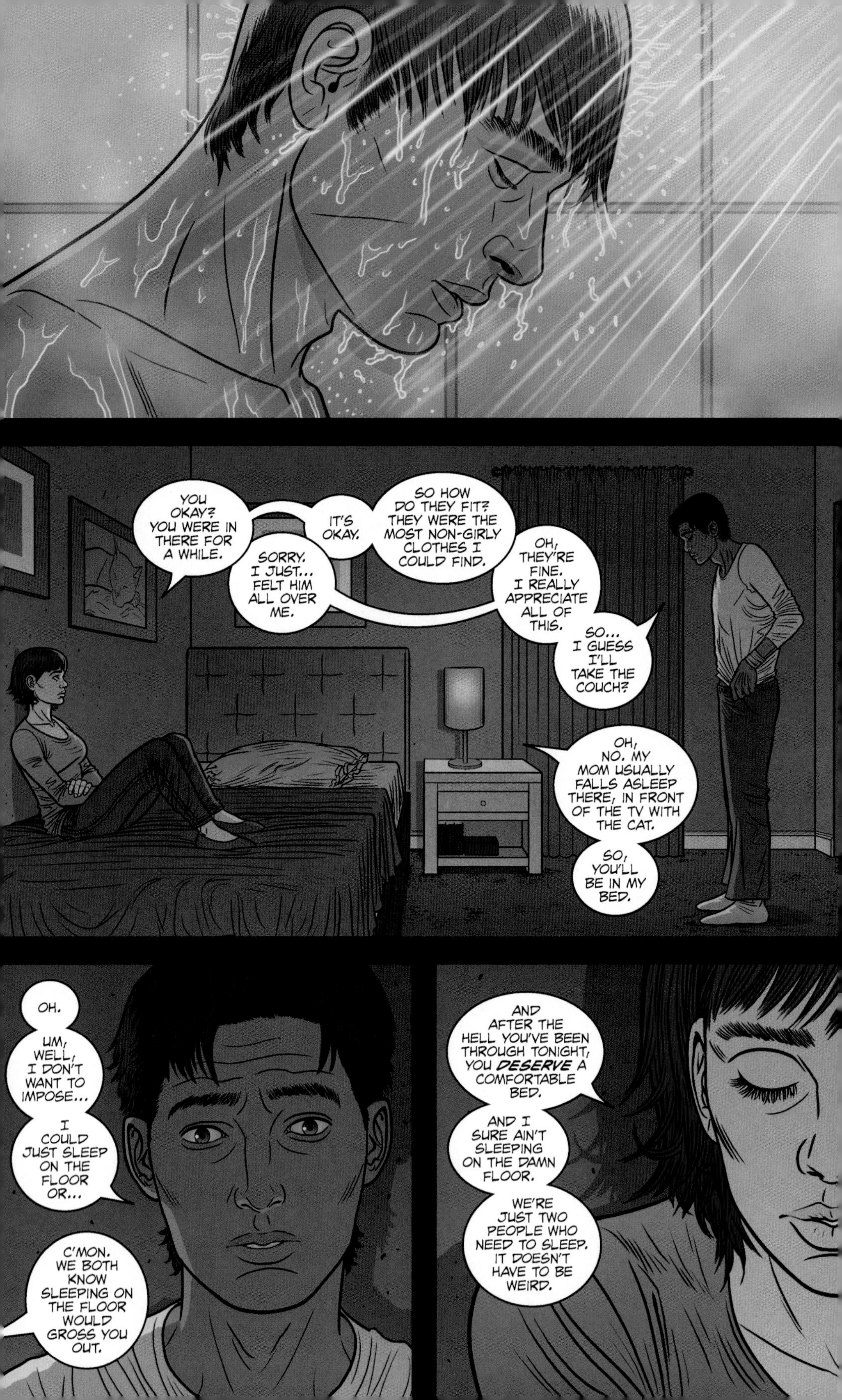
YOU OKAY? YOU WERE IN THERE FOR A WHILE.
SORRY. I JUST... FELT HIM ALL OVER ME.
IT'S OKAY.
SO HOW DO THEY FIT? THEY WERE THE MOST NON-GIRLY CLOTHES I COULD FIND.
OH, THEY'RE FINE. I REALLY APPRECIATE ALL OF THIS.
SO... I GUESS I'LL TAKE THE COUCH?
OH, NO. MY MOM USUALLY FALLS ASLEEP THERE, IN FRONT OF THE TV WITH THE CAT.
SO, YOU'LL BE IN MY BED.
OH.
UM, WELL, I DON'T WANT TO IMPOSE...
I COULD JUST SLEEP ON THE FLOOR OR...
C'MON. WE BOTH KNOW SLEEPING ON THE FLOOR WOULD GROSS YOU OUT.
AND AFTER THE HELL YOU'VE BEEN THROUGH TONIGHT, YOU ***DESERVE*** A COMFORTABLE BED.
AND I SURE AIN'T SLEEPING ON THE DAMN FLOOR.
WE'RE JUST TWO PEOPLE WHO NEED TO SLEEP. IT DOESN'T HAVE TO BE WEIRD.

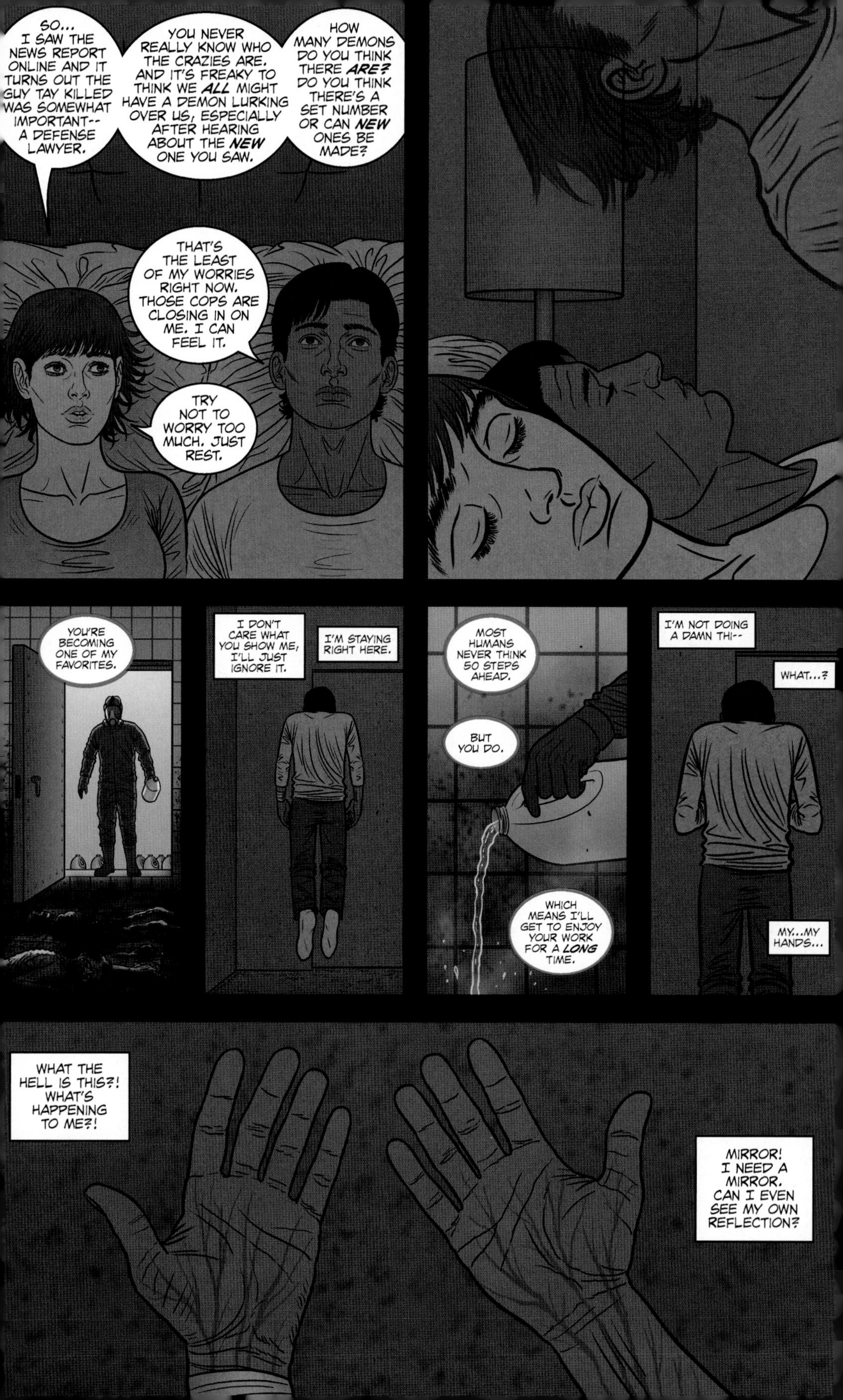

SO... I SAW THE NEWS REPORT ONLINE AND IT TURNS OUT THE GUY TAY KILLED WAS SOMEWHAT IMPORTANT-- A DEFENSE LAWYER.
YOU NEVER REALLY KNOW WHO THE CRAZIES ARE. AND IT'S FREAKY TO THINK WE ALL MIGHT HAVE A DEMON LURKING OVER US, ESPECIALLY AFTER HEARING ABOUT THE NEW ONE YOU SAW.
HOW MANY DEMONS DO YOU THINK THERE ARE? DO YOU THINK THERE'S A SET NUMBER OR CAN NEW ONES BE MADE?
THAT'S THE LEAST OF MY WORRIES RIGHT NOW. THOSE COPS ARE CLOSING IN ON ME. I CAN FEEL IT.
TRY NOT TO WORRY TOO MUCH. JUST REST.
YOU'RE BECOMING ONE OF MY FAVORITES.
I DON'T CARE WHAT YOU SHOW ME, I'LL JUST IGNORE IT.
I'M STAYING RIGHT HERE.
MOST HUMANS NEVER THINK 50 STEPS AHEAD.
BUT YOU DO.
WHICH MEANS I'LL GET TO ENJOY YOUR WORK FOR A LONG TIME.
I'M NOT DOING A DAMN THI--
WHAT...?
MY...MY HANDS...
WHAT THE HELL IS THIS?! WHAT'S HAPPENING TO ME?!
MIRROR! I NEED A MIRROR. CAN I EVEN SEE MY OWN REFLECTION?

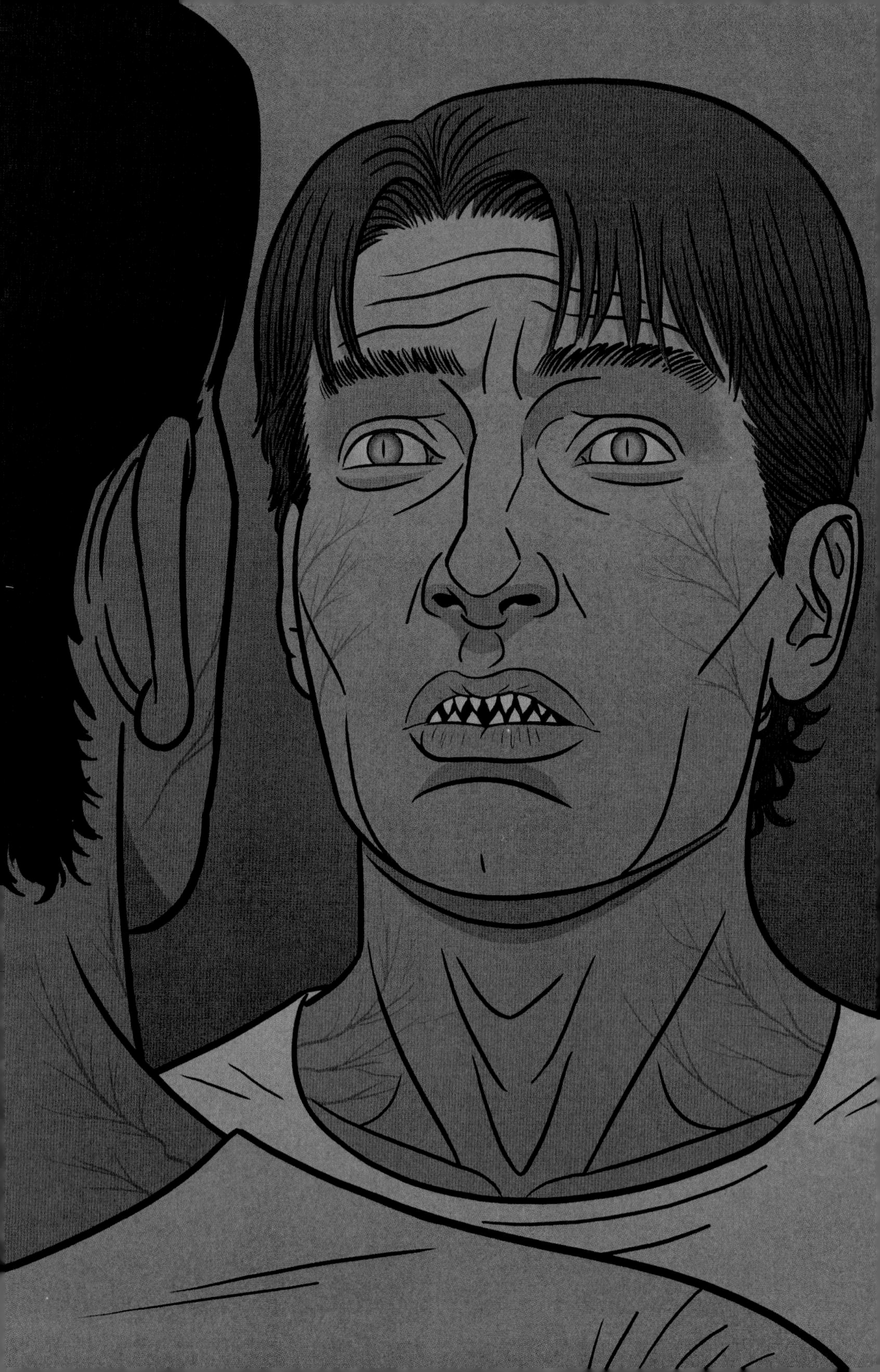

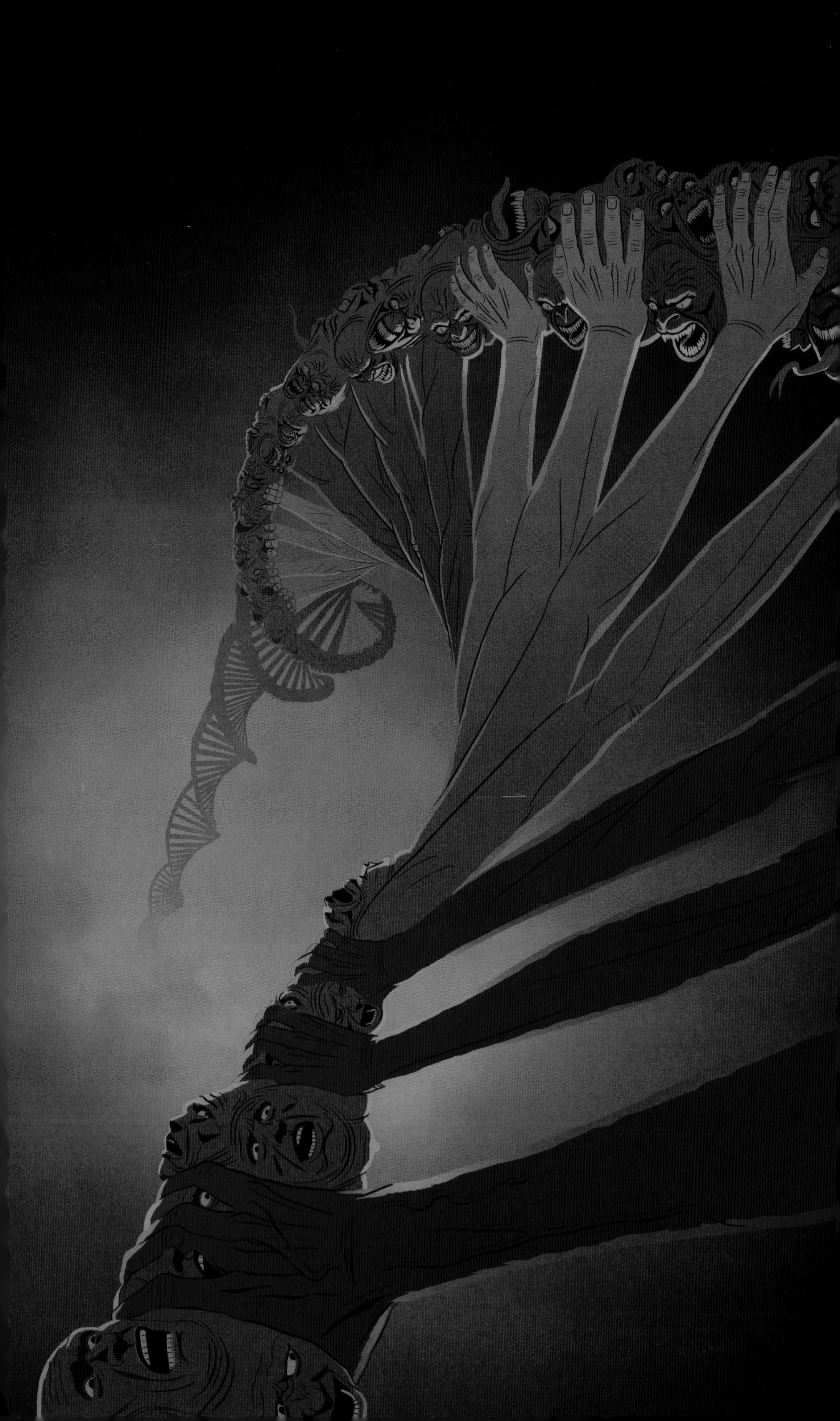

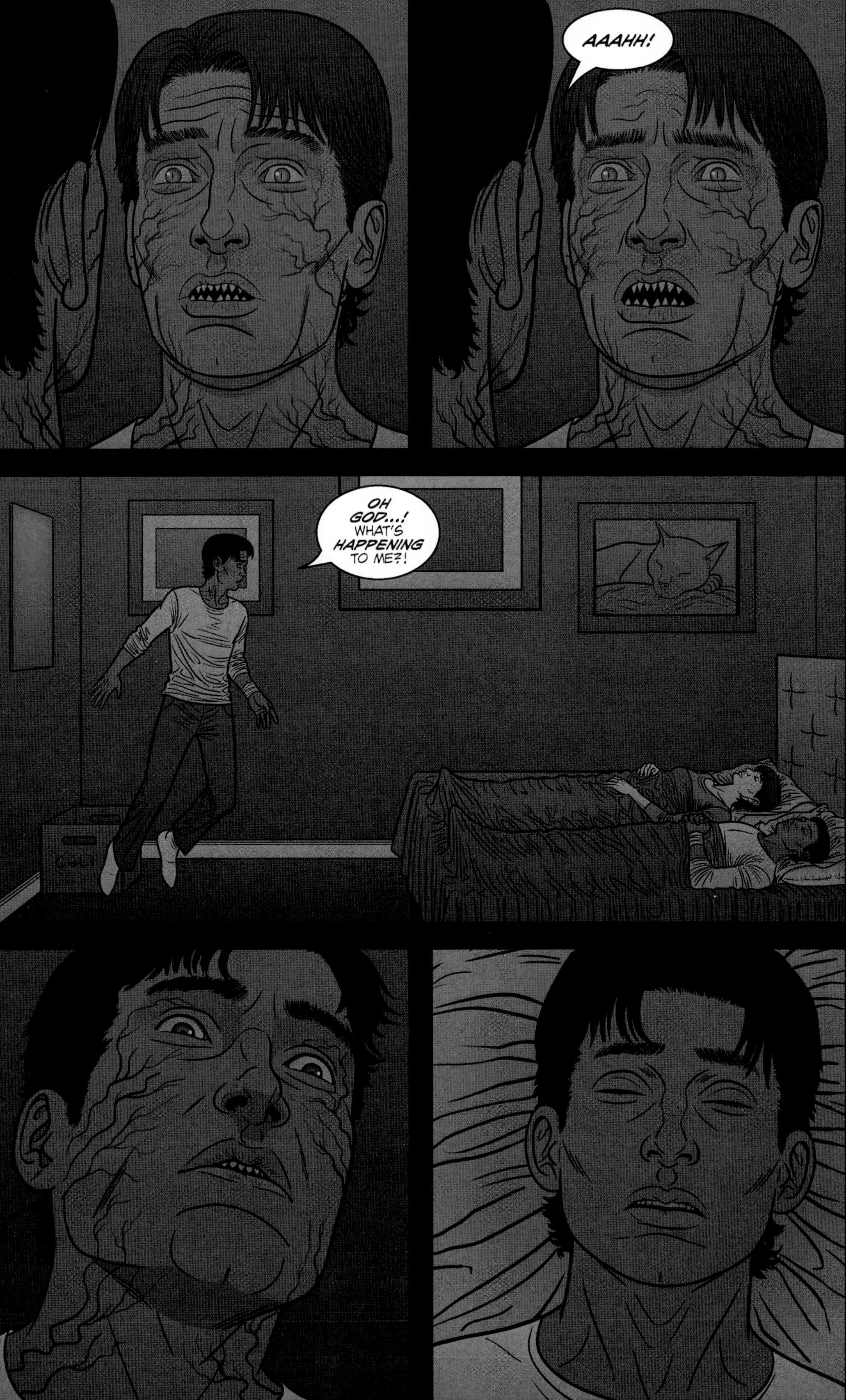
AAAHH!
OH GOD...! WHAT'S HAPPENING TO ME?!

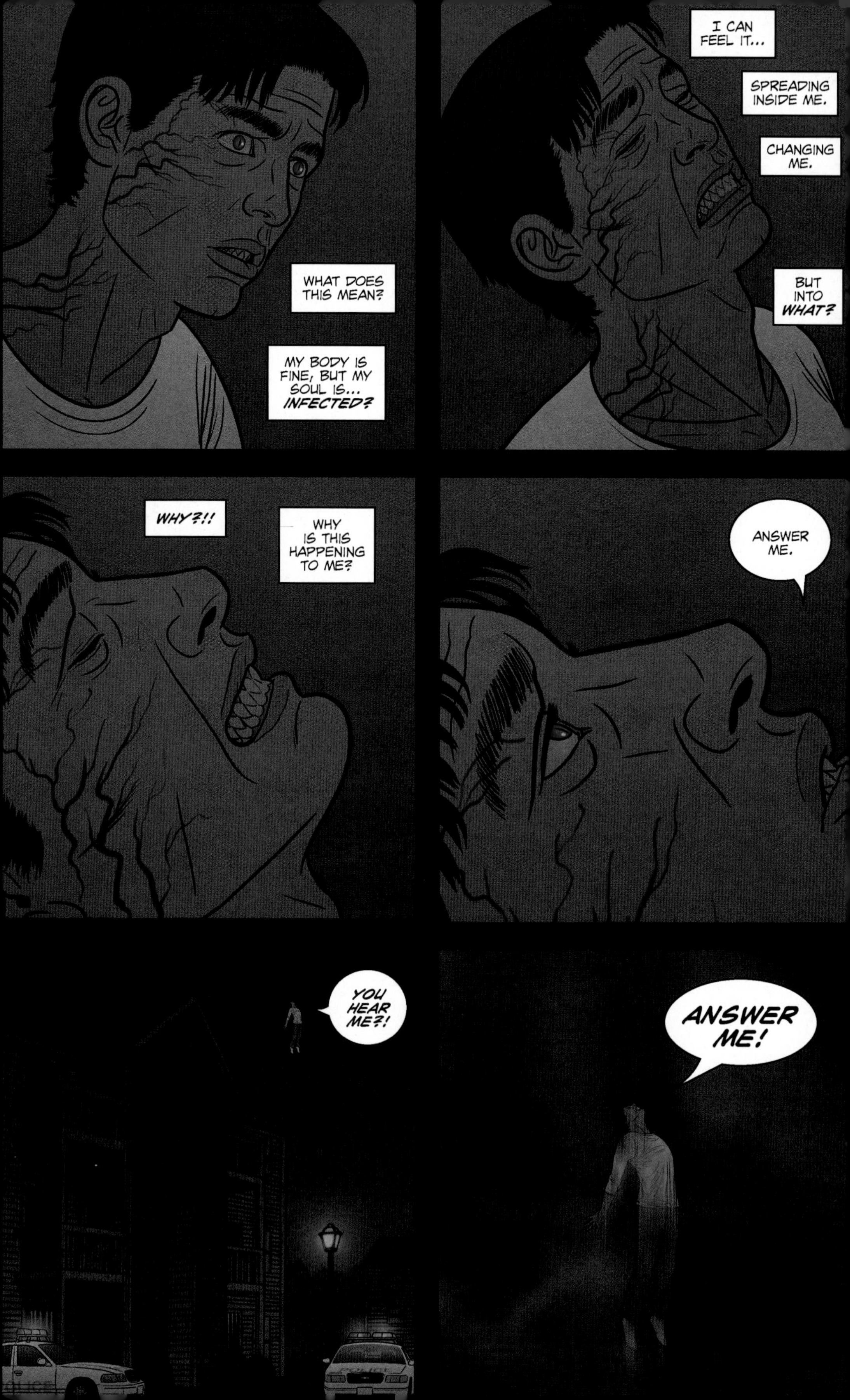
WHAT DOES THIS MEAN?
MY BODY IS FINE, BUT MY SOUL IS... *INFECTED?*
I CAN FEEL IT...
SPREADING INSIDE ME.
CHANGING ME.
BUT INTO *WHAT?*
WHY?!!
WHY IS THIS HAPPENING TO ME?
ANSWER ME.
YOU HEAR ME?!
ANSWER ME!

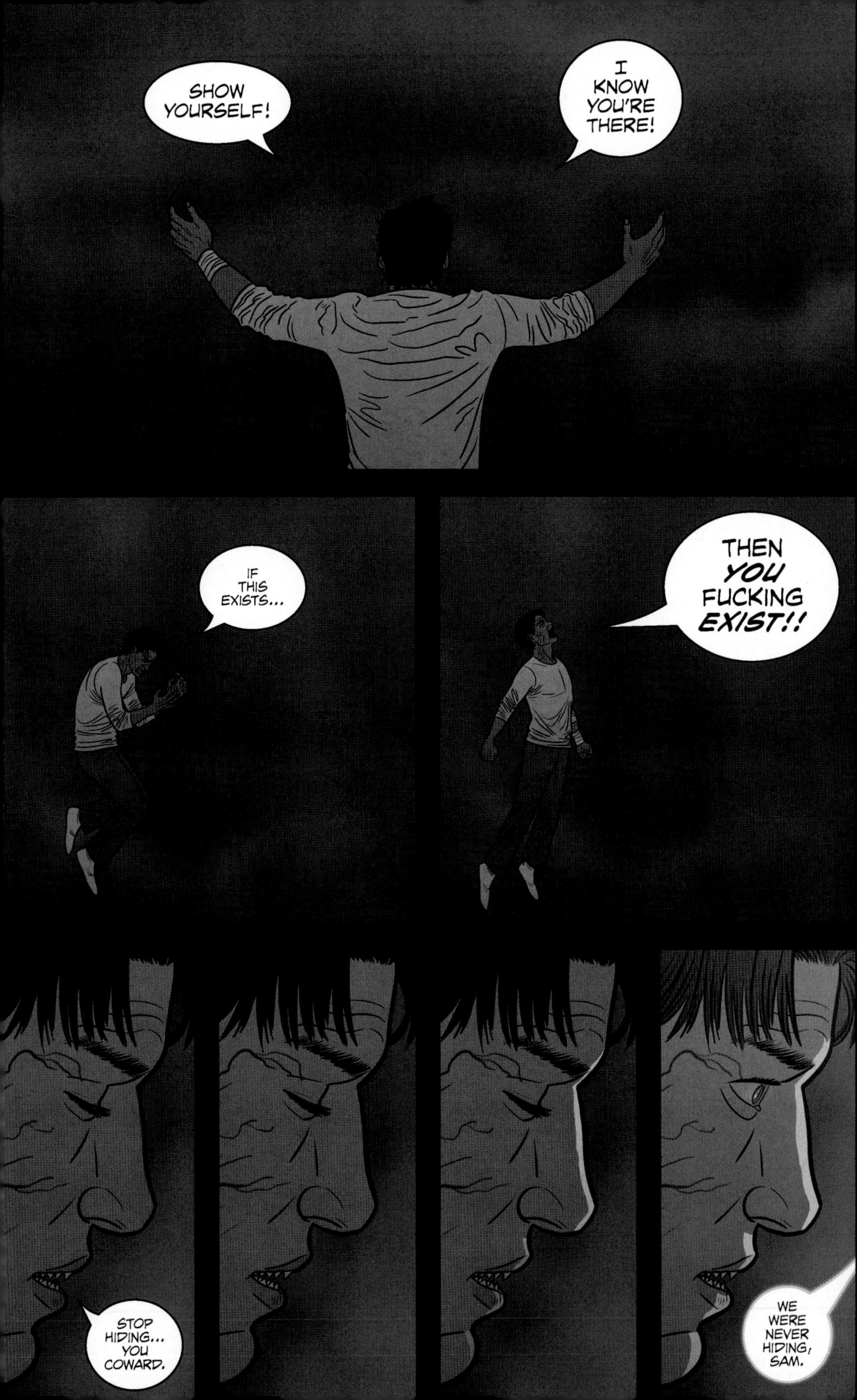
SHOW YOURSELF!
I KNOW YOU'RE THERE!
IF THIS EXISTS...
THEN *YOU* FUCKING *EXIST!!*
STOP HIDING... YOU COWARD.
WE WERE NEVER HIDING, SAM.

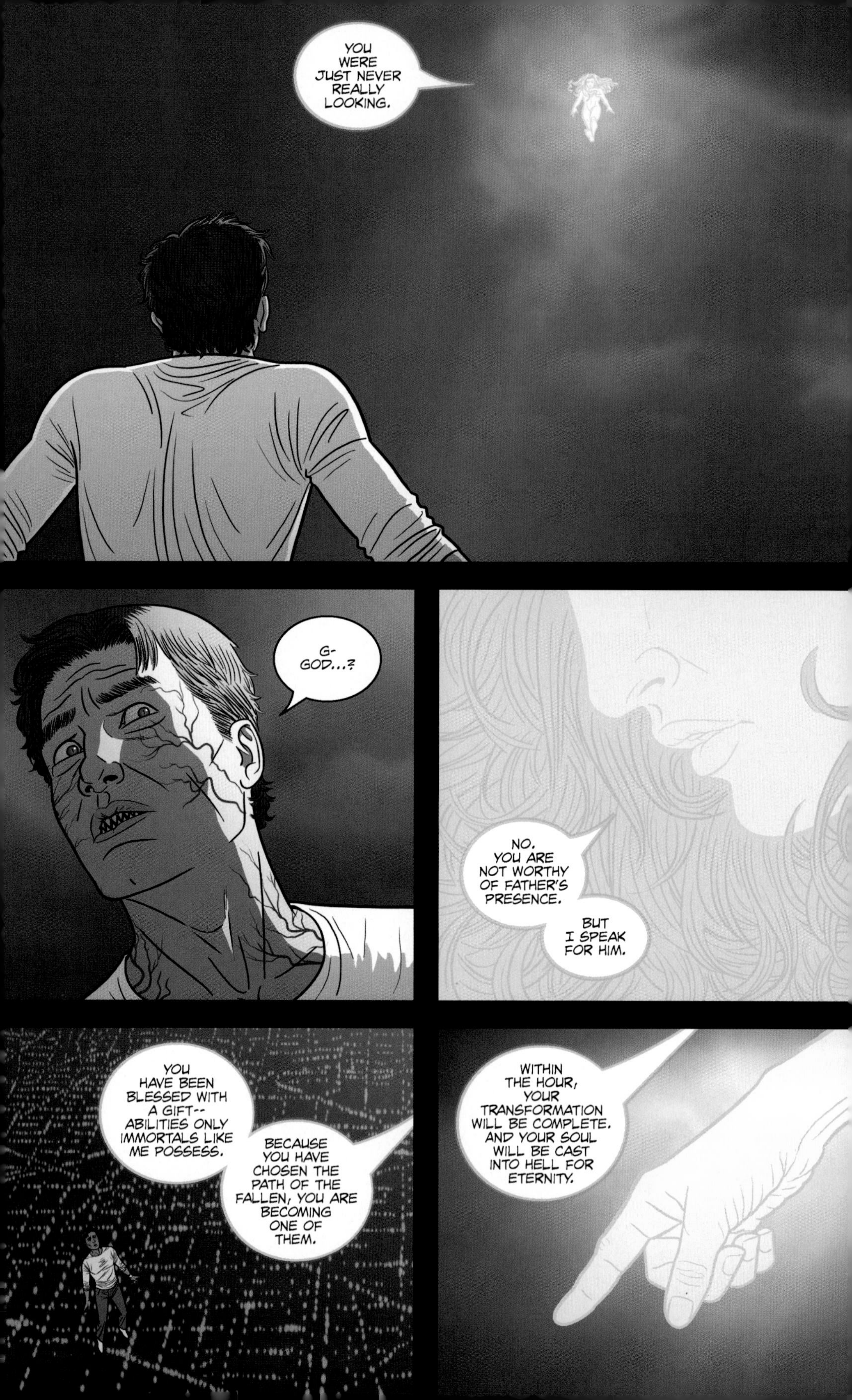
YOU WERE JUST NEVER REALLY LOOKING.
G-GOD...?
NO. YOU ARE NOT WORTHY OF FATHER'S PRESENCE.
BUT I SPEAK FOR HIM.
YOU HAVE BEEN BLESSED WITH A GIFT-- ABILITIES ONLY IMMORTALS LIKE ME POSSESS.
BECAUSE YOU HAVE CHOSEN THE PATH OF THE FALLEN, YOU ARE BECOMING ONE OF THEM.
WITHIN THE HOUR, YOUR TRANSFORMATION WILL BE COMPLETE. AND YOUR SOUL WILL BE CAST INTO HELL FOR ETERNITY.

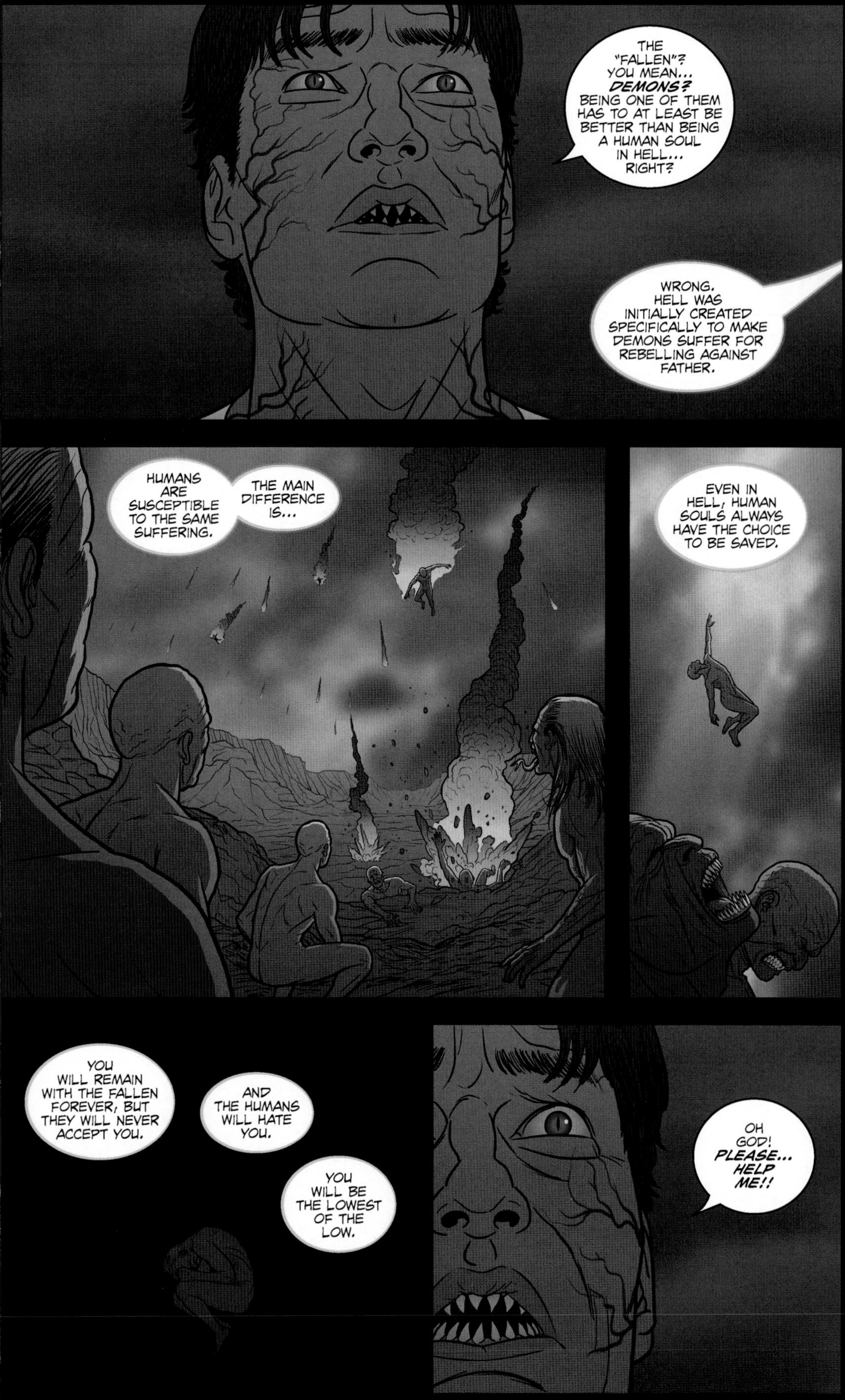
THE "FALLEN"? YOU MEAN... DEMONS? BEING ONE OF THEM HAS TO AT LEAST BE BETTER THAN BEING A HUMAN SOUL IN HELL... RIGHT?
WRONG. HELL WAS INITIALLY CREATED SPECIFICALLY TO MAKE DEMONS SUFFER FOR REBELLING AGAINST FATHER.
HUMANS ARE SUSCEPTIBLE TO THE SAME SUFFERING.
THE MAIN DIFFERENCE IS...
EVEN IN HELL, HUMAN SOULS ALWAYS HAVE THE CHOICE TO BE SAVED.
YOU WILL REMAIN WITH THE FALLEN FOREVER, BUT THEY WILL NEVER ACCEPT YOU.
AND THE HUMANS WILL HATE YOU.
YOU WILL BE THE LOWEST OF THE LOW.
OH GOD! PLEASE... HELP ME!!

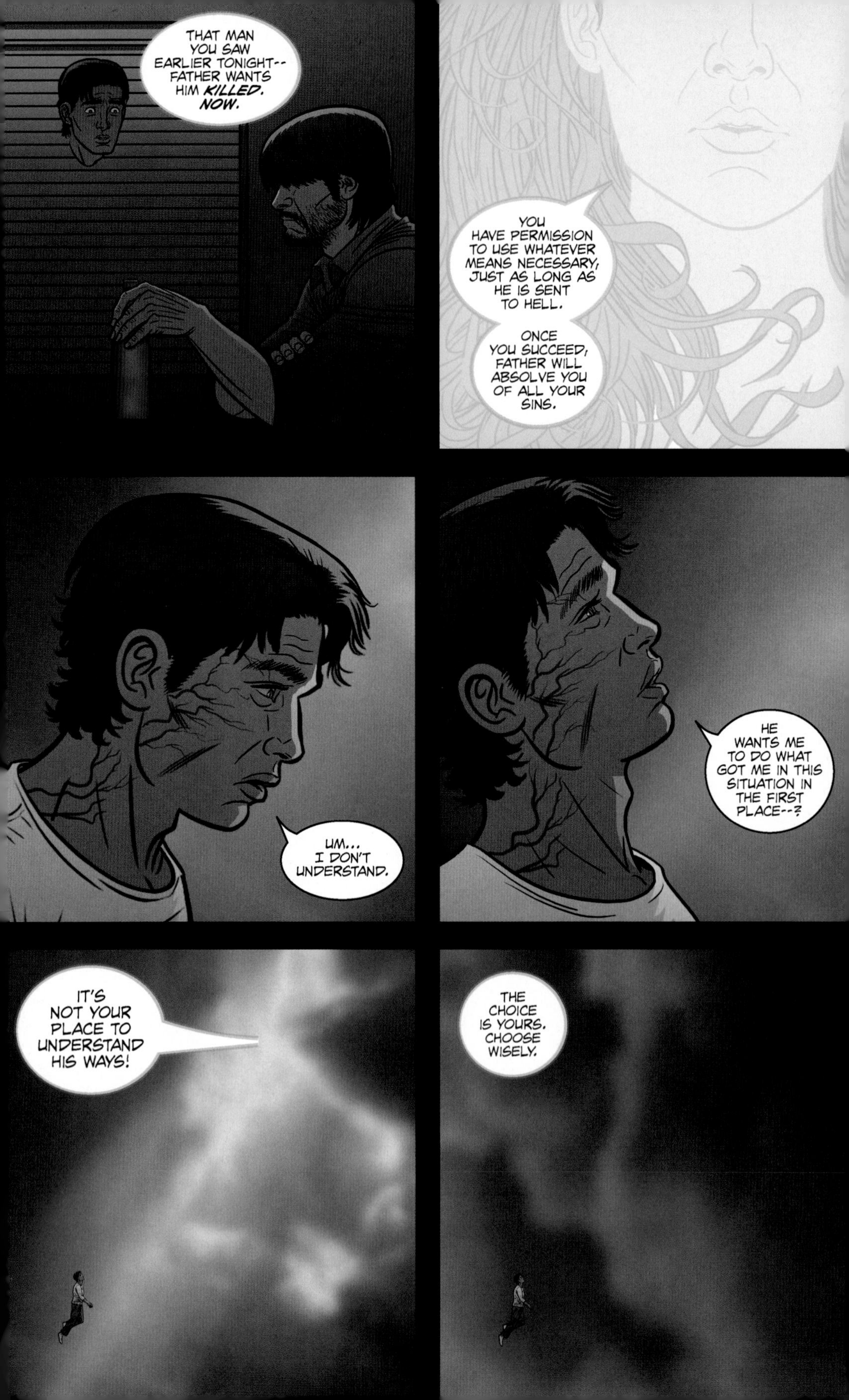
THAT MAN YOU SAW EARLIER TONIGHT-- FATHER WANTS HIM KILLED. NOW.
YOU HAVE PERMISSION TO USE WHATEVER MEANS NECESSARY, JUST AS LONG AS HE IS SENT TO HELL.
ONCE YOU SUCCEED, FATHER WILL ABSOLVE YOU OF ALL YOUR SINS.
UM... I DON'T UNDERSTAND.
HE WANTS ME TO DO WHAT GOT ME IN THIS SITUATION IN THE FIRST PLACE--?
IT'S NOT YOUR PLACE TO UNDERSTAND HIS WAYS!
THE CHOICE IS YOURS. CHOOSE WISELY.

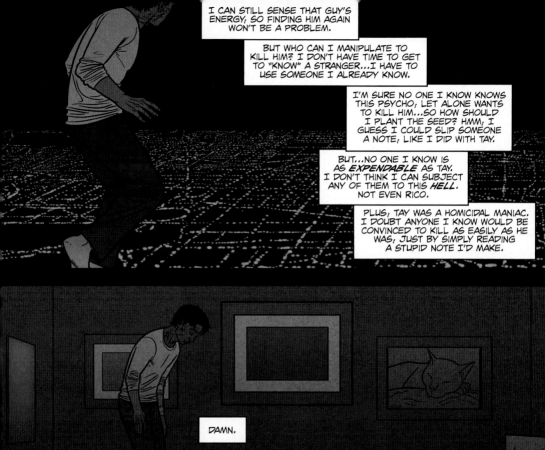

I CAN STILL SENSE THAT GUY'S ENERGY, SO FINDING HIM AGAIN WON'T BE A PROBLEM.

BUT WHO CAN I MANIPULATE TO KILL HIM? I DON'T HAVE TIME TO GET TO "KNOW" A STRANGER...I HAVE TO USE SOMEONE I ALREADY KNOW.

I'M SURE NO ONE I KNOW KNOWS THIS PSYCHO, LET ALONE WANTS TO KILL HIM...SO HOW SHOULD I PLANT THE SEED? HMM, I GUESS I COULD SLIP SOMEONE A NOTE, LIKE I DID WITH TAY.

BUT...NO ONE I KNOW IS AS *EXPENDABLE* AS TAY. I DON'T THINK I CAN SUBJECT ANY OF THEM TO THIS *HELL*. NOT EVEN RICO.

PLUS, TAY WAS A HOMICIDAL MANIAC. I DOUBT ANYONE I KNOW WOULD BE CONVINCED TO KILL AS EASILY AS HE WAS, JUST BY SIMPLY READING A STUPID NOTE I'D MAKE.

DAMN.

WHAT THE HELL AM I GOING TO DO?

NNNGG...

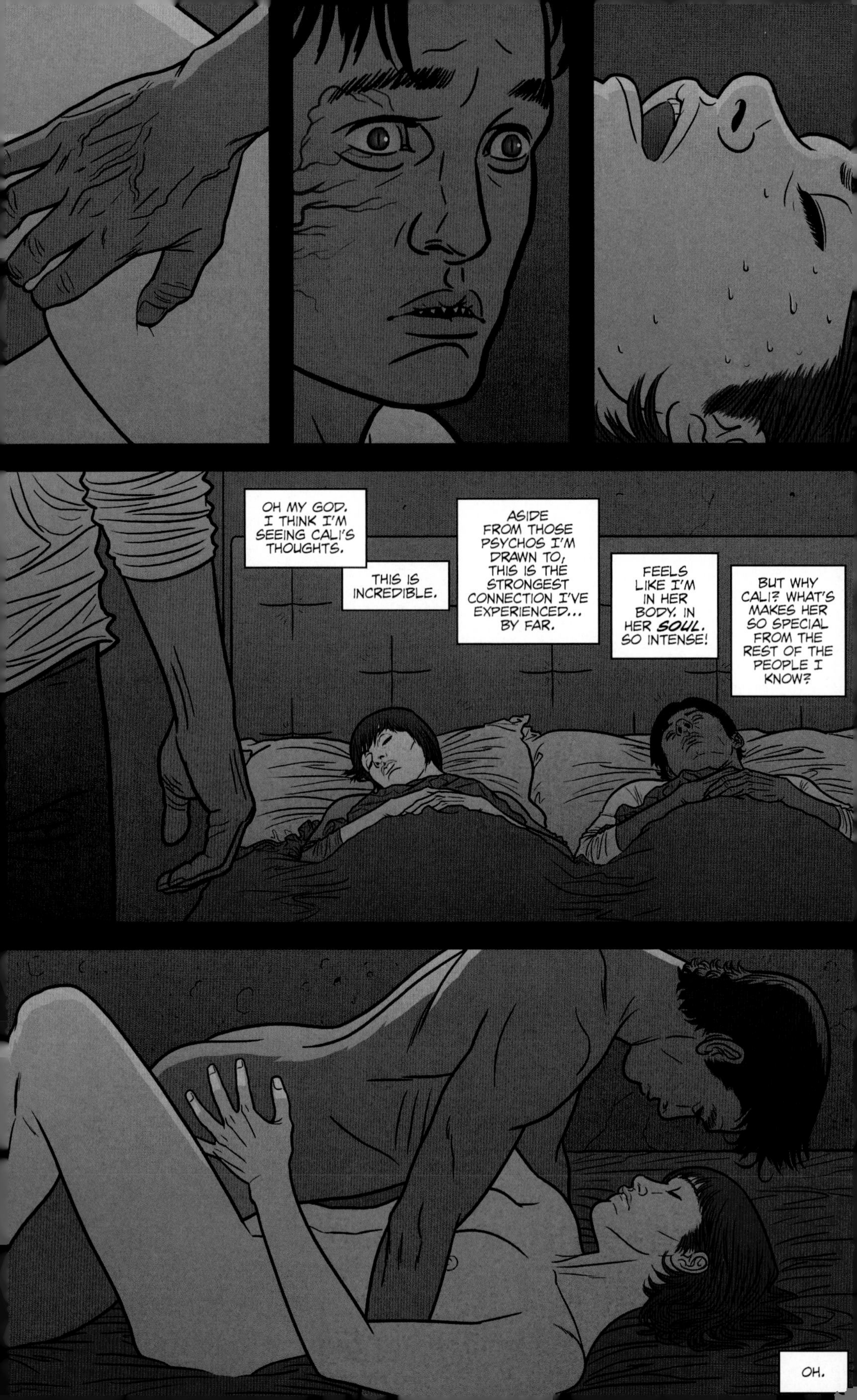
OH MY GOD. I THINK I'M SEEING CALI'S THOUGHTS.
THIS IS INCREDIBLE.
ASIDE FROM THOSE PSYCHOS I'M DRAWN TO, THIS IS THE STRONGEST CONNECTION I'VE EXPERIENCED... BY FAR.
FEELS LIKE I'M IN HER BODY. IN HER SOUL. SO INTENSE!
BUT WHY CALI? WHAT'S MAKES HER SO SPECIAL FROM THE REST OF THE PEOPLE I KNOW?
OH.

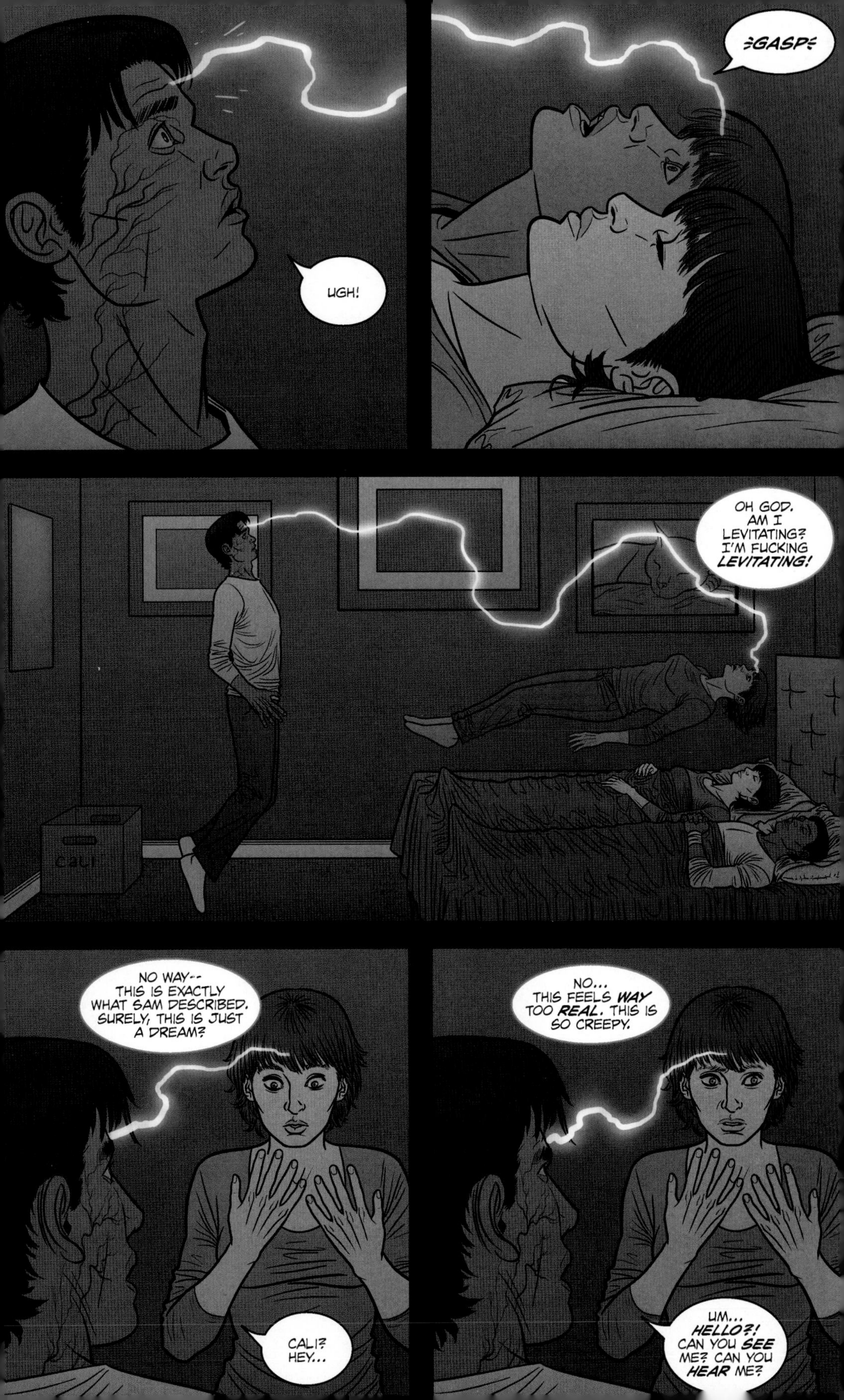
UGH!
GASP
OH GOD. AM I LEVITATING? I'M FUCKING LEVITATING!
CALI
NO WAY-- THIS IS EXACTLY WHAT SAM DESCRIBED. SURELY, THIS IS JUST A DREAM?
CALI? HEY...
NO... THIS FEELS WAY TOO REAL. THIS IS SO CREEPY.
UM... HELLO?! CAN YOU SEE ME? CAN YOU HEAR ME?

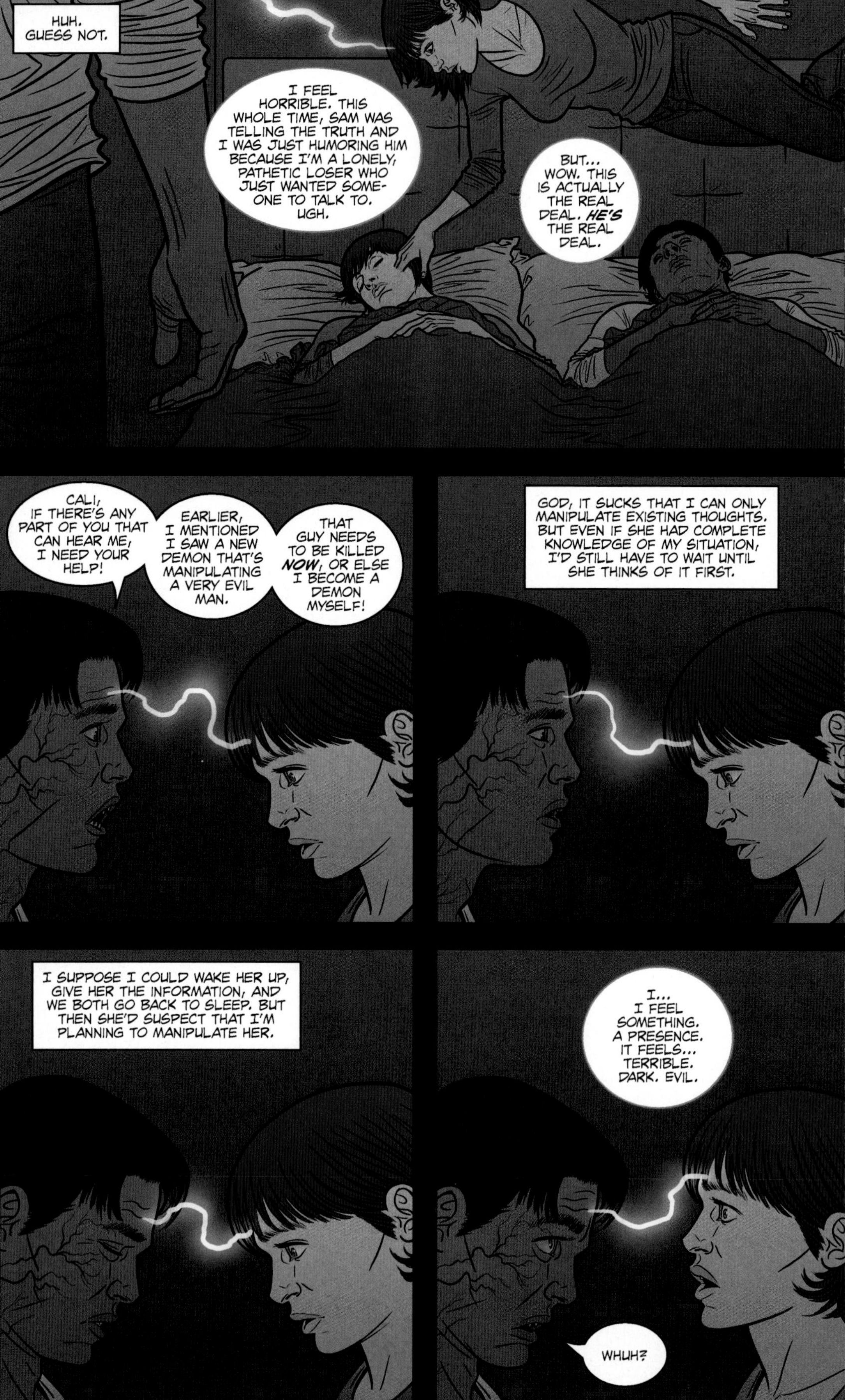
HUH. GUESS NOT.
I FEEL HORRIBLE. THIS WHOLE TIME, SAM WAS TELLING THE TRUTH AND I WAS JUST HUMORING HIM BECAUSE I'M A LONELY, PATHETIC LOSER WHO JUST WANTED SOME-ONE TO TALK TO. UGH.
BUT... WOW. THIS IS ACTUALLY THE REAL DEAL. *HE'S* THE REAL DEAL.
CALI, IF THERE'S ANY PART OF YOU THAT CAN HEAR ME, I NEED YOUR HELP!
EARLIER, I MENTIONED I SAW A NEW DEMON THAT'S MANIPULATING A VERY EVIL MAN.
THAT GUY NEEDS TO BE KILLED *NOW*, OR ELSE I BECOME A DEMON MYSELF!
GOD, IT SUCKS THAT I CAN ONLY MANIPULATE EXISTING THOUGHTS. BUT EVEN IF SHE HAD COMPLETE KNOWLEDGE OF MY SITUATION, I'D STILL HAVE TO WAIT UNTIL SHE THINKS OF IT FIRST.
I SUPPOSE I COULD WAKE HER UP, GIVE HER THE INFORMATION, AND WE BOTH GO BACK TO SLEEP. BUT THEN SHE'D SUSPECT THAT I'M PLANNING TO MANIPULATE HER.
I... I FEEL SOMETHING. A PRESENCE. IT FEELS... TERRIBLE. DARK. EVIL.
WHUH?

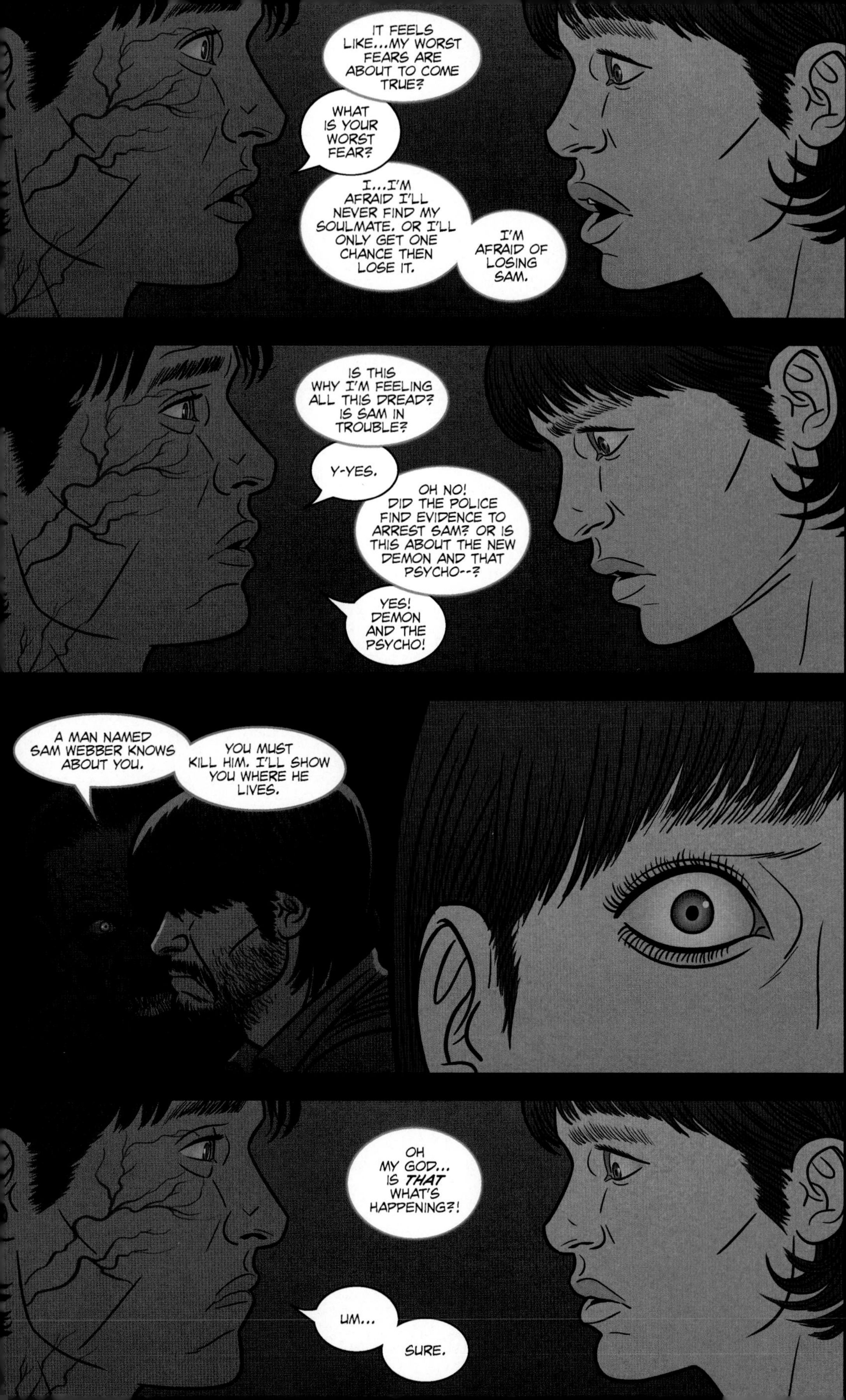
IT FEELS LIKE...MY WORST FEARS ARE ABOUT TO COME TRUE?
WHAT IS YOUR WORST FEAR?
I...I'M AFRAID I'LL NEVER FIND MY SOULMATE. OR I'LL ONLY GET ONE CHANCE THEN LOSE IT.
I'M AFRAID OF LOSING SAM.
IS THIS WHY I'M FEELING ALL THIS DREAD? IS SAM IN TROUBLE?
Y-YES.
OH NO! DID THE POLICE FIND EVIDENCE TO ARREST SAM? OR IS THIS ABOUT THE NEW DEMON AND THAT PSYCHO--?
YES! DEMON AND THE PSYCHO!
A MAN NAMED SAM WEBBER KNOWS ABOUT YOU.
YOU MUST KILL HIM. I'LL SHOW YOU WHERE HE LIVES.
OH MY GOD... IS *THAT* WHAT'S HAPPENING?!
UM...
SURE.

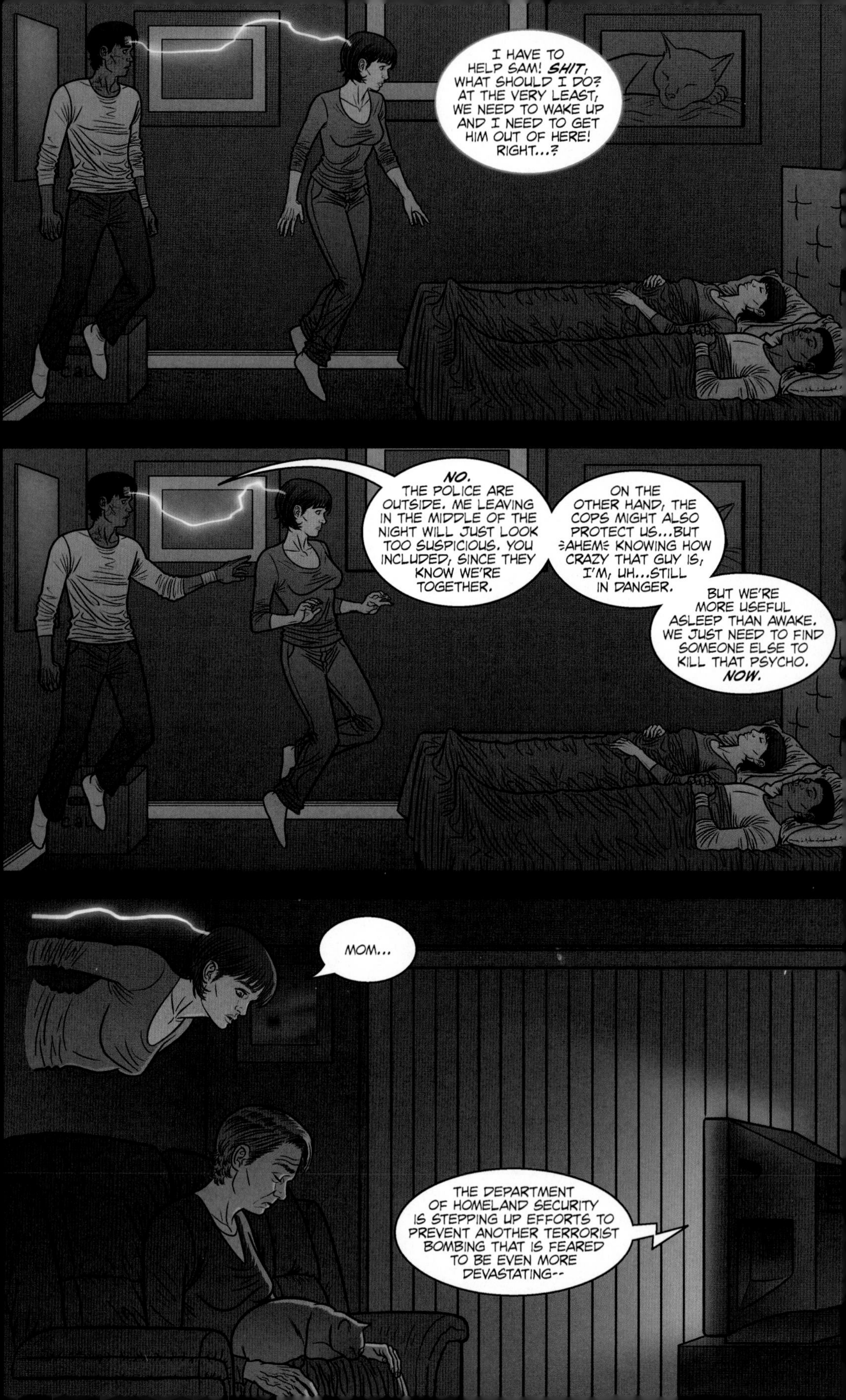
I HAVE TO HELP SAM! SHIT, WHAT SHOULD I DO? AT THE VERY LEAST, WE NEED TO WAKE UP AND I NEED TO GET HIM OUT OF HERE! RIGHT...?
NO. THE POLICE ARE OUTSIDE. ME LEAVING IN THE MIDDLE OF THE NIGHT WILL JUST LOOK TOO SUSPICIOUS. YOU INCLUDED, SINCE THEY KNOW WE'RE TOGETHER.
ON THE OTHER HAND, THE COPS MIGHT ALSO PROTECT US...BUT AHEM KNOWING HOW CRAZY THAT GUY IS, I'M, UH...STILL IN DANGER.
BUT WE'RE MORE USEFUL ASLEEP THAN AWAKE. WE JUST NEED TO FIND SOMEONE ELSE TO KILL THAT PSYCHO. NOW.
MOM...
THE DEPARTMENT OF HOMELAND SECURITY IS STEPPING UP EFFORTS TO PREVENT ANOTHER TERRORIST BOMBING THAT IS FEARED TO BE EVEN MORE DEVASTATING--

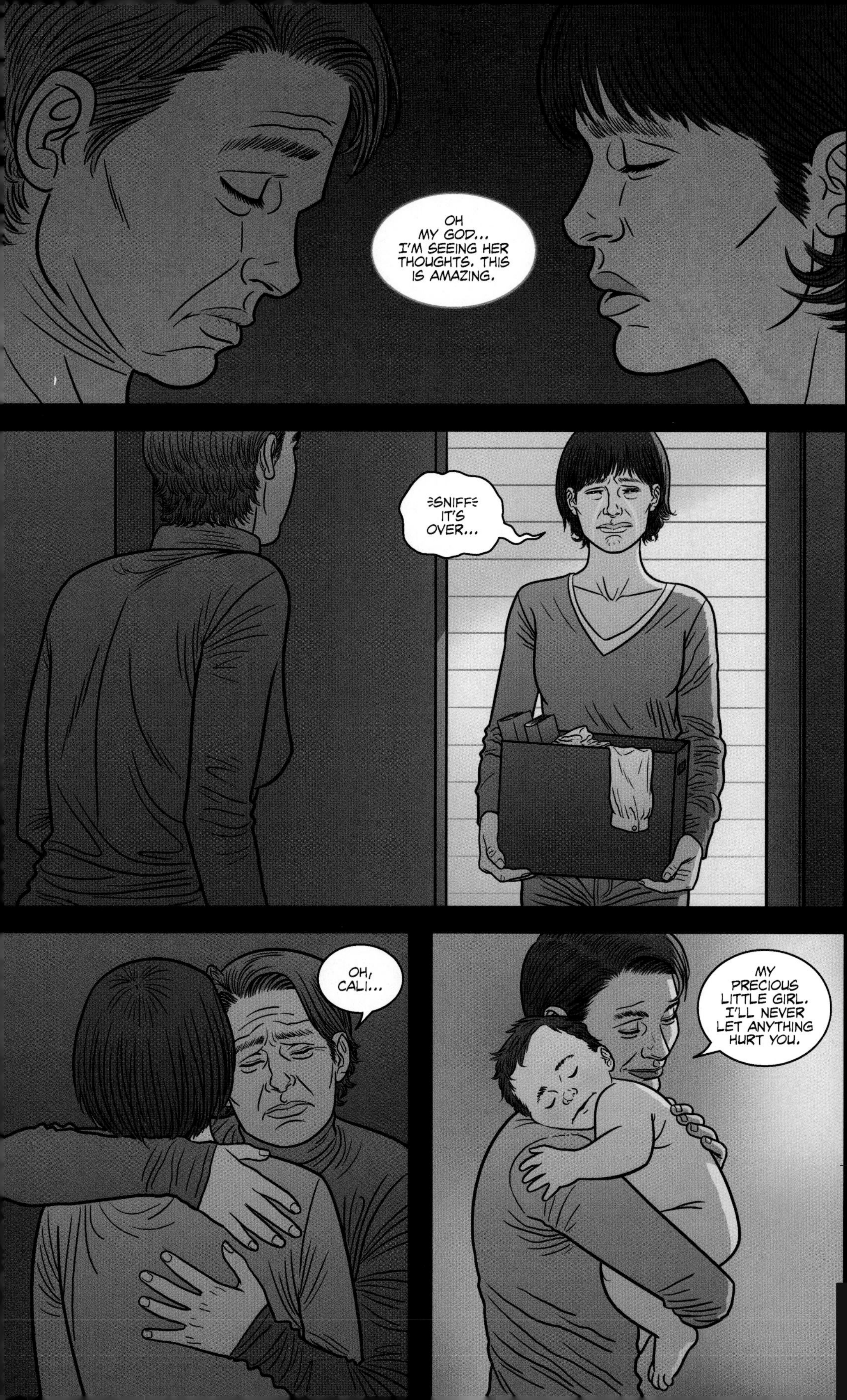
OH MY GOD... I'M SEEING HER THOUGHTS. THIS IS AMAZING.
≈SNIFF≈ IT'S OVER...
OH, CALI...
MY PRECIOUS LITTLE GIRL. I'LL NEVER LET ANYTHING HURT YOU.

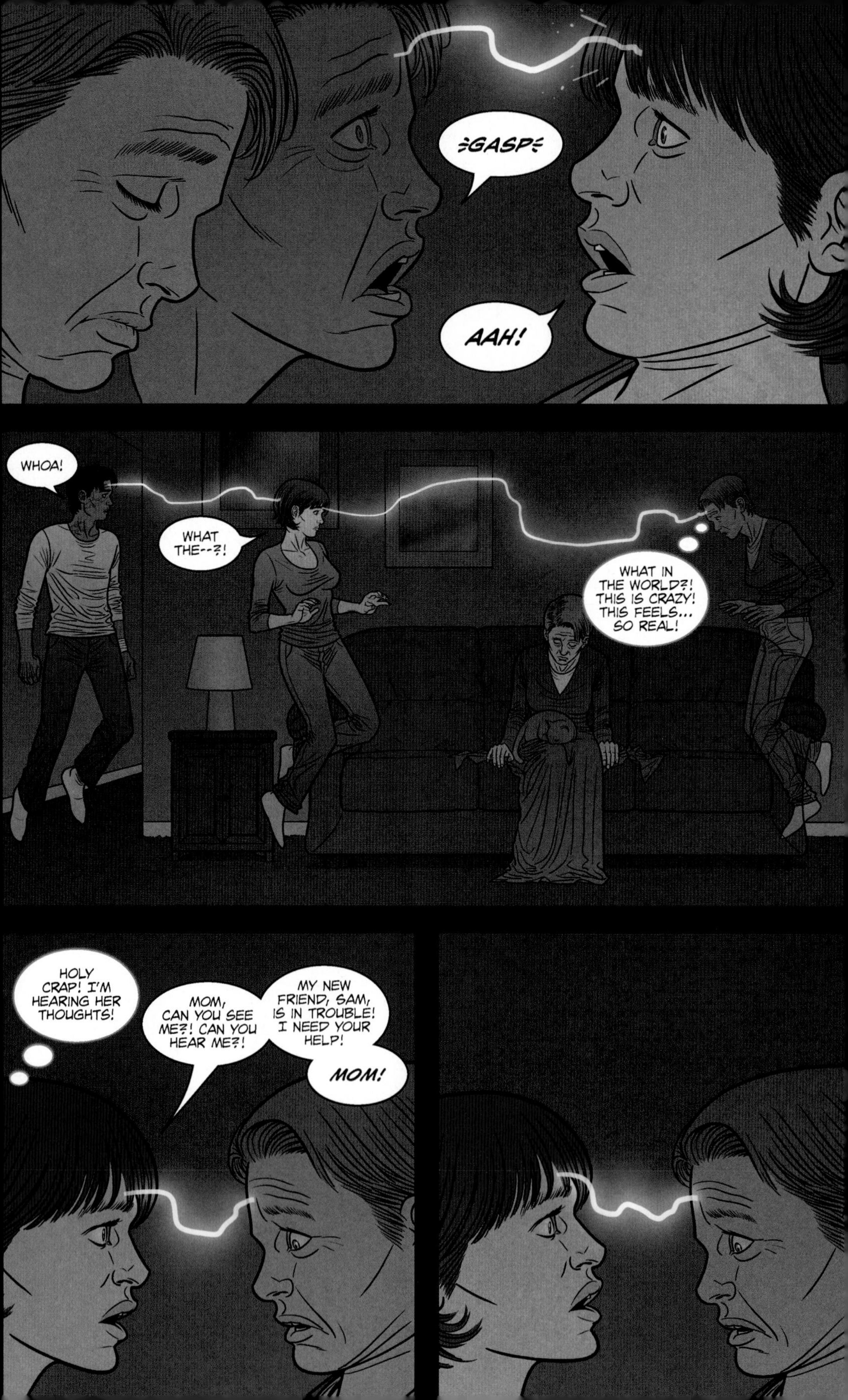

=GASP=
AAH!
WHOA!
WHAT THE--?!
WHAT IN THE WORLD?! THIS IS CRAZY! THIS FEELS... SO REAL!
HOLY CRAP! I'M HEARING HER THOUGHTS!
MOM, CAN YOU SEE ME?! CAN YOU HEAR ME?!
MY NEW FRIEND, SAM, IS IN TROUBLE! I NEED YOUR HELP!
MOM!

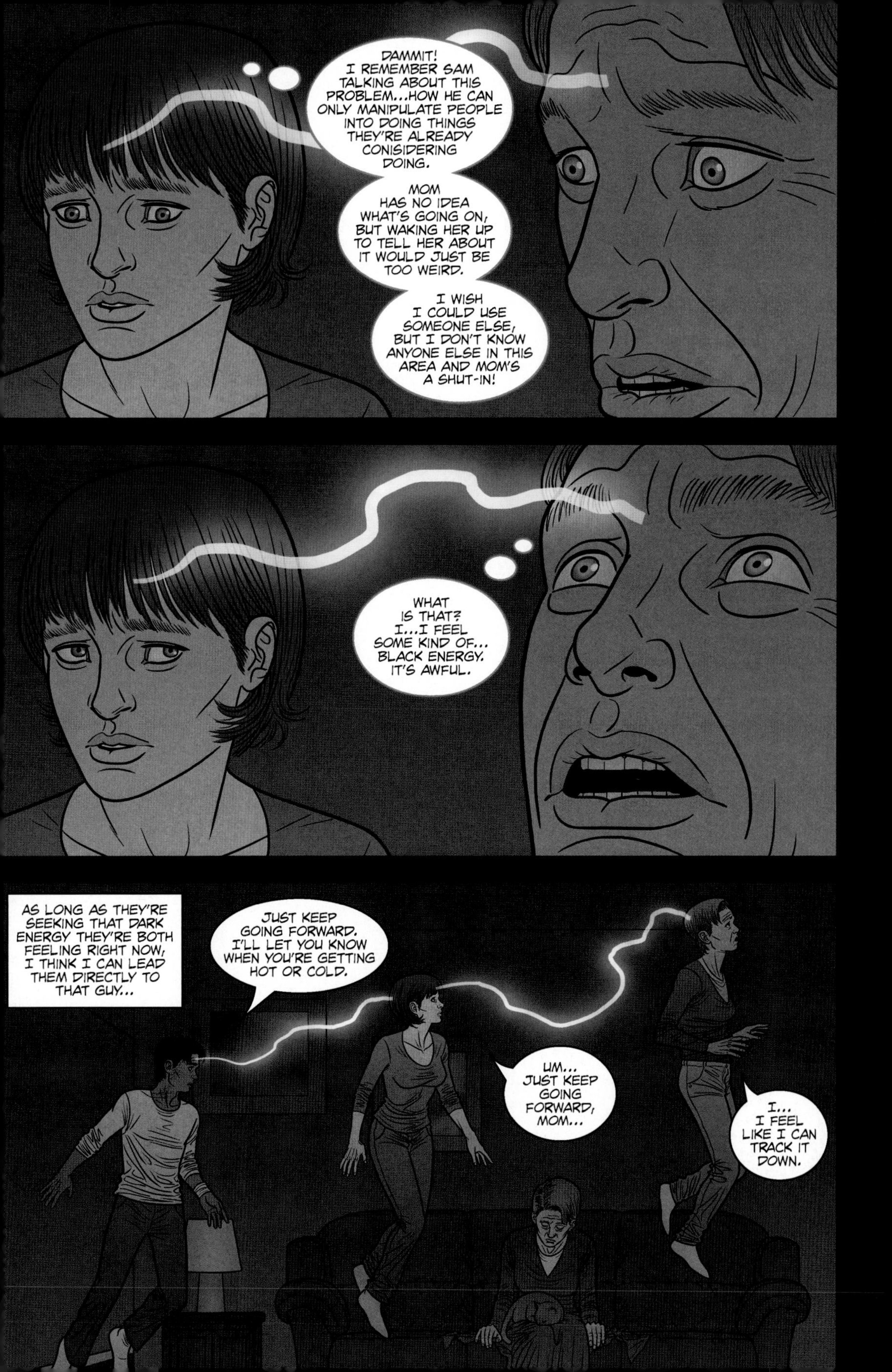
DAMMIT! I REMEMBER SAM TALKING ABOUT THIS PROBLEM...HOW HE CAN ONLY MANIPULATE PEOPLE INTO DOING THINGS THEY'RE ALREADY CONISIDERING DOING.
MOM HAS NO IDEA WHAT'S GOING ON, BUT WAKING HER UP TO TELL HER ABOUT IT WOULD JUST BE TOO WEIRD.
I WISH I COULD USE SOMEONE ELSE, BUT I DON'T KNOW ANYONE ELSE IN THIS AREA AND MOM'S A SHUT-IN!
WHAT IS THAT? I...I FEEL SOME KIND OF... BLACK ENERGY. IT'S AWFUL.
AS LONG AS THEY'RE SEEKING THAT DARK ENERGY THEY'RE BOTH FEELING RIGHT NOW, I THINK I CAN LEAD THEM DIRECTLY TO THAT GUY...
JUST KEEP GOING FORWARD. I'LL LET YOU KNOW WHEN YOU'RE GETTING HOT OR COLD.
UM... JUST KEEP GOING FORWARD, MOM...
I... I FEEL LIKE I CAN TRACK IT DOWN.

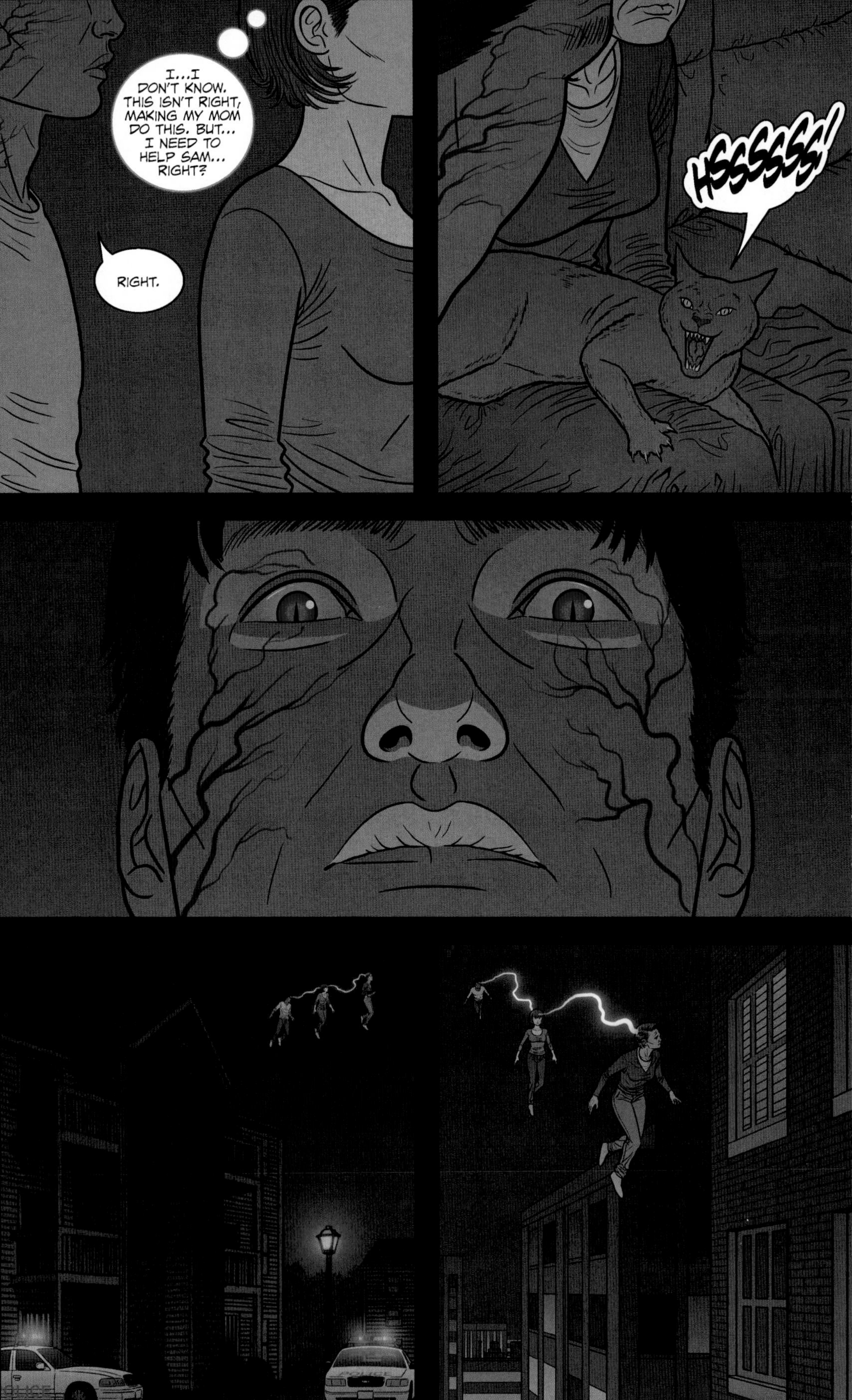
I...I DON'T KNOW. THIS ISN'T RIGHT, MAKING MY MOM DO THIS. BUT... I NEED TO HELP SAM... RIGHT?
RIGHT.
HSSSSSS!

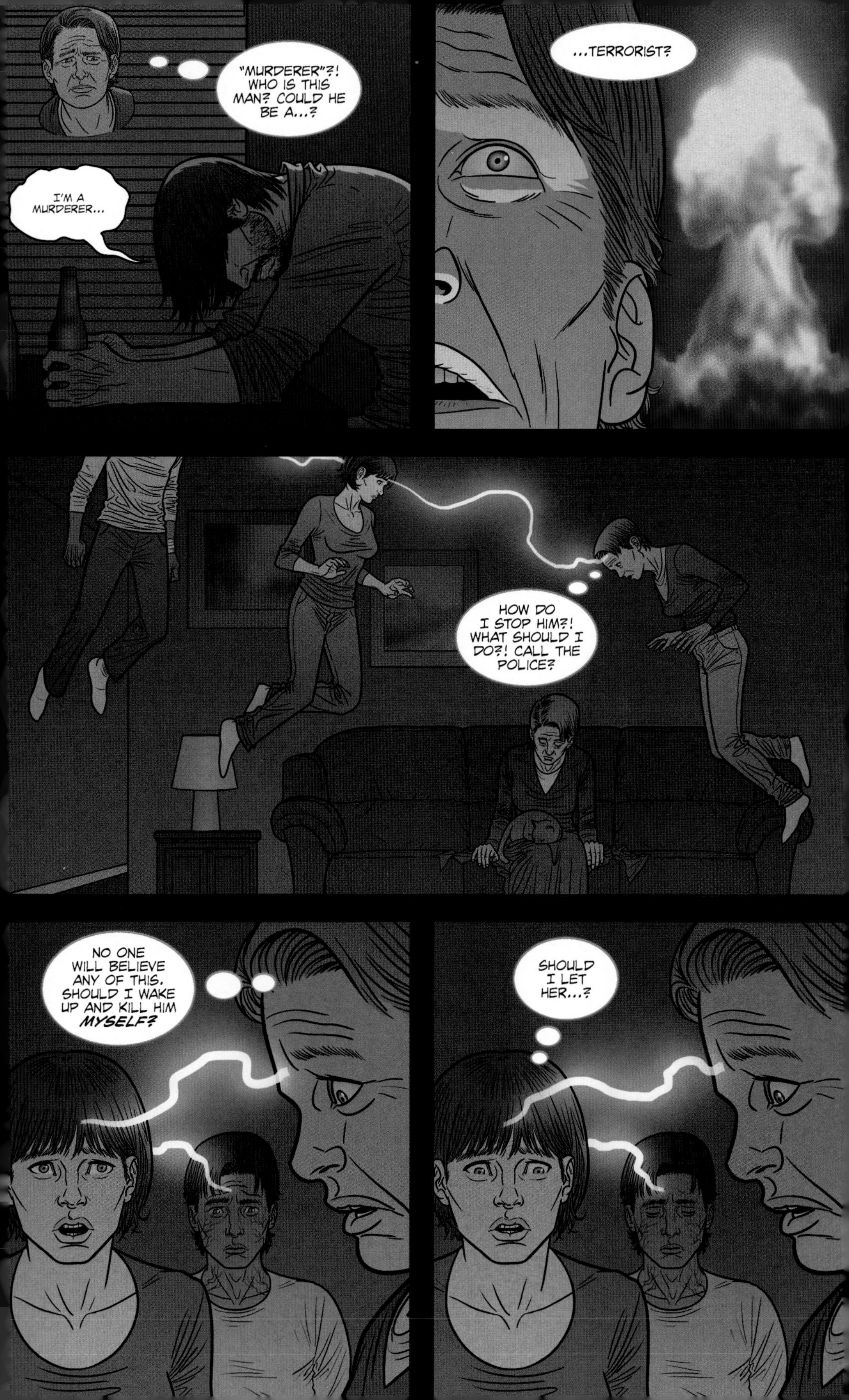
"MURDERER"?! WHO IS THIS MAN? COULD HE BE A...?
I'M A MURDERER...
...TERRORIST?
HOW DO I STOP HIM?! WHAT SHOULD I DO?! CALL THE POLICE?
NO ONE WILL BELIEVE ANY OF THIS. SHOULD I WAKE UP AND KILL HIM *MYSELF?*
SHOULD I LET HER...?

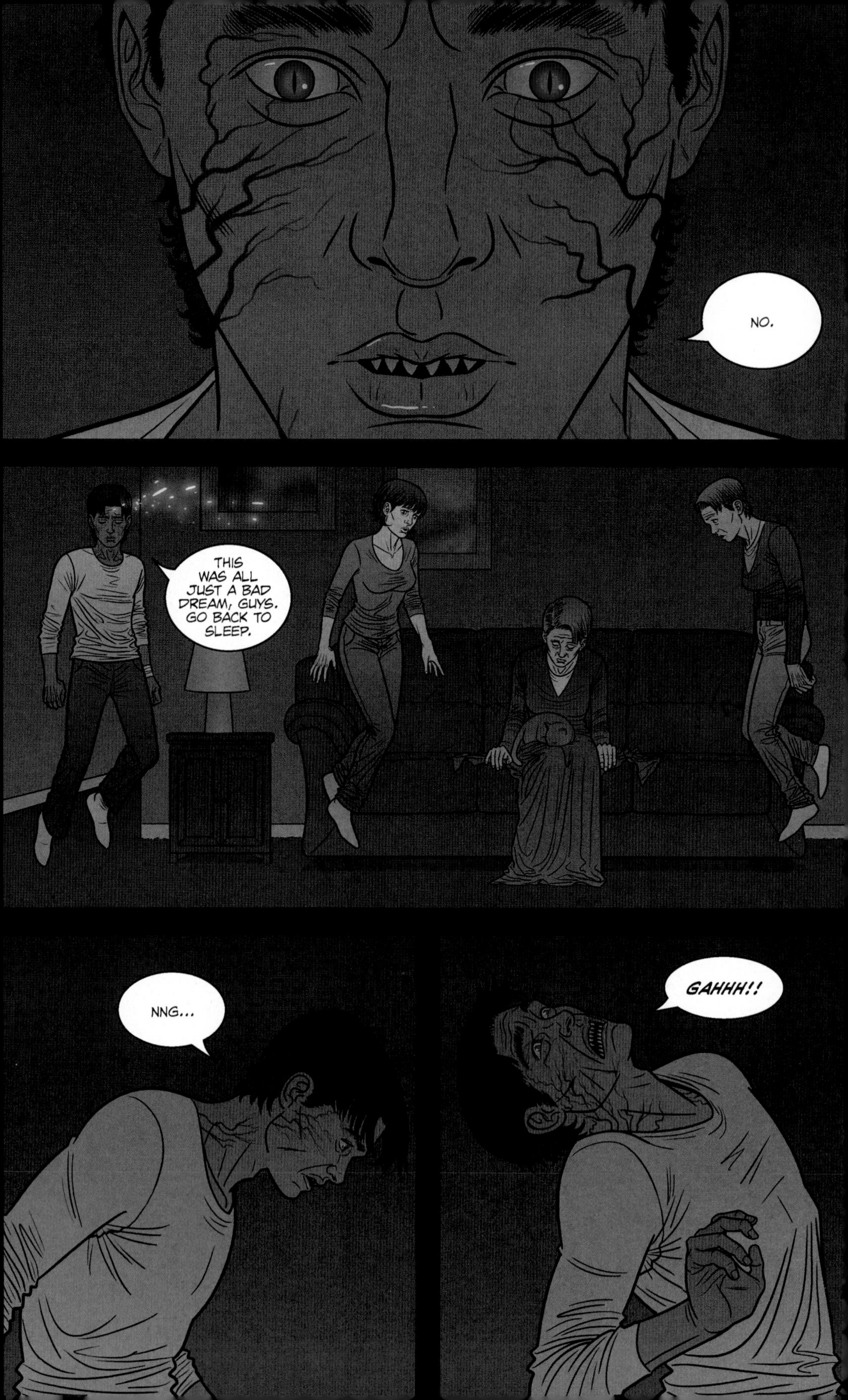
NO.
THIS WAS ALL JUST A BAD DREAM, GUYS. GO BACK TO SLEEP.
NNG...
GAHHH!!

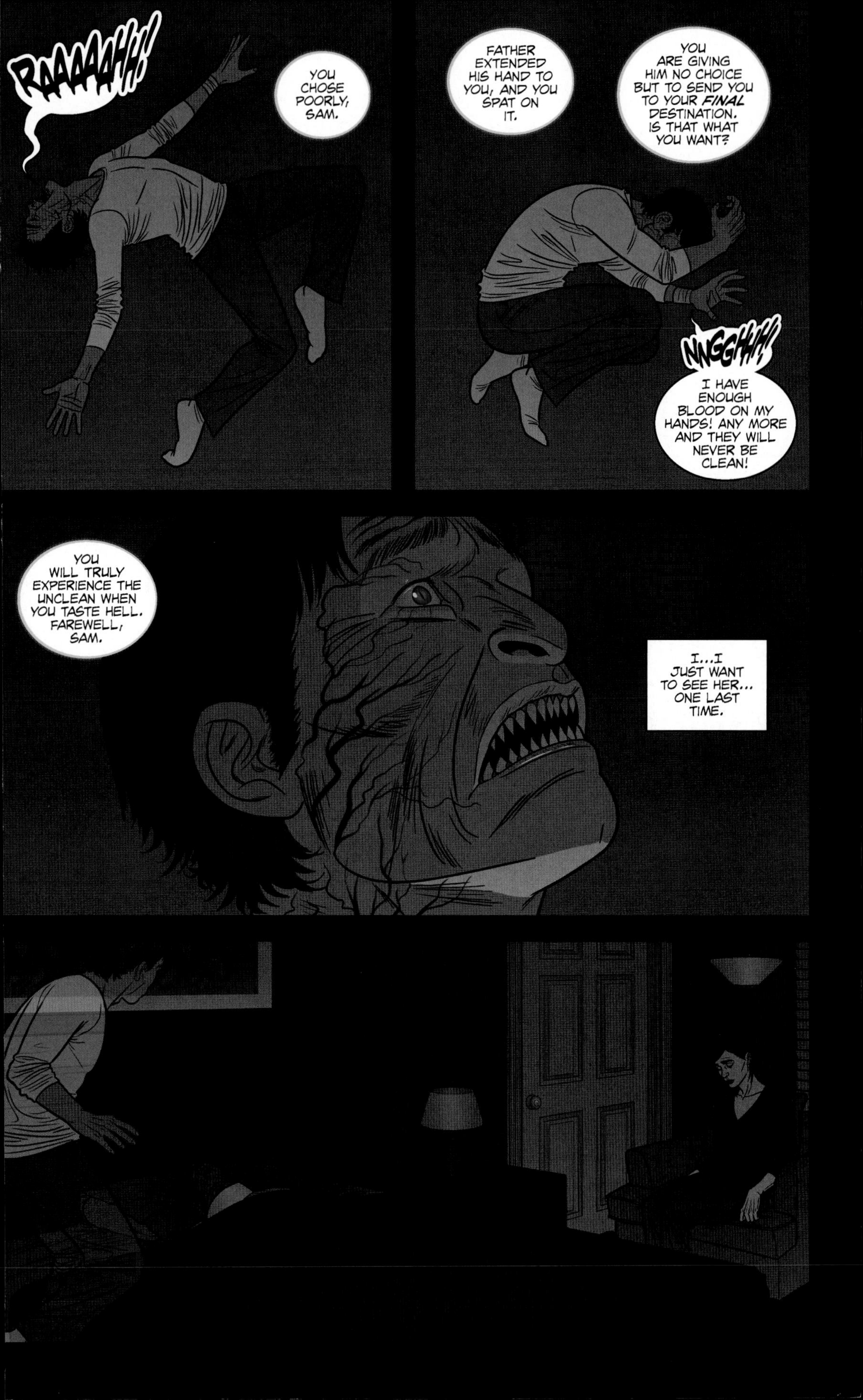
RAAAAAHH!
YOU CHOSE POORLY, SAM.
FATHER EXTENDED HIS HAND TO YOU, AND YOU SPAT ON IT.
YOU ARE GIVING HIM NO CHOICE BUT TO SEND YOU TO YOUR *FINAL* DESTINATION. IS THAT WHAT YOU WANT?
NNGGHHH!
I HAVE ENOUGH BLOOD ON MY HANDS! ANY MORE AND THEY WILL NEVER BE CLEAN!
YOU WILL TRULY EXPERIENCE THE UNCLEAN WHEN YOU TASTE HELL. FAREWELL, SAM.
I...I JUST WANT TO SEE HER... ONE LAST TIME.

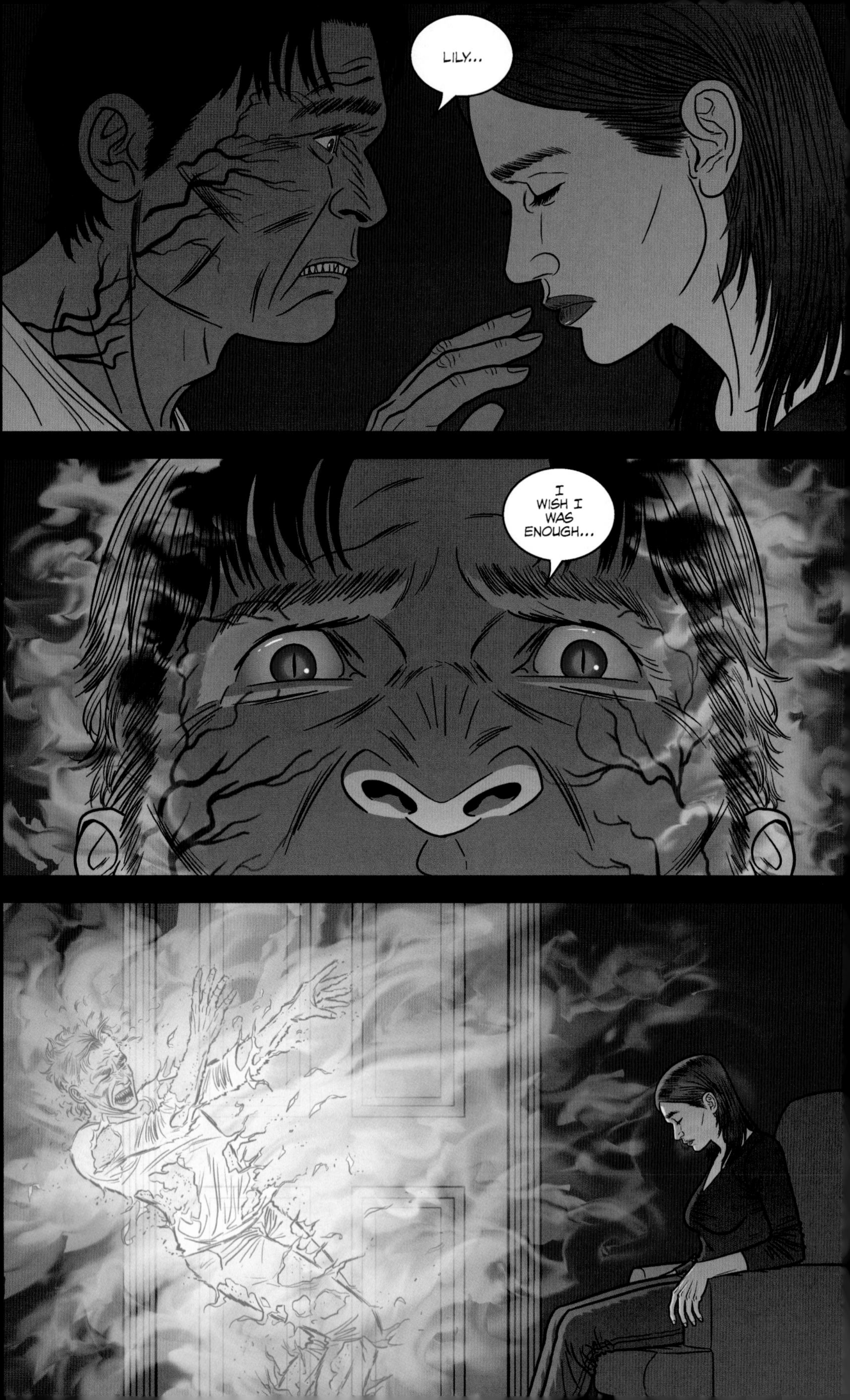
LILY...
I WISH I WAS ENOUGH...

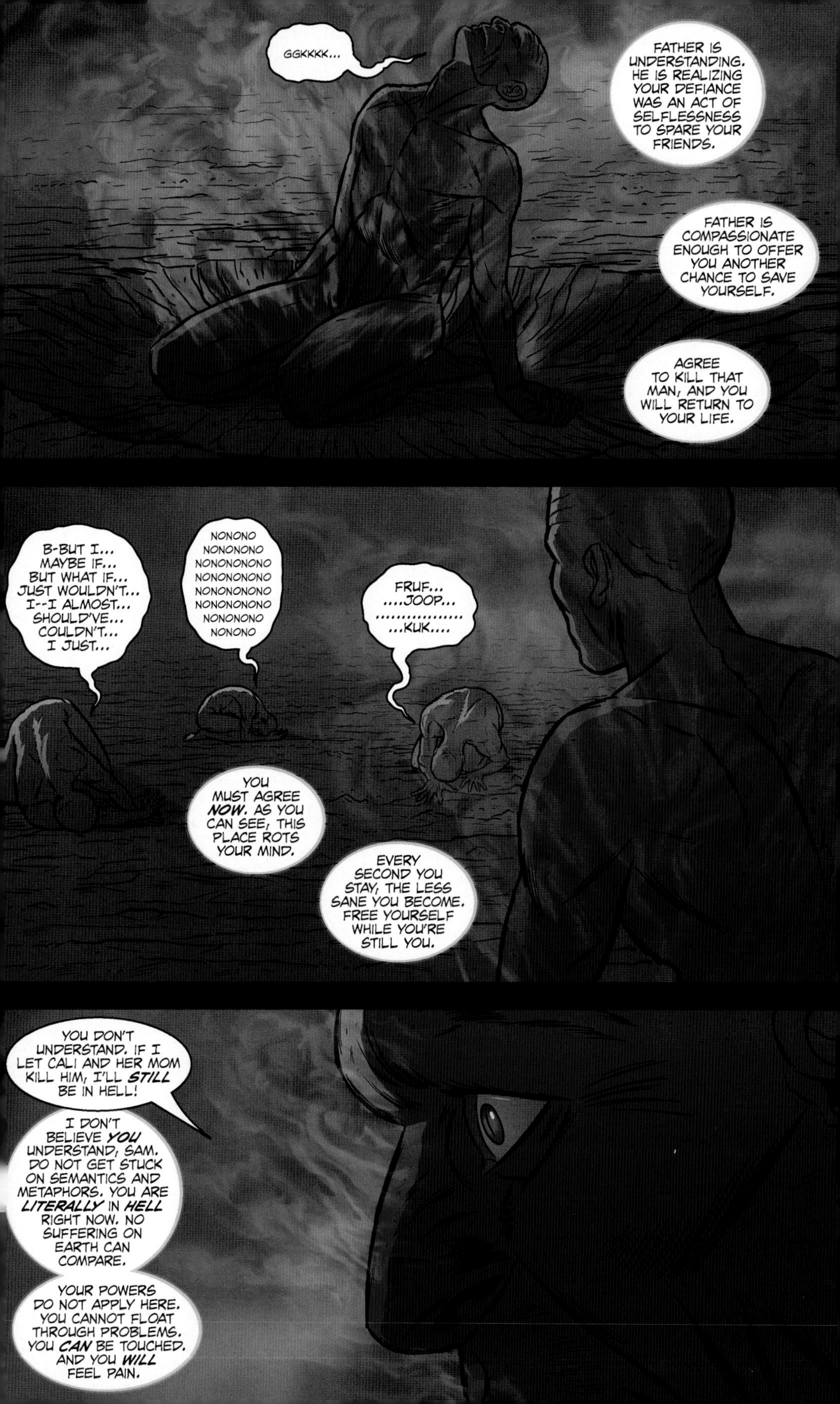
GGKKKK...
FATHER IS UNDERSTANDING. HE IS REALIZING YOUR DEFIANCE WAS AN ACT OF SELFLESSNESS TO SPARE YOUR FRIENDS.
FATHER IS COMPASSIONATE ENOUGH TO OFFER YOU ANOTHER CHANCE TO SAVE YOURSELF.
AGREE TO KILL THAT MAN, AND YOU WILL RETURN TO YOUR LIFE.
B-BUT I... MAYBE IF... BUT WHAT IF... JUST WOULDN'T... I--I ALMOST... SHOULD'VE... COULDN'T... I JUST...
NONONO NONONONO NONONONONO NONONONONO NONONONONO NONONONONO NONONONO NONONO
FRUF... ....JOOP... ....KUK....
YOU MUST AGREE *NOW*. AS YOU CAN SEE, THIS PLACE ROTS YOUR MIND.
EVERY SECOND YOU STAY, THE LESS SANE YOU BECOME. FREE YOURSELF WHILE YOU'RE STILL YOU.
YOU DON'T UNDERSTAND. IF I LET CALI AND HER MOM KILL HIM, I'LL *STILL* BE IN HELL!
I DON'T BELIEVE *YOU* UNDERSTAND, SAM. DO NOT GET STUCK ON SEMANTICS AND METAPHORS. YOU ARE *LITERALLY* IN *HELL* RIGHT NOW. NO SUFFERING ON EARTH CAN COMPARE.
YOUR POWERS DO NOT APPLY HERE. YOU CANNOT FLOAT THROUGH PROBLEMS. YOU *CAN* BE TOUCHED. AND YOU *WILL* FEEL PAIN.

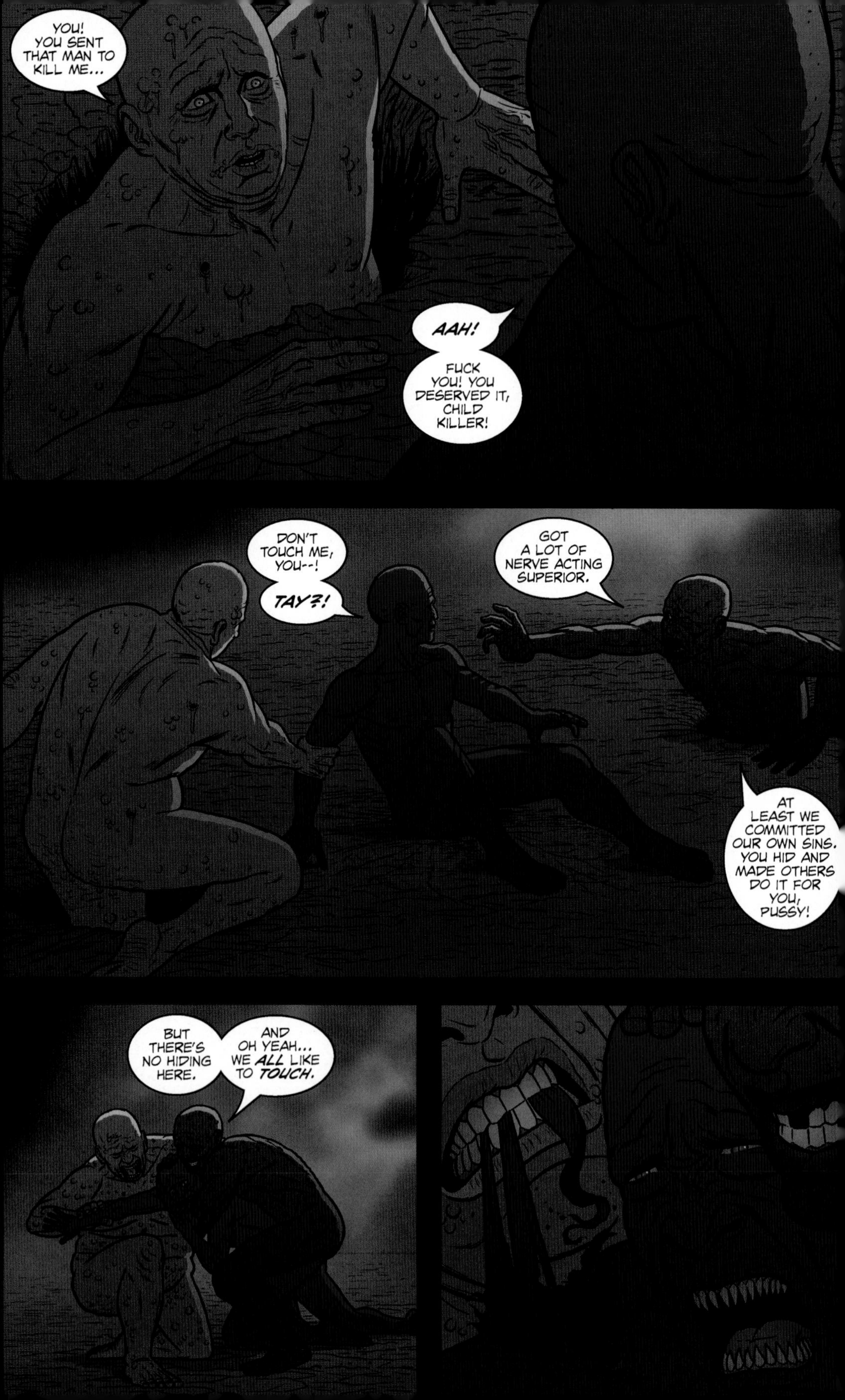
YOU! YOU SENT THAT MAN TO KILL ME...
AAH!
FUCK YOU! YOU DESERVED IT, CHILD KILLER!
DON'T TOUCH ME, YOU--!
TAY?!
GOT A LOT OF NERVE ACTING SUPERIOR.
AT LEAST WE COMMITTED OUR OWN SINS. YOU HID AND MADE OTHERS DO IT FOR YOU, PUSSY!
BUT THERE'S NO HIDING HERE.
AND OH YEAH... WE ALL LIKE TO TOUCH.

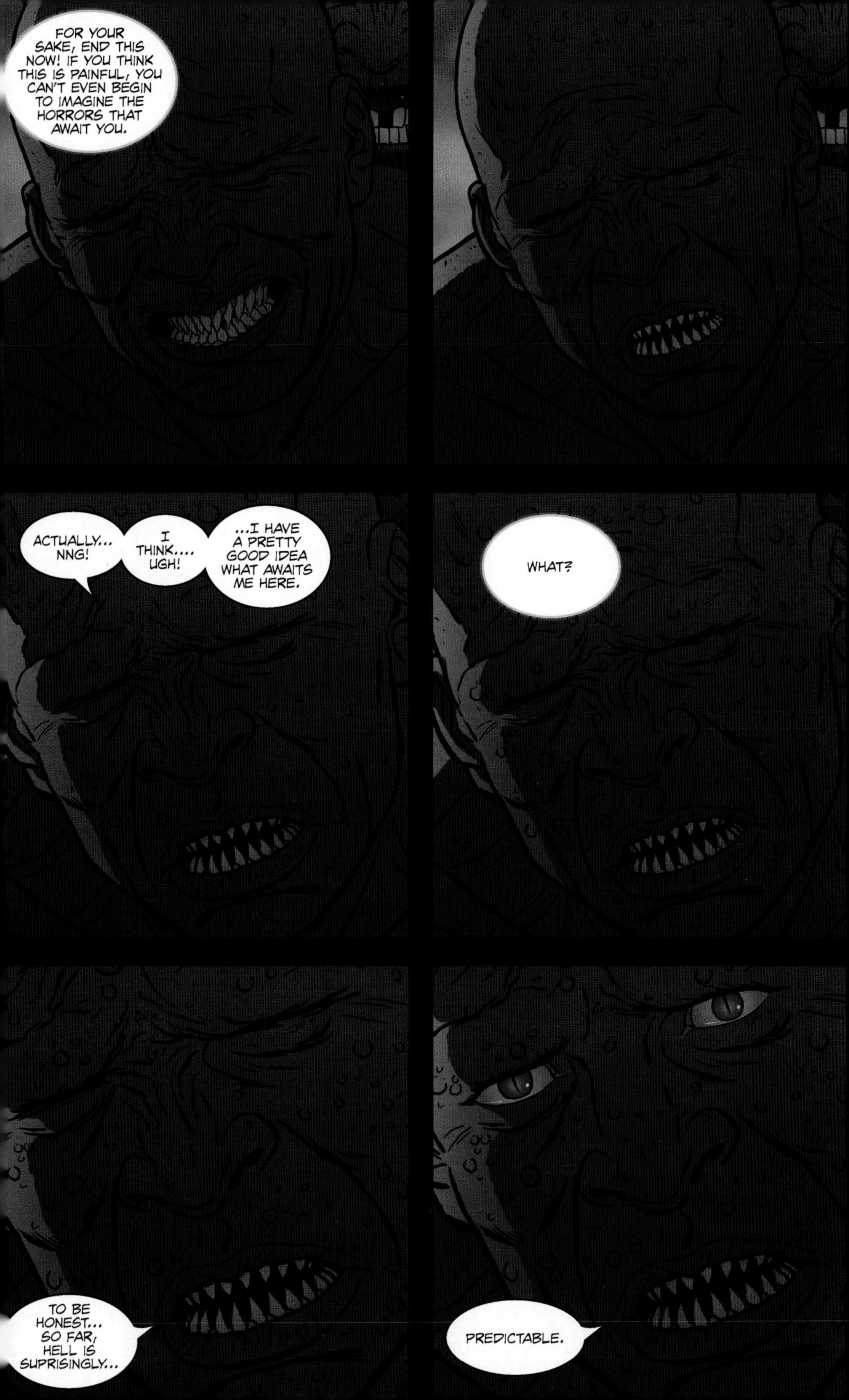
FOR YOUR SAKE, END THIS NOW! IF YOU THINK THIS IS PAINFUL, YOU CAN'T EVEN BEGIN TO IMAGINE THE HORRORS THAT AWAIT YOU.
ACTUALLY... NNG!
I THINK.... UGH!
...I HAVE A PRETTY GOOD IDEA WHAT AWAITS ME HERE.
WHAT?
TO BE HONEST... SO FAR, HELL IS SUPRISINGLY...
PREDICTABLE.

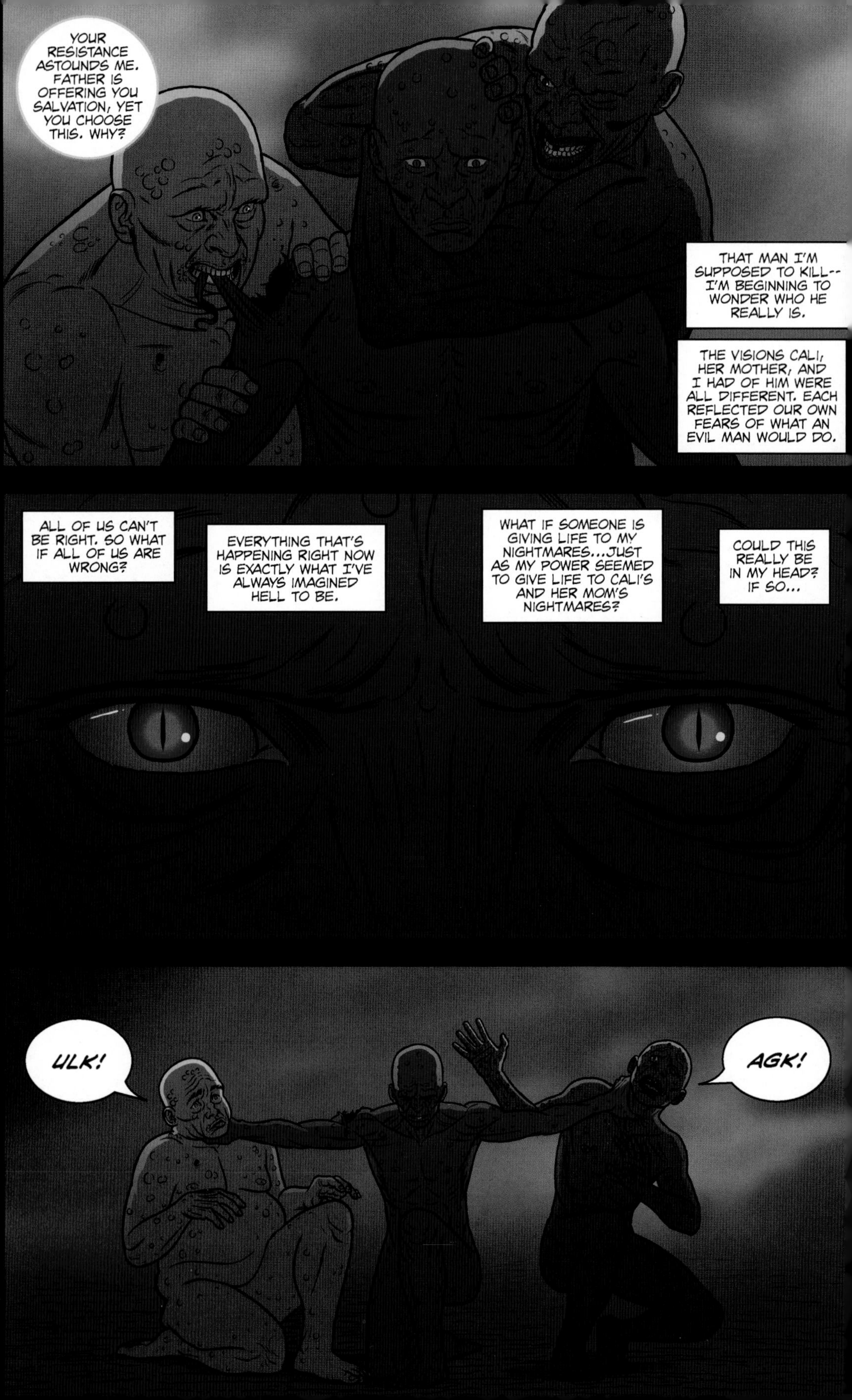
YOUR RESISTANCE ASTOUNDS ME. FATHER IS OFFERING YOU SALVATION, YET YOU CHOOSE THIS. WHY?
THAT MAN I'M SUPPOSED TO KILL-- I'M BEGINNING TO WONDER WHO HE REALLY IS.
THE VISIONS CALI, HER MOTHER, AND I HAD OF HIM WERE ALL DIFFERENT. EACH REFLECTED OUR OWN FEARS OF WHAT AN EVIL MAN WOULD DO.
ALL OF US CAN'T BE RIGHT. SO WHAT IF ALL OF US ARE WRONG?
EVERYTHING THAT'S HAPPENING RIGHT NOW IS EXACTLY WHAT I'VE ALWAYS IMAGINED HELL TO BE.
WHAT IF SOMEONE IS GIVING LIFE TO MY NIGHTMARES...JUST AS MY POWER SEEMED TO GIVE LIFE TO CALI'S AND HER MOM'S NIGHTMARES?
COULD THIS REALLY BE IN MY HEAD? IF SO...
ULK!
AGK!

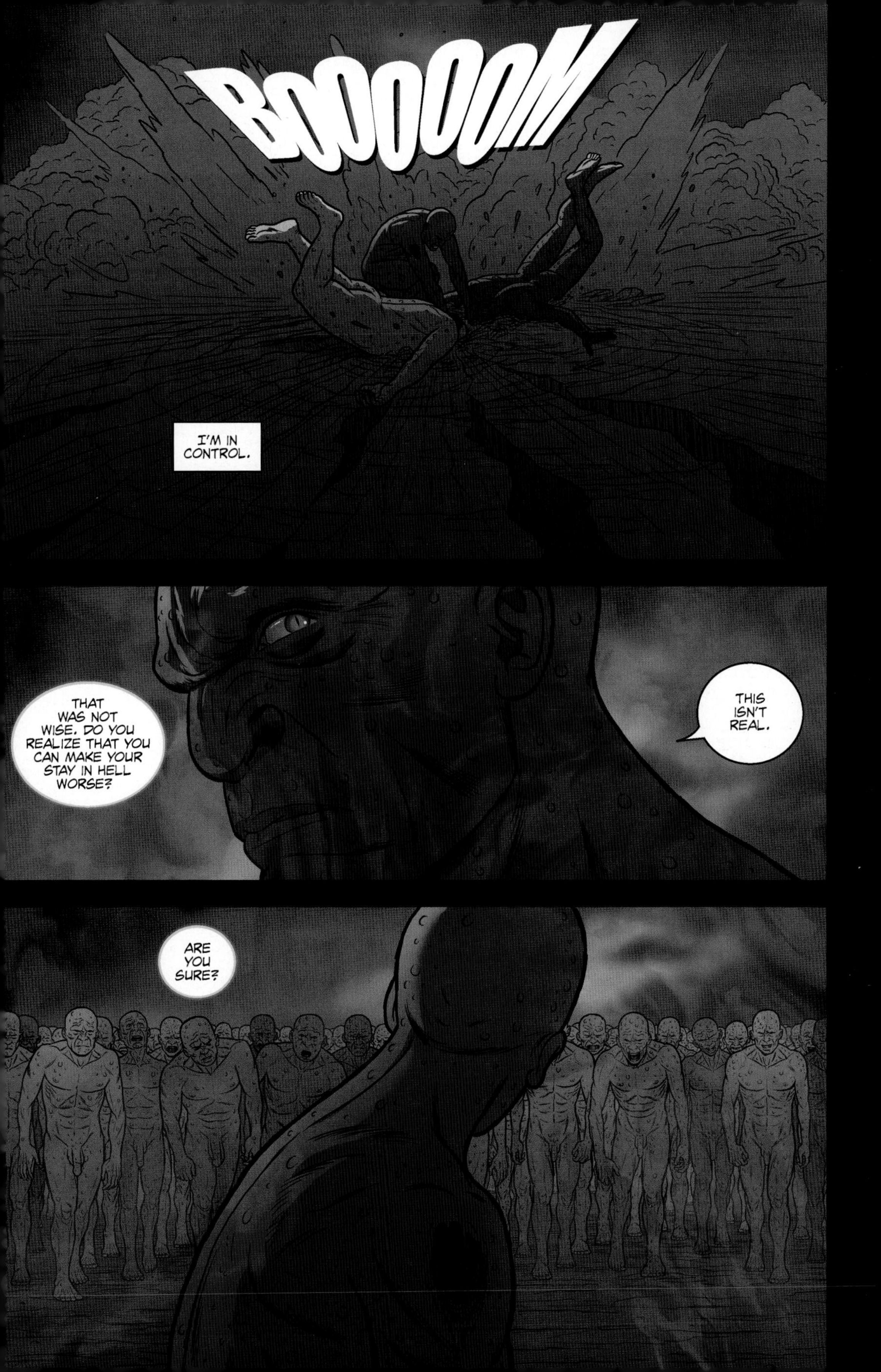
BOOOOOM
I'M IN CONTROL.
THAT WAS NOT WISE. DO YOU REALIZE THAT YOU CAN MAKE YOUR STAY IN HELL WORSE?
THIS ISN'T REAL.
ARE YOU SURE?

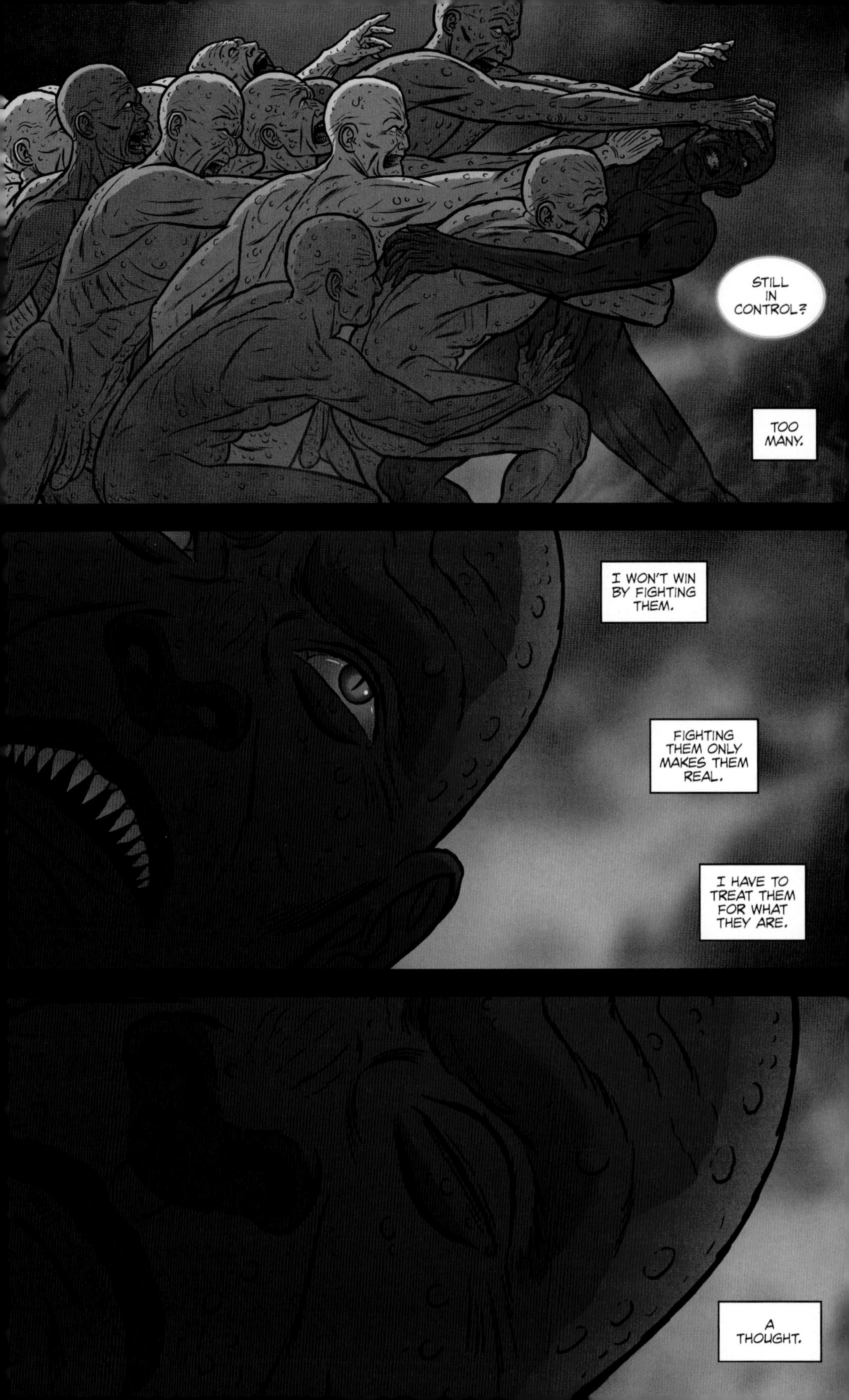
STILL IN CONTROL?
TOO MANY.
I WON'T WIN BY FIGHTING THEM.
FIGHTING THEM ONLY MAKES THEM REAL.
I HAVE TO TREAT THEM FOR WHAT THEY ARE.
A THOUGHT.

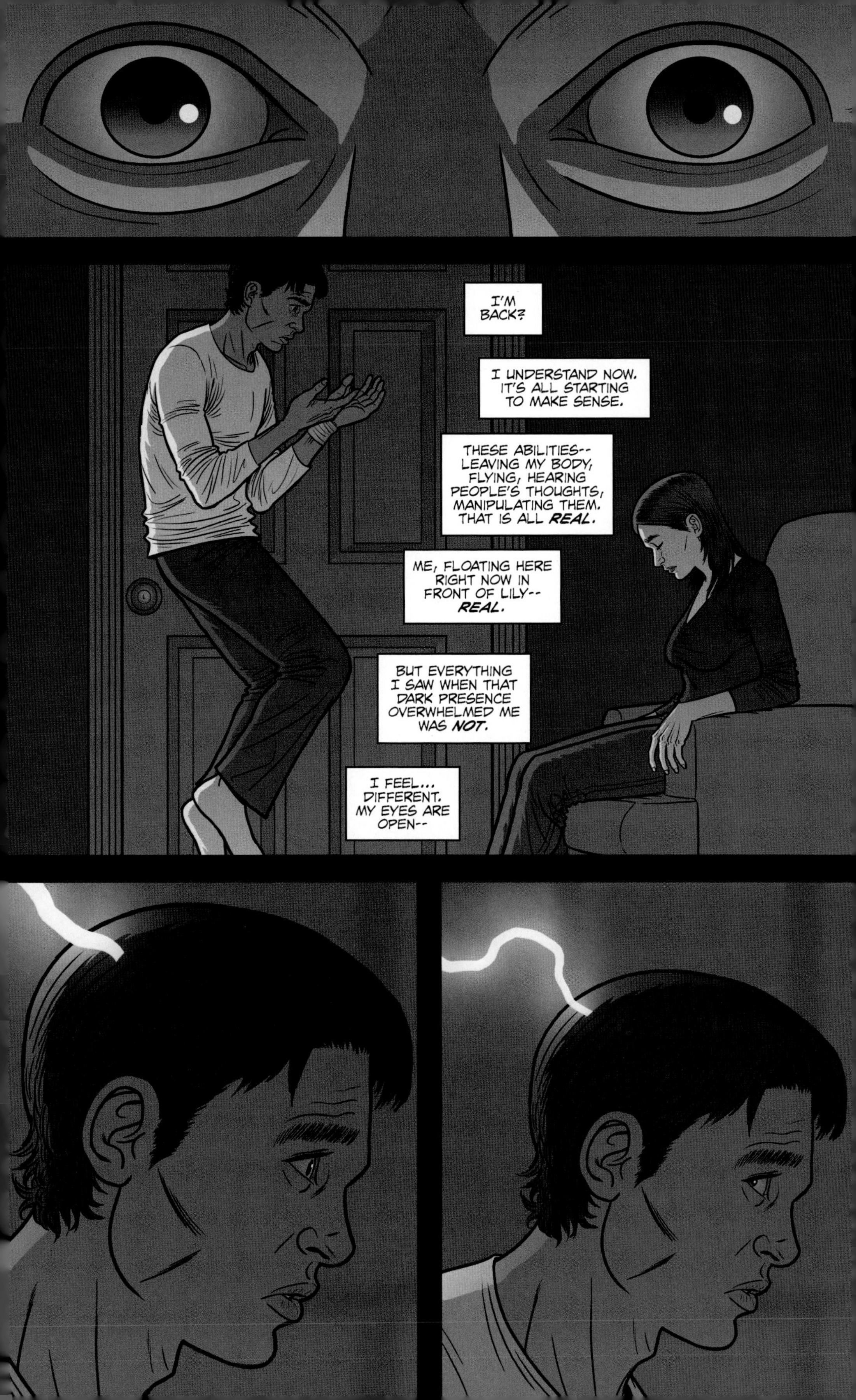
I'M BACK?
I UNDERSTAND NOW. IT'S ALL STARTING TO MAKE SENSE.
THESE ABILITIES--LEAVING MY BODY, FLYING, HEARING PEOPLE'S THOUGHTS, MANIPULATING THEM. THAT IS ALL REAL.
ME, FLOATING HERE RIGHT NOW IN FRONT OF LILY--REAL.
BUT EVERYTHING I SAW WHEN THAT DARK PRESENCE OVERWHELMED ME WAS NOT.
I FEEL... DIFFERENT. MY EYES ARE OPEN--

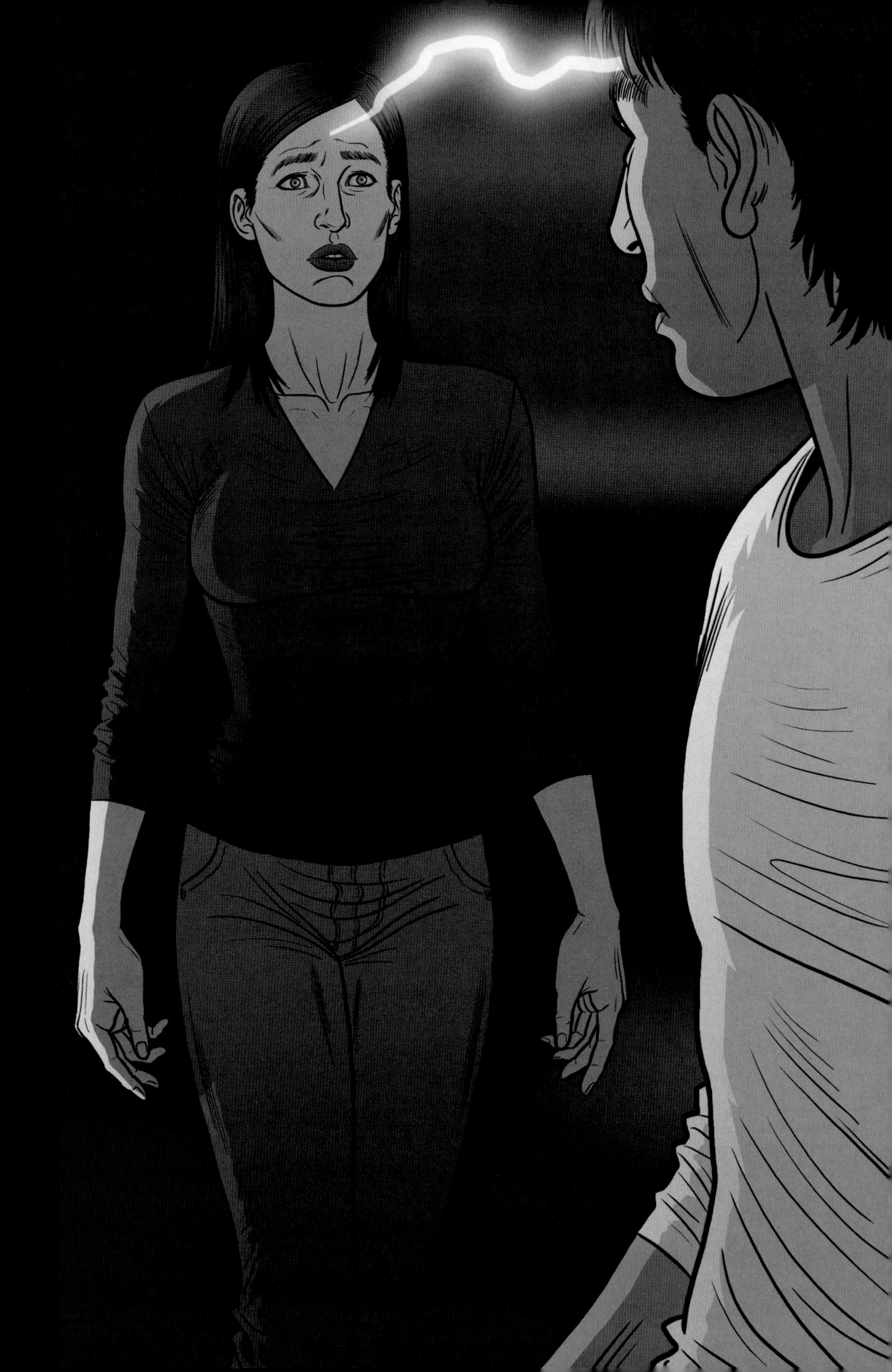

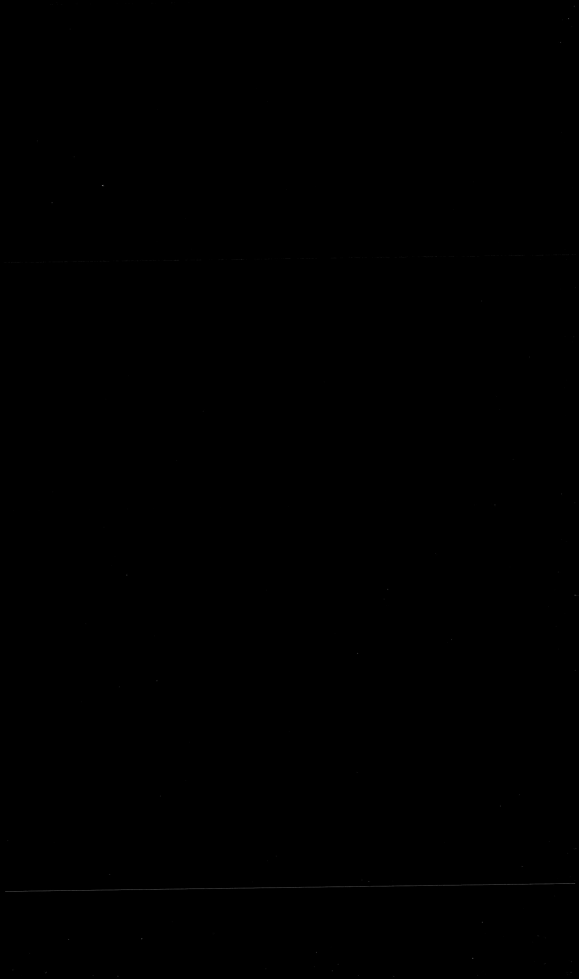

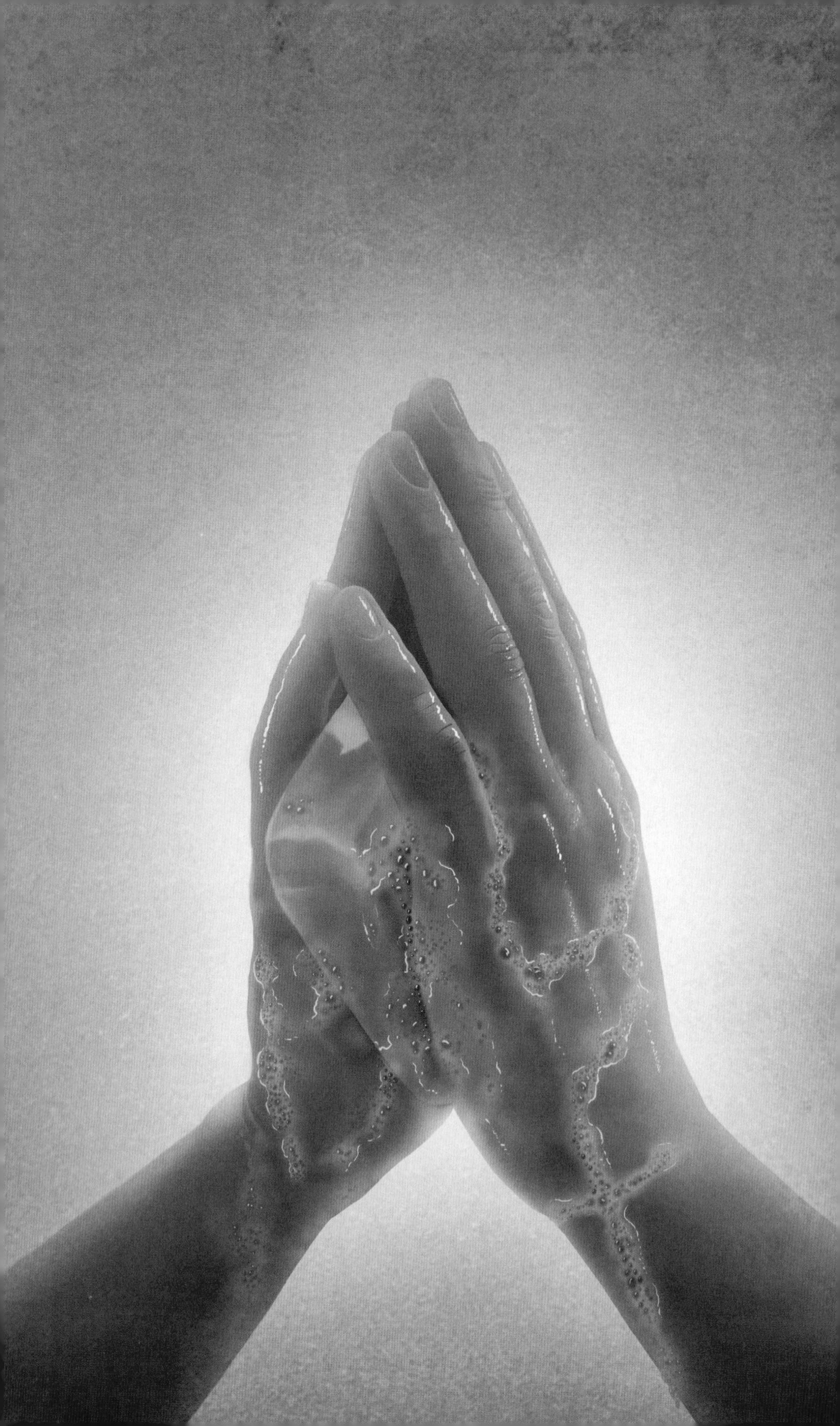

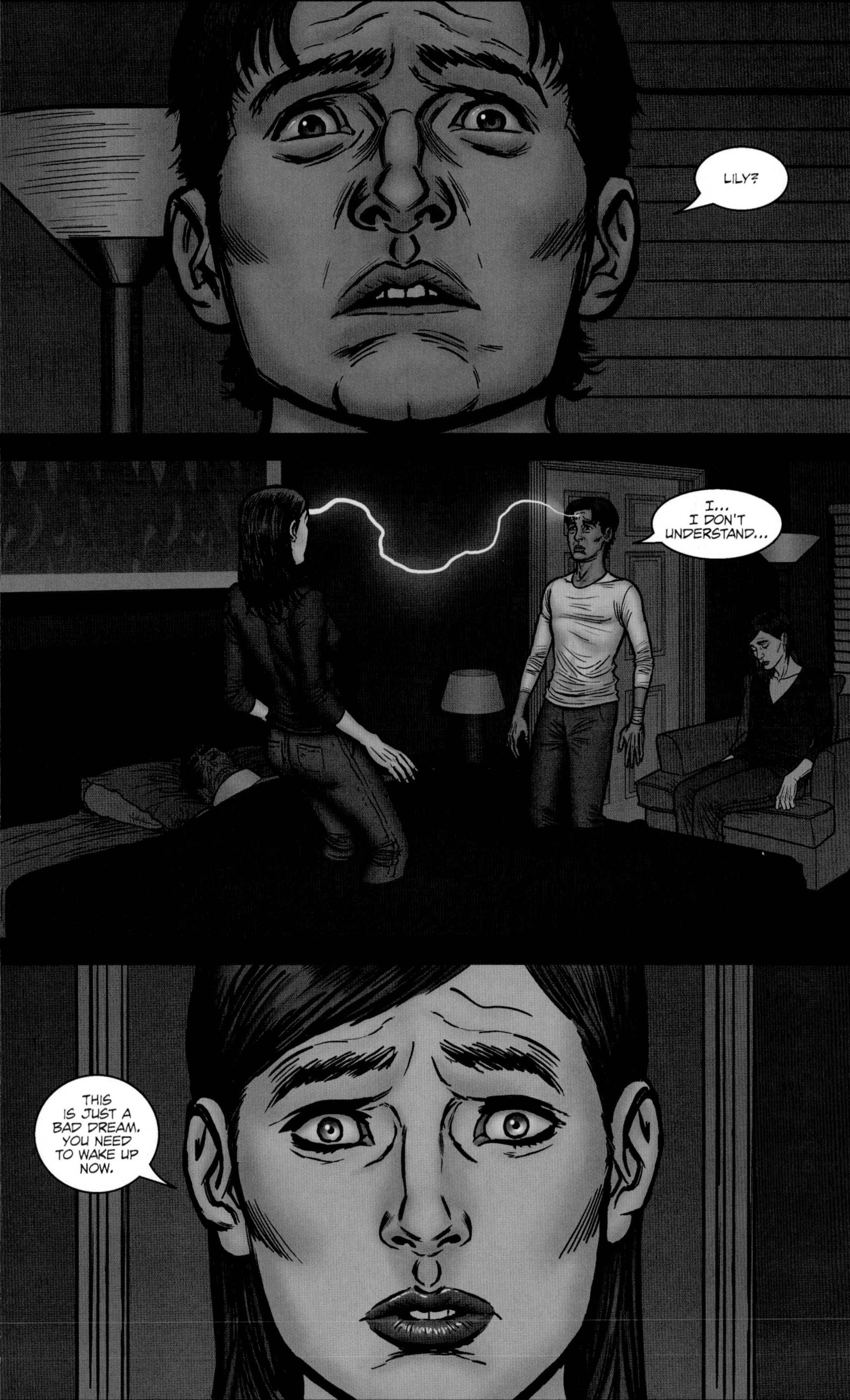
LILY?
I... I DON'T UNDERSTAND...
THIS IS JUST A BAD DREAM. YOU NEED TO WAKE UP NOW.

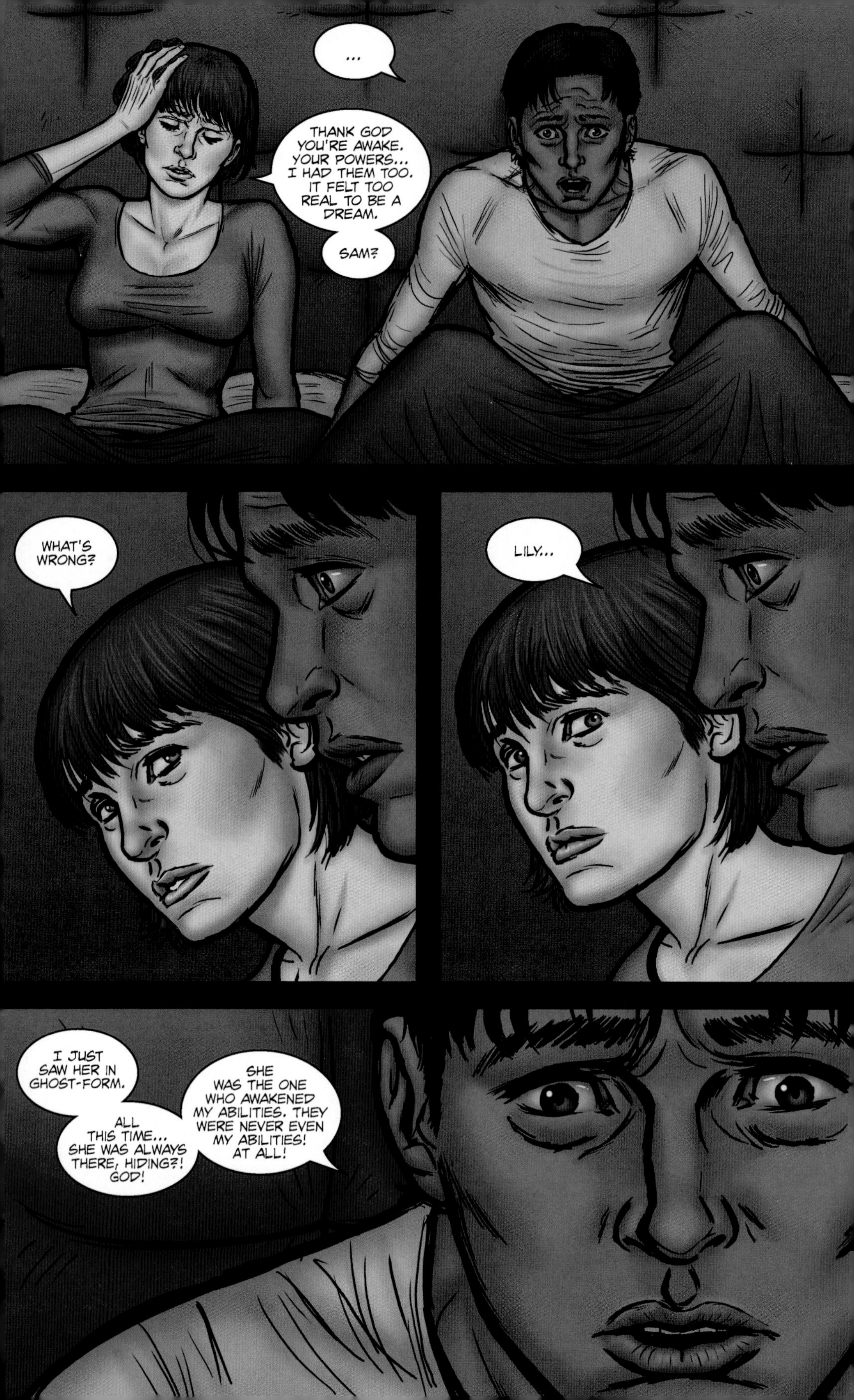
...
THANK GOD YOU'RE AWAKE. YOUR POWERS... I HAD THEM TOO. IT FELT TOO REAL TO BE A DREAM.
SAM?
WHAT'S WRONG?
LILY...
I JUST SAW HER IN GHOST-FORM.
ALL THIS TIME... SHE WAS ALWAYS THERE, HIDING?! GOD!
SHE WAS THE ONE WHO AWAKENED MY ABILITIES. THEY WERE NEVER EVEN MY ABILITIES! AT ALL!

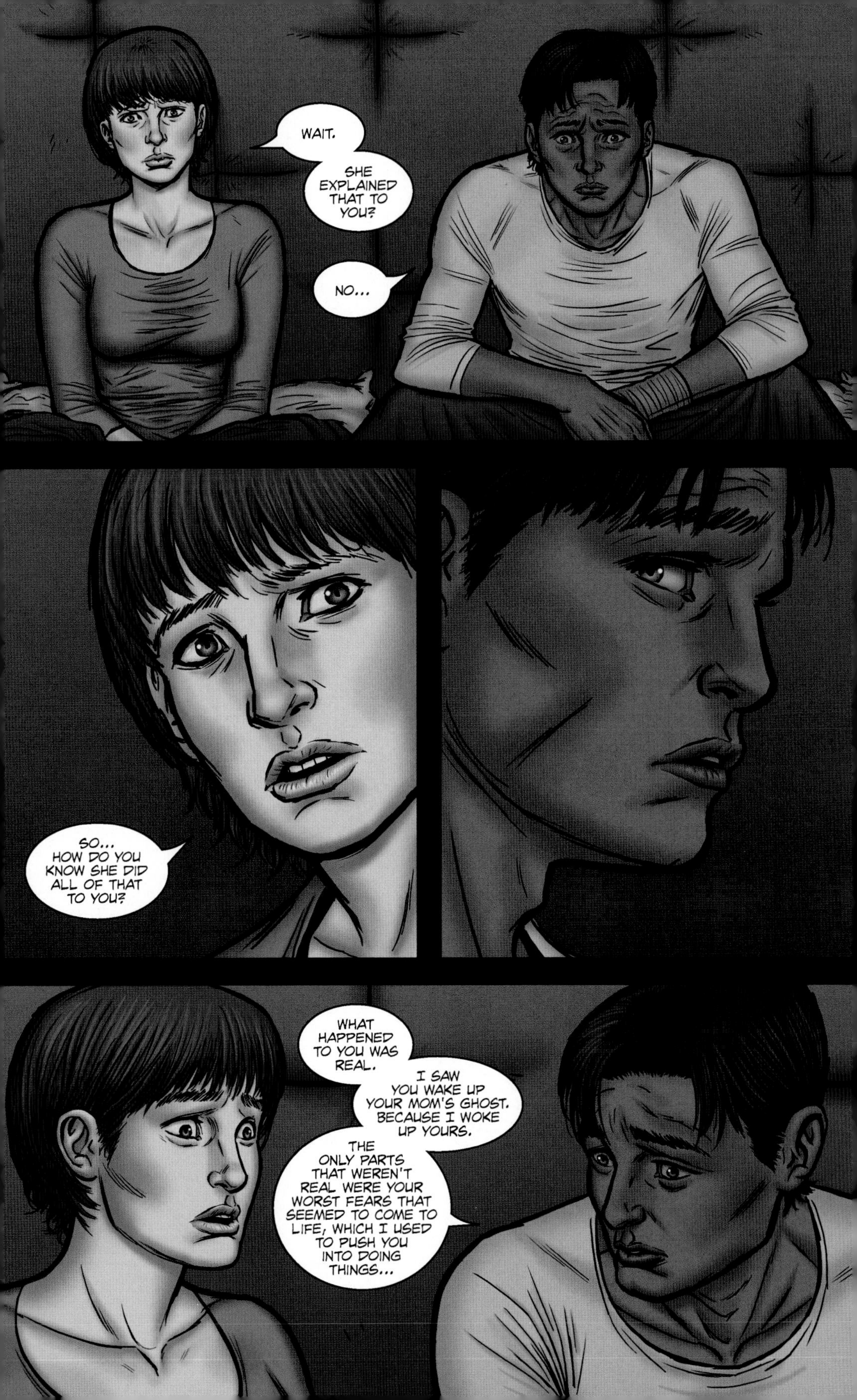
WAIT.
SHE EXPLAINED THAT TO YOU?
NO...
SO... HOW DO YOU KNOW SHE DID ALL OF THAT TO YOU?
WHAT HAPPENED TO YOU WAS REAL.
I SAW YOU WAKE UP YOUR MOM'S GHOST. BECAUSE I WOKE UP YOURS.
THE ONLY PARTS THAT WEREN'T REAL WERE YOUR WORST FEARS THAT SEEMED TO COME TO LIFE; WHICH I USED TO PUSH YOU INTO DOING THINGS...

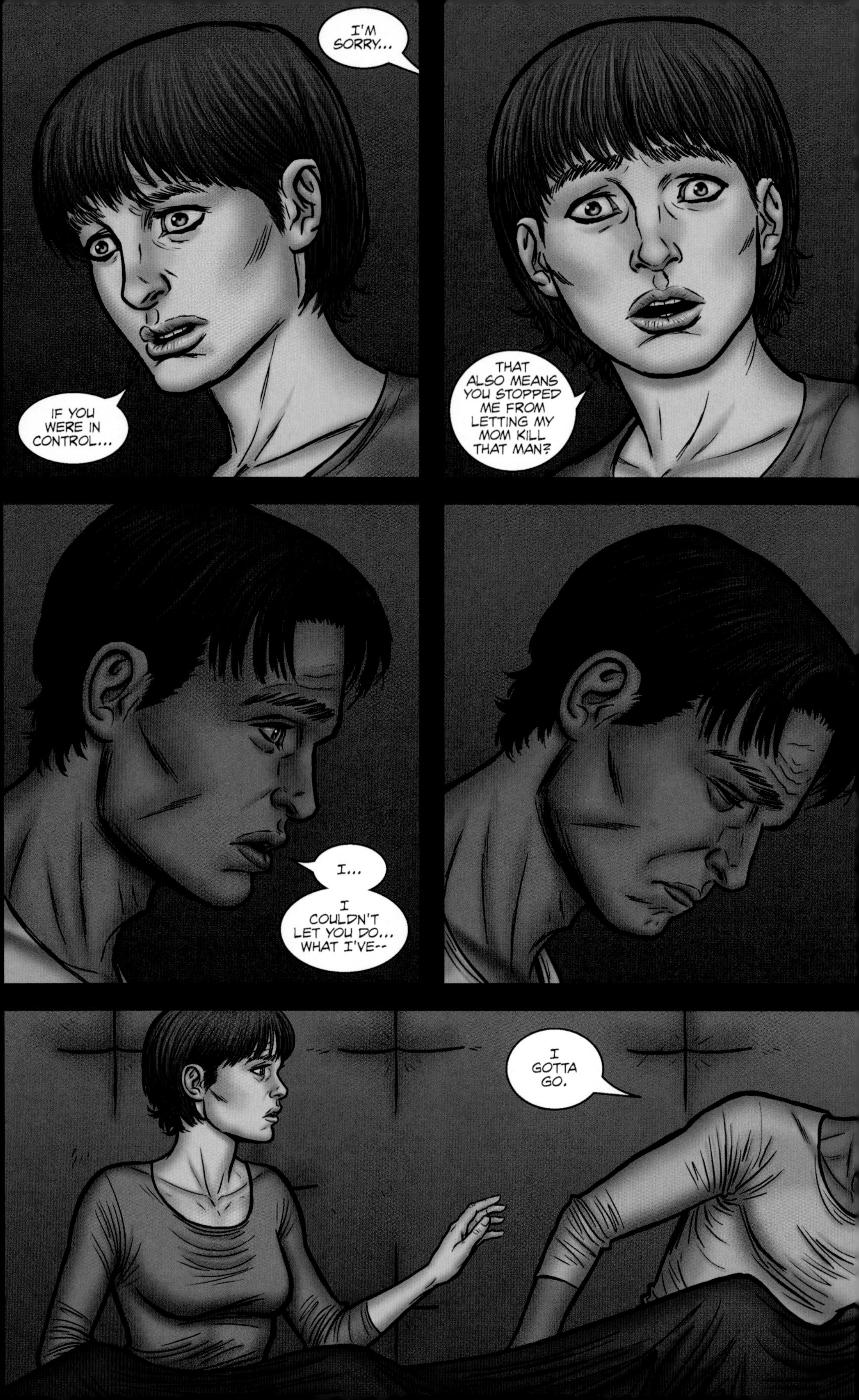
I'M SORRY...
IF YOU WERE IN CONTROL...
THAT ALSO MEANS YOU STOPPED ME FROM LETTING MY MOM KILL THAT MAN?
I...
I COULDN'T LET YOU DO... WHAT I'VE--
I GOTTA GO.

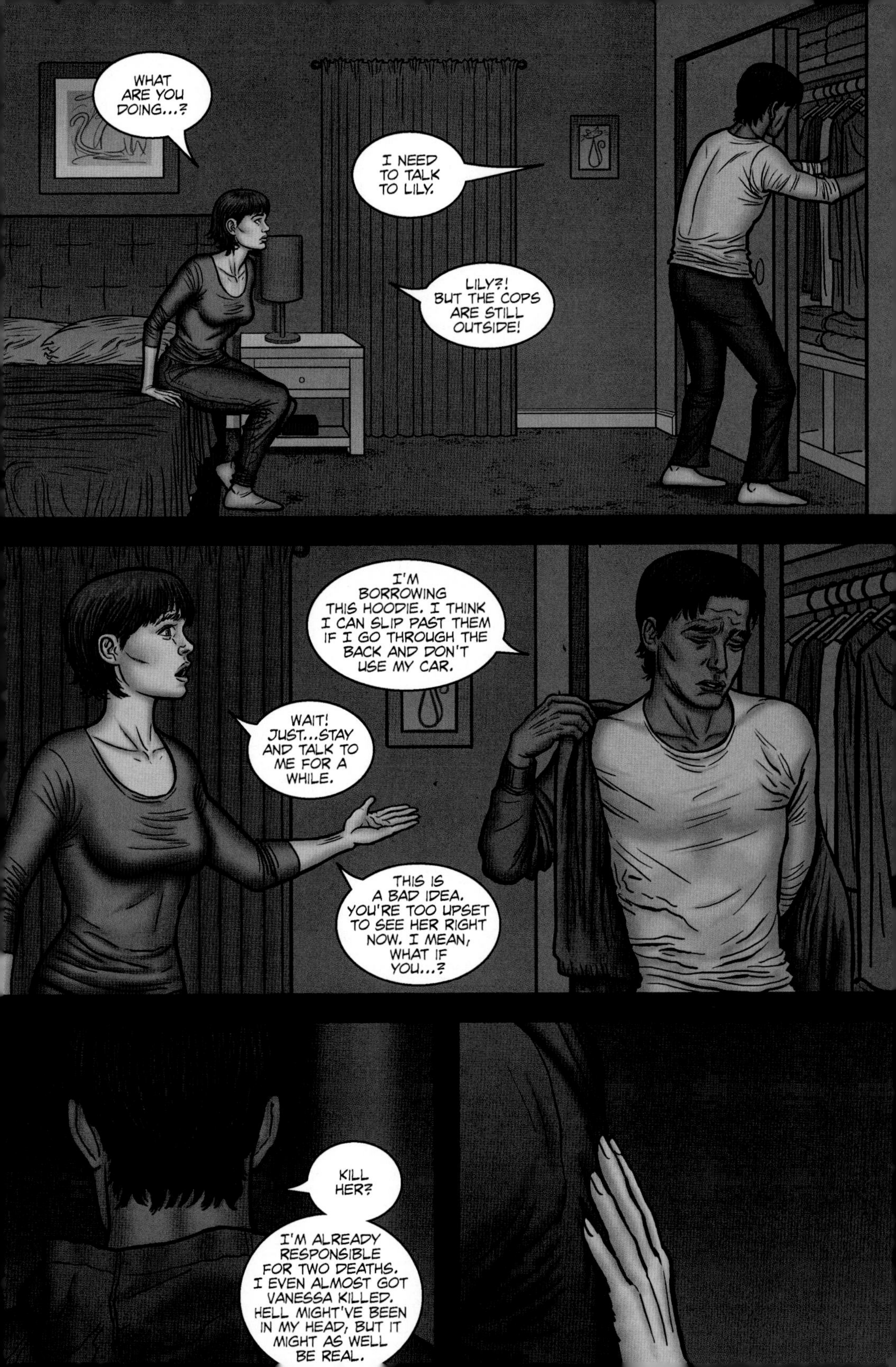
WHAT ARE YOU DOING...?
I NEED TO TALK TO LILY.
LILY?! BUT THE COPS ARE STILL OUTSIDE!
I'M BORROWING THIS HOODIE. I THINK I CAN SLIP PAST THEM IF I GO THROUGH THE BACK AND DON'T USE MY CAR.
WAIT! JUST...STAY AND TALK TO ME FOR A WHILE.
THIS IS A BAD IDEA. YOU'RE TOO UPSET TO SEE HER RIGHT NOW. I MEAN, WHAT IF YOU...?
KILL HER?
I'M ALREADY RESPONSIBLE FOR TWO DEATHS. I EVEN ALMOST GOT VANESSA KILLED. HELL MIGHT'VE BEEN IN MY HEAD, BUT IT MIGHT AS WELL BE REAL.

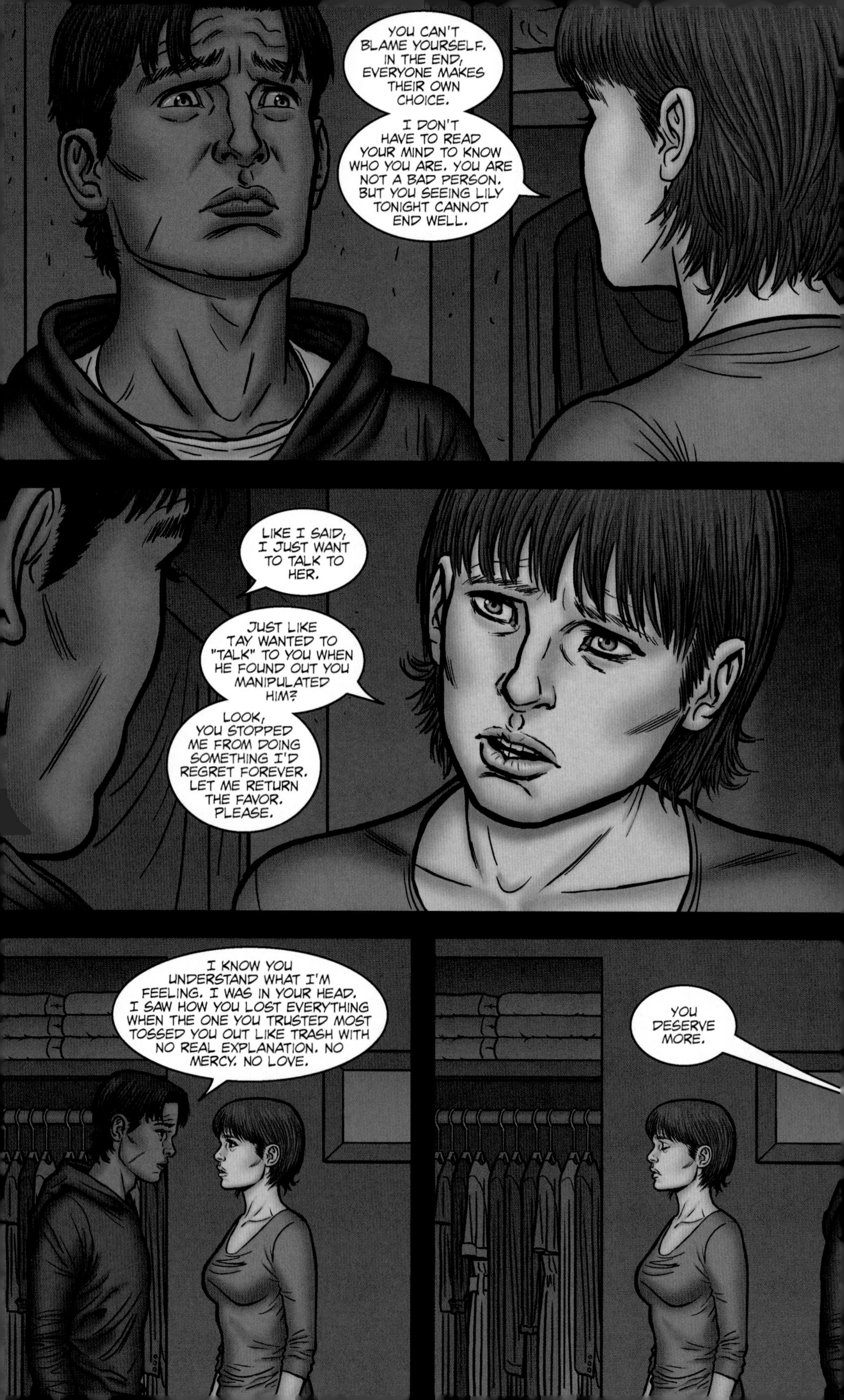
YOU CAN'T BLAME YOURSELF. IN THE END, EVERYONE MAKES THEIR OWN CHOICE.
I DON'T HAVE TO READ YOUR MIND TO KNOW WHO YOU ARE. YOU ARE NOT A BAD PERSON. BUT YOU SEEING LILY TONIGHT CANNOT END WELL.
LIKE I SAID, I JUST WANT TO TALK TO HER.
JUST LIKE TAY WANTED TO "TALK" TO YOU WHEN HE FOUND OUT YOU MANIPULATED HIM?
LOOK, YOU STOPPED ME FROM DOING SOMETHING I'D REGRET FOREVER. LET ME RETURN THE FAVOR. PLEASE.
I KNOW YOU UNDERSTAND WHAT I'M FEELING. I WAS IN YOUR HEAD. I SAW HOW YOU LOST EVERYTHING WHEN THE ONE YOU TRUSTED MOST TOSSED YOU OUT LIKE TRASH WITH NO REAL EXPLANATION. NO MERCY. NO LOVE.
YOU DESERVE MORE.

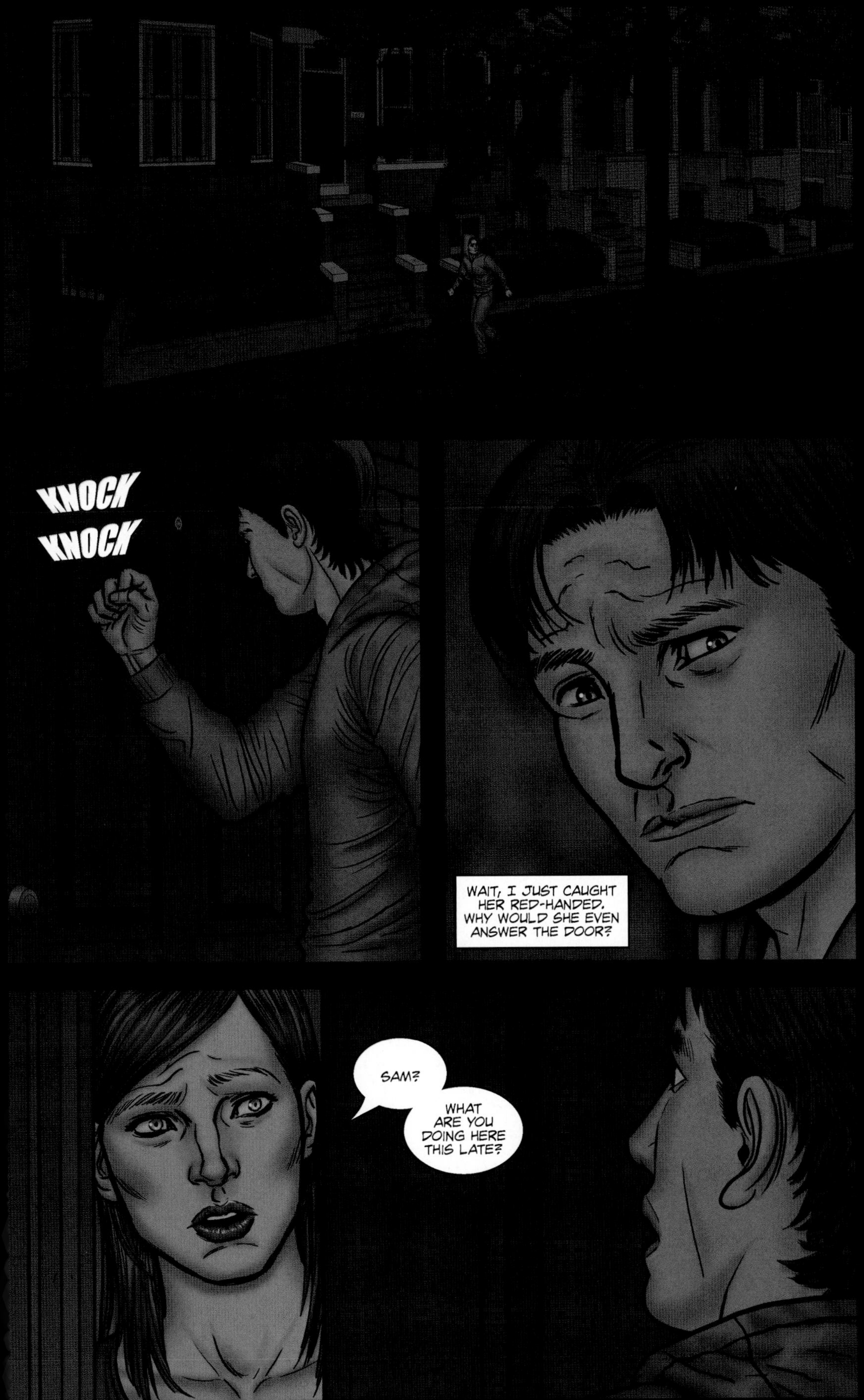
KNOCK
KNOCK
WAIT, I JUST CAUGHT HER RED-HANDED. WHY WOULD SHE EVEN ANSWER THE DOOR?
SAM?
WHAT ARE YOU DOING HERE THIS LATE?

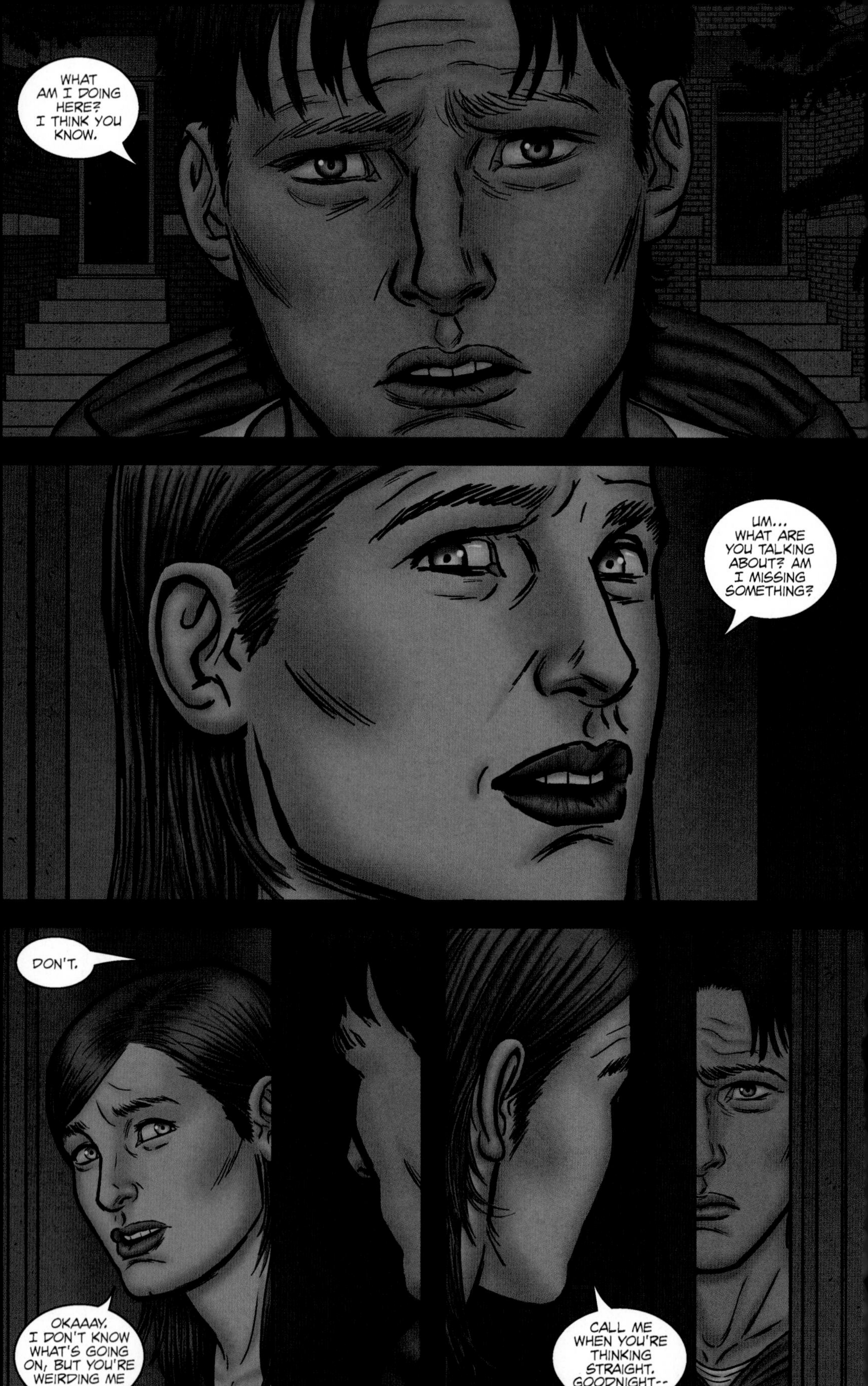
WHAT AM I DOING HERE? I THINK YOU KNOW.
UM... WHAT ARE YOU TALKING ABOUT? AM I MISSING SOMETHING?
DON'T.
OKAAAY. I DON'T KNOW WHAT'S GOING ON, BUT YOU'RE WEIRDING ME OUT.
CALL ME WHEN YOU'RE THINKING STRAIGHT. GOODNIGHT--

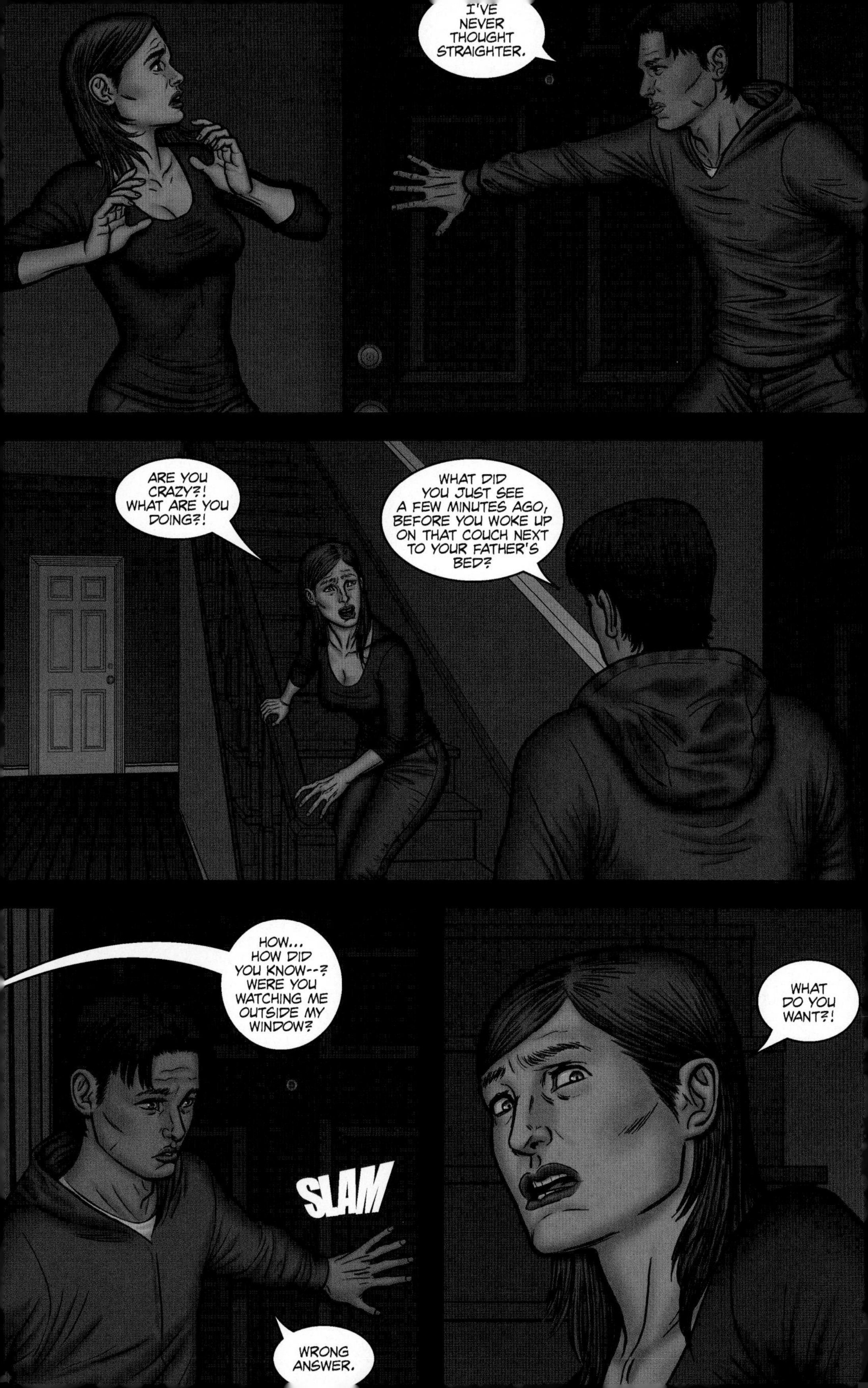
I'VE NEVER THOUGHT STRAIGHTER.
ARE YOU CRAZY?! WHAT ARE YOU DOING?!
WHAT DID YOU JUST SEE A FEW MINUTES AGO, BEFORE YOU WOKE UP ON THAT COUCH NEXT TO YOUR FATHER'S BED?
HOW... HOW DID YOU KNOW--? WERE YOU WATCHING ME OUTSIDE MY WINDOW?
SLAM
WRONG ANSWER.
WHAT DO YOU WANT?!

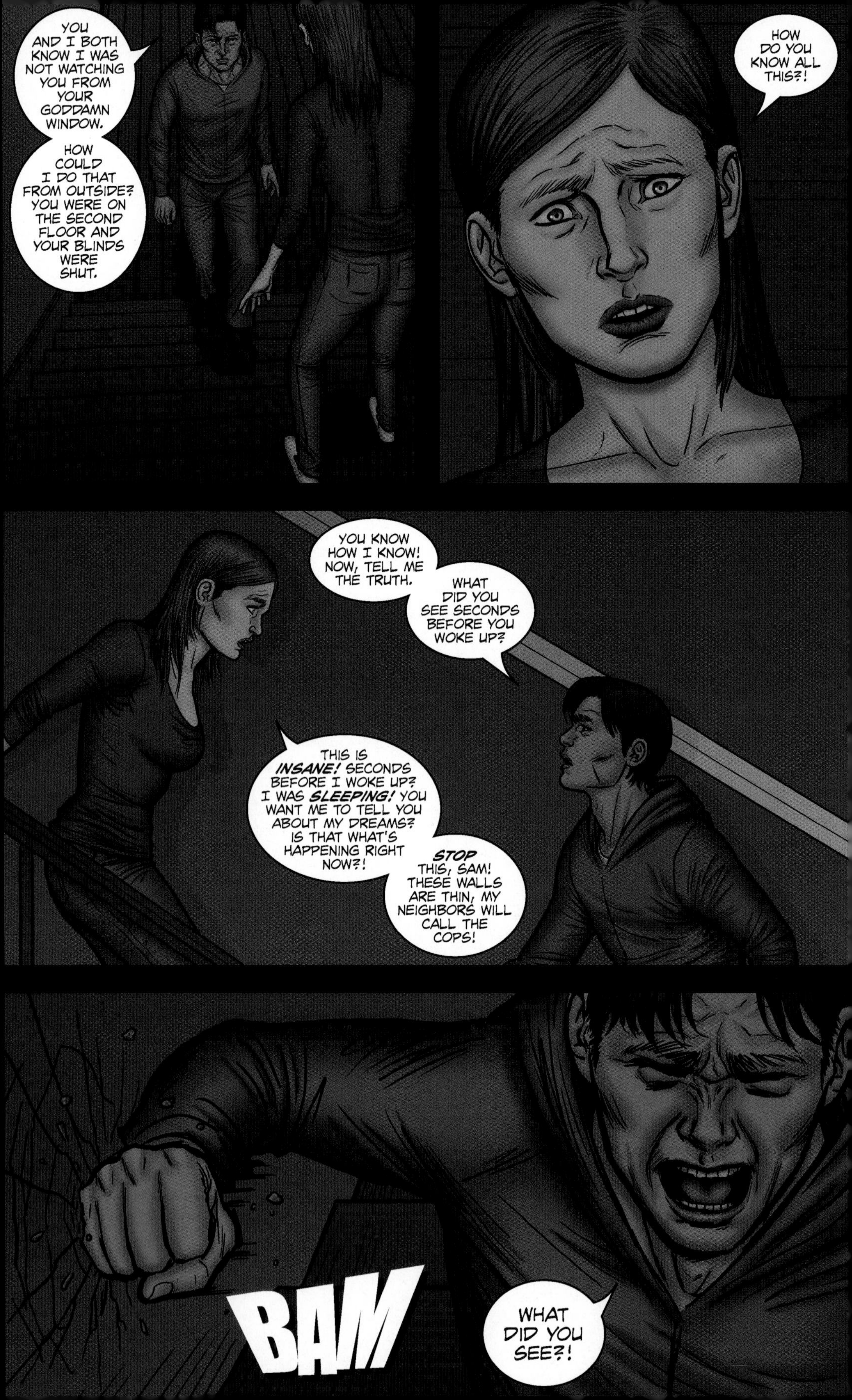
YOU AND I BOTH KNOW I WAS NOT WATCHING YOU FROM YOUR GODDAMN WINDOW.
HOW COULD I DO THAT FROM OUTSIDE? YOU WERE ON THE SECOND FLOOR AND YOUR BLINDS WERE SHUT.
HOW DO YOU KNOW ALL THIS?!
YOU KNOW HOW I KNOW! NOW, TELL ME THE TRUTH.
WHAT DID YOU SEE SECONDS BEFORE YOU WOKE UP?
THIS IS *INSANE!* SECONDS BEFORE I WOKE UP? I WAS *SLEEPING!* YOU WANT ME TO TELL YOU ABOUT MY DREAMS? IS THAT WHAT'S HAPPENING RIGHT NOW?!
STOP THIS, SAM! THESE WALLS ARE THIN, MY NEIGHBORS WILL CALL THE COPS!
BAM
WHAT DID YOU SEE?!

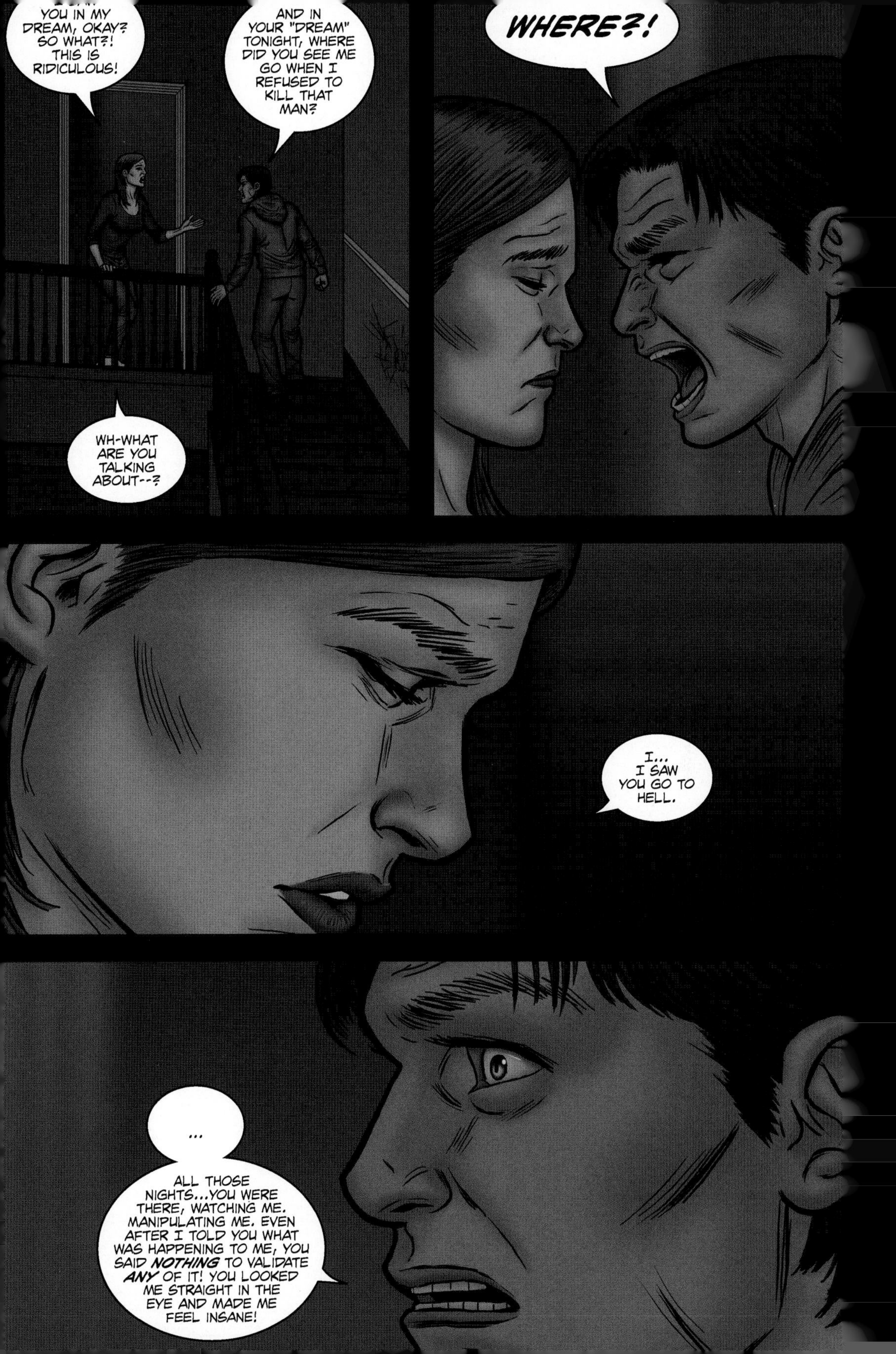
YOU IN MY DREAM, OKAY? SO WHAT?! THIS IS RIDICULOUS!
AND IN YOUR "DREAM" TONIGHT, WHERE DID YOU SEE ME GO WHEN I REFUSED TO KILL THAT MAN?
WH-WHAT ARE YOU TALKING ABOUT--?
WHERE?!
I... I SAW YOU GO TO HELL.
...
ALL THOSE NIGHTS...YOU WERE THERE, WATCHING ME. MANIPULATING ME. EVEN AFTER I TOLD YOU WHAT WAS HAPPENING TO ME, YOU SAID NOTHING TO VALIDATE ANY OF IT! YOU LOOKED ME STRAIGHT IN THE EYE AND MADE ME FEEL INSANE!

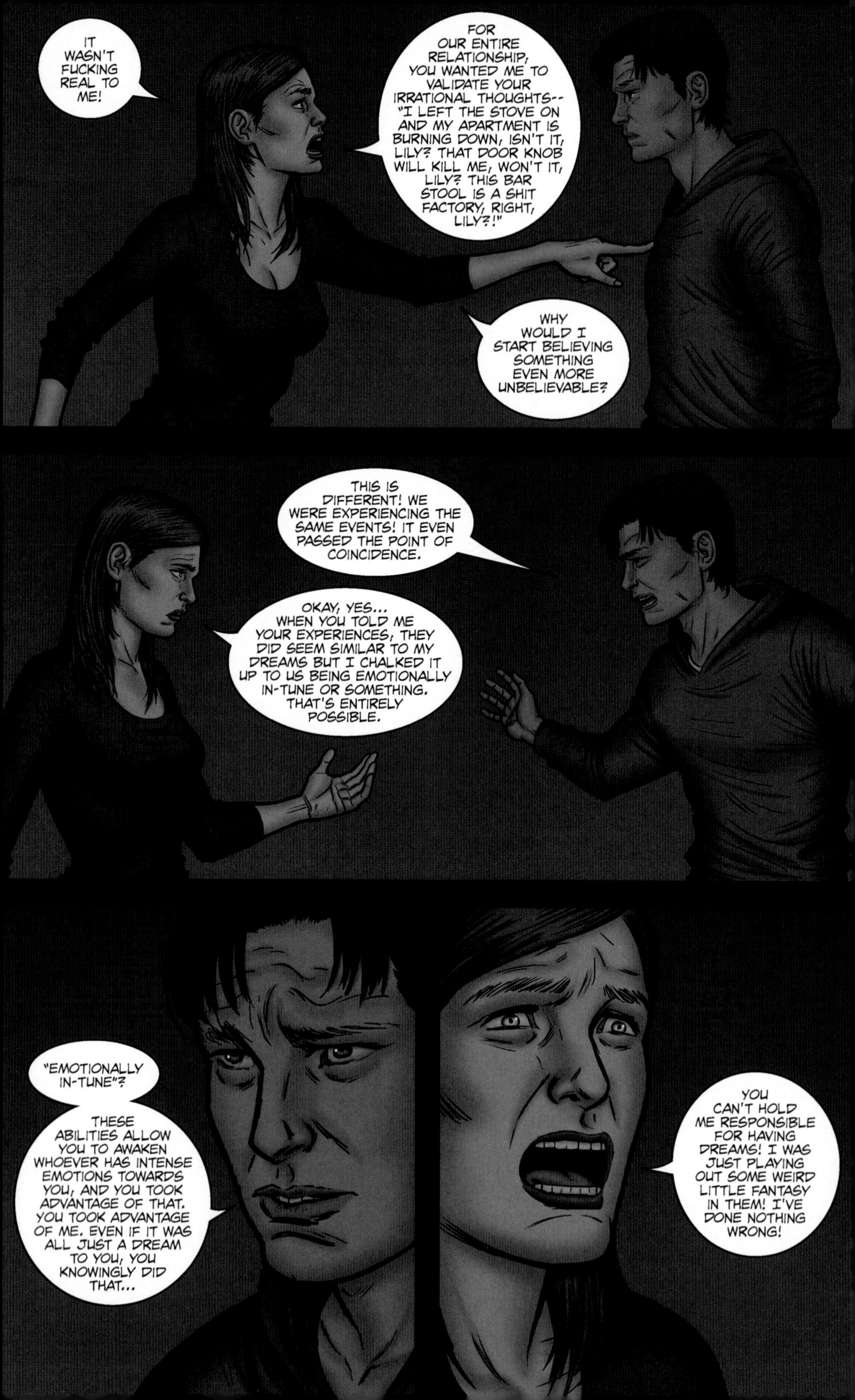
IT WASN'T FUCKING REAL TO ME!
FOR OUR ENTIRE RELATIONSHIP, YOU WANTED ME TO VALIDATE YOUR IRRATIONAL THOUGHTS-- "I LEFT THE STOVE ON AND MY APARTMENT IS BURNING DOWN, ISN'T IT, LILY? THAT DOOR KNOB WILL KILL ME, WON'T IT, LILY? THIS BAR STOOL IS A SHIT FACTORY, RIGHT, LILY?!"
WHY WOULD I START BELIEVING SOMETHING EVEN MORE UNBELIEVABLE?
THIS IS DIFFERENT! WE WERE EXPERIENCING THE SAME EVENTS! IT EVEN PASSED THE POINT OF COINCIDENCE.
OKAY, YES... WHEN YOU TOLD ME YOUR EXPERIENCES, THEY DID SEEM SIMILAR TO MY DREAMS BUT I CHALKED IT UP TO US BEING EMOTIONALLY IN-TUNE OR SOMETHING. THAT'S ENTIRELY POSSIBLE.
"EMOTIONALLY IN-TUNE"?
THESE ABILITIES ALLOW YOU TO AWAKEN WHOEVER HAS INTENSE EMOTIONS TOWARDS YOU, AND YOU TOOK ADVANTAGE OF THAT. YOU TOOK ADVANTAGE OF ME. EVEN IF IT WAS ALL JUST A DREAM TO YOU, YOU KNOWINGLY DID THAT...
YOU CAN'T HOLD ME RESPONSIBLE FOR HAVING DREAMS! I WAS JUST PLAYING OUT SOME WEIRD LITTLE FANTASY IN THEM! I'VE DONE NOTHING WRONG!

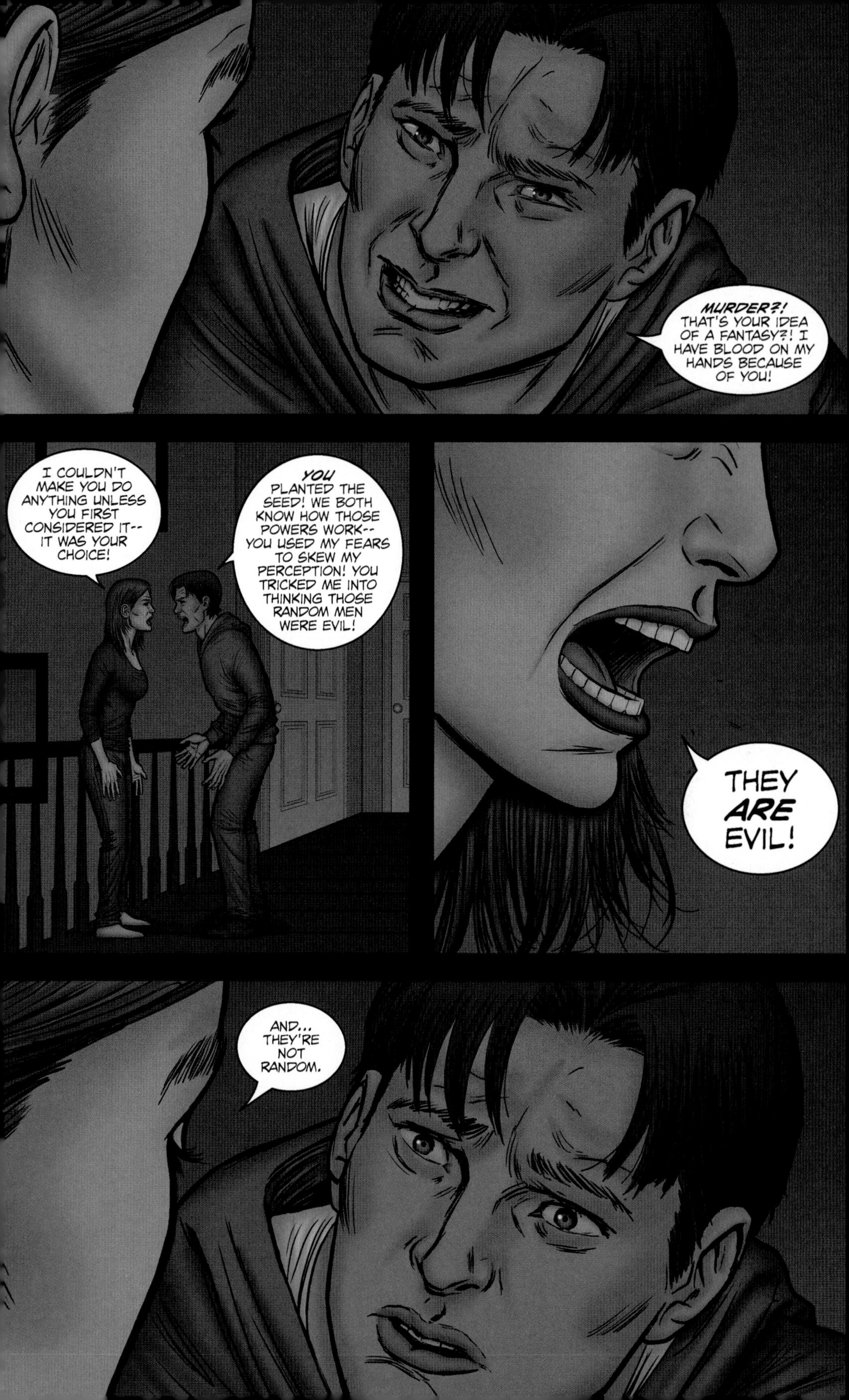
MURDER?! THAT'S YOUR IDEA OF A FANTASY?! I HAVE BLOOD ON MY HANDS BECAUSE OF YOU!
I COULDN'T MAKE YOU DO ANYTHING UNLESS YOU FIRST CONSIDERED IT-- IT WAS YOUR CHOICE!
YOU PLANTED THE SEED! WE BOTH KNOW HOW THOSE POWERS WORK-- YOU USED MY FEARS TO SKEW MY PERCEPTION! YOU TRICKED ME INTO THINKING THOSE RANDOM MEN WERE EVIL!
THEY ARE EVIL!
AND... THEY'RE NOT RANDOM.

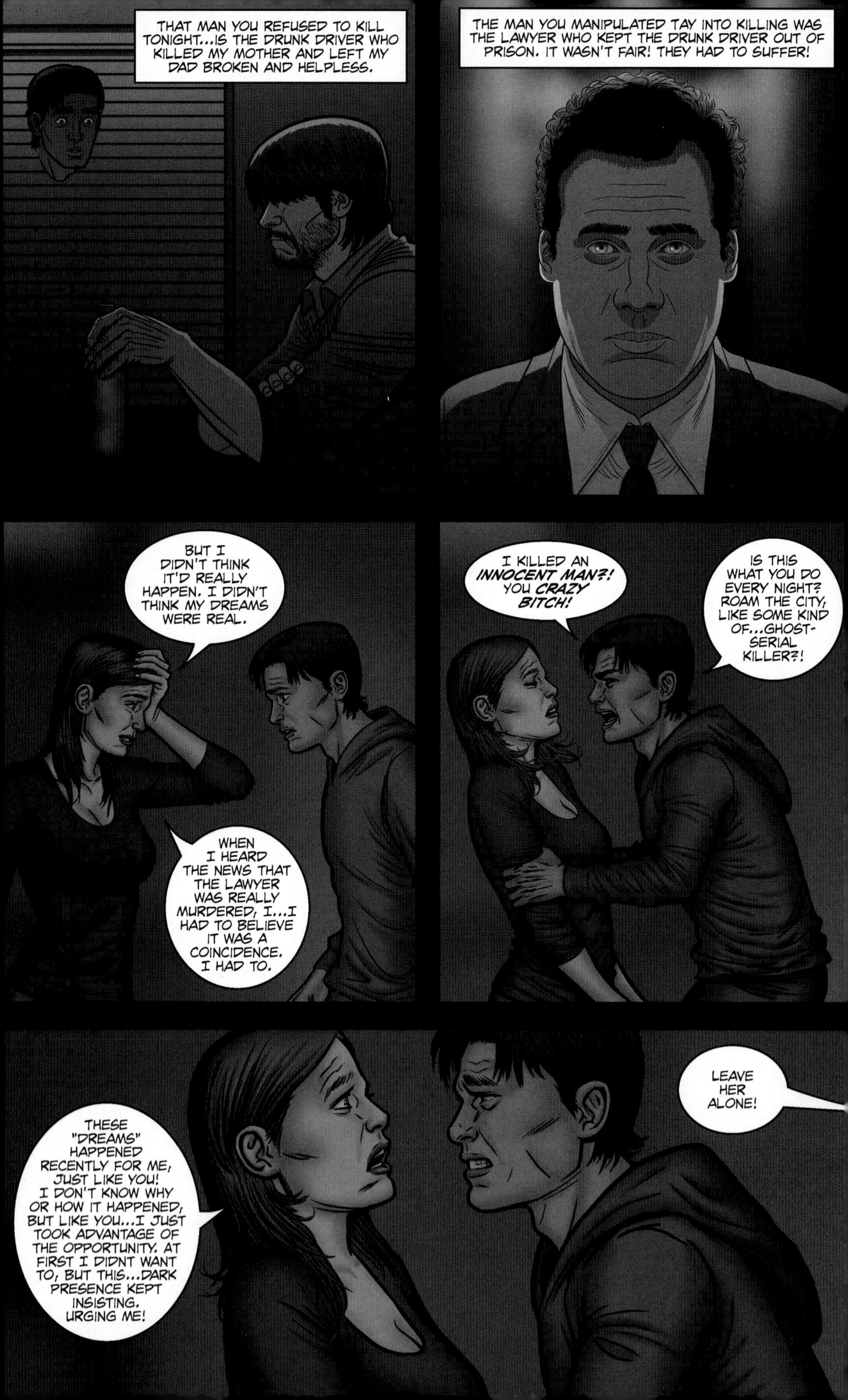
THAT MAN YOU REFUSED TO KILL TONIGHT...IS THE DRUNK DRIVER WHO KILLED MY MOTHER AND LEFT MY DAD BROKEN AND HELPLESS.
THE MAN YOU MANIPULATED TAY INTO KILLING WAS THE LAWYER WHO KEPT THE DRUNK DRIVER OUT OF PRISON. IT WASN'T FAIR! THEY HAD TO SUFFER!
BUT I DIDN'T THINK IT'D REALLY HAPPEN. I DIDN'T THINK MY DREAMS WERE REAL.
WHEN I HEARD THE NEWS THAT THE LAWYER WAS REALLY MURDERED, I...I HAD TO BELIEVE IT WAS A COINCIDENCE. I HAD TO.
I KILLED AN *INNOCENT MAN?!* YOU *CRAZY BITCH!*
IS THIS WHAT YOU DO EVERY NIGHT? ROAM THE CITY, LIKE SOME KIND OF...GHOST-SERIAL KILLER?!
THESE "DREAMS" HAPPENED RECENTLY FOR ME, JUST LIKE YOU! I DON'T KNOW WHY OR HOW IT HAPPENED, BUT LIKE YOU...I JUST TOOK ADVANTAGE OF THE OPPORTUNITY. AT FIRST I DIDNT WANT TO, BUT THIS...DARK PRESENCE KEPT INSISTING. URGING ME!
LEAVE HER ALONE!

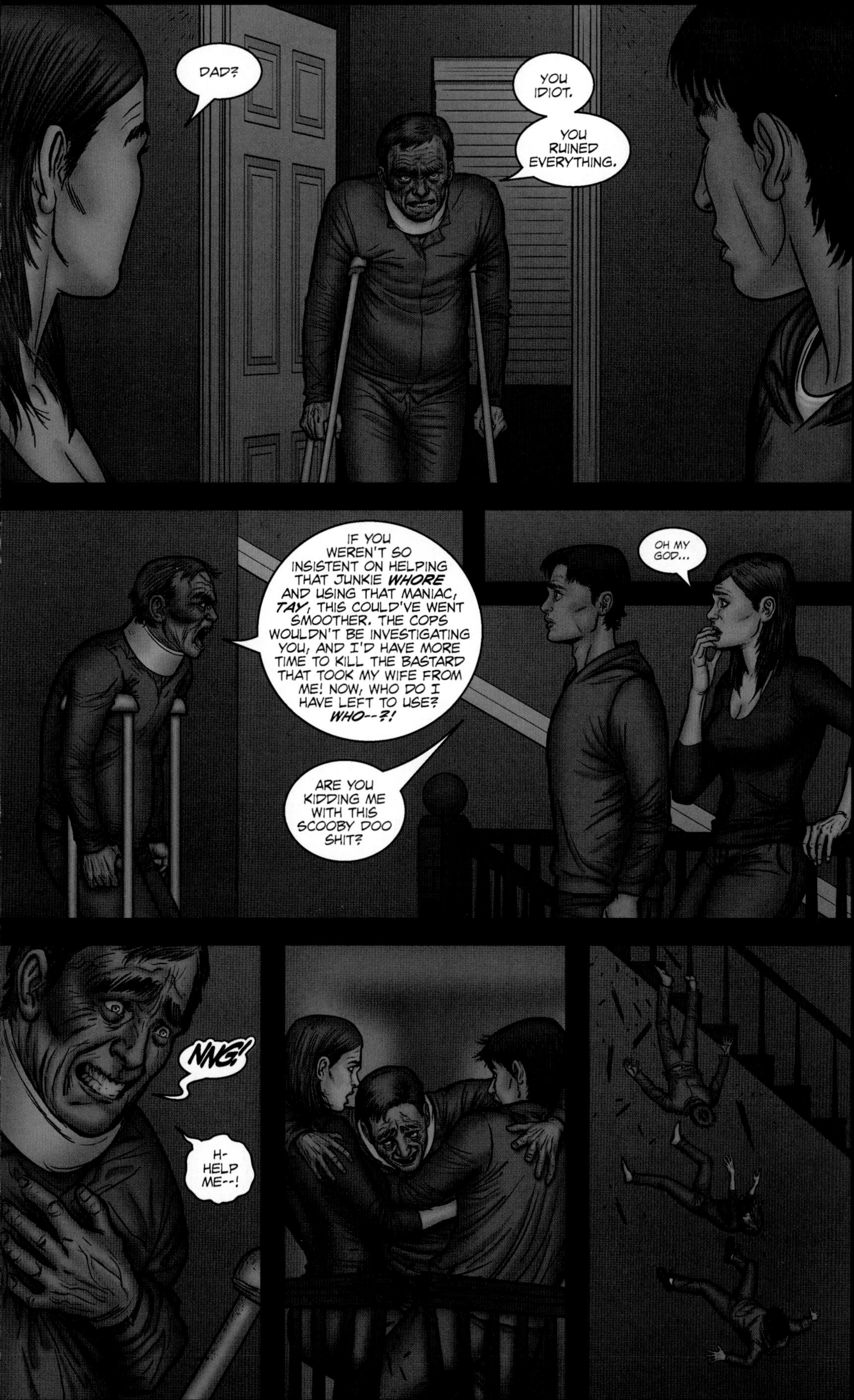
DAD?
YOU IDIOT.
YOU RUINED EVERYTHING.
IF YOU WEREN'T SO INSISTENT ON HELPING THAT JUNKIE *WHORE* AND USING THAT MANIAC, *TAY*, THIS COULD'VE WENT SMOOTHER. THE COPS WOULDN'T BE INVESTIGATING YOU, AND I'D HAVE MORE TIME TO KILL THE BASTARD THAT TOOK MY WIFE FROM ME! NOW, WHO DO I HAVE LEFT TO USE? *WHO--?!*
OH MY GOD...
ARE YOU KIDDING ME WITH THIS SCOOBY DOO SHIT?
NNG!
H-HELP ME--!

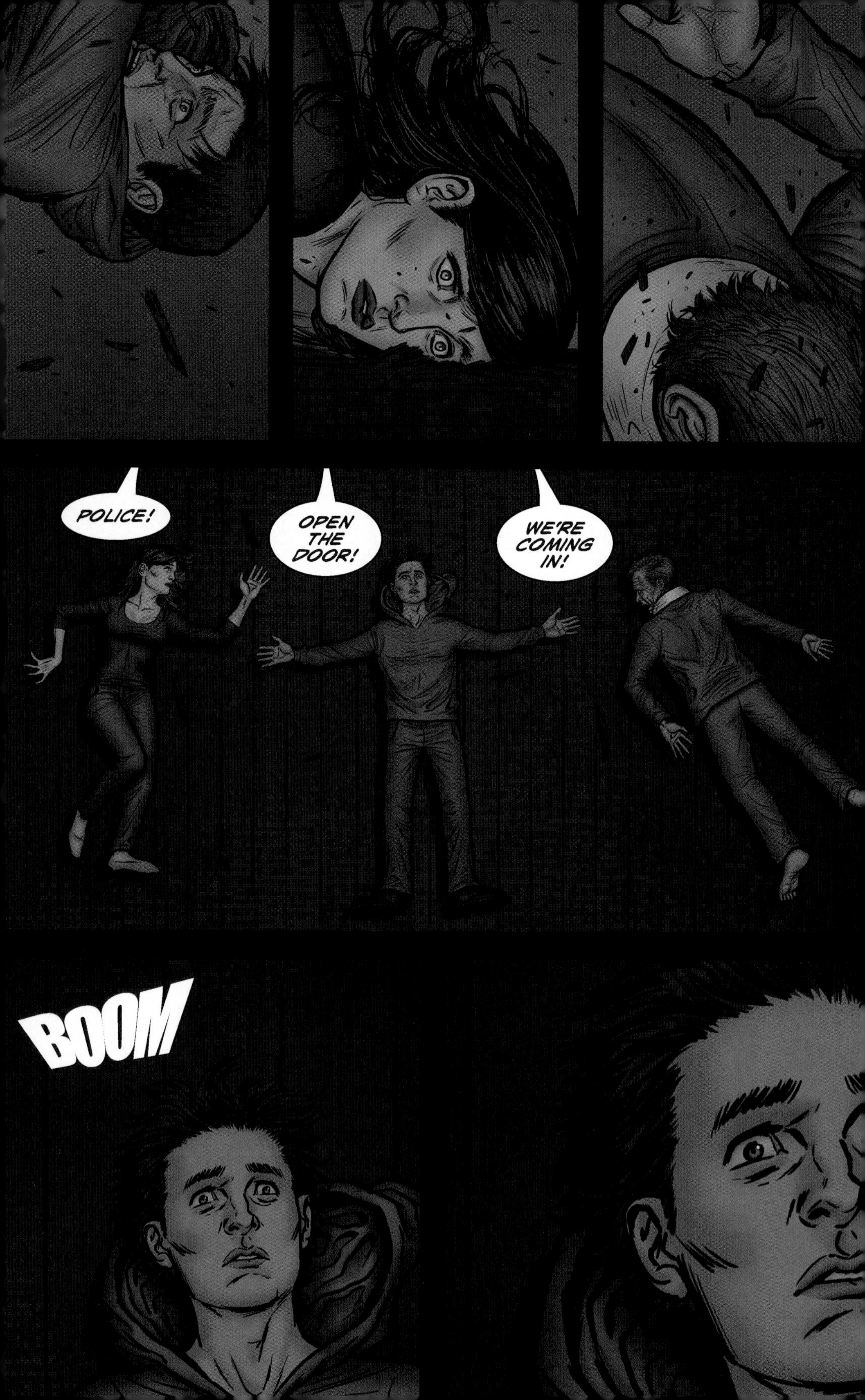
POLICE!
OPEN THE DOOR!
WE'RE COMING IN!
BOOM

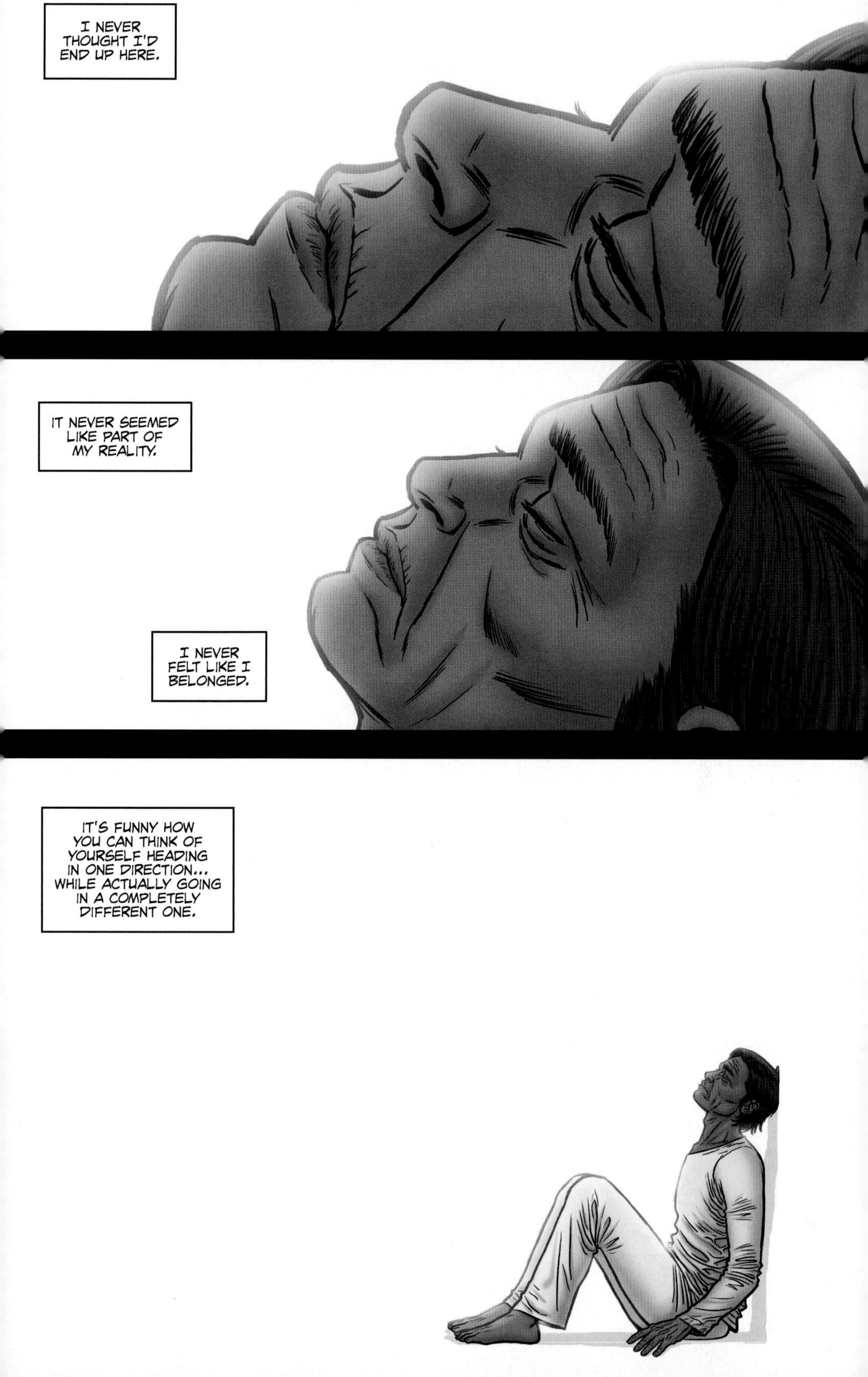
I NEVER THOUGHT I'D END UP HERE.
IT NEVER SEEMED LIKE PART OF MY REALITY.
I NEVER FELT LIKE I BELONGED.
IT'S FUNNY HOW YOU CAN THINK OF YOURSELF HEADING IN ONE DIRECTION... WHILE ACTUALLY GOING IN A COMPLETELY DIFFERENT ONE.

TODAY IS ANOTHER ANNIVERSARY.

THAT NIGHT IS STILL CLEAR IN MY MIND.

I WAS ASKED TO CONFRONT MY THOUGHTS AND FEELINGS ABOUT IT. I STILL CAN'T TELL IF THAT HELPS OR HURTS ME.

WITHOUT A SHRED OF DOUBT, I KNOW I DID NOT MURDER LILY AND HER FATHER. YET, I NEVER ONCE PUT UP A FIGHT.

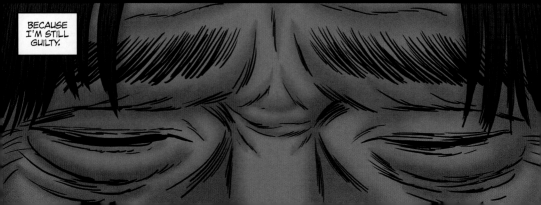

BECAUSE I'M STILL GUILTY.

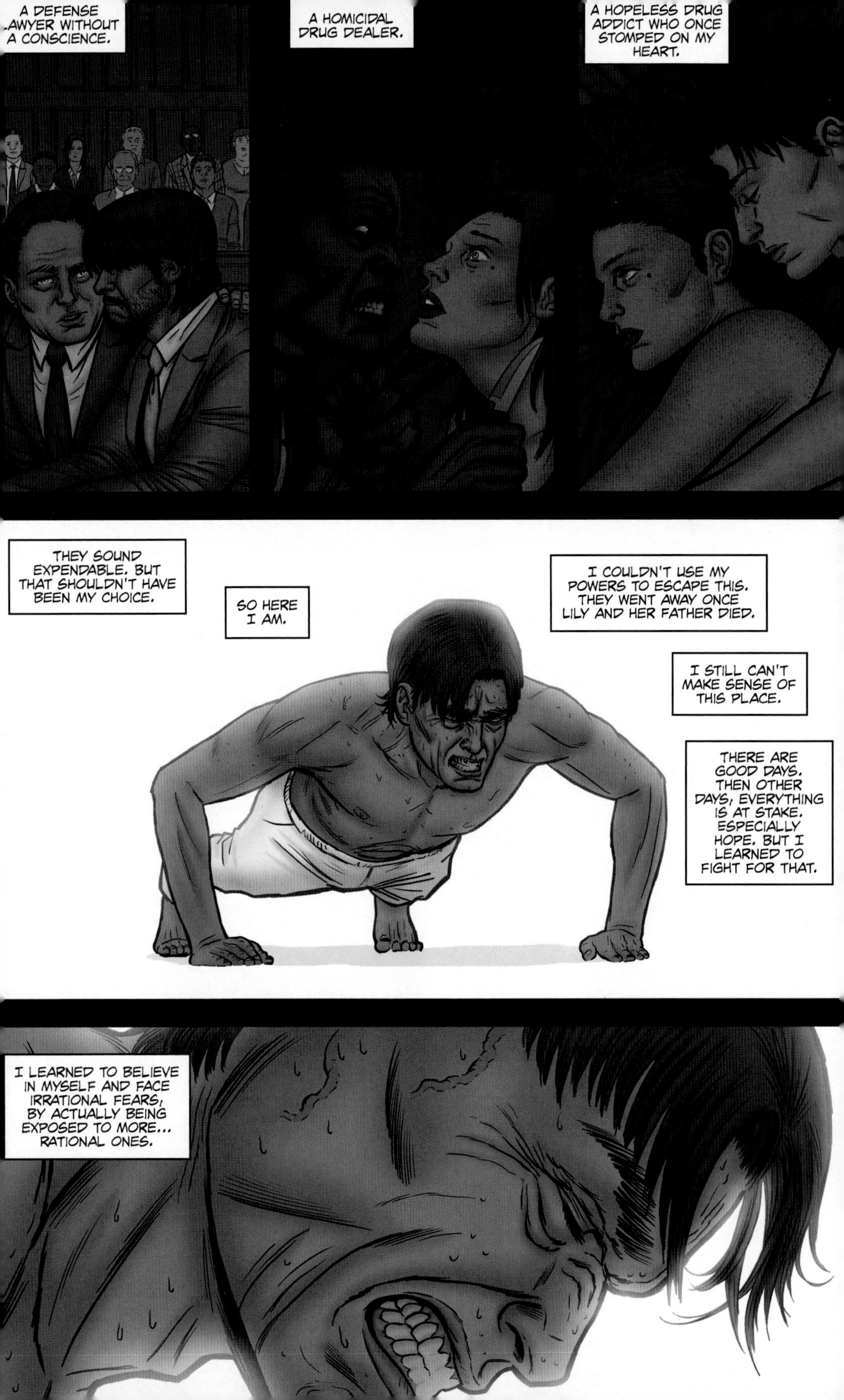
A DEFENSE LAWYER WITHOUT A CONSCIENCE.
A HOMICIDAL DRUG DEALER.
A HOPELESS DRUG ADDICT WHO ONCE STOMPED ON MY HEART.
THEY SOUND EXPENDABLE. BUT THAT SHOULDN'T HAVE BEEN MY CHOICE.
SO HERE I AM.
I COULDN'T USE MY POWERS TO ESCAPE THIS. THEY WENT AWAY ONCE LILY AND HER FATHER DIED.
I STILL CAN'T MAKE SENSE OF THIS PLACE.
THERE ARE GOOD DAYS. THEN OTHER DAYS, EVERYTHING IS AT STAKE. ESPECIALLY HOPE. BUT I LEARNED TO FIGHT FOR THAT.
I LEARNED TO BELIEVE IN MYSELF AND FACE IRRATIONAL FEARS, BY ACTUALLY BEING EXPOSED TO MORE... RATIONAL ONES.

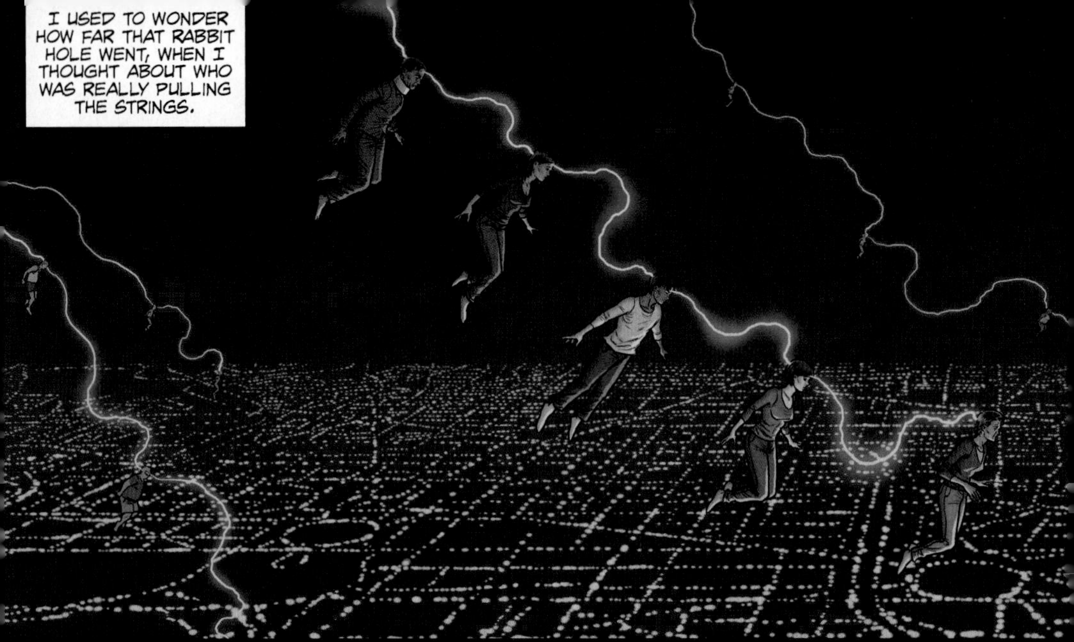
I USED TO WONDER HOW FAR THAT RABBIT HOLE WENT, WHEN I THOUGHT ABOUT WHO WAS REALLY PULLING THE STRINGS.

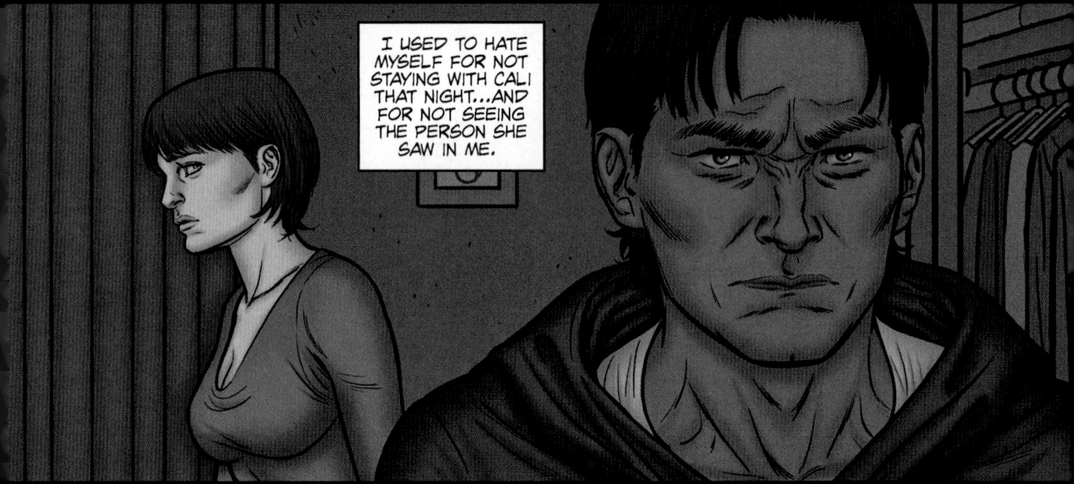
I USED TO HATE MYSELF FOR NOT STAYING WITH CALI THAT NIGHT...AND FOR NOT SEEING THE PERSON SHE SAW IN ME.

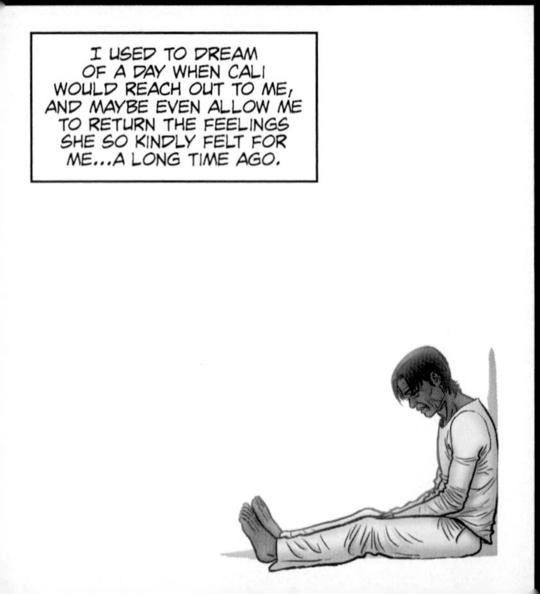
I USED TO DREAM OF A DAY WHEN CALI WOULD REACH OUT TO ME, AND MAYBE EVEN ALLOW ME TO RETURN THE FEELINGS SHE SO KINDLY FELT FOR ME...A LONG TIME AGO.

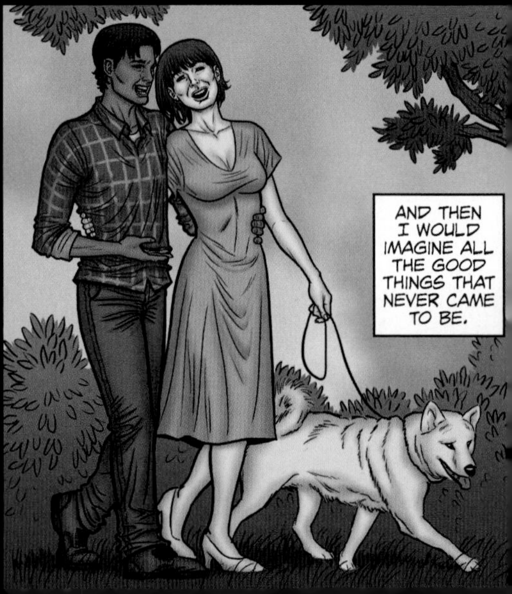
AND THEN I WOULD IMAGINE ALL THE GOOD THINGS THAT NEVER CAME TO BE.

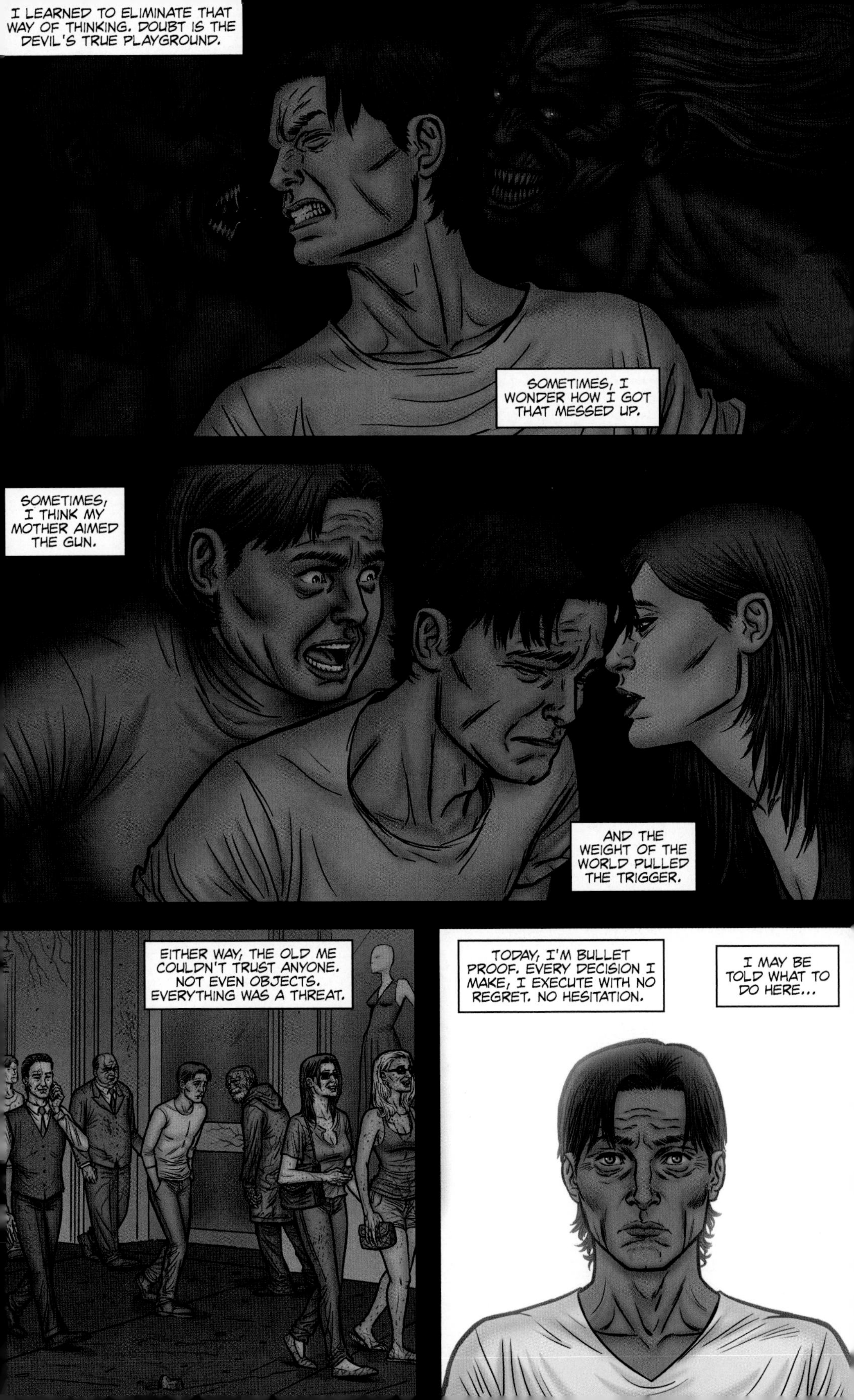
I LEARNED TO ELIMINATE THAT WAY OF THINKING. DOUBT IS THE DEVIL'S TRUE PLAYGROUND.
SOMETIMES, I WONDER HOW I GOT THAT MESSED UP.
SOMETIMES, I THINK MY MOTHER AIMED THE GUN.
AND THE WEIGHT OF THE WORLD PULLED THE TRIGGER.
EITHER WAY, THE OLD ME COULDN'T TRUST ANYONE. NOT EVEN OBJECTS. EVERYTHING WAS A THREAT.
TODAY, I'M BULLET PROOF. EVERY DECISION I MAKE, I EXECUTE WITH NO REGRET. NO HESITATION.
I MAY BE TOLD WHAT TO DO HERE...

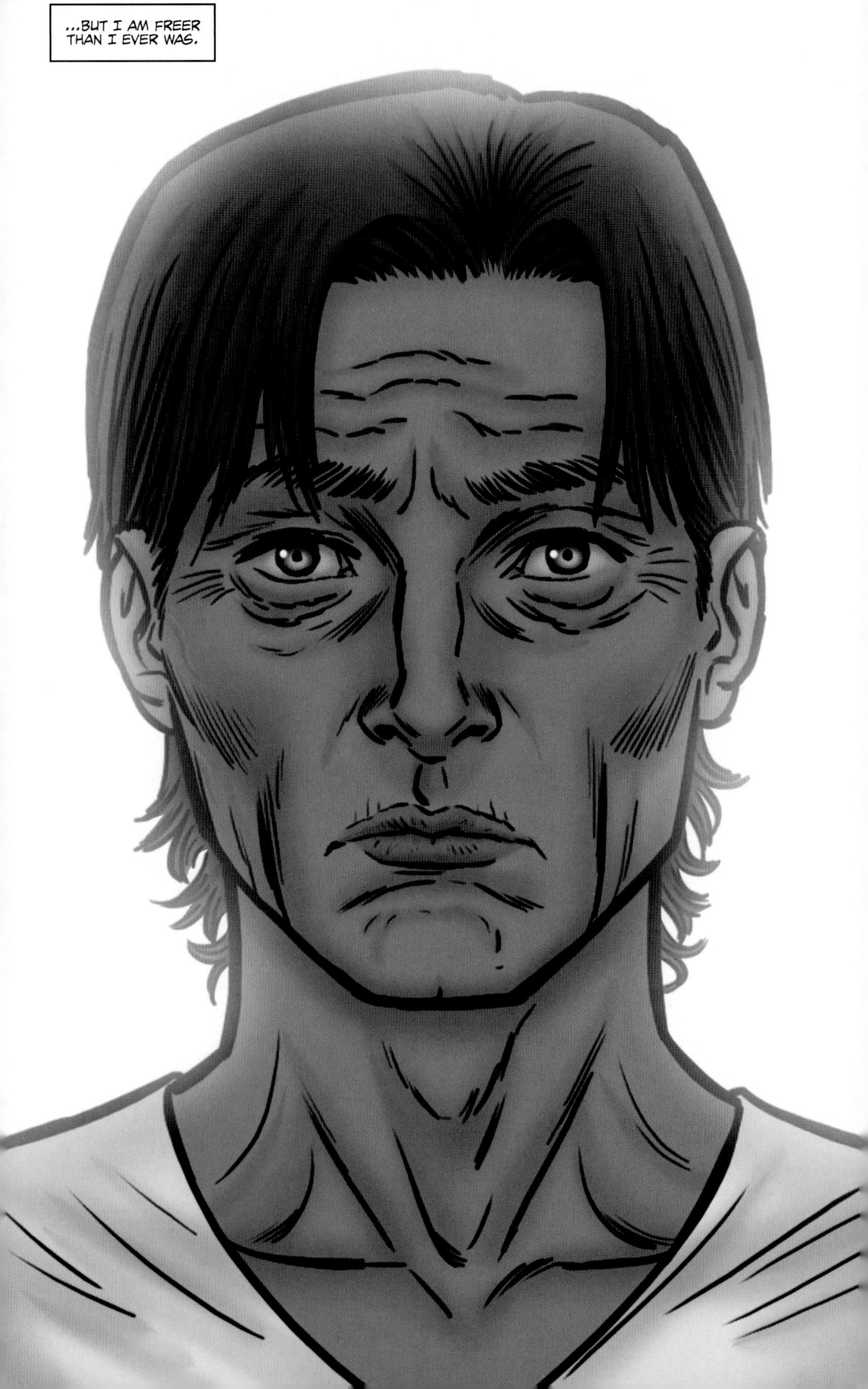
...BUT I AM FREER THAN I EVER WAS.

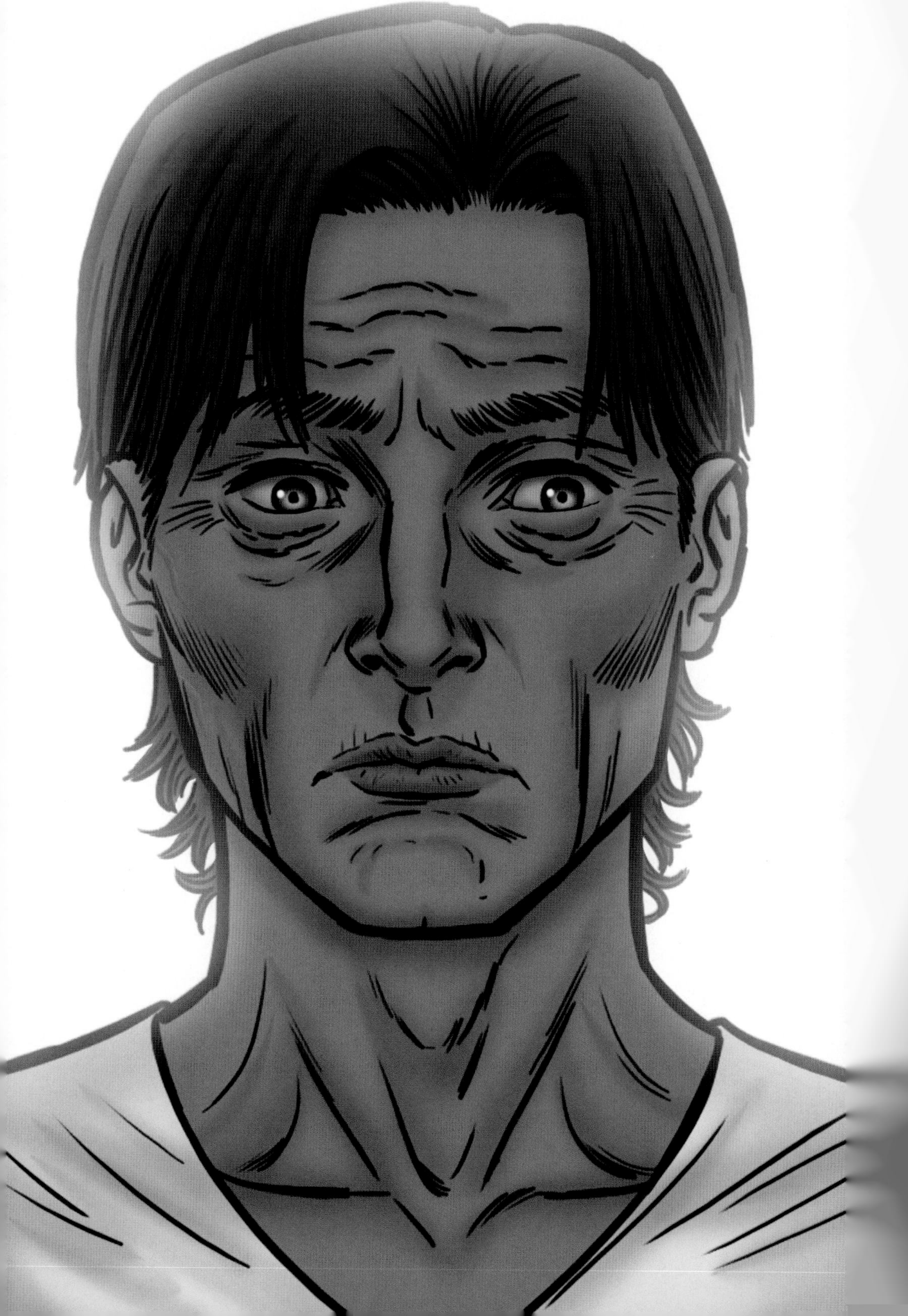

Dear Reader,

Thank you for picking up this book. If you have been reading Whispers since the release of the first issue, I owe you even greater gratitude. Without your support, I would have found the long periods of "silence" even more difficult to push through.

For as long as I can remember, I always had a need to create. I remember early memories of myself crafting homemade comic books, clumsily stapling stacks of lined paper together, writing and drawing random stories that came to my head, purely for my own enjoyment. I never stopped making comic books since. When I broke into the comic book industry, primarily as a writer, I discovered a new set of challenges once my hobby suddenly became a career. I wasn't prepared for the pressure of exercising a muscle I hadn't truly worked to its fullest capacity, which meant I essentially had to learn how to write stories in front of an audience.

Years later, I decided to take on my solo debut with Whispers. Now having years of experience in the industry, I figured it would be reasonably straight forward to achieve. I even went so far to wonder why more artists didn't take on solo comic book projects. I found out why. Even though I'd become more confident as a writer, I realized my drawing muscle had somewhat atrophied. Sure, I had drawn random pin-ups, sketches, and detailed layouts during my career thus far, but I completely underestimated the amount of work and time it would take to create and complete a comic book series all by myself. Once again, I learned in front of you.

I always thought I needed my art to be presented and packaged "perfectly," in its most distilled, final form. Free of all mistakes, missteps, and behind-the-scenes glimpses into the often clumsy process of creating something out of nothing. Ironically, even while writing this letter, that need is strong. What I learned is that there really is freedom and beauty in imperfection.

However, I also believe in finding out who you are by facing challenges head-on and pushing yourself to the limit, and for me that means writing and drawing stories like I did as a kid (minus the lined paper this time, of course). Sam's journey doesn't seem so different from mine now. Uncertainty will always be present, but it's up to you whether it holds you back or pushes you forward. As Sam found his voice, so did I.

Thank you for your patience and support throughout Whispers. I hope you're as excited as I am for my next opportunity to face uncertainty head-on... and emerge with a new story to tell.

Both muscles currently working hard.

Sincerely,

Joshua Luna

Stay tuned for updates or contact me at:

(Facebook page) www.facebook.com/joshualunacreations

(Twitter) @Joshua_Luna

(official website) www.joshualuna.com.

(Email) contact@joshualuna.com